P9-DXE-997

THE HOME INSULATION BIBLE

BY S. BLACKWELL DUNCAN

TAB BOOKS Inc.

BLUE RIDGE SUMMIT, PA. 17214

FIRST EDITION

FIRST PRINTING

Copyright © 1982 by TAB BOOKS Inc.

Printed in the United States of America

Library of Congress Cataloging in Publication Data

Duncan, S. Blackwell.
    The home insulation bible.

    Includes index.
    1. Dwellings—Insulation—Amateurs' manuals.
I. Title.
TH1715.D86   693.8′3   81-9277
ISBN 0-8306-0040-X   AACR2
ISBN 0-8306-1348-X (pbk.)

Cover courtesy of Johns-Manville.

Contents

Introduction

The weather is always with us; there's no escaping it. In this country, vast as it is, the weather tends to run to extremes and cycle through an amazing repertoire of vagaries. Across the nation, temperatures of over 100 F are commonplace. The record high is 134 F. Temperatures of − 30 F are just as common. The record low in the continental United States is − 69.7 F and in Alaska it is − 79.8 F. In 1936, the temperature in one part of North Dakota didn't rise above zero degrees Fahrenheit for 47 consecutive days. Heat waves occur frequently, and temperatures often remain above 100 F for days. Seasonal storm winds often top 100 mph; the highest recorded speed is nearly 232 mph. Relative humidity zips up and down the scale with startling rapidity. We are periodically inundated with several inches of rain or several feet of snow at one time. Precipitation varies from 2 inches annually in some places to 200 inches annually in others. Snow-days run from less than 1 to 80 or more. Precipitation days range from less than 20 to over 200. Hours of sunshine run from less than 1800 to over 3500 annually. We are beset by blizzards, tornadoes, freezing fogs, ice storms, hailstorms, hurricanes, and thunderstorms, and other less worrisome weather phenomena. One way or another, we must adjust to all this and live with an incredible variety of weather.

As a matter of protection and self-preservation, we have devised sophisticated shelters in which we can hide from the elements in reasonable safety, security, and comfort. Not only are these structures stoutly built and cunningly designed (some more so than others) to withstand the powerful ravages of time and Mother Nature, they are also fitted with various sorts of mechanical equipment to heat, cool, and ventilate interior environments, to compensate for wide swings in weather conditions. In order to live enveloped as continuously as possible in an accustomed comfort zone of about 65 F to 75 F, we have precisely engineered equip-

4

ment and systems to perform—for the most part automatically—to remarkably high standards. We have learned to control indoor weather in defiance of whatever might happen outdoors.

Millions of man-hours and dollars have gone into researching, developing, and producing heating/cooling systems and equipment. Millions more have gone into purchasing, installing, and operating them. It's expensive to generate artificial heat within a house and it is getting more expensive all the time. It's even more expensive to extract heat from the air within a house and getting more so all the time. That controlled interior of benign weather conditions is a necessity that carries a luxury price tag.

Fuel/energy supplies are sometimes short and can at any time be interrupted or curtailed. Meeting heating/cooling operating and maintenance expenses is a difficult proposition for many folks, and unfortunately it has become impossible for a few. At best, keeping that expensive mechanically generated heat inside a house during cold weather is a tough chore. Keeping warm air outside during hot weather and cooling the interior of a house is even more difficult. The challenge in both respects is an on-going one that is made increasingly urgent by the difficult political, social, and economic realities that we now face.

For today's homeowner, the most important aspect of that challenge is to reduce heating/cooling costs to the lowest possible practical point and at the same time maintain reasonable comfort levels in the house (or perhaps even improving them). Part of that goal can be met by the incorporation of the latest in heating/cooling designs, technology, techniques, equipment, and systems, In many cases this is feasible. In many existing houses, this cannot be accomplished. For most owners of homes or for those homes still on the drawing board, the most practical approach lies in the central key to an energy-efficient structure—thermal insulation. Without thermal insulation, not even the finest equipment can function properly.

Whether you are a current homeowner or a prospective homeowner who merely wants to have done whatever is necessary in order to live comfortably with low heating/cooling costs or a do-it-yourselfer who wants to improve an existing house or build top thermal efficiency into a new one, a thorough knowledge of what thermal insulation is, how it works, and what it can do for you is essential. The starting point is with the laws of thermodynamics.

Does that sound complicated? It is or it can be. But not here. In simplified fashion, the first part of this book deals with what heat is, how it acts and reacts, what it does and why, so that you can understand what you're working with and how to go about winning the struggle to reduce heat losses/gains. Next is a full discussion of the various kinds of insulants that you can use to thermally protect your house. There is information on their characteristics, properties, and general uses. Then you'll find out how to calculate the actual heat losses or gains of a house using simple techniques and formulas. This fundamental process is the most important of all—and probably the least understood by the layperson—in making intelligent judgments about insulation installation projects.

There are a good many outside influences that bear upon the overall effectiveness of the thermal performance of a house. This includes the effects of building orientation, building design, the materials used in construction, control of moisture, ventilation, control of infiltration, and similar matters. There is a complete discussion of insulation applications and what parts of the house must be insulated. This is followed by instructions on how to properly install different kinds of insulation.

It's unfortunate that thermal insulation and the ways to achieve top-notch thermal performance in a house by proper assessment, application, and installation are poorly understood and so often given short shrift by so many homeowners. Even today, with the tremendous impetus to conserve energy and reduce heating/cooling costs, the preponderance of home-owners and (even more dismayingly) far too many do-it-yourselfers, amble along largely in ignorance of the substantial benefits they are missing. I assume that this has nothing to do with orneriness, rugged individualism, reactionaryism against the establishment, or even lack of interest. Primarily, I think, it's because most of the necessary information is scattered here and there and from time to time throughout numerous generalized books and periodicals. This piecemeal state of affairs discourages optimum results and makes for very difficult development of a comprehensive, knowledgeable overview of the subject by busy home-owners who have many other claims on their time and attention.

I hope that this book will, to some small extent, help correct that situation. While I make no claim that the subject is covered here in its entirety, at least the fundamentals are set forth. Using this book, you can proceed along whatever course best suits your purposes. For the most part, you should be able to achieve maximum heating/cooling comfort for minimum cost.

These days, that's a worthwhile goal.

Heat Basics

Insulation can be used to minimize the passage of vibration, electricity, sound, heat, or cold. *Insulation* is a term used to denote a certain group of special building materials called *insulants*. They are manufactured from several raw materials, sometimes in conjunction with one another, and are specifically designed, engineered, and produced for a number of applications in the building industry. Most insulation serves one purpose in particular and that is to impede the transfer of heat. To a far lesser degree, some types of insulation are used for sound insulation.

Although there is a wide variety of insulants available, a general knowledge of them—as well as of the expertise needed to make an effective installation of them—seems sometimes to be in short supply. The theory and practice of effective thermal insulation in residences has in the past been perhaps one of the most misunderstood and misapplied (when not ignored altogether) phases of small building construction. The result is that most residences—including far too many expensive, custom-designed and custom-built ones—are either underinsulated, improperly insulated, or ineffectively insulated (and sometimes all three).

Certainly this need not be so. The subject is not difficult to grasp, the details of residential insulation practices are not terribly complex, and the skills needed for proper insulation application and installation are easily and quickly learned. The most common problem seems to be a failure to comprehend the basics of the subject and to recognize all of the details involved in effectively minimizing heat transfer in a house or similar small building. In order to gain a full understanding of the whys and wherefores and to get an overall picture of just what must be done and how, you need to start at the very beginning.

ENERGY

Starting a discussion of insulation by talking about energy might seem a bit surprising until you realize that the entire purpose of installing insulation is to cope adequately with energy of one type or another. The concept of energy is a difficult one for many people to grasp. Although we know we are surrounded by energy, the concept seems elusive and somehow almost magical.

Energy is found in two fundamental forms: *potential energy* and what might be called *actual energy* or *active energy*. Potential energy is stored within objects or substances and it is ready to be released upon application of the right stimulus. Actual energy results from the proper triggering and subsequent release of potential energy. This book contains potential energy. If you drop the book to the floor, energy will be released. A match contains a certain amount of potential energy. If you light the match, potential energy will be released in a different fashion. If you set fire to the book with the match, more energy will be released.

Stored potential energy, when released, becomes actual or "real" energy. The opposite of potential energy is *kinetic energy*. This is the energy of motion. Any moving object, like a revolving door, a truck rolling down a turnpike, or the proverbial speeding bullet, is releasing potential energy as kinetic energy. Note that this also applies to molecular motion. The molecules that make up all of the matter that surrounds us (including our own bodies) are in constant, ceaseless motion. The molecules that comprise the ink and paper of this page are jostling about at incredibly high speeds, though within the fixed parameters of their ranges and the form and substance of the page, and will continue to do so in one guise or another forever.

This gives rise to several familiar types of energy *(electrical, mechanical, radiant, heat)*. These forms of energy interact with one another, or are made to do so, to produce the different kinds of work that we want done.

Electrical Energy

Electrical energy comes about as a consequence of electron flow (current) through conductors (such as wires and cables), which can then be converted by various means into effective work. The work producer might be a glowing light bulb, a portable heating unit, a power saw or any one of thousands of similar items. Electricity can be generated by mechanical or chemical means.

Electrical energy is also present in natural phenomena, like lightning, Saint Elmo's fire, the aurora borealis, and assorted kinds of static electricity. In addition, electrical energy is present all around us in minute quantities, unseen but forever operational during our daily lives—as in our nervous systems. Electrical energy can readily be converted to other kinds of energy.

Mechanical Energy

Mechanical energy is perhaps best exemplified by the internal combustion engine. In this example, fuel is burned to release energy that causes the engine to run. This transmits motion to the driving wheels of the vehicle through a series of gears and shafts. Similarly, an electric motor is another example of mechanical energy at work. Electrical energy causes the armature (in most cases) of the motor to revolve. The rotating armature shaft is mechanically connected to some other tool or device that performs work. Mechanical energy results from the conversion of another form of energy. Conversely, mechanical energy can be used to provide another form of energy as when electricity is generated by a turbine.

Radiant Energy

The greatest source of radiant energy—the one upon which all life upon earth depends—is the sun. Practically all of the energy that exists on this planet was, and is being, derived from solar radiation (or to use the more technical term, *insolation*). Although sunlight is the ultimate source of radiant energy, there are many secondary sources as well. Some sources are natural and others have been devised by man. Radiant energy is what makes fireflies flicker and glowworms glow. In both examples, the luminescence derives from a natural conversion of chemical energy. The glittering lights of a big city that you see from an airplane are comprised of visible radiant energy (light) converted from "man-made" electrical energy. Fire, or combustion of any sort, creates radiant energy which involves both electrical and chemical energy conversion. Invisible radiant energy can also be emitted by man-made devices such as cables or panels expressly designed for the purpose.

There is some confusion about radiant energy in relation to heat that has brought about an incorrect amalgamation of terms—something called "radiant heat." Actually, there is no such thing. Heat does not radiate; radiant energy does radiate. To clarify, first be aware that radiant energy is a part of the *electromagnetic spectrum* and, specifically, the *infrared* portion. This spectrum includes light in all its colors, radio waves, X-rays and other waves. The infrared or thermal portion is the deepest red just at the edge of the visible light band. These waves travel at the same speed as that of visible light. You cannot normally see it, but infrared radiation surrounds you all the time. Every object, every bit of matter, is in a continual process of emitting and absorbing radiant energy. The hotter the object the more energy is emitted.

Because radiant energy is largely invisible, we seldom pay much attention to it—but it is constantly at work. Radiant energy is emitted by everything, but absorbed only by an object cooler in temperature than the emitting body. Sometimes there is a balance and the amount emitted is equal to the amount absorbed. When radiant energy is absorbed by an object—like a table, a carpet, or your own body—heat energy is released by conversion from radiant energy. The electromagnetic infrared waves thereby will become sensorially noticeable.

Heat Energy

Heat energy, of course, is ultimately the most important form of energy to consider because the whole object of insulating a building is to either retain or to block out heat. Tremendous quantities of heat energy reach us each day in the form of converted solar radiation. Most of this energy remains unused in the active sense of turning it to our own purposes. We grow crops and gardens, we sunbathe, or perhaps we draw the curtains to keep the sun's heat out. Only a few curious souls have concerned themselves with converting solar radiation into heat for direct use in modern homes, offices, and factories.

In addition to sunlight, one of the most frequently used sources of heat energy known to man is fire. With fire, heat energy results as a conversion from chemical energy by a rearrangement, through chemical reaction, of the molecular structure of the fuel into different substances. As the reaction takes place, heat is released.

Heat is also generated when other forms of energy are converted for one purpose or another. For example, when an automobile engine runs, it produces a great deal of heat as a byproduct. So much so that if not properly cooled it will overheat and quit. Light bulbs produce a considerable amount of heat as a result of emanating light. Refrigerators and freezers produce quantities of heat in the process of chilling. And electric motors generate heat as they perform their functions. Even the human body throws off large quantities of heat as it goes about its normal functions.

ENERGY LOSS

Energy loss is a physical impossibility. This is a point that deserves special mention in order to avoid confusion over the term "energy loss" as it is sometimes casually used. Just as the laws of physics state that matter can neither be created nor destroyed, so energy can neither be gained nor lost. The amount of energy surrounding us at any given point in time is a constant. No amount of conversion, transference, or transformation from one form to another makes any impact whatsoever on the total amount of energy that exists. When a transformation process takes place, every single bit of energy will be accounted for in one fashion or another. If you burn a lump of coal, the lump disappears and becomes a few bits of ash and clinker. The potential energy that was stored in that piece of coal is released as chemical energy, electrical energy, radiant energy, and other forms of energy. All of which add up to 100 percent of the energy that originally existed in that lump of coal (Fig. 1-1).

Energy can, however, be "lost" during a series of conversions or during transmission or transference. What this means is that not all of the energy that you begin with can be converted to specific useful purposes. You might burn that lump of coal for heat, but only a percentage of the total energy involved will actually become heat. Therefore, as far as the person burning the coal is concerned, part of that process has resulted in an energy loss or a power loss (Fig. 1-2).

These so-called losses are usually translated in terms of the efficiency of the energy conversion process. No complete energy conversion or transmission system can be 100 percent efficient; there are always losses somewhere along the chain—often large ones. On the other hand, certain individual segments of a conversion chain can be close to 100 percent efficient. An example is when electrical energy is converted to heat a home.

HEAT

We habitually think in terms of heat and cold as being relative to our bodily comfort. We say that temperatures around 65 F to 75 F are neither "hot" nor "cold," but "comfortable." Objects of 100 F or more are "hot" to us, while objects down around the freezing mark (32 F) or below are "cold." Actually, objects with a temperature of zero degrees Fahrenheit also contain heat. So do objects at −100 F. Molecular activity, and therefore the release of heat energy, does not stop until a low of −460 F, or *absolute zero*, is reached (Fig. 1-3).

Absolute zero is the point at which there is no appreciable molecular activity. From that point upward, the heat in an object is dependent upon the speed of the molecules which make up that object. Higher speed means higher molecular temperatures. This process works in two ways. Greater molecular activity can be induced by various means and the result is a higher output of kinetic energy and more heat. Or the object can absorb heat from warmer outside sources and the result is increased molecular activity and larger amounts of heat.

Heat Transmission

Just as water always seeks its own level, heat also seeks to equalize itself. The flow of heat goes on continuously all around us and always travels from the warmer object or body to the cooler. In a tiny sphere of

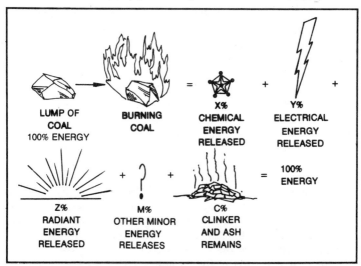

Fig. 1-1. The energy contained in a lump of coal (or any other object) is dispersed in various ways when the object changes form.

11

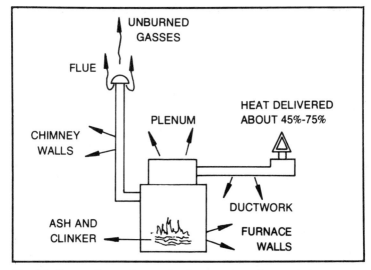

Fig. 1-2. Energy "losses" can arise in a number of ways during energy conversion and transmission processes.

interest, or a microclimate, there can be temperature equalization between two or more areas or objects for a short period of time. On a cloudy and calm 70 F day, your house interior can also stand at 70 F and there is no general, widespread heat transfer (though transfer does continue in hundreds of localized, small areas). As the sphere of interest enlarges, there are always temperature differentials everywhere that are seeking to equalize themselves (Fig. 1-4). This continual, universal process of equalization occurs in three basic ways; *convection, conduction,* and *radiation.*

Convection

Convection is by definition a process of *conveying*. Heat is convected, or transported if you will, by storing it temporarily in another substance and physically moving that substance from point to point—along with its cargo of heat. Air is commonly used in heating systems as a convecting medium and so are liquids, generally either plain water or some sort of antifreeze solution.

The air surrounding the stove picks up heat, and because heated air is lighter than cooler air, the warm air rises and the heat is transported in the gentle air currents by what is called *natural convection* (Fig. 1-5). If you add a fan to the stove so that cool air is sucked through or past the hot stove elements—picking up heat on the way by and being driven away as hot air—this is called *forced convection* (Fig. 1-6).

Similarly, the water in a water heater is always hottest at the top because the heat is transported upward by natural convection currents in the stored water.

If a pump is added to mechanically circulate the water, the convection is forced. Convection also occurs as a result of wind currents. Wind is nothing more than air in motion from natural causes and it will convect heat away from (or to) an object or body.

Conduction

Conduction is a matter of *transfer* of heat from one body or object to another that is in direct contact with the heat source. As always, the

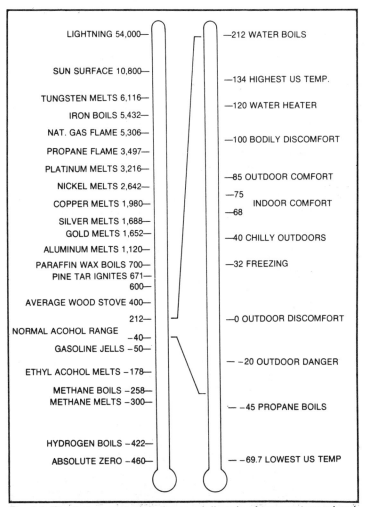

Fig. 1-3. The listing on the left shows a full scale of temperature-related phenomena and represents maximum range. Contrast it with the scale on the right which shows a temperature range that can be described as running from "incredibly cold" to "scalding hot."

13

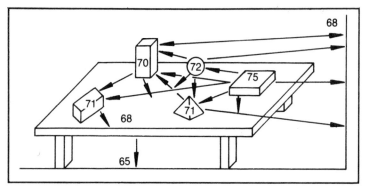

Fig. 1-4. Heat travels endlessly from object to object in a ceaseless attempt at equalization. This sketch is highly simplified.

direction of heat flow is from the warmer to the cooler body. Direct contact must be made so that there is interaction between the molecules of the two objects. If there is only a minute space between them, there is no interaction and conduction cannot take place (Fig. 1-7). If you sit down upon a cold rock, your nether regions will soon commence to feel chilly. This is because you are in contact with the rock (through layers of clothing) and your body heat is immediately transferred to the cooler rock in an attempt at equalization of temperature. Similarly, if you place a hot pot on a cool

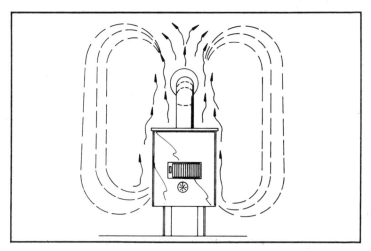

Fig. 1-5. Following the physical law that warmer air rises and cooler air falls, the airflow past and around this wood stove naturally pulls cool air up from the floor and continuously warms it as it passes the hot stove body. The warm air circulates outward as it hits the ceiling, cools as it moves away from the influence of the stove, and slowly settles to begin the cycle all over again. This sketch is stylized; seldom do natural convective air currents perform in such neat patterns.

14

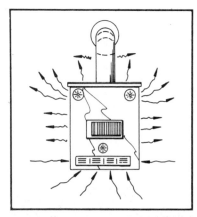

Fig. 1-6. When the natural convective air flow is supplanted with a fan, forced convection takes place. Here, suction created by the fans at the top corners of a wood stove pulls cool air in at the bottom of the stove jacket, up past the hot stove body, and exhausts it through the corner grilles as hot air. A certain amount of natural convection around the stove takes place as well.

stove mat, the pot will immediately begin to transfer heat to the mat and the mat will begin to warm up.

When heat is conducted between two objects, there is a molecular interaction between the two at all points of direct contact. But conduction can also take place in an individual object, from one end to another, or one side to another, Apply heat to one end of a length of copper wire and eventually a certain amount of that heat will be transferred, by conduction through molecular motion, to the other end of the wire (Fig. 1-8). Stick the head of a branding iron into the hot coals of a fire and eventually the head of the iron will become extremely hot—perhaps cherry red. Heat will also be conducted along the shank of the iron. The temperature will lessen toward the handle.

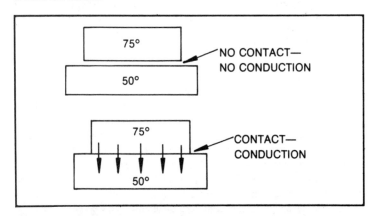

Fig. 1-7. If two bodies of different temperatures are separated from one another, no heat transfer can take place by means of conduction. It can by radiation and/or convection (above). Once the two objects are in physical contact, heat transfer by conduction takes place, but does not by either convection or radiation (below). The closer and tighter the contact, the better the conduction.

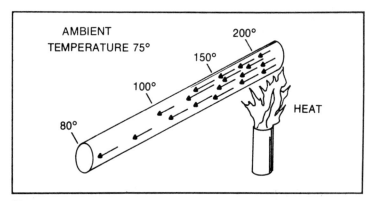

Fig. 1-8. If a heat source is held at one end of a copper wire, heat will transfer by conduction through the material and diminish in temperature as the distance from the heat source increases.

But not all materials conduct heat in equal measure. Some substances are excellent conductors, while other are not (Fig. 1-9). The measure of a given material's ability to conduct heat is called its *conductivity*. Conversely, the ability of a given material to oppose the conduction of heat—its resistance to heat transfer—is known as *resistivity*. Materials with high resistivity can make good insulators.

If you leave a silver spoon in a pot of bubbling-hot stew for a long enough period of time, the spoon handle will become so hot that you cannot hold it. Silver has a high rate of conductivity. On the other hand, you can leave a wooden spoon in a pot of hot stew indefinitely and have no difficulties in grasping the handle. Wood has a low rate of conductivity or a high measure of resistance to heat conduction. In this instance, it is an insulator. The steel shank of a branding iron might be too hot to hold. If fitted with a wooden handle, the end of the shank and the inside of the handle itself might well be of nearly the same temperature. Yet, you can pick up the wooden-handled iron with no discomfort. This is because the wood is a poor conductor and is reluctant to give up its heat to your hand. The heat transfer will eventually be made if you hang on long enough, but it will happen so slowly that the process will not be bothersome.

Heat conduction is so important to a discussion of insulants and home insulating that another example is in order. To approach the matter from a slightly different angle, consider three separate objects at a temperature of 40 F; a pane of glass, a piece of plywood, and a square of thick carpet. If you place the palm of your hand on each object successively, you will immediately feel a sensation of cold from the glass. The wood will feel cool, but to a much lesser degree than the glass. With the carpet, you will probably notice little change. Yet the temperature of your hand has remained constant—as has that of the three objects—except during the brief period of contact when the process of attempted temperature equalization is under way.

16

The reason for the differences in temperature sensation has to do with the conductivity of the three different materials. The glass has a high rate of conductivity and absorbs or releases heat rapidly, so the heat is quickly withdrawn from the palm of your hand at a much faster rate than it can be replaced by your body, and your hand immediately feels cold. Wood is not a particularly good conductor of heat. Although heat is being withdrawn from your palm during the contact period, the rate is slow and the change much less noticeable than with the glass. The heavy carpet is a good insulator in this situation and has low conductivity. The heat from your hand is absorbed so slowly by the carpet and replaced so quickly by your body that there is little or no noticeable change. But note that in all cases there *is* transfer of heat by conduction in various degrees.

Substances and materials of virtually any kind can be tested and given a rating to determine exactly how much heat can be transferred through them in a given period of time.

Radiation

The third method whereby heat is transferred is radiation. This is the conveyance of energy by electromagnetic waves (Fig. 1-10). This radiation is largely invisible and is confined to the infrared portion of the electromagnetic spectrum. Radiation takes place continuously all around us but we usually can't see it. This is almost always the case when the temperatures involved are less than about 885 F. When the temperature of the emitting body rises above that point, however, a small portion of the emission does become visible.

A good example of this is an ordinary sheet-metal wood stove. With a normal, small fire burning in the stove, no radiation is noticeable. As the fire burns hotter, the face of the stove will turn deep cherry red. At this

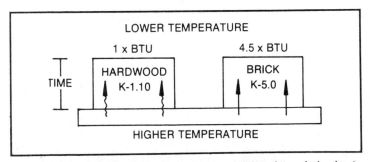

Fig. 1-9. Different materials have different capabilities of transfering heat. If a block of hardwood and a block of brick, each the same size, are positioned with higher temperature on one side and lower temperature on the other, heat will transfer through the materials from the higher to the lower temperature. But the brick will transfer 4.5 times as much heat over a given time period as will the hardwood. The brick has 4.5 times the conductivity as the hardwood; the hardwood has only 22% of the conductivity of brick. Conversely, the hardwood has 4.5 times the resistivity of the brick; the brick has only 22% of the resistivity of the hardwood.

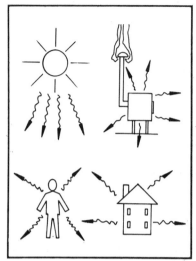

Fig. 1-10. Some of the most common emitters of radiant energy are the sun (top left), a stove (top right), the human body (bottom left), and a heated house in a cold environment (bottom right).

point, the temperature of the emitting surface is probably in excess of 900 F and the color that you see is the result of a slight shift in the wave emissions from infrared electromagnetic waves toward the red of the visible light spectrum. As the temperature rises, the shift in color will continue through bright red to orange, to yellow, and eventually to a bright white (though actually a stove is most unlikely to become this hot). This is visible radiation, but the greater proportion still remains in the thermal infrared range.

The effects of infrared radiation are practically instantaneous because the waves travel at the speed of light. When the waves strike another object they immediately become converted to heat. If you walk into a room where a stove is glowing deep red, you immediately feel the heat. How much heat you can feel depends upon the distance between you and the stove. It also depends to some extent upon where you are standing with relation to the stove and the physical shape and size of the stove itself. A flat surface will radiate a large portion of its electromagnetic waves straight outward, but there is some radiation in all directions. A curved surface will spread its radiation in a somewhat different pattern. The intensity of the radiation increases as the receiving body nears the source, and depends also to some degree upon the angular relationship with the emitting body. Put another way, the farther away from the stove (emitting body) the waves travel, the less their intensity will be and some waves will have less intensity than others depending upon what angle they leave the stove.

Exact amounts of radiation can be determined mathematically through a series of rather complicated geometric calculations. Radiation intensity is at its greatest when the receiving body is very close to and directly in front of the emitting body. If you hold the red-hot tip of a poker a quarter of an inch from a piece of newspaper, the paper will quickly char and curl. If you hold the poker 2 feet away, nothing will happen. At that distance, the intensity of radiation is insufficient to allow the release of enough heat energy quickly enough to char the paper. And because of the diverging angles of the waves being radiated most of them miss the paper and are dissipated in the air or travel to other objects. The radiation is still taking place. Some of the electromagnetic waves are being converted to heat energy when they strike the newspaper, in dispersed and weakened fashion and to no great effect.

Radiation travels nicely through air, of course, and it is also the only way that heat can be transported or transmitted through a vacuum. But radiation, or infrared rays, cannot travel through most solid objects. As soon as the rays strike the surface of an object, they are converted to heat. There are a few exceptions to this (Fig. 1-11). Glass will allow a certain amount of radiation to pass through; how much is dependent upon the characteristics of the particular type of glass. Infrared rays will penetrate water only for a short distance. That's one reason why when you swim in a pond on a sunny day you will find the shallows warm but the deeper water much colder. There are also a few minerals and particular compositions of plastics that will allow the passage of infrared rays. Although most objects absorb infrared radiation, there are some cases where the rays will be reflected instead of absorbed or passed. This is particularly true of shiny and light-colored surfaces—especially metal.

Comfort heating by infrared ray-emitting surfaces can be accomplished by means of direct radiation and reradiation (convection and

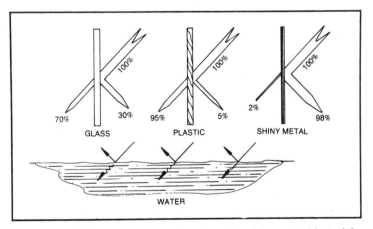

Fig. 1-11. When radiant energy (as from the sun) strikes most objects, it is converted to heat energy. Much of the energy passes through glass or transparent plastic that can be manufactured to admit/exclude various amounts of radiant energy. Practically all radiant energy is reflected away from both shiny metal and water surfaces; only a tiny amount is converted to heat.

conduction also play their parts, but disregard this for the moment). If a radiant energy source, such as a heater, is activated in a room, the infrared radiation will travel to whatever objects are directly in the path of the rays. This is essentially a straight-line proposition. No rays will travel beyond or around any objects that block them.

However, as those objects begin to warm through the release of heat energy, they will reradiate in different directions to other cooler objects. These objects will gain heat and reradiate again, and so forth. The result is a network of radiation traveling in all directions which eventually brings everything in the room to an essentially equal temperature. If the exterior temperatures happen to be cooler than the interior, radiation will also transfer heat to the exterior. All of this is a constant and continuing process of action and interaction. The initial source of radiation can just as easily be the sun as an electrical device designed to produce infrared radiation.

Radiation is the principal means whereby heat is transferred over an appreciable distance between objects. That distance might be just a matter of inches or less. In the case of the sun, it amounts to millions of miles. You can see for yourself approximately how radiation works by doing a bit of simple experimenting. Stand out in the sun on a cold winter day and point your face directly into the sun's rays. You will immediately feel warmth as a result of the radiation. Your back, however, will feel cold. This is because the radiation is directional and hits you only in the front. The area behind you is much colder than you are. Consequently, your body is receiving radiation from the front, but emitting it from the rear into the cold air and snow behind you in the universal attempt at temperature equalization (Fig. 1-12).

If you hang up a sheet of black plastic film and step behind it, you will be in the shade and you will feel cold. The direct radiation from the sun no longer reaches you and your body itself is radiating heat away in all directions. Within a matter of moments, the black plastic sheet will begin to reradiate the heat it has gained from the sun and you again feel the warmth. If you were to place a large sheet of polished and highly reflective aluminum propped at the proper angle behind you, you would quickly feel warmth on both sides. This is because the infrared radiation from the sun is reflected from the aluminum onto your back (Fig. 1-13). Your sides, however, will probably still feel cold because they are radiating off in those directions.

HEAT FORMS

There are two different forms of heat: *sensible* and *latent*. The principal reason for differentiating is that clear definitions of heat energy components are necessary.

Sensible Heat

Sensible heat is heat that you can actually feel. If you touch a hot stove lid you feel sensible heat. Any heat that is detectable by touch is sensible heat. Radiant energy is not sensible heat, but it becomes so after being absorbed by an object and converted to heat energy. Sensible heat is associated with objects or substances that remain in steady state. They do not change their form or phase.

Latent Heat

Latent heat is involved when a change takes place in the physical condition of a substance. Substances exist in any one of three states: gas, liquid, or solid. Water (liquid) can be transformed into ice (solid) or water vapor (gas) and oxygen gas can be converted to liquid oxygen. When one of these changes takes place, latent heat is required to accomplish the task. When the process is reversed and the change back to the original state is made, latent heat is released.

When you heat a pot of water, the temperature of the water rises and sensible heat is given off. When the boiling point is reached, there is no further rise in temperature. Instead, the water begins to change form to vapor and "uses up" latent heat (mostly from the water itself) in the process. If the resulting water vapor is captured and condensed, an identical amount of latent heat will be released during the condensation process.

The firewood you burn in your stove contains a certain amount of moisture. As the wood burns, this moisture is released in the form of vapor and additional vapor is formed during the combustion process itself. The vapor contains latent heat, taken from the burning wood, that is later released and converted to sensible heat when the moisture condenses. Unfortunately, most of this heat generally escapes the heating system (up the flue) and serves no useful purpose.

TEMPERATURE

We often tend to think of heat and temperature as being the same. They are not. While heat is a form of energy, temperature is a measure of

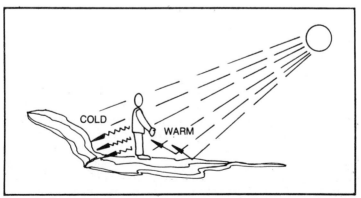

Fig. 1-12. A person standing facing the sun on a cold day will be warmed in front by both direct and reflected radiant energy from the sun, but feel cool in back because body energy is radiating away into the shaded, cooler area.

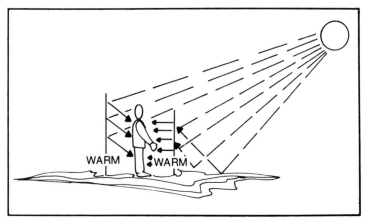

Fig. 1-13. Black plastic sheeting intercepts radiant energy from the sun and then reradiates it to warm the person from the front. Meantime, radiant energy from the sun reflects from the shiny aluminum sheet and warms from the rear. The sides remain cool because energy radiates away in those directions.

the intensity of heat. The most familiar scale to us is Fahrenheit. Celsius is the other temperature scale. Temperature does not have anything to do with heat quantity. The temperature of molecules moving at high speed is high. The temperature of molecules moving at a lower speed is correspondingly lower. The quantity of heat involved depends upon the combined kinetic energy of all molecules in a given object. If there are only a few high-speed molecules in that object, the molecular temperature is high, but the total heat quantity is low because the total kinetic energy is low. If there are many high-speed molecules in the object, there is high molecular temperature and a high heat output quantity because of the large amount of total kinetic energy being released. The same *quantity* of heat can be contained in a small pot of boiling water, a large tub of cool water or a huge cake of ice. The *temperatures* of the three objects are obviously vastly different (Fig. 1-14).

A high temperature does not equate with heat quantity. For example, if you fire up a blowtorch in your workshop, the temperature of the flame, especially the blue portion, will be quite high and enable you to melt solder or whatever. You could let the torch run all day without elevating the room temperature to any appreciable degree. The total quantity of heat being released is far too small to have any impact upon the total quantity of heat within the room.

On the other hand, a lower temperature does not mean that large quantities of heat are not present. Great amounts of heat, sufficient to provide for the heating needs of a residence, can be extracted from a suitable volume of air at 32 F or even less by a device known as a heat pump. Such equipment is now in common use in this country for comfort heating.

22

HEAT ENERGY CONTENT

Just as temperature is a necessity for measuring heat intensities on a comparative scale, other units are essential for determining heat quantity, or heat energy content. Energy in its various kinds is measured by a great many different units—all with varying definitions. A *calorie* is a basic measure of heat quantity. A *gram* or *small calorie* equals the amount of heat required to raise the temperature of 1 gram of water 1 degree centigrade. Another kind of calorie, called the *kilogram* or *large calorie*, is the amount of heat required to raise the temperature of 1 kilogram of water 1 degree Celsius. This is the unit used in calculating the heat or energy-producing value of foods and it is equal to 1000 gram calories.

One *Btu,* or *British thermal unit,* equals 252 small calories. One Btu is defined as the amount of heat needed to increase the temperature of 1 pound (about a pint) of water by 1 degree Fahrenheit.

The Btu is a relatively small unit of heat quantity, but it is the one most commonly used in the heating and air conditioning fields. A large proportion of the equipment used for such purposes is rated in terms of Btu input and output. Many calculations for heating or cooling requirements are couched in terms of the Btu. To give you some idea of the relative size of a Btu, consider that if you down 2000 calories in your meals during a day, you will have provided yourself with just a bit less than 8000 Btu's. A 100-watt light bulb left burning for 1 hour consumes 0.1 kilowatt-hour of electricity, equivalent to 341 Btu. An 800-watt toaster operating for 2 minutes releases approximately 90 Btu's of heat.

POWER AND ENERGY UNITS

Energy is the capacity to do work. *Power* includes a time factor so that the *amount* of work being done can be conveniently calculated or discus-

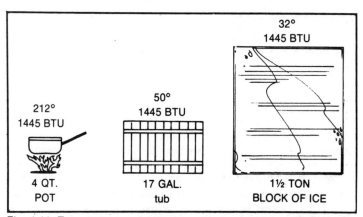

Fig. 1-14. Temperature and heat quantity do not equate. Though the temperatures of the 4 quarts of water, the 17 gallons of water, and the 1.5 tons of ice are far different, each contains an identical quantity of heat in Btu's.

sed. Power is the time rate at which work is done or energy is emitted or transferred. There are numerous terms used to designate power or the emission or transference of a particular amount of energy over a particular period of time. Probably the best-known of these terms is *horsepower*. Another is the *watt*, 746 of which equal 1 horsepower.

To further explain the concept of power, consider for example, that a gallon of fuel oil (or a lump of coal, a stick of wood or a roll of newspaper) contains a certain amount of heat energy. This can be released as mostly sensible heat, along with some latent heat, by igniting the material. By controlling the combustion process, the oil can be made to burn fast and furiously or slowly over a much longer period of time. In either case, the total amount of heat energy released is the same and so is the quantity of sensible heat produced. However, the first heat release happens at a rapid rate while the second occurs at a slow rate. Fast burning results in a high-power situation. Slow burning produces a lower power level. The differences lie in the time span over which the identical amounts of heat are released (Fig. 1-15).

One of the most common methods of expressing heat power, and the one you will often encounter in discussions of this sort, is the rating in terms of British thermal units per hour, expressed as Btu/h or Btuh. This simply means the total number of Btu's that are emitted or transferred during an hour's time.

A typical oil-fired furnace, for example, might have an input rating of 100,000 Btuh. In an hour, it can burn sufficient fuel oil to provide that much total heat release. The output of the furnace, or the amount of sensible heat which actually enters the area being heated, depends upon numerous factors. This includes the efficiency of both the furnace and the heat conveyance system. This output can also be measured in Btuh.

Similarly, the thermal conductivity of materials is also measured in Btuh. In this case, two additional factors are included in the formula so that direct comparisons can be made between all kinds of materials. The rating is done in terms of Btuh per degree Fahrenheit difference in temperature between the two bounding surfaces of the material, per square foot of material.

The *watt* is another term widely used in respect to heat energy that is released by electrical devices. The watt is used as a matter of convenience for rating electric heating devices and calculating heat losses or gains directly into power requirements for electrical heating or cooling systems. Actually, Btuh or watts can be used because they are readily convertible from one to the other. One watt is the equivalent of 3.413 Btuh. Conversely, one Btuh is equal to 0.293 watts. An electric heater of 1000-watt rating has a capability of 3413-Btuh heat production. If left running for a full hour, 3413 Btu's will be produced to consume 1000 watts of power, or one *kilowatt*—abbreviated *kw* (1 kilowatt equals 1000 watts). During the process, 1000 *watt-hours* of electrical energy or *1 kilowatt-hour* (abbreviated *kwh*) will be transferred.

HEAT STORAGE

Heat storage capacity is usually referred to in terms of the *specific heat* of the particular substance involved. This is defined as the amount of heat required to raise a unit weight of a substance by 1 degree of temperature at either constant volume or constant pressure. One common formulation is to express specific heat in terms of calories per gram per degree centigrade. It can also be done in terms of Btu's per pound per degree Fahrenheit. By the latter method, wood has a specific heat of about 0.6. Silver, on the other hand, has a rating of only 0.056. The greater the number, the greater the heat storage capability.

Heat storage can be an important factor in making heating/cooling calculations and judgements. For example, when the sun shines down on your roof for a long period of time during the warm summer days, the entire roof structure will slowly gain heat. This heat will be transferred into the attic, to the ceiling joists and the ceiling, and perhaps to a certain extent down into the living quarters as well. When the sun goes down, a certain amount of this heat will remain in storage, to be dissipated slowly during the night hours. This situation could greatly increase a potential cooling load.

Heat storage can also have a bearing upon how rapidly the temperature level within a structure moves up and down as heating and cooling takes place by mechanical means. If the various elements that make up the structure have a high capacity for heat storage, they will absorb heat when the heating system is on and release it slowly when the heating system is off. This flywheel effect, as it is often called, makes for a much more even

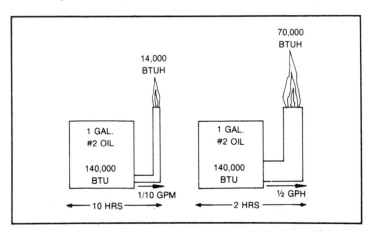

Fig. 1-15. Power represents the time rate at which energy is emitted or transferred. If a gallon of fuel oil is burned over 10 hours, 14,000 Btu of heat is emitted per hour; over 2 hours, 70,000 Btu of heat is emitted per hour. In both cases, 1 gallon of oil was burned and the same total of heat (140,000 Btu) emitted. But the 10-hour burn is at much lower power than the 2-hour burn.

ambient temperature than would be the case if the structure components had a low heat storage capacity.

The entire concept of heat storage and flywheel effect has come in for much closer scrutiny over the past few years as energy conservation has become more important and the development of solar heating systems has accelerated. Considerable emphasis is just now beginning to be placed upon heat storage as a useful adjunct to a comfort heating system. This is the concept of *thermal mass* and it is essential to the design of either passive or active solar heating systems. Such designs use large quantities of materials with relatively high heat storage capacity that can absorb heat from the sun (or other sources) to be slowly released during periods of darkness or cloudy skies.

HEAT AND COMFORT

There are a number of factors that influence our sense of comfort as we go about our daily chores. The ambient air temperature, or the temperature of the air that immediately surrounds the body, is most often measured by what is called the *dry bulb* method. This does not take into account one of the more important factors governing bodily comfort—that of humidity. If the temperature is taken by the *wet bulb* method, which includes the evaporative cooling rate of mositure in the air, results are likely to be quite different.

On an extremely hot day in an arid region, the dry bulb temperature might rest at 100 F; yet a person accustomed to that situation could feel perfectly comfortable. A wet bulb temperature measurement shows one reason why. That reading might lie at about the 70-degree mark because of the effect of low humidity. On the other hand, a dry bulb temperature of a moderate 80 F might well feel most uncomfortable with a high humidity causing the wet bulb temperature to be on the order of 77 F. The amount of moisture in the air has a definite effect upon our feeling of comfort. This is true regardless of whether we are indoors or outdoors.

Another important factor is movement of the surrounding air. When we are outdoors in warm weather, we don't pay too much attention to air movement unless the wind happens to be particularly strong. A breeze mostly serves to make a warm day more pleasant because of its evaporative cooling effect upon our bodies. As temperatures slip below 70 F or 75 F, air movement becomes much more noticeable. With the *wind chill factor*, air motion and ambient temperature can be measured to calculate an accurate temperature (Table 1-1). For example, if the ambient temperature is 30 F and the wind speed is 30 miles per hour, the effective temperature as far as our bodies are concerned is—2F.

In an indoor environment, air movements are called *drafts* and we don't like them. Drafts become particularly noticeable as the outdoor temperature drops and we are trying to maintain a relatively high indoor temperature. In such situations, even a very slight air movement, perhaps only the current caused by someone walking by, is often noticeable and can produce a feeling of discomfort. Air movement is something we can seldom get away from completely, but the less there is, to a point, the more comfortable we feel. At least this is true in most artificially-heated indoor environments. Some air motion is essential for proper heat distribution and reasonable comfort. The trick is to eliminate cold drafts and at the same time maintain uniform and unobtrusive interior air circulation.

Another factor that influences our perception of comfort has to do with the temperature of some of the elements in our immediate surroundings. We would normally consider a room temperature of 75 F to be a perfectly comfortable one, if not perhaps a bit warm. If the floor or walls of the room are at a much lower temperature, such as 50 F, most people invariably perceive the room temperature to be considerably less than it actually is. Large expanses of window glass can create the same impression.

Interestingly enough, this situation can sometimes work in reverse. If there is a radiant heat source in the room and you arrange yourself directly before it, well enclosed in a comfortable armchair (which acts as a partial insulating cocoon), you might find yourself quite cozy even though the room temperature is low. That source of radiant energy could be the sun streaking in through a window or it could be a wood stove or an electrical radiant heat panel. The effect remains the same.

The type of activity in which you are engaging at any given moment also has a bearing upon your perception of environmental comfort. If you sit quietly reading or knitting, you might well find an ambient air temperature of 72 F to be a bit chilly. Your body is largely at rest and is not producing excess heat. On the other hand, if you are busy in your workshop building cabinets or engaged in scrubbing floors or a little impromptu dancing, you might find a temperature of 65 F to be more than adequate. Your body is producing plenty of heat to keep you warm.

A certain amount of our perception of comfort has to do with *psychophysical conditioning*. In other word, a set of conditions different than those you have habitually lived with for years might produce a certain amount of discomfort. In this country, we are not only used to—but almost entirely dependent upon—central heating systems which pump out enormous quantities of heat and maintain an indoor ambient temperature so high that visitors from many other countries find the atmosphere stifling. Our

Table 1-1. Wind Chill Chart.

	Dry bulb temperature (°F)																		
	45	40	35	30	25	20	15	10	5	0	-5	-10	-15	-20	-25	-30	-35	-40	-45
4	45	40	35	30	25	20	15	10	5	0	-5	-10	-15	-20	-25	-30	-35	-40	-45
5	43	37	32	27	22	16	11	6	0	-5	-10	-15	-21	-26	-31	-36	-42	-47	-52
10	34	26	22	16	10	3	-3	-9	-15	-22	-27	-34	-40	-46	-52	-58	-64	-71	-77
15	29	23	16	9	2	-5	-11	-18	-25	-31	-38	-45	-51	-58	-65	-72	-78	-85	-92
20	26	19	12	4	-3	-10	-17	-24	-31	-39	-46	-53	-60	-67	-74	-81	-88	-95	-103
25	23	16	8	1	-7	-15	-22	-29	-36	-44	-51	-59	-66	-74	-81	-88	-96	-103	-110
30	21	13	6	-2	-10	-18	-25	-33	-41	-49	-56	-64	-71	-79	-86	-93	-101	-109	-116
35	20	12	4	-4	-12	-20	-27	-35	-43	-52	-58	-67	-74	-82	-89	-97	-105	-113	-120
40	19	11	3	-5	-13	-21	-29	-37	-45	-53	-60	-69	-76	-84	-92	-100	-107	-115	-123
45	18	10	2	-6	-14	-22	-30	-38	-46	-54	-62	-70	-78	-85	-93	-102	-109	-117	-125

Wind speed (mi/h)

heating/cooling range is very narrow (usually considered to be about 65 F - 75 F) and we find that attempting to accomodate ourselves to other conditions can be unpleasant. Yet, this is not terribly difficult to do and it is a matter of becoming **mentally** and physically attuned to higher or lower temperature ranges or to a broader or different comfort range altogether.

All of the above factors must be tempered to some degree by the physical characteristics of each individual involved. Some folks are more susceptible to heat or cold than others and accordingly require higher or lower ambient air temperatures or comfort levels. The state of one's health has a bearing.

Clothing plays an important part. Some people insist upon wandering about in T-shirts and shorts when the exterior temperature hovers around zero; others wear their blue serge suits on 100 F days. Dressing for the conditions at hand not only allows greater comfort, but can also reduce the load on a heating/cooling system—thereby cutting costs as well. There is much to be said for the idea of keeping the body warm or cool, rather than the entire space that it regularly occupies.

AIR MOVEMENT

No matter how well-built a building is there is always a certain amount of interior air movement. This is unavoidable, if only because doors are constantly being opened and closed as people come and go. Human movement within a building creates air currents. Air also begins to move as the temperature increases or decreases. The general movement is upward or downward and there may be some lateral movement as well.

In enclosed spaces, the warmer air will collect along the ceiling level, while the cooler air remains below. Air can also stratify in horizontal thermal layers. As the density of layers changes with heating and cooling, the layers will begin to shift.

Colder air always falls. You can prove this to yourself by holding your hand beneath the interior sill of a window on a cold day. You will be able to feel the cold air current as it passes over your hand. A lighted cigarette held in the same position will produce a trail of smoke curling toward the floor. As this air gains warmth from its surroundings, it will begin to rise.

Another curious phenomenon is called the *stack effect*. This is actually an *air pressure differential* created in a building on a cold day. The effect is much more severe in multistoried buildings, but it is also present to a degree in small houses. Warm air inside the house is much more buoyant than the cold air outside. The warm air inside rises and eventually finds its way outside. In equalization of the pressure differential, cold air then works its way in around the lower portion of the building. This creates drafts and increases the heating load. In serious cases, this effect can be so drastic in tall buildings as to make closing doors at ground level a difficult struggle because of the air pressure.

In most small buildings, the *neutral pressure level* is about midway up the building wall (Fig. 1-16). Above this point, warm air is moving out (higher pressure), while below it the cold air is being drawn in (lower pressure). The resulting pressure differential within a building creates some interesting problems in cold weather that go unnoticed or might not occur at other times. For example, a tiny leak in the lower portion of a house that might admit little, if any, air during warm weather suddenly becomes the equivalent of a pressurized air hose, pumping cold air into the interior at a tremendous rate. At the same time, a small crack or aperture around the eaves or ridge of the building streams warm air out into the cold atmosphere at a horrendous clip. This can happen when the air is perfectly calm on the inside and outside.

Pressure differentials can also be created within the house as a result of wind driving up against and curling around a structure. Wind can change the neutral pressure zone of a house by varying it in all sorts of ways depending upon the wind velocity, direction and turbulence. The effect upon the interior atmosphere is also variable. This depends upon the number, size and location of any openings in the structure such as chimneys, vent pipes and the like. This in turn has an effect upon air movement within the structure and consequently upon heat production, distribution and regulation. In addition, air leakage (in and out) will be amplified by the wind as well as the pressure differential. The opening and closing of doors or windows will also play a part.

STRUCTURAL HEAT TRANSFER

Heat transfer in a building of any sort is continually taking place. At no time is there complete temperature equalization. In certain climates and at

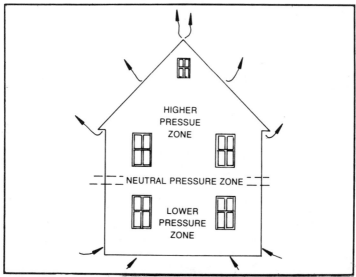

Fig. 1-16. In most residences, when the stack effect is operative the neutral pressure zone lies about halfway up the house walls. Cold air enters in the lower pressure zone and warm air exits in the higher pressure zone.

certain times of the year, we pay little attention to this and seldom notice the process. However, when the time comes to turn on the heating or cooling system so that we can adjust our microclimates to our personal tastes and comfort, the business of overall structural heat transfer becomes extremely important.

Heat entering a building through the building components from the outside during the hot weather is a *structural heat gain*. Heat which is lost by transfer from the inside of a building to the outdoors during cold weather is a *structural heat loss*.

Heat losses take place by transmission through the building sections—walls, floors, ceilings, doors and windows—and because of the flow of air through the structure by virture of pressure differentials, leakage, operation of fans and vents, open chimney stacks and so forth. In addition, various temperature differentials between the interior and exterior of the building section must be taken into consideration. The presence or absence of adequate vapor barriers and proper ventilation of the structure also plays a part.

An element, sometimes called the *experience factor*, is important too. This involves a series of extremely variable factors that includes the living habits of the occupants of the building, how often the doors are open and closed, whether or not the heat will be turned down for lengthy periods of time, whether the building is constantly occupied or is sometimes empty, the number of people who occupy, use, or visit the building, and so on.

Other elements that must be taken into account include sun, wind and weather, the design and quality of the structure, and similar assorted items. Many of these factors are difficult to pin down with any degree of accuracy. Often they are well worth considering in a general way.

Heat gains occur in several ways. Direct sunlight passing through transparent sections of the building produces a solar heat gain. Heat is also transmitted through the solid building sections to the interior. Heat can be gained by air flow and infiltration through doors, windows, vent pipes and cracks. Most buildings also contain internal sources of heat that must be figured into the overall heat gain. These sources include equipment and machinery, lights, appliances, and people. Latent heat components must also be included as a part of the overall heat gain in a building. Latent heat appears along with outdoor air that inflitrates, from people in the building, and occasionally from some of the other internal heat loads.

All of these various factors involved in structural heat gains and losses are important to any discussion of insulating calculations and techniques. They are treated individually and in considerable depth in later portions of this book.

Heat Transfer

Heat is transmitted, is transferred, moves, or flows from one point to another by three different means: conduction, convection, or radiation. While at any given point at any one given moment only one of these functions might be taking place, in the overall picture all three functions work concurrently in the transfer of heat. The direction of heat flow is always from the warmer to the cooler area. This takes place through materials or objects, around them, over them, or under them. Like electricity, heat seeks the paths of least resistance in its quest for equalization.

Thermal transmission is symbolized by q. Simply stated, this equals the quantity of heat that flows as a result of all three heat transfer mechanisms over a specific period of time and under the specific conditions that prevail during that time. The measurement of q can be expressed either in Btuh or W (watts). For the most part, I will be using the Btuh term. If we were to make heating or cooling load calculations specifically for electric heating/cooling units, you could just as easily make them in watts.

All of the various aspects of thermal transmission comprise the basic key to designing and constructing houses that are thermally efficient, to calculating heating and cooling loads, and to sizing heating and cooling equipment and systems. In addition, and most importantly to this particular subject, they are the key to discovering how much insulation is required in a particular house under specific conditions, where the insulation might best be placed for given house designs, and what the cost-effectiveness over given periods of time will be for different insulations or combinations thereof.

Your body is a producer of heat. If the ambient temperature of the air surrounding your body is sufficiently high, and is even, no gross heat transfer will take place. As the ambient temperature falls, you must put on clothing in order to slow down the rate at which heat escapes your body in order to keep from feeling chilly or cold. The lower the temperature, the more clothing is necessary to retain enough heat to keep warm. No matter how much clothing you put on, there is always a constant heat transfer from your body to the colder surrounding atmosphere. The shell of the house, like the clothing you wear, is incapable of producing any heat. All it can do is restrain the generated heat from escaping into the outside atmosphere.

If the house shell has good restraint capabilities, the amount of heat that escapes can be slowed and minimized. If it does not, large amounts of heat will escape. The colder the outside temperature and the stronger the wind, the greater the heat loss. Although a person can put on more clothing to increase heat-restraint capability, no such thing can be done with a house. Once a structure is built, adding to the heat-restraining capability is difficult, expensive, and sometimes practically impossible. This means that the structure should be designed and built for worst-case conditions, within reason, at the outset. And just as with the clothed human body, the heat loss to the outside is a continuous process whenever the exterior temperature is lower than the interior temperature. If you think of a house as a huge radiator of heat, with the heat traveling out and away in all directions, you'll get the picture. Much the same happens in the summertime except that in the summer heat travels inward from the outside and is a heat gain.

In order to construct a thermally efficient house, the process of heat transfer, either from the inside out or the outside in, has to be minimized as much as is possible from a practical standpoint. In order to accomplish this, you must know just how, where, and when such heat transfer takes place. In addition, it's helpful to know the fundamental terminology involved and how to make the necessary judgements and calculations. That's what this chapter is all about. Unfortunately, there's no choice but to get a bit technical. If you take things a step at a time, you'll find that this is not as difficult a subject as it first appears.

CONDUCTIVITY AND CONDUCTANCE

Thermal conductivity is thermal transmission, or transmission of heat, by conduction only (radiation or convection play no part) through a unit area of an infinite slab in unit time, in a direction perpendicular to the surface, when the unit difference in temperature between the two surfaces of the slab is known. The translation of that is simple enough and it becomes more obvious when particular units are assigned to the process. The usual method, at least in this country, is to consider the slab in terms of 1-square-foot chunks, the thickness of the slab in inches, the unit time in hours, and the temperature in degrees Fahrenheit. Written out, this reads: Btu per inch per hour per square foot per degree F difference. The symbol for thermal conductivity is k.

Now for a practical example. The k of practically all common materials has been tested at one time or another. The specific values that are conventionally used can be found in reference tables made up for the purpose. The figures shown in Table 2-1 are typical and were taken from a larger and more complete table. Medium-density particle board has a listed k of 0.94. Suppose you had a piece of this particle board that measures 1 foot square and is 1 inch thick. Assume that the temperature on one side of the piece is 70 F and the temperature on the other side is 30 F. The temperature difference (which is sometimes expressed as Δt) is 40 F ($t_i - t_0 = 70 - 30 = 40$). Heat will travel through the particle board from the warm side to the cold side at the rate of 0.94 Btu (k values are expressed in terms of Btu) every hour for every degree difference in temperature. In an hour's time, assuming that the inside and outside temperatures remain stable and 40 F apart, 0.94 x 40 Btu of heat, or 37.6 Btu, will travel through that piece of particle board every hour (Fig. 2-1). Now suppose that your piece of particle board is not 1 inch thick, but is only one-half inch thick. Note that this does not cut the k value in half, but rather doubles it. Because the material is only half as thick, it has only half the thermal resistance and twice as much heat can pass through in the same time period. If the particle board is 2 inches thick, *then* only half as much heat could pass through in an hour because the thermal resistance would be doubled (Fig. 2-2).

Figures such as these are used, by convention, in making various kinds of heat calculations for residential (or other) heat loss or gain. But it is important to realize that these are not fixed, inviolate numbers. They are based on certain test parameters and assumptions and they were developed by controlled laboratory tests. In the real world there are always variables. For example, the figures are established on the basis of a specific mean temperature, a particular direction and orientation of the heat transmission, the fact that transmission is only taking place by conduction, the material being tested is of a certain particular density, and of a certain moisture content, and so on.

Table 2-1. Representative Conductivity (k) Factors at Specified Densities and Mean Temperature of 75 F of Several Common Homogeneous Materials.

MATERIAL	DENSITY lbs/cu ft	CONDUCTIVITY k
Particle board, med. density	50	0.94
Douglas fir plywood	34	0.80
Common brick	120	5.00
Sandstone	---	12.50
Sawdust	8-15	0.45
Hardboard siding	40	1.49
Gypsum plaster, sand aggregate	105	5.60
Perlite	5-8	0.37
Oak	45	1.10
Snow (32F)	34.7	3.24
Still air (32F)	---	0.157
Soft rubber	58	1.00

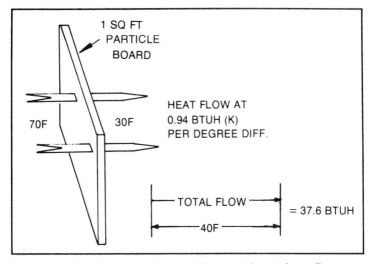

Fig. 2-1. Heat transfers through a material at a certain rate depending upon its conductivity or conductance. Particle board has a k of 0.94 and that means 0.94 Btu of heat will transfer from the warmer side to the cooler side, per inch of thickness, per square foot of surface area, per degree of temperature difference between the two sides, per hour. If the temperature difference is 40 F, then 37.6 Btu of heat will be transferred through 1 square foot of the particle board every hour.

Note, too, that the k factor is used only with materials that are homogeneous. The materials are of the same makeup and structure all the way through, with no significant variations in composition. But your piece of particle board, even though it is stamped "medium-density," might actually have a density of 47 pounds per cubic foot instead of 50, or it might have picked up some moisture. Of course it will not be put to work in a constant, controlled temperature of 75 F, and so on. The actual k for your particle board will almost surely be something different than what the table says.

As you can imagine, the minute variations that can take place in k or any other factors are infinite. Trying to cope with them all would be, from a practical standpoint of someone in the field trying to work out heat loss calculations, an impossible task. That's why the figures that you'll find in the reference tables are the ones that are generally used. They are uniform and universally employed and make calculations much easier.

Keep in mind as you make heat loss/gain calculations that the results of your calculations will always be approximations regardless of what those calculations are or how carefully you do them. The degree of error or inaccuracy is never sufficient to cause any particular difficulties, provided that you follow the approved methods of calculations and work carefully.

To carry the k factor business a bit further, we can recap by saying that k equals the number of Btu's of heat that will pass from the warm side to the cool side of a 1-square-foot piece of material in an hour for every degree of difference in temperature from one side to the other of the piece. The *k* of a common brick is 5.0, the *k* of sawdust is 0.45, the *k* of a sand-aggregate gypsum plaster is 5.6, and the *k* of oak is 1.10. For molded-bead expanded polystyrene insulating board, the *k* is 0.28. Insulating materials have much lower *k*-factors than most building materials; the higher the *k* value, the lower the insulating value, and vice versa. So, if you know the *k* of any given material, you can quickly compare one to the other and determine just how effective it may be in resisting the flow of heat.

Suppose that the material in question is not of the same construction or makeup all the way through. This is true of a great many building materials, of course, so we need to have a different way of expressing the material's capability of conducting heat. Here we use the *C* factor; this stands for *thermal conductance*. This is the thermal transmission in unit time through a unit area of a particular body or assembly having defined surfaces, with a unit average temperature difference between the surfaces known. The *C* factor works in much the same way as the *k* factor. The principal difference is that the *C* factor is for a material of stated construction and stated thickness, rather than being homogeneous and 1 inch thick.

In practice, the *C* factor is used with a great many standard building materials that are available only in certain thicknesses or made up in certain constructions (Table 2-2). For example, consider a concrete block. Obviously it is not homogeneous because it has cores and webs, and certainly concrete blocks are not built only 1 inch thick. The thermal conductance is expressed as a particular figure for each different kind of concrete block. An 8-inch-thick block made with sand and gravel aggregate

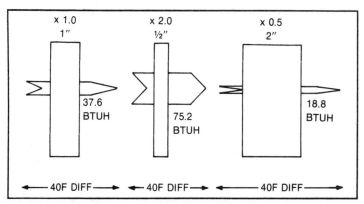

Fig. 2-2. With 37.6 Btuh, it will transfer through 1 square foot of 1-inch thick particle board every hour (× 1.0) at a temperature difference of 40 F. However, if the thickness of the particle board is halved, twice as much heat transfer (× 2.0) takes place over the same time period and the amount is doubled to 75.2 Btuh. If the thickness is doubled, the heat transfer is halved (× 0.5) to 18.8 Btuh. A change in thickness of a material results in a change in heat transfer, in inverse proportion.

Table 2-2. Representative Conductance (C) Factors at 75 F Mean Temperature for Some Common Nonhomogeneous Building Materials.

MATERIAL	CONDUCTANCE C
Concrete block - 3 oval core, sand and gravel aggregate, 8″	0.90
Cinder block, 3 oval core, 8″	0.58
Asbestos-cement board, ⅛″	33.00
Hardboard underlay, ¼″	0.82
Aluminum siding over sheathing	1.61
Asphalt roof shingles	2.27
Wood bevel siding, lapped, ½″ x 8″	1.23
Hardwood flooring, ¾″	1.47
Fiberboard sheathing, ½″	0.76

and with three oval cores has a C of 0.90. The same type of block made with a cinder aggregate has a C of 0.58. And as with k, the higher the C value, the greater the material's ability to conduct heat and consequently the less value it has as an insulating material.

As with k, C factors have been developed on the basis of certain testing procedures—all of which seldom will be found in the field. Nonetheless, the listed factors are the ones to use. To take an example of the C factor in action, consider the concrete blocks mentioned above. With a temperature difference of 40 F between one side of the blocks and the other, 36 Btu (0.09 x 40) will pass through the sand-and-gravel block every hour. Only 23.2 Btu (0.58 x 40) will pass through the cinder block. Other things being equal, you'd get better thermal performance from a basement made with cinder blocks than with concrete blocks.

To sum up, k is thermal conductivity with values expressed in Btu and used in conjunction with materials that are homogeneous and 1 inch thick. C, on the other hand, is thermal conductance, also expressed in Btu but used in respect to nonhomogeneous materials or assemblies of stated construction and thickness. Both express the amount of heat that travels through a square foot of the material of assembly every hour, per degree of temperature difference between one surface and the other.

SURFACE CONDUCTANCE

Surface conductance, or *film conductance* as it is sometimes called, is another important consideration. Not only can heat be conducted through a solid object, or from one object to another in close contact, but also along the surface of an object or material. When you stop to think about it, all exposed surfaces are surrounded or covered by air. There is a very thin film of air always in contact with the surface of an object. Because there is contact, there can be conductance from the object to the air film or vice versa. The symbol for this surface conductance is h and the conductance values under certain conditions have been developed and formed into a standard table (Table 2-3) where the values are expressed, just as with C and k, in terms of Btu per square foot per hour per degree temperature difference. Surface conductance is affected by the relative position of the surface, whether the air contacting the surface is still or moving, and the surface emittance of the surface with which the air is in contact.

In practice, three divisions are established with respect to air motion. Air inside a structure, or within parts of a structure, is considered as *still*. Outside air is considered as *moving* at 15 miles per hour in the winter and 7.5 miles per hour in the summer. The latter two designations are arbitrary ones that are generally used in developing heat loss/gain calculations. They can be adjusted for different conditions. Still air is classed in five positions, as you can see in Table 2-3. As to the third factor, I will have to digress for a moment to explain what surface emittance is all about.

The symbol for *surface emittance* is the Greek letter epsilon, or ϵ. By strict definition, it is the ratio of the radiant flux emitted by a specimen to that emitted by a blackbody at the same temperature. For our purposes, it is the relative degree of reflectivity of surfaces and only three categories are of concern (see Table 2-4). A nonreflective surface has an ϵ of 0.90, a

Table 2-3. Surface Conductances and Resistances (Reprinted with Permission from the 1977 Fundamentals Volume, ASHRAE HANDBOOK & Product Directory).

Position of Surface	Direction of Heat Flow	Surface *Emittance*					
		Non-reflective $\varepsilon = 0.90$		Reflective $\varepsilon = 0.20$		Reflective $\varepsilon = 0.05$	
		h_i	R	h_i	R	h_i	R
STILL AIR							
Horizontal	Upward	1.63	0.61	0.91	1.10	0.76	1.32
Sloping—45 deg	Upward	1.60	0.62	0.88	1.14	0.73	1.37
Vertical	Horizontal	1.46	0.68	0.74	1.35	0.59	1.70
Sloping—45 deg	Downward	1.32	0.76	0.60	1.67	0.45	2.22
Horizontal	Downward	1.08	0.92	0.37	2.70	0.22	4.55
MOVING AIR (Any Position)		h_0	R	h_0	R	h_0	R
15-mph Wind (for winter)	Any	6.00	0.17				
7.5-mph Wind (for summer)	Any	4.00	0.25				

Table 2-4. Reflectivity and Emittance Values of Various
Surfaces and Effective Emittances of Air Spaces (Reprinted with Permission
from the 1977 Fundamentals Volume, ASHRAE HANDBOOK & Product Directory).

Surface	Reflectivity in Percent	Average Emittance ε	Effective Emittance E of Air Space	
			One surface emittance ε; the other 0.90	Both surfaces emittances ε
Aluminum foil, bright	92 to 97	0.05	0.05	0.03
Aluminum sheet	80 to 95	0.12	0.12	0.06
Aluminum coated paper, polished	75 to 84	0.20	0.20	0.11
Steel, galvanized, bright. . .	70 to 80	0.25	0.24	0.15
Aluminum paint	30 to 70	0.50	0.47	0.35
Building materials: wood, paper, masonry, nonmetallic paints	5 to 15	0.90	0.82	0.82
Regular glass	5 to 15	0.84	0.77	0.72

highly reflective surface has an ϵ of 0.05, and a moderately reflective surface has an ϵ of 0.20. Only these three classes are considered in determining the value of surface conductances: 0.90 for virtually all ordinary building materials, 0.20 for foil-faced insulations or other materials, and occasionally 0.05 where extremely bright and highly reflective aluminum foil or similar surfaces are encountered.

The h of any surface of an assembly or building section that is being analyzed for its thermal efficiency is an important factor that must always be taken into consideration. Just as a sheet of particle board, a layer of shingles or a pane of glass has a certain C or k, so does the surface film of air against every surface have a certain conductance value.

For example, suppose you are going to determine the thermal efficiency of a wall (Fig. 2-3) with an eye toward calculating heat loss. There is obviously a surface film on the inside and another on the outside. The inside surface film is still and the wall is vertical. The direction of heat flow is assumed to be horizontal. Because neither surface is reflective, you would use the nonreflective section of Table 2-3 under "still air, vertical surface position, horizontal heat flow." The h_i for the inside surface (the i stands for indoor or inside) equals 1.46. The exterior surface film is usually considered to be moving air at 15 mph, and the h_o equals 6.00 (winter conditions).

To take another example, if the building section under consideration is a finished attic with sloping ceilings, the surface position for the inside still-air surface would be at an angle. Assuming heat gain calculations are being made, rather than heat loss, the direction of heat flow would then be downward and the h_i would equal 1.32 if kraft paper-faced insulation were installed in the roof, or 0.60 with reflective foil-faced insulation. The exterior surface film would be considered to be subject to moving air at 7.5 mph (summer conditions) and therefore the h_o would equal 4.00

REFLECTIVITY AND EFFECTIVE EMITTANCES

Now we have to get back for a moment to surface emittance, or ϵ, reflectivity, and effective emittance, or E. All surfaces reflect or absorb heat to varying degrees (Table 2-5). The degree to which they can reflect heat or light is known as *reflectivity*. As an example, bright, polished aluminum foil will reflect from 92 to 97 percent of the heat directed against it. This in turn leads to an average ϵ of 0.05. On the other hand, a wood wall will only reflect 5 to 15 percent of the heat directed against it; the rest is absorbed. This leads to an average ϵ, for conventional calculation purposes, of 0.90. The higher the reflectivity in percent, the lower the average ϵ.

This brings us to a new value called the effective emittance E. It is used in determining the particular thermal conductances or resistances of air spaces. The effective emittance is the combined effect of the surface emittances, or ϵ, of the surfaces that form the boundaries of an air space. This consideration comes into play only when the air space is of large dimensions compared to the distance between the surfaces. An example would be the hollow space in a wall construction, bounded by the inside

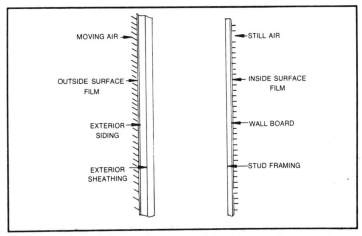

Fig. 2-3. Every building section is comprised of the separate materials from which it is made, plus a surface film and an air layer on each side. This wall section is exposed to still air on the inside surface, moving air on the outside and there are surface films between the air layers and the actual wall surfaces. Each individual element of the section is considered when making heat loss/gain calculations.

Table 2-5. Typical Reflectivity Values in Percent of Various Types of Surfaces.

MATERIAL	REFLECTIVITY Percent
Silver Plate (New)	96
Fresh White Plaster	93
New Top-grade Mirror	88
Aluminum Foil	85
White Paint	80
Aluminum Paint	55
Chromium	51
Green Paint	50
Red Brick	45
Granite	45
Concrete	40
Grass	33
Desert	25
Gray Paint	25
Dark Green Paint	20
Dark Brown Paint	15
Dark Wood	10
Tarpaper	7
Flat Black Paint	4
Lamp Black	2
Black Velvet	1
Theoretical Black Body	0

faces of the interior and exterior sheathing, and the sides of the two studs forming the wall cavity.

Let's say that the inside surface of the exterior wall is nonreflective, with an ϵ of 0.90, while the inside surface of the interior wall is foil-faced. With Table 2-4, you can see that this works out to an effective emittance E of 0.20. If both surfaces are reflective, the E would be 0.11. An airspace within a building section always has a certain E that is dependent upon the nature of the inside surfaces of the space. Never fear, the point of all this will become clear very soon.

RESISTANCE AND RESISTIVITY

In making calculations for either heat losses or heat gains, we are not especially interested in the conductance or the conductivity of building materials or sections. What we really want to know is how well the material or section can *resist* the transfer of heat. This is the object of the entire exercise. The capability of a particular material to resist the transfer of heat is the opposite number of its capability to conduct heat. Put another way, resistance is the reciprocal of conductance. It is written as R. The resistivity of a material to thermal transfer is the reciprocal of its conductivity and thermal resistivity is written as r. In common practice, the term resistance or R is generally used as the reciprocal for either conductivity (k) or conductance (C), and I will follow that pattern.

What is a reciprocal? It's very confusing if you don't know and very simple when you do. The reciprocal of any number is 1 divided by that number. Finding reciprocals invariably results in a whole lot of decimal places and it can be a tedious job if you use scratch paper and a pencil. If you want, you can look them up in reciprocals tables—but there's an easier way. By all means, if you don't already have one, invest $10 or so in a small electronic pocket calculator; it needn't be anything fancy for these purposes.

Let's go back to the common brick, with a *k* of 5.0. To find the *R* of common brick, punch the number 1 into your calculator, hit the divide button, and punch the 5 button. Pressing the equal button results in a figure of 0.2 *R* for the brick. Do the same thing for oak, with a *k* of 1.10, and you come up with 0.909 (which could be rounded to 0.91). Note that with both the brick and the oak you have taken the reciprocal of *k*. This represents the thermal conductivity *per inch thickness* of material. If the brick is laid in a wall as a stretcher brick and if it is 4 inches thick, the total *R* for the construction thickness would be 4 times 0.20 per inch, or a total of 0.80. Similarly, if the oak is a plank 2 inches thick, its *R* would be 2 × 0.91, or 1.82.

Suppose you were to take the reciprocal of the *C* of wood fiberboard acoustical tile, one-half inch thick. The *C* of this tile is 0.80 which when divided into 1 results in an *R* of 1.25. This is the *R* factor or value for that particular tile type in that particular thickness—the stated material and thickness.

As you've probably noticed, the higher the R the greater the resistance of the material to the transfer of heat. In other words, the better it is as an insulator. All building materials have a certain degree of insulating value which can be readily determined by finding the *C* or *k* of the material and then finding its reciprocal. When the *R* is already known, by simply noting which material has the higher *R* value, you immediately know which will have the greater effectiveness as an insulator. Many commercial insulation products are rated in just this way. The familiar *R* value rating is generally stamped on the product. The popular 3½-inch-thick fiberglass insulation so commonly used in walls, for example, carries an *R* value of 11.

From a practical standpoint, when working with R values for residential insulating purposes, R values are considered to be cumulative or additive. If you add an R-4 layer of insulation to an R-9 layer, the result will be, for purposes of calculation, R-13. The values are subtractive as well. The thermal conductance and resistance of an assembly or a material can be a function of its thickness. A particular assembly might have a greater thermal resistance proportionately in one thickness than it does in a lesser thickness. Because there are so many other variables as well, such as the effects of atmospheric pressure, presence of water vapor, ambient air temperature, and so on, the calculations are essentially estimates and for practical purposes this added variable has little appreciable effect.

AIR SPACE RESISTANCE

Enclosed air spaces found within building sections also have a certain resistance to the transfer of heat. This includes such spaces as those found in uninsulated floor, wall, or ceiling sections, the shallow gap between dished-in thermal blanket insulation and wallboard, or similar areas in floors and ceilings. Often such spaces are deliberately built into the structure to provide additional thermal insulating value by virtue of the air space or to allow maximum efficiency of reflective faces on building materials which would otherwise be negated if the reflective face were tight against the surface of another building material. The thermal resistance of plane air spaces can be approximated by consulting Tables 2-6A and 2-6B once the effective emittance E has been determined, as discussed in the section on reflective emittance.

Suppose, for example, that you install foil-faced blanket insulation in a wall and dish the insulation in so that there is a three-fourth inch gap left between the face of the insulation and the inside surface of the wallboard. The first step in finding the thermal resistance of the air space is to determine the effective emittance E of the space. In this case, one surface is of aluminum-coated paper, with an average ϵ of 0.20, while the other is nonreflective ($\epsilon = 0.90$). From Table 2-4, the effective emittance E of the air space is then 0.20. The position of the air space is vertical and the direction of heat flow is horizontal. If you assume a mean temperature of 50 F and a temperature difference of 30 F, reading across in the proper column of the table in Table 2-6A you can see that the air space has a value of 2.01 (in the 0.2 column).

Air spaces of up to 3.5 inches in depth can be determined by using this table. Where specific mean temperatures and temperature differences are not known, calculations can be made on a worst-case basis. Note that the air spaces must be completely blocked off and contain only still air (the small eddy currents and thermal convection loops that are frequently present in so-called "dead-air" spaces are not considered for these purposes). Multiple air spaces in a given building section can be calculated in the same way, but must be done with great care. Spaces of greater than 3.5 inches in depth have virtually no more effectiveness than those that are 3.5 inches or less.

COEFFICIENTS OF TRANSMISSION

Working with R values is handy enough when you are buying thermal insulation or when you're comparing certain individual materials. The problem is that houses are not built of insulation or of single, individual building materials. Almost invariably there are several materials involved in any particular building section. There are exceptions, of course, such as panes of glass, solid wood doors, and occasionally even wall sections as in the case of the so-called flat-milled or solid-timber log houses or a poured concrete foundation. For the most part, you will have to determine the value of the thermal transmittance of various composite building sections.

Trying to do this in terms of R values is cumbersome and also gives relative rather than specific information. For simplicity and convenience, another factor is used. This is the *U value* or *coefficient of transmission*. As with the other factors, *U* values are expressed in terms of Btu per hour per square foot per degree Fahrenheit difference in temperature from one side to the other of the material (or the building section).

The *U* value of either a material or a building section is the overall coefficient of heat transfer or the total amount of heat flowing through either a single material or any combination of materials that makes up an assembly, including air spaces. This is the ultimate factor that is used in the calculation of heat losses and gains in residences. *U* is simply the reciprocal of the sum total of the *R* values found in any given building section. In the case of a single material, it is the reciprocal of the *R* value of that material. Sounds complicated, but it really isn't—here's how it works.

Suppose you want to find that coefficient of transmission or *U* of a house wall. Reading from the inside out, the wall is composed of one-half inch gypsum wallboard, a one-half inch air space, 3.5-inch fiberglass blanket insulation with a foil face, one-half inch fiberboard sheathing, and one-half inch plywood exterior siding (Fig. 2-4). The first step is to determine the *k* or *C* of each material, and then find the reciprocal of each to obtain the *R*-value. (If you have tables on hand that directly list the *R* values of building materials, there is no need to go through the business of finding the reciprocals of *k* or *C*.) Then add up all of the *R* values to find R_t (t = total).

In this case, the air space happens to be reflective on one surface, the mean temperature is assumed to be 50 F, and the temperature difference is assumed to be 30 F, for a value of 1.84. Adding this *R* to the values of the building materials results in an R_t of 15.23. The values of the inside and outside surface films must also be added—for a total of 16.08. The reciprocal of this figure is 0.062. This is the *U* value for this particular construction of wall *between the studs*. The value at the points where studs are located is different by virtue of the presence of the studs themselves. In other words, 16.08 Btu of heat will flow through every square foot of this particular building section every hour for every degree of difference in temperature between the inside surface and the outside surface.

There are published tables available in reference works that list a good many different composite building sections and give the particular *U* value for each. The problem is that first you must find the tables and then you must use only those particular values listed. Or you can try to guesstimate what the value of a different building section might be. There are any number of variables involved and trying to tabulate all of them would be a horrendous chore. If you know or can find the *k, C,* or *R* of any given material, you can work out the U-value for any possible combination of materials that you would like to use.

Bear in mind that every building material has a certain capability of retarding the flow of heat, however little that might be. This means that

All resistance values expressed in (hour)(square foot)(degree Fahrenheit temperature difference) per Btu

Values apply only to air spaces of uniform thickness bounded by plane, smooth, parallel surfaces with no leakage of air to or from the space.

Thermal resistance values for multiple air spaces must be based on careful estimates of mean temperature differences for each air space.

See the Caution section, under Overall Coefficients and Their Practical Use.

Table 2-6A. Thermal Resistances of Plane Air Spaces.[d,e] (Reprinted with permission from the 1977 Fundamentals Volume, ASHRAE HANDBOOK & Product Directory).

Position of Air Space	Direction of Heat Flow	Mean Temp[b] (F)	Temp Diff[g] (deg F)	0.5-in. Air Space — Value of E[b,c]					0.75-in. Air Space — Value of E[b,c]				
				0.03	0.05	0.2	0.5	0.82	0.03	0.05	0.2	0.5	0.82
Horiz.	Up	90	10	2.13	2.03	1.51	0.99	0.73	2.34	2.22	1.61	1.04	0.75
		50	30	1.62	1.60	1.29	0.96	0.75	1.71	1.66	1.35	0.99	0.77
		50	10	2.13	2.05	1.60	1.11	0.84	2.30	2.21	1.70	1.16	0.87
		0	20	1.73	1.70	1.45	1.12	0.91	1.83	1.79	1.52	1.16	0.93
		0	10	2.10	2.04	1.70	1.27	1.00	2.23	2.16	1.78	1.31	1.02
		-50	20	1.69	1.66	1.49	1.23	1.04	1.77	1.74	1.55	1.27	1.07
		-50	10	2.04	2.00	1.75	1.40	1.16	2.16	2.11	1.84	1.46	1.20
45° Slope	Up	90	10	2.44	2.31	1.65	1.06	0.76	2.96	2.78	1.88	1.15	0.81
		50	30	2.06	1.98	1.56	1.10	0.83	1.99	1.92	1.52	1.08	0.82
		50	10	2.55	2.44	1.83	1.22	0.90	2.90	2.75	2.00	1.29	0.94
		0	20	2.20	2.14	1.76	1.30	1.02	2.13	2.07	1.72	1.28	1.00
		0	10	2.63	2.54	2.03	1.44	1.10	2.72	2.62	2.08	1.47	1.12
		-50	20	2.08	2.04	1.78	1.42	1.17	2.05	2.01	1.76	1.41	1.16
		-50	10	2.62	2.56	2.17	1.66	1.33	2.53	2.47	2.10	1.62	1.30
Vertical	Horiz.	90	10	2.47	2.34	1.67	1.06	0.77	3.50	3.24	2.08	1.22	0.84
		50	30	2.57	2.46	1.84	1.23	0.90	2.91	2.77	2.01	1.30	0.94
		50	10	2.66	2.54	1.88	1.24	0.91	3.70	3.46	2.35	1.43	1.01
		0	20	2.82	2.72	2.14	1.50	1.13	3.14	3.02	2.32	1.58	1.18
		0	10	2.93	2.82	2.20	1.53	1.15	3.77	3.59	2.64	1.73	1.26
		-50	20	2.90	2.82	2.35	1.76	1.39	2.90	2.83	2.36	1.77	1.39
		-50	10	3.20	3.10	2.54	1.87	1.46	3.72	3.60	2.87	2.04	1.56
45° Slope	Down	90	10	2.48	2.34	1.67	1.06	0.77	3.53	3.27	2.10	1.22	0.84
		50	30	2.64	2.52	1.87	1.24	0.91	3.43	3.23	2.24	1.39	0.99
		50	10	2.67	2.55	1.89	1.25	0.92	3.81	3.57	2.40	1.45	1.02
		0	20	2.91	2.80	2.19	1.52	1.15	3.75	3.57	2.63	1.72	1.26
		0	10	2.94	2.83	2.21	1.53	1.15	4.12	3.91	2.81	1.80	1.30
		-50	20	3.16	3.07	2.52	1.86	1.45	3.78	3.65	2.90	2.05	1.57
		-50	10	3.26	3.16	2.58	1.89	1.47	4.35	4.18	3.22	2.21	1.66
Horiz.	Down	90	10	2.48	2.34	1.67	1.06	0.77	3.55	3.29	2.10	1.22	0.85
		50	30	2.66	2.54	1.88	1.24	0.91	3.77	3.52	2.38	1.44	1.02
		50	10	2.67	2.55	1.89	1.25	0.92	3.84	3.59	2.41	1.45	1.02
		0	20	2.94	2.83	2.20	1.53	1.15	4.18	3.96	2.83	1.81	1.30
		0	10	2.96	2.85	2.22	1.53	1.16	4.25	4.02	2.87	1.82	1.31
		-50	20	3.25	3.15	2.58	1.89	1.47	4.60	4.41	3.36	2.28	1.69
		-50	10	3.28	3.18	2.60	1.90	1.47	4.71	4.51	3.42	2.30	1.71

Table 2-6B. Thermal Resistances of Plane Air Spaces (Reprinted with Permission from the 1977 Fundamentals Volume, ASHRAE HANDBOOK & Product Directory).

Position of Air Space	Direction of Heat Flow	Mean Temp,[b] (F)	Temp Diff,[g] (deg F)	1.5-in. Air Space[d] — Value of E[b,c] 0.03	0.05	0.2	0.5	0.82	3.5-in. Air Space[d] — Value of E[b,c] 0.03	0.05	0.2	0.5	0.82
Horiz	Up	90	10	2.55	2.41	1.71	1.08	0.77	2.84	2.66	1.83	1.13	0.80
		50	30	1.87	1.81	1.45	1.04	0.80	2.09	2.01	1.58	1.10	0.84
		50	10	2.50	2.40	1.81	1.21	0.89	2.80	2.66	1.95	1.28	0.93
		0	20	2.43	2.35	1.63	1.23	0.97	2.25	2.18	1.79	1.32	1.03
		0	10	2.55	2.47	1.80	1.35	1.04	2.71	2.62	2.07	1.47	1.12
		-50	20	1.94	1.91	1.68	1.36	1.06	2.65	2.58	2.18	1.67	1.20
		-50	10	2.37	2.31	1.99	1.55	1.26	2.65	2.58	2.18	1.67	1.33
45° Slope	Up	90	10	2.92	2.73	1.86	1.14	0.80	3.18	2.96	1.97	1.18	0.82
		50	30	2.14	2.06	1.61	1.12	0.84	2.26	2.17	1.67	1.15	0.86
		50	10	2.88	2.74	1.99	1.29	0.94	3.12	2.95	2.10	1.34	0.96
		0	20	2.30	2.23	1.82	1.34	1.04	2.42	2.35	1.90	1.38	1.06
		0	10	2.79	2.69	2.12	1.49	1.13	2.98	2.87	2.23	1.54	1.16
		-50	20	2.71	2.64	1.88	1.54	1.21	2.87	2.29	1.97	1.54	1.25
		-50	10	2.71	2.64	2.23	1.69	1.35	2.87	2.79	2.33	1.75	1.39
Vertical	Horiz.	90	10	3.99	3.66	2.25	1.27	0.87	3.69	3.40	2.15	1.24	0.85
		50	30	2.58	2.46	1.84	1.23	0.90	2.67	2.55	1.89	1.25	0.91
		50	10	3.79	3.55	2.39	1.45	1.02	3.63	3.40	2.32	1.42	1.01
		0	20	2.76	2.66	2.10	1.48	1.12	2.88	2.78	2.17	1.51	1.14
		0	10	3.51	3.35	2.51	1.67	1.23	3.49	3.33	2.30	1.67	1.23
		-50	20	3.31	3.21	2.18	1.66	1.33	2.82	2.75	2.30	1.73	1.37
		-50	10	3.31	3.21	2.62	1.91	1.48	3.40	3.30	2.67	1.94	1.50
45° Slope	Down	90	10	5.07	4.55	2.56	1.36	0.91	4.81	4.33	2.49	1.34	0.90
		50	30	3.58	3.36	2.31	1.42	1.00	3.51	3.30	2.28	1.40	1.00
		50	10	5.10	4.66	2.85	1.60	1.09	4.74	4.36	2.73	1.57	1.08
		0	20	3.85	3.85	2.68	1.74	1.37	3.81	3.63	2.65	1.74	1.27
		0	10	4.92	4.62	3.16	1.94	1.54	4.59	4.32	3.02	1.88	1.34
		-50	20	4.67	4.47	2.80	2.01	1.54	3.77	3.64	2.90	2.05	1.57
		-50	10	4.67	4.47	3.40	2.29	1.70	4.50	4.32	3.31	2.25	1.68
Horiz.	Down	90	10	6.09	5.35	2.79	1.43	0.94	10.07	8.19	3.41	1.57	1.00
		50	30	6.27	5.63	3.18	1.70	1.14	9.60	8.17	3.86	1.88	1.22
		50	10	6.61	5.90	3.27	1.73	1.15	11.15	9.27	4.09	1.93	1.24
		0	20	7.03	6.43	3.91	2.19	1.49	10.90	9.52	4.87	2.47	1.62
		0	10	7.73	6.66	4.00	2.22	1.51	11.97	10.32	5.08	2.52	1.64
		-50	20	8.09	7.20	4.77	2.85	1.99	11.64	10.49	6.02	3.25	2.18
		-50	10	8.09	7.52	4.91	2.89	2.01	12.98	11.56	6.36	3.34	2.22

[b] Interpolation is permissible for other values of mean temperature, temperature differences, and effective emittance E. Interpolation and moderate extrapolation for air spaces greater than 3.5 in. are also permissible.

[c] Effective emittance of the space E is given by $1/E = 1/\epsilon_1 + 1/\epsilon_2 - 1$, where ϵ_1 and ϵ_2 are the emittances of the surfaces of the air space.

[d] Credit for an air space resistance value cannot be taken more than once and only for the boundary conditions established.

[e] Resistances of horizontal spaces with heat flow downward are substantially independent of temperature difference.

[f] Thermal resistance values were determined from the relation $R = 1/C$, where $C = h_c + Eh_r$, is the conduction-convection coefficient, Eh_r is the radiation coefficient $\approx 0.00686 E [(460 + t_m)/100]^3$, and t_m is the mean temperature of the air space. For interpretation from Table 2 to air space thicknesses less than 0.5 in. (as in insulating window glass), assume $h_c = 0.795 (1 + 0.0016)t_m$ and compute R-values from the above relations for an air space thickness of 0.2 in.

* Based on National Bureau of Standards data presented in Housing Research Paper No. 32, Housing and Home Finance Agency 1954, U. S. Government Printing Office, Washington 20402.

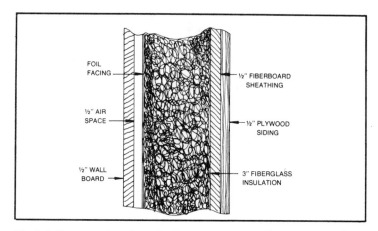

Fig. 2-4. Cross section of a typical wall construction. Each individual item is assessed for its thermal performance to develop a final factor for heat loss/gain computations.

you can juggle building materials around—and that includes finish and decorating materials like carpeting—to achieve maximum U values for the least number of dollars.

THE CONCEPT OF OVERALL U

The time-honored procedure for making residential heat loss/gain calculations is to break out each individual building section and figure it separately and then add up the results. This is generally done for each heated or cooled room or area of the house. But there are times when it is useful to know, or when it is easier to work with, combined U-factors. These combined factors are known as U_0 or overall U. The concept of overall U can be applied to building sections of any size that are composed of one or more different elements or it can be applied to an entire structure. The concept sometimes has practical value in determining the overall heat loss or gain of a house.

In some areas, building codes specify minimum heat loss standards, in one fashion or another. This is not yet being done with cooling, but it might eventually happen. In some locales, local building codes require that the insulation in a house be of a certain thickness and type. In such cases there is nothing to do but follow the regulations. Often these are minimal requirements and it is both permissable and worthwhile to exceed them with heavier insulation. The regulations might specify that walls or roof must be insulated to certain R values. This gives the home builder more leeway.

The greatest flexibility in structural design is possible when local building officials recognize the validity of the overall U concept and have established standards of minimum overall heat loss from an entire house as a unit rather than approaching the problem on a piecemeal, building-section basis. Using the overall U concept, thermal insulation, as well as other building materials and architectural features, can be placed where they will do the most overall good with thermal efficiency and a desirable, liveable house design.

For example, the exterior walls of a solid-timber house might have a U value of only 0.192 (R-5.2), whereas local building regulations might require an exterior wall to be filled with R-7 blanket insulation (U-0.143) or perhaps to have a minimum opaque-wall (that is, not including windows) U value of 0.125 or whatever. This would mean that the house design would then have to be changed to include some such arrangement as covering those lovely interior wood wall surfaces with rigid foam insulation topped with paneling or planking in order to achieve a higher thermal efficiency. If the overall U concept is followed, this would mean that the walls could be left as solid wood and the ceilings or roof insulated to a greater degree to make up the difference.

There is another practical advantage to using U_0. It's easier, in some respects, to work with when making the final calculations for heat loss/gain in a large house that is composed of a good many different kinds of building sections and a sizable number of individual sections.

Though the formula for determining U_0 looks complicated, it really isn't. By using it, you can determine the U factor for gross wall areas, gross floor areas, and gross ceiling or roof areas. These in turn can be combined. Here's how it works, using a single wall as an example.

The makeup of the hypothetical wall is as follows: dimensions, 8 feet high and 30 feet long; 2×4 stud frame construction with one-half inch plasterboard covering on the inside, one-half inch plywood exterior sheathing, 3½-inch fiberglass insulation; exterior siding consists of brick veneer on the lower half, three-eighth inch plywood siding on the upper half; a pair of 4×5 double-glazed windows; one 6/8×3/0 solid wood exterior door with no storm door; one 6/8×6/0 double-glazed sliding patio door.

Each of these construction sections has a different U value and each encompasses a certain area of the total wall section. The areas are worked out by simple multiplication and the U values are derived from the tables. Those values are: wall with wood siding = 0.089; brick-veneered wall = 0.087; windows = 0.58; wood door = 0.46; patio door = 0.55.

The basic formula for finding U_0 is as follows:

$$U_0 = \frac{U_{section\ 1}A_{section\ 1} + U_{section\ 2}A_{section\ 2} + etc.}{A_0}$$

where

U_0 = the average thermal transmittance of the gross area, Btu/hr/sq ft/F

$U_{section}$ = the thermal transmittance of any given construction section, Btu/hr/sq ft/F

^{A}section = area of the section, sq ft

A_0 = gross area of sections, sq ft

You are looking for the overall U of a wall, so U_0 can become U_{wall}. Similarly, you can substitute the various sections found in the wall for both $U_{section}$ and $A_{section}$; i.e., $U_{brick\ wall}$, $U_{wood\ wall}$, $U_{windows}$, and so on. All you need do is multiply the U of each section times its area, add them all up, and finally divide the sum by the gross area of the wall.

$$U_0 = \frac{(0.089 \text{x} 60) + (0.087 \text{x} 60) + (0.58 \text{x} 40) + (0.46 \text{x} 20) + (0.55 \text{x} 40)}{240} =$$

$$\frac{5.34 + 5.22 + 23.2 + 9.2 + 22}{240} = \frac{64.96}{240} = 0.27$$

As you can see, by simply setting up $U \text{x} A$ for whatever sections you want to include in the overall U, you have full flexibility. To carry the above example to its logical conclusion, the hourly heat loss through the entire composite wall section, on average, would be 0.27 x 240 (U_0 x sq ft), or 64.8 Btuh.

CALCULATING SURFACE TEMPERATURES

The temperature of interior structural surfaces of building sections that are exposed to the outdoors can be very important from a number of standpoints. Sometimes it is necessary to determine during the design process, rather than after the building has been constructed, whether or not there will be sufficient insulation in a particular building section to eliminate any danger of condensation forming on interior surfaces under given conditions of humidity. This might be the case, for example, when designing an earth-sheltered house with poured concrete walls or roof assembly.

More commonly, though, determining the inside surface temperatures of walls, floors and ceiling exposed to the outside—particularly in areas where harsh winter weather prevails—is important from the standpoint of the comfort of the occupants of the house. You know from your own experience that if you stand before a big window or sliding glass patio doors on a cold winter day, you will immediately feel an uncomfortable sensation of cold (provided the furnace isn't blowing a blast of hot air up between you and the glass).

This takes us back to the business of radiation. Your body will radiate large quantities of heat toward an object or surface that is appreciably colder than you are, leaving you with the sensation of being chilly. The phenomenon is not confined to big windows. It can take place as your body radiates heat toward floors, walls, or ceilings that are colder on their inside surfaces than they should be for bodily comfort. In other words, if you want to be fully comfortable within a house, all of the interior surfaces of building sections that are exposed to the outdoors must be relatively warm.

There is nothing very exact, really, about what this surface temperature should be because people react differently under varying conditions. If you are normally comfortable in an ambient temperature of 70 F, for example, the surrounding surface temperatures should probably be on the order of 66 F to 68 F. If you are perfectly happy with a 65 F ambient temperature, perhaps about 62 F is adequate for bodily comfort. Of course, the level of the interior relative humidity will also play a part and so will the degree of air motion within the heated space, and other factors.

However, you cannot get the interior surfaces too warm for winter comfort. Because that's not a concern, when designing a structure, it's just as well to have the surface temperatures as high as possible and practical. The way this is done is by adding thermal insulation and/or increasing the thickness of the building section and/or using alternative building material components in the construction of the section that are of higher R value. Of course, infiltration of outside cold air must also be reduced as much as possible. In an uninsulated house of frame construction, a temperature even as high as 85 F may be insufficient in many cases to prevent the occupants from becoming chilled. They loose tremendous amounts of body heat to the cold surfaces and cannot absorb enough from the warm air being pumped out by the heating system to counterbalance the loss.

Finding inside surface temperatures is not a difficult chore and you can easily run two or more sets of calculations to determine what combination of building materials/thermal insulation might be best and most practical as well as most cost-effective. You can use the same method to find out whether you would prefer to have double or triple glazing instead of single or if the addition of storm doors would be worthwhile. This is true at least from a surface-temperature standpoint; this calculation does not deal directly with the heat losses that are involved in such choices.

Here's how it works. First, determine your inside ambient temperature—let's say 70 F. Suppose you want to find the inside surface temperature of the outside walls. Find the U factor for your wall construction (proposed or existing). We'll call it 0.081. We'll also suppose that since 0 F is about the lowest temperature you will experience in your area, that's the temperature you'll use for the outside surface of the walls. Now all you need is the U value of the inside wall surface, which from the Table 2-3, is 0.68. What we are looking for is T_s (the surface temperature) As a formula, this reads $T_s = T_i - (R_i \times U)(t_i - t_o)$, where t_i is the inside ambient temperature, U_s is the U value of the inside surface film, U_w is the U value of the wall, and t_0 is the outdoor temperature. Subtracting the outdoor temperature from the indoor temperature gives 70. Multiplying the inside surface film U times the wall U times the temperature difference looks like this: $70 - (1.46 \times 0.081 \times 70)$ or $70 - 8.28$, or 61.72. Thus, the T_s for this particular wall under these particular conditions is just a bit less than 62 F. This wall, which happens to be a very common construction, is obviously a bit cool in severe winter conditions.

CALCULATING INTERFACE TEMPERATURES

An *interface* is defined as a surface forming a common boundary of two bodies or spaces. In this context, an interface would be, for example, the two abutting surfaces of two materials in a building section. This might be the backside of exterior wall siding and the outside surface of the wall sheathing, or the underside of a layer of roofing felt and the top surface of the roof sheathing, or the foil face of blanket insulation and the surface film of air contacting it in an air space in a wall. You can determine the temperature of any of these interfaces under any given conditions by using a simple formula.

One practical application of this would be to find the interface temperatures of the components of a wall section to determine whether or not there is any possibility of condensation occurring under whatever potential climatic conditions might come about. Condensation within a wall has a disastrous effect upon its thermal resistance. Or you can use the method to determine the surface temperatures of an air space within a wall so that you can find the temperature difference and relate it to the table of thermal resistances of plane air spaces (Table 2-6A) to obtain a correct value for calculation. The mean temperature can be approximated by finding the arithmetic mean of the two surface temperatures and related to the table in the same way.

The temperature drop through any component of a wall or other building section is proportional to its resistance. Suppose that you want to know the temperature of the interior surface of the plasterboard on the inside of an exterior wall when the inside temperature is 70 F and the outside temperature is 10 F. We'll call that temperature T_i, for interface temperature. We need to know the thermal resistance of the wallboard, or R_w, and the total thermal resistance of the wall section, or R_t. The formula will be: $T_i = R_w (t_i - t_0 / R_t$. The $(t_i - t_0)$ is the inside temperature minus the outside temperature, or 60. Let's assume R_w to be 0.45 (for one-half inch plasterboard), and the R_t to be 12.3. This gives us: $T_i = 0.45(60)/12.3$, or 27/12.3, or 2.195. The temperature drop from the warm side of the wallboard to the cooler side is approximately 2.2 degrees. Under the given conditions the backside surface temperature of the wallboard is 70 F − 2.2, or 67.8 F.

If you wanted to find the temperature difference between the two surfaces that bound the air space, you would run the same calculation for the opposite surface of the air space and subtract the lesser from the greater. The mean temperature can be found by adding the two air-space surface temperatures and dividing by 2.

HEAT STORAGE

I have emphasized the point that all materials, objects, and substances have a certain capability to conduct or to resist the transfer or flow of heat through them. In years past, the determination of home insulation and home heating requirements and equipment has been based almost entirely upon these specifics. But there's another factor that is of equal importance, even though it has been almost totally ignored until recently, and that is that objects, materials, and substances also have a certain capability of storing heat. With today's quest for better heating methods and lower energy consumption, heat storage has suddenly become of great importance. In most solar heating designs, it is an essential characteristic and without careful application the system simply will not work.

Materials can be assigned a value known as the *specific heat* of the material. This is defined as the number of Btu required to raise 1 pound of the material by 1 F. Water is the commonly used example. To raise the temperature of 1 pound of water by 1 F, 1 Btu of heat is needed. It would take 100 Btu to raise 100 pounds of water—roughly 12 gallons—by 1 F. This is true if the starting temperature of the water is 40 F; the specific heat of a material varies slightly as the temperature of the material or substance varies. For practical purposes, the differences are minimal and cause no problems. You can use whatever standard published figures are available in making approximate calculations.

Specific heat is written in terms of Btu per pound per degree F. It takes 0.22 Btu to raise the temperature of 1 pound of concrete by 1 F. Tables showing the specific heat (Table 2-7) for a great variety of different substances and materials are available. However, most of the entries are of little interest insofar as construction is concerned.

All substances and materials also have a certain weight per unit volume. This is referred to as *density*. The terms most often used in this country to express density are the weight in pounds per unit of 1 cubic foot. Water has a density of 62.5 pounds per cubic foot. Concrete has a density of 144 pounds per cubic foot (Table 2-8). There are some variables involved. For example, concrete is made up primarily of cement, sand, and/or gravel. Depending upon exactly how that concrete is mixed, the density might actually be somewhat more or somewhat less than 144. For our purposes, these variables really have little meaning and can be disregarded.

The *heat capacity* of a given material, as the term will be used in this discussion, depends upon the specific heat and the density of the material. From a scientific standpoint, the definition is somewhat different and there is both *mean heat capacity* and *true heat capacity* to deal with. However, there is no need to get wrapped up in differential equations. It is suffice to say that multiplying the specific heat times the density of the given material results in the amount of heat needed to raise the temperature of 1 cubic foot of the material by 1 F.

Using water again, multiplying 1.00 (specific heat) times 62.5 (density) equals 62.5 Btu needed to raise the temperature of a cubic foot of water by 1 F (Table 2-9). Similarly, for concrete you multiply 0.22 times 144, for a total of 31.7 Btu required. To carry this a step further, in order to raise the temperature of a 1-cubic-foot block of concrete by 10 F, 317 Btu would be needed. Now turn that around. If the temperature of the concrete cube is raised by 10 F, the block will have stored within it 317 Btu of heat.

If you have a concrete wall that contains 1000 cubic feet of concrete and you raise its temperature by 10 F, that concrete wall will contain 317,000 Btu of heat. By the same token, a 1000-cubic-foot tankful of water (nearly 7500 gallons) would need 625,000 Btu of heat to raise the temperature of the water by 10 F. If you did raise the temperature by 10 F, the water would store that 625,000 Btu of heat. As the temperature rises, every object, material, or substance affected by the temperature rise will store, or contain, a certain quantity of heat (depending upon its characteristic).

Note the interaction of specific heat and density. Water has a very high specific heat and a low density. Because of the high specific heat, it has an excellent heat capacity. Steel, on the other hand, has a very high density of 489 pounds per cubic foot, but a low specific heat of 0.12. The result is that steel has an only slightly lower heat capacity (5.87) than water. Materials with a low specific heat and low density also have a very low heat capacity. Fiberglass is a good example; it has a heat capacity of only 0.51. In other words, it has almost no capability at all of storing any appreciable amount of heat.

THERMAL MASS

Thermal mass is the whole point of the discussion about heat capacity of materials. Let's go back to that 1000-cubic-foot concrete wall. That's a

Table 2-7. Specific Heat Values for Several Common Materials.

MATERIAL	SPECIFIC HEAT Btu/lb/deg F
Water	1.000
Kerosene	0.500
Cork	0.485
Wood, 12% Moisture	0.391
Wood, Dry	0.295
Gypsum	0.259
Adobe	0.240
Air	0.240
Asphalt	0.220
Limestone	0.217
Aluminum	0.214
Marble	0.210
Brick	0.200
Stone	0.200
Sand	0.191
Soda-lime Glass	0.180
Fiberglass Wool	0.157
Concrete	0.156
Cast Iron	0.120
Mild Steel	0.120
Copper	0.092

huge mass of concrete and it is also a substantial thermal mass. That big chunk of concrete has the capability of containing and storing for a time, depending upon conditions, a substantial amount of heat. If, for example, the temperature surrounding the wall or block of concrete is elevated from 60 F to 70 F and kept there until the entire concrete mass reached the same temperature, the concrete would contain 317,000 Btu of heat. That's as much heat as a 2000-watt electric heater will put out in 46 hours of continuous running. A block of steel of the same size would contain considerably more heat and a tank of water would hold more yet.

Many of the materials that are ordinarily used in the construction of houses can be deliberately used to store large quantities of heat. By utilizing materials perhaps not quite so common to residential construction or by using common materials in greater quantities and in different ways, a house can be specifically designed to become a huge thermal mass. It will be a great quantity, in the aggregate, of materials that will absorb heat from whatever sources are available and store it. This can be readily done by pouring extra-thick concrete floors, building concrete walls, constructing massive masonry fireplaces and chimneys (rock has good heat capacity), introducing drums or tanks of water, and by a variety of other methods.

Table 2-8. Density Values for the Materials Listed in Table 2-7.

MATERIAL	DENSITY lbs/cu ft
Copper	556
Mild Steel	489
Cast Iron	450
Aluminum	171
Marble	162
Soda-lime Glass	154
Concrete	144
Asphalt	132
Brick	123
Adobe	106
Limestone	103
Sand	95
Stone	95
Gypsum	78
Water	62.5
Kerosene	51.2
Black Locust	48.2
N. Red Oak	44
Red Maple	37.7
White Spruce	28
Ponderosa Pine	26.6
E. White Pine	24.5
W. Red Cedar	22.4
Cork	5.4
Fiberglass Wool	3.25
Air	0.075

Table 2-9. Heat Capacity Values for the Materials Listed in Figs. 2-5 and 2-6.

MATERIAL	HEAT CAPACITY Btu/cu ft/deg F
Water	62.50
Mild Steel	58.68
Cast Iron	54.00
Copper	51.15
Aluminum	36.59
Marble	34.04
Asphalt	29.04
Soda-lime Glass	27.72
Kerosene	25.60
Adobe	25.44
Brick	24.60
Concrete	22.46
Limestone	22.35
Gypsum	20.20
Stone	19.00
Black Locust	18.85
Sand	18.14
N. Red Oak	17.20
Red Maple	14.74
White Spruce	10.95
Ponderosa Pine	10.40
E. White Pine	9.58
W. Red Cedar	8.76
Cork	2.62
Fiberglass Wool	0.51
Air	0.018

You're probably thinking that this is all well and good, but you know perfectly well that your concrete foundation walls lose heat at a tremendous rate. Everybody realizes that concrete and stone are mighty poor insulators and can cause a substantial heat loss in a house. Of course they can.

Let's consider 1,000-cubic-foot concrete wall again. Assume that it is a basement foundation wall 1 foot thick, 8 feet high, and 125 feet long. The k of 140 pounds-per-cubic-foot concrete is 12.0, for a rather miserable 0.08 R per inch of thickness—0.96 for a foot-thick wall. That's a U of 1.04, not counting surface films. If the inside temperature of the wall is 70 F and the outside temperature is 30 F, every exposed square foot of that wall will lose 41.6 Btu per hour (40 x 1.04). Because 1000 square feet of wall is exposed to the lower temperature, the total loss is 41,600 Btu every hour—bad news!

The key is that when the thermal mass concept is to be used as a part of the house design and as a adjunct to comfortable and economical heating, the entire thermal mass must be *within* the house envelope. Here's how it works.

To start with, let's take a partial exception. You've probably heard that log houses are easier to heat than comparable conventional wood-frame buildings, and that they also maintain a more even interior temperature. That's often true, other things being equal, and it's because of the thermal mass that is an integral part of even an ordinary log house that has not been designed with thermal mass in mind. Even though the floor and the roof might be of conventional construction, the walls are of thick, heavy logs, there might well be some log interior partitions, and perhaps some massive interior roof trusses of log or timber. All of this adds to the total mass. A fairly substantial mass is within the house envelope. A large mass makes up a good proportion of the house envelope itself.

One side of the exterior log walls obviously is exposed to the outdoors. But, unlike concrete (or ordinary frame walls), the logs themselves have a good R value—an average thickness of 10 inches would result in about R-12.5, for example—and at the same time the walls have a reasonably good heat capacity. This is nowhere near as good as concrete, but it is sufficient to store a fair amount of heat that doesn't escape very rapidly because of the relatively high resistance of the wood to thermal transmission. In this case, there is sufficient thermal mass in the building to be of noticeable value to the occupants by comparison with an ordinary frame house.

Although the log house is a partial thermal mass by nature, it in turn is nowhere near as efficient as a house that is designed with thermal mass specifically in mind. Rather than the mass just being part of or within the house envelope, the entire thermal mass should, for best results, be completely within the *thermal* envelope of the house—that is, *inside* the insulation. To make the most use of the heat stored within the thermal mass, it must be prevented from escaping to the outdoors and allowed only to replenish heat lost through various mechanisms within the house.

Standard practice in this country for many, many years has been to install whatever insulation is used—and that almost invariably has been far too little—*inside* the house envelope. The concrete basement walls are furred out on the inside and the spaces filled with fiberglass insulation or, more lately, with rigid panels. The frame wall cavities are filled with fiberglass insulation or blown mineral wool. The attic floor or the underside of the roof is insulated in much the same way. You can see the result immediately. Whatever mass there might be is to the outside of the heated area, where it does little good. The mass of a conventional wood-frame house is pretty small anyway.

Thermal mass is a very important design tool that you can incorporate readily into a new house. There are also a number of ways in which a certain amount of thermal mass can be retrofitted to an existing house (although in that situation the efficiency and effectiveness may be reduced and there may also be a question of reasonable cost-effectiveness). But the incorporation of thermal mass in a house can do several things for you. The mass itself in a new house becomes a part of the structure or a part of the overall architectural or decorative design. You kill two birds with one stone. After a certain period of heating time, the thermal mass becomes "charged," and stores a certain amount of heat. Only a small amount of this heat can escape to the outdoors (a certain loss is inevitable) and most of it remains within the mass as long as the temperature remains fairly stable.

Let's assume that your house is not a solar design, but is conventionally heated (electric baseboard, oil-fired furnace, wood stove) and that there is a 5,000-cubic-foot concrete thermal mass within the insulation envelope. The temperature in the house is 60 F and you turn on the heat to raise the temperature to 70 F. After a certain length of time, the thermal mass will become charged and will store about 150,000 Btu of heat. As long as the surrounding temperature is 70 F, the thermal mass will also be at 70 F and contain that amount of heat. When you retire for the evening, you set the thermostat back to 60 F. As the temperature within the house begins to fall because of inescapable losses to the outdoors, the thermal mass begins to release into the house some of those Btu's it has stored. In effect, it becomes a radiator.

This release of heat slows the rate of temperature descent within the house. If you waited long enough, all of the heat that had been stored would be released when the temperature of the thermal mass reached 60 F again. By this time, the air temperature would undoubtedly be lower (if the heating system is still off), because the air in the house will lose its heat faster than the thermal mass. But before that happens, assuming that the heat loss characteristics of the house and the size and properties of the thermal mass were properly calculated for whatever specific conditions under which they are to function, you would have gotten up in the morning before the air temperature reached 60 F, turned the thermostat back up to 70 F, and the whole cycle begins again. Therefore, you are getting better use from the heat generated by your heating plant as well as a more comfortable interior environment.

Obviously, the fuel that was used to generate the heat that warmed the interior of the house and charged the thermal mass had a certain cost. Whether or not that cost is less than for a comparable house of identical thermal resistance characteristics, but without the thermal mass, is an open question and something that has to be calculated for each individual circumstance. But it is equally obvious that if the heat used to charge the thermal mass were free, overall heating costs would be reduced by a certain degree. This free heat can come from the sun.

In a solar design, the thermal mass is situated in such a way that it can absorb and store heat generated as sunlight streaming into the house. This can be done by direct contact with the sun's rays, a concrete intercept wall (Fig. 2-5), storage cylinders of water placed directly in the sun (Fig. 2-6), or indirectly, where the thermal mass absorbs heat from the interior environment without necessarily being directly in the sun.

Often as not, both methods are used together. The result is that the house becomes a heat trap. Sunlight enters the building, the radiant energy is transformed to heat energy, and a substantial proportion of that heat energy cannot escape the house envelope. How much does escape is dependent upon the thermal efficiency of the house shell.

The heat remaining in the house is absorbed and stored by the thermal mass. When the sun goes down in the afternoon or is obscured during cloudy spells, the stored heat is released from the thermal mass as the interior temperature begins to fall. This is a passive solar arrangement. An active system uses the same principles, but obtains the heat from special exterior solar collectors. The heat is transferred by mechanical means to a thermal mass which can be in the form of a heat storage element such as a huge bin of crushed rock or a tank of water or to a stone or concrete mass

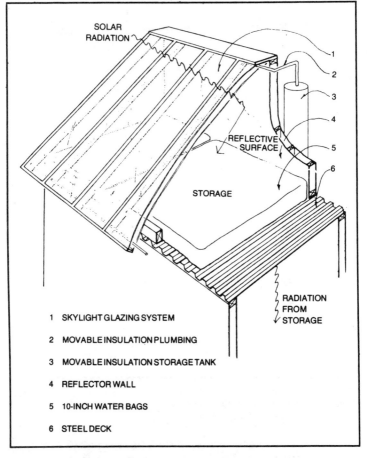

1 SKYLIGHT GLAZING SYSTEM

2 MOVABLE INSULATION PLUMBING

3 MOVABLE INSULATION STORAGE TANK

4 REFLECTOR WALL

5 10-INCH WATER BAGS

6 STEEL DECK

Fig. 2-5. An example of thermal mass/storage at work. Heat from the sun is stored in the large bags of water and radiated downward into the living space in this solar design.

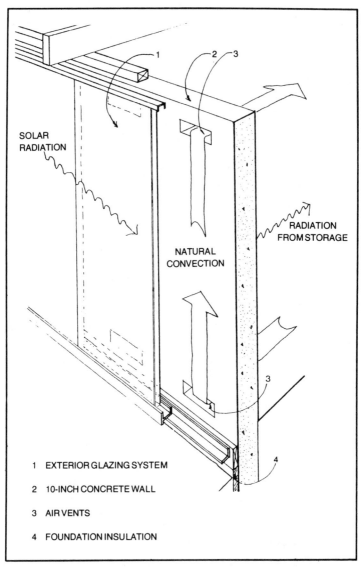

SOLAR
RADIATION

NATURAL
CONVECTION

RADIATION
FROM STORAGE

1   EXTERIOR GLAZING SYSTEM

2   10-INCH CONCRETE WALL

3   AIR VENTS

4   FOUNDATION INSULATION

Fig. 2-6. This method of utilizing reradiation of solar energy by means of thermal mass/storage employs a massive concrete wall with natural convection ports for heat dispersion.

that is part of the house structure. Whatever the specifics of the arrangements, the idea remains the same. Heat is released by the thermal mass into the interior atmosphere as the air temperature falls below that of the mass.

THE FLYWHEEL EFFECT

The *flywheel effect* comes about as a result of a phenomenon called *thermal lag*. In this context, thermal lag simply means that the temperature within an unheated (or uncooled) building will rise and fall with relation to changes in the outside temperature, but not at the same time. The changes inside will always lag behind those outside. The rate of change is also less abrupt. As the outdoor temperature plummets rapidly, the indoor temperature will remain stable for a short time. As the structure loses heat to the outside, the inside temperature begins to fall—but more slowly. If, after a time, the outdoor temperature swings upward again, the indoor temperature will continue to fall for a while until the structure is sufficiently warmed from the outside for the effect to begin to take place on the inside. The inside temperature will then slowly start to rise in an attempt to equalize with the outside temperature. This cyclical rise and fall continues endlessly.

However, the more isolated the interior environment is from the exterior, the more gradual and the less consequential these ups and downs of inside temperature become with relation to the outside temperature. A chart of the outside temperatures would show abrupt ups and downs in the form of sharp, spiky curves in the temperature line. On the same chart, the curves for the interior temperature would become flatter and gentler and approach a straight line as the degree of isolation between inside and outside increases.

You might know that the ambient temperature in deep mines remains relatively constant all the time. Miners working there do so in an environment of, say, 50 F that never varies more than a degree or so in either direction, night or day and regardless of the weather topside. This is because the mine environment is shielded from any weather or temperature changes at the surface by a good many hundreds of feet of earth and rock. This buffer zone completely averages out and damps down all the cyclical changes.

Much the same situation is true of those earth-sheltered houses that are completely buried to a substantial depth. Studies made by The Underground Space Center at the University of Minnesota show that the wide daily swings in air temperature are almost completely eliminated at a depth of less than 1 foot below the ground surface. At 10 feet below the surface, daily temperature chances are negated and even seasonal temperature swings are restricted to a range of only 20 F or so in a harsh climate. Lag time for below-ground changes is as much as 3 months or a whole season. When the lowest ground temperature has been reached, spring is already in progress topside. At depths of about 25 feet and below, there is virtually no change whatsoever. The soil temperature line is almost straight.

The protection of an inside environment from an outside one, and consequently a leveling-out of the interior temperature curves compared to the outside, is accomplished by the insertion of a thermal mass. The important property here is *thermal inertia*, between the two environments. The greater the thermal mass and the thermal inertia , the flatter will be the temperature curves inside, by comparison to what happens outside. With regard to an above-ground house, the greater the thermal mass of its shell, the more even the inside temperature will remain. It cannot respond quickly to changes in outside temperature.

For example, a conventional wood-frame house has an almost negligible thermal mass in its shell. Comparatively, it is very lightweight and is composed entirely of a few pieces of wood, fiberboard, and mineral wool. If the power goes off in your "stick-built" house on a cold winter day, you know perfectly well that it doesn't take very long for the inside temperature to drop. Within just a few short hours it's almost as cold inside as it is out. On the other hand, the temperature inside a tightly-built cabin made of 12-inch logs and with massive log roof trusses and a huge masonry fireplace might not drop below the comfort level even if the power outage lasted several hours. The log house has greater thermal mass and thermal inertia and is much better protected from the outdoor temperature swing.

If the interior of a house responds rapidly to outdoor temperature fluctuations, the heating system must be of large capacity, sufficient to quickly compensate for wide and drastic swings in worse-case conditions. There will be a few times during the heating season when the system will be called upon to produce tremendous quantities of heat in a short period of time. But most of the time that large capacity remains unused and in normal heating situations it is also very likely to be inefficient and comparatively costly to operate. If a house responds very slowly to outside temperature cycles, all that is required is a modest, or even a tiny, heating system that will produce just enough heat over a given period of time to compensate for the mild swings in indoor temperature by comparison with the more pronounced outside changes. Because the outdoor temperature swings are averaged out on the inside over a period of two or three days, or even a week, once the indoor temperature reaches a comfortable level at the beginning of the heating season, not much is required to keep it that way. All of this presupposes, that the house not only has a substantial thermal mass, but is also properly insulated so that heat losses are minimized to the greatest practical extent.

Insulants

Virtually all substances have the capability to conduct heat or to resist the passage or flow of heat. Generally, the higher the density of the material, the greater the ability of the material to conduct heat and the lower its resistance to the passage of heat. A chunk of granite, for example, is very dense and has a very low R. Some natural substances, however, have relatively high R values. Wood averages about R-1. However, the different species vary in their R value according to their density. Cork is another natural material with high R. The tough outer bark of the cork oak tree *(Quercus Suber)* was once widely employed for various purposes because of its capability to float and to resist the passage of heat. But there are no naturally occurring substances that have a very high resistance to the transfer of heat that are readily available and easily adaptable for that purpose—with one exception. The exception is dry, still air when it is enclosed in small and/or shallow spaces. This forms the basis for modern thermal insulants.

In the residential construction field (and in building construction in general) all of the building materials used have a certain R value. All of them will resist the transfer of heat to a certain degree. Decades ago, little thought was given to this characteristic. As the years went by, the demand for living comfort increased, methods of construction changed and costs and other attendant problems of heating and cooling because of increasingly greater consequence.

This fostered investigation and testing of various substances and combinations of materials that might be suitable for the specific purpose of retarding heat flow into and out of buildings. Research has led to the development of a particular class of building materials designed to prevent the transmission of heat through building sections. (Note that a few of these materials do include a certain amount of structural or decorative function as a secondary purpose.) These special materials technically are thermal insulants and are commonly called thermal insulation or just insulation. This can be misleading because there are several kinds of insulants—electrical, acoustic, vibration, and so on.

Actually, there is nothing new at all about the general idea of thermal insulation. The methods and products used today for residential thermal insulation, however, are highly specialized. Most of these special materials gain their effectiveness by incorporating millions of tiny air cells within the base material. It is the still dry air that provides the high insulating value, not the base material or matrix itself. One type of material, plain aluminum foil, that is classed as an insulation really is not, in the usual sense, though the net effect is much the same. The foil depends upon a high reflectivity and actually is a heat shield or radiation barrier. Some thermal insulations combine a highly reflective surface with the dead air spaces and so are able to retard heat flow via two separate mechanisms.

PROPERTIES AND APPLICATIONS

There is a wide variety of specific insulation products from which to choose; many of them have slightly differing properties and characterstics. How do you choose which one to use? Well, the way *not* to go about it is to run right out and buy a bale of fiberglass (though after due consideration that might turn out to be exactly what you need).

Some thought should be given to which insulant might do the best job for your particular application. This does not mean that you should use the same kind of insulation throughout your house. Some parts of the house will call for one kind of insulation and other parts might be better served by installing a different type. Situations arise during retrofitting of insulants in an existing house where the choice of certain kinds of insulating materials will make for a much easier installation without tearing the whole house apart. There are a number of characteristics that should be considered.

Obviously, the R value of a particular insulation is of primary importance. After all, that's what you're buying the material for in the first place. The R value of an insulant is only one factor among many and it must be balanced against the other properties of the material. A 6-inch fiberglass batt has an R of about 19, but that won't do you much good if you only have a 3-inch space to fit it into. If you need R-19, you'll have to find something with a higher R value per inch of thickness or change the construction of the section.

Often some compromise is necessary by virtue of balancing the R value of the insulant against its other properties to get the most effective overall installation. Keep in mind that whatever R value (or better, U value) you might not be able to gain in one building section, you might be able to make up for in another (in terms of overall U).

Cost is also an important factor, but once again this should not be the final determinant. A very expensive insulation does not necessarily do the best job in a given application, nor does the least expensive necessarily prove least efficient or effective. Insulating materials are often priced on a per-square-foot basis or by the roll or bundle containing so many square feet—which amounts to much the same thing. But price per square foot is not a good way to judge your insulation purchase. The price of a square foot of fiberglass insulation might be considerably less than that of a square foot of rigid foam board. But what does that prove? More to the point is to consider how much thermal efficiency you are purchasing with your dollars. R value is based upon square feet, too, so you can easily calculate the cost per R unit. Economy is always a factor. In this instance, economy is best judged upon overall heat loss (or gain) reduction through the completed building section, for lowest cost commensurate with the other properties of the insulant and also of the building section itself (thickness, appearance, ease of construction, general suitability for the application).

The different insulating materials also have differing physical characteristics. Some insulations can be used for some purposes and not for others. A few are quite versatile in application, some are very specialized, and others lie in the middle ground where they are useful for some things but not for others. But there is no such thing as a universal insulating material. An individual house might conceivably have as many as four or five different kinds of insulation installed in one place or another. The following are a few of the nonthermal characteristics of insulants that you should keep in mind as you go about making your selection.

Appearance

Most of the time the appearance of an insulant makes no difference whatsoever because it is hidden within a building section. There are circumstances, though, when this might not be true. Suppose, for instance, you want to retrofit an insulant to the walls of your house. You can tear out the inside wall covering and install fiberglass—quite a job. You can tear off the exterior siding and add a layer of exterior insulating sheathing—also quite a job. You might be able to install an interior prefinished sandwich-type paneling against the original wall covering—much simpler, and attractive. If the insulant, or a building material in which an insulant is enclosed, will be exposed to view anywhere, the appearance factor has some importance.

Fire Safety

Fire safety is an important factor in choosing an insulant. This is particularly true if the material is to be used essentially within the living space of the house or in areas where the fire hazard might be potentially higher than normal. Some insulants will not support flame, and/or will not burn; they will just melt or—in a hot enough surrounding fire—be consumed or incinerated.

Fiberglass is a noncombustible insulation, but if it has a kraft paper facing, the paper will burn merrily. Other kinds of insulation will burn to a certain extent, but it will have a low flame-spread rating. Flames will spread across the surface of the material only at a slow rate. Other materials are quite combustible.

A factor associated with combustibility is that of whether or not the material will give off toxic gases or heavy, thick smoke as it burns or smolders. Some do and some do not. Insulants are seldom avoided specifically because they do. Nonetheless, the factor is worth considering. This is particularly true if a high degree of life-safety is one of your house design goals (and it's a good one).

Moisture Absorption

The presence of excessive amounts of water vapor in insulation will diminish its ability to retard the flow of heat. Certain insulations can absorb, or entrap water vapor to varying degrees. Certain insulants also will retain water to a greater degree than others. The presence of free moisture can entirely destroy the insulating value of a material and in certain circumstances it can destroy the material itself. This can happen rather abruptly or can be an ongoing process of degradation over a fairly long period of time. This means that certain insulations should be protected from the passage of water vapor to as great a degree as possible and they must also be protected from damage by free moisture, such as might occur from a leak in a roof or sidewall. Those insulants that are prone to damage by moisture cannot be used in applications where contact with free moisture is either a possibility or a periodic reality. An example would be insulant installed around the perimeter of a concrete slab foundation.

Resistance to Crushing

Because of the different ways in which insulants are made, some are far more resistant to crushing under load than other. Fiberglass blanket, for instance, can be flattened completely with only a slight pressure of the hand. Some of the foam boards, on the other hand, are relatively resistant to crushing; it is even possible to walk upon them, provided they are fully supported from beneath.

Some of the so-called rigid insulations are not suitable for use beneath a concrete slab because they will eventually crush to a certain degree and lose part of their insulating value. There are certain kinds of rigid insulants that are extremely tough and highly resistant to crushing that can be used for such applications. Where relative crushability is a design factor, only those insulants with high crush resistance can be used, regardless of their other characteristics. Most such insulants also have a relatively high k; if necessary, two or more layers can be used to gain a higher R value.

Odor

Most insulants are odorless, but there are exceptions. In some applications, it makes no difference whether an insulant has an odor or not. Only if the insulant is essentially with the living space is this factor of much consequence. The possibility of outgassing of fumes from an insulant also can be a problem when the insulant is within the living space envelope. If an insulant has an unsavory odor or the potential for exuding fumes, it is best not used in the living-space areas.

Resistance to Pests

Pests are attracted to certain kinds of insulation. There are certain kinds of flies that like to lie dormant and also breed in the filaments of fiberglass insulation. Mice love to make nests in mineral wool or cellulose insulations. Some insulants contain starch and similar organic compounds such as cellulose that attract certain insects because the material can serve as food; termites are a notable example. This should not be considered a fault of the insulation. Such insulations should be sealed off and protected from the incursion of pests. Failing that, a type of insulation that has little or no susceptibility to damage by pests should be employed.

Corrosiveness

There sometimes is a possibility that certain insulants will react adversely with surrounding building materials that they come in contact with. It has been found, too, that some fire retardant chemicals that are used to treat cellulose or sawdust insulation, for instance, can have a corrosive effect in certain circumstances. Though this is not a common occurrence and is not likely to be a problem in most residential applications, nonetheless it is a point to keep in mind.

Physical Characteristics

Different kinds of insulation have entirely different physical characteristics. Some are loose particles, others are solid, some are limp, others are stiff, some are fully rigid while others are bendable, some have high impact resistance while others do not, some can be poured from the bag while others must be blown in place, and so on. Then there are also the standard trade sizes or packages of insulation. Fiberglass batts and rolls come in certain widths to fit between framing members, and in standard lengths and thicknesses. Rigid sheets can be obtained in 2 and 4 foot widths, and several lengths and thicknesses. Other types are packed so many cubic feet to the bag. The installation procedures vary from type to type; some are easy while others are more difficult. Installation of some types require only the simplest of tools, while others require highly specilized equipment. Some types are a snap for the do-it-yourselfer to install, while others must be installed only by professionals. Obviously, all of these physical characteristics must be considered in advance and they should be joined with the other pertinent factors to arrive at a final conclusion of which insulant, and even which particular insulant product, will be the best for your own purposes.

TYPES AND CHARACTERISTICS

All of the several types of thermal insulants that are available today in the general construction materials marketplace are suitable for use in one application or another in residential construction. Many of these insulants are sold under trade names and sometimes the actual materials used are not denoted. In other cases, the material is obvious. To further add to the confusion, though the R values of nearly all insulations are noted on the material or in the accompanying literature they might vary somewhat from product to product, they generally are rounded off to the nearest whole figure (R-4, R-10, etc.) rather than being carried out to a more accurate two decimal places. The R value noted for a given product might not coincide particularly well with the value for the generic insulating material as listed in published coefficient of heat transmission tables.

In addition, the R values of the insulation products are developed from a series of static testing procedures carried out under controlled conditions in a laboratory and are not the result of dynamic testing done over periods of time under actual operating conditions in the field. Most "in-use" properties of insulants under varying conditions of actual operation have not been evaluated to any substantial degree and specifics of either thermal or nonthermal in-the-field performance of most materials are rather sketchy. There are other problems, too, such as the uncertain effects of thickness on the measurement of thermal transmission properties of some kinds of insulation. While new testing procedures and equipment are being developed and new data is being accumulated in different ways, we have little recourse but to follow the usual accepted information.

Some of these particular details, as they affect certain kinds of insulants, will be mentioned in the individual discussions of those insulants on the next few pages. The effects of the varying temperatures under which insulants actually perform, however, can be considered in general. The listed R value of an insulant as derived from laboratory tests at a standard mean temperature of 75 F does not remain the same for other mean temperatures. And, of course, insulants are not much called upon to perform at a mean temperature of 75 F under real application conditions. Rather, the mean temperature that is experienced is usually considerably higher or lower.

As you can see from the values in Table 3-1, the performance of insulants in general becomes somewhat better as the mean temperature drops and somewhat worse as it rises. Note that fiberglass, for instance, has an R of 3.16 (per 1-inch thickness) at 75 F, but that increases to 3.57 at 40 F and decreases to 2.81 at 100 F. Thermal insulations calculated according to their standard 75 F ratings and installed primarily to guard against heat loss in winter will actually perform better with lower temperatures. The lower the temperature the better the performance. On the other hand, just the opposite is true for thermal insulations installed to decrease heat gain in summer.

This would lead you to the logical supposition that you can safely install insulation at the standard rating in heating applications and expect somewhat better performance than indicated. But for heat gain applications you might well want to increase insulant R-levels somewhat above the listed ratings in order to maintain full performance. Further, because the summer performance listed in Table 3-1 of the various insulants averages about 9.2 percent poorer than at design temperature, it probably would not be amiss to increase R factors for summer heat gain applications by about 10 percent. This, of course, would further increase winter performance at the same time and that would be all to the good. As a matter of interest, consider the differences in *k* factors for the loose-fill insulants shown in Table 3-2, as tested at different mean temperatures than the usual 75 F.

Though some generalizing can be done concerning the mean temperature effect upon insulation performance, it cannot with respect to many other pertinent factors. In order to discuss the various characteristics of insulants, you will have to look at them type by type. Bear in mind that there are a good many permutations of the basic varieties of insulants— slight differences in properties, *R* values, physical characteristics and attributes, application details, and so on—and the products that your lumberyard or building supplies dealer carries might not exactly match up with those insulants discussed here.

Rock and Slag Wool

Rock and slag wool are generally known under the generic name rock wool. They are made from two different (and yet somewhat similar) substances. Rock wool is made from many kinds of natural rock by melting the rock and then fiberizing it while it is in a molten state. Slag wool is made in the same way, but from the left-over material, or dross, that results from smelting metal-bearing ores—particularly iron. While rock wool is a product; slag wool is a byproduct.

Originally, rock and slag wool were manufactured by passing a stream of molten material in front of a high-pressure steam jet. This fiberized the liquid and produced a continuous stream of droplets, each of which trailed a fine fiber tail, much like a hair, behind it. Only the fibers could be used and the solidified droplets had to be recycled. The problem was that many of the droplets wound up in the insulating material. This effectively reduced its insulating value by virtue of the relatively large amount of high-*k* solid material contained in it.

Other processes were later developed that were based upon the concept of "spinning" long filaments out by centrifugal force. This minimized the quantity of droplets, called "shot," in the insulation and improved its performance. But the shot content remained fairly high and—along with other problems such as the availability of coke to fire the

Table 3-1. Thermal Performance of Various Insulants Under Winter, Summer, and Design Temperature Conditions.

Mean Temperature			Apparent Thermal Conductivity, Btu-in/hrft²°F					Thermal Resistance, hrft²°F/Btu per 1″ Thickness				
Condition	F	Fiberglass[1]	Cellulose[2]	Molded Polystyrene[3]	Extruded Polystyrene[4]	Urea Formaldehyde[5]		Fiberglass	Cellulose	Molded Polystyrene	Extruded Polystyrene	Urea Formaldehyde
Winter	40	0.28	0.26	0.225	.185	0.22		3.57	3.85	4.44	5.41	4.54
Design	75	0.316	0.27	0.25	.200	0.24		3.16	3.70	4.0	5.00	4.17
Summer	110	0.355	0.28	0.275	.215	0.26		2.81	3.57	3.65	4.65	3.85

1. Conforming to an R11 product at 75 F.
2. Loose-fill at 2.5 lb/ft³ (average results from Reference 28).
3. Molded polystyrene at 1.0 lb/ft (average results).
4. Extruded polystyrene at 2 lb/ft³.
5. At 0.7 lb/ft³.

Table 3-2. Thermal Conductivity (k) of Various Industrial Insulants (Reprinted with Permission From the 1977 Fundamentals Volume, ASHRAE HANDBOOK & Product Directory).

Expressed in Btu per (hour)(square foot)(degree Fahrenheit temperature difference per in.)

Form / Material Composition	Accepted Max Temp for Use, °F*	Typical Density (lb/ft³)	Typical Conductivity k at Mean Temp °F													
			−100	−75	−50	−25	0	25	50	75	100	200	300	500	700	900
BLANKETS & FELTS																
MINERAL FIBER																
(Rock, slag or glass)																
Blanket, metal reinforced	1200	6–12									0.26	0.32	0.39	0.54		
	1000	2.5–6									0.24	0.31	0.40	0.61		
Mineral fiber, glass																
Blanket, flexible, fine-fiber organic bonded	350	0.65				0.25	0.26	0.28	0.30	0.33	0.36	0.53				
		0.75				0.24	0.25	0.27	0.29	0.32	0.34	0.48				
		1.0				0.23	0.24	0.25	0.27	0.29	0.32	0.43				
		1.5				0.21	0.22	0.23	0.25	0.27	0.28	0.37				
		2.0				0.20	0.21	0.22	0.23	0.26	0.26	0.33				
		3.0				0.19	0.20	0.21	0.23	0.23	0.24	0.31				
Blanket, flexible, textile-fiber organic bonded	350	0.65				0.27	0.28	0.29	0.30	0.31	0.32	0.50	0.68			
		0.75				0.26	0.27	0.28	0.29	0.31	0.32	0.48	0.66			
		1.0				0.24	0.25	0.26	0.27	0.29	0.31	0.45	0.60			
		1.5				0.22	0.23	0.24	0.25	0.27	0.29	0.39	0.51			
		3.0				0.20	0.21	0.22	0.23	0.24	0.25	0.32	0.41			
Felt, semirigid organic bonded																
Laminated & felted	400	3–8				0.24	0.24	0.24	0.25	0.26	0.27	0.35	0.44	0.45		
	850	3				0.21	0.21	0.21	0.22	0.23	0.24	0.35	0.35	0.35		
Without binder	1200	7.5	0.16	0.17	0.18	0.19	0.20									
VEGETABLE & ANIMAL FIBER																
Hair Felt or Hair Felt plus Jute	180	10					0.26		0.28	0.29	0.30					
BLOCKS, BOARDS & PIPE INSULATION																
ASBESTOS																
Laminated asbestos paper	700	30									0.40	0.45	0.50	0.60		
Corrugated & laminated asbestos																
Paper																
4-ply	300	11–13								0.54	0.57	0.68				
6-ply	300	15–17								0.49	0.51	0.59				
8-ply	300	18–20								0.47	0.49	0.57				
MOLDED AMOSITE & BINDER	1500	15–18									0.32	0.37	0.42	0.52	0.62	0.72
85% MAGNESIA	600	11–12									0.35	0.38	0.42			
CALCIUM SILICATE	1200	11–13									0.38	0.41	0.44	0.52	0.62	0.72

	1800	12-15												0.63	0.74	0.95
CELLULAR GLASS	800	8.5			0.32	0.33	0.35	0.36	0.38	0.40	0.42	0.48	0.55			
DIATOMACEOUS SILICA	1600	21-22												0.64	0.68	0.72
	1900	23-25												0.70	0.75	0.80
MINERAL FIBER																
Glass,																
Organic bonded, block and boards	400	3-10	0.16	0.17	0.18	0.19	0.20	0.22	0.24	0.25	0.26	0.33	0.40			
Nonpunking binder	1000	3-10									0.26	0.31	0.38	0.52		
Pipe insulation, slag or glass	350	3-4					0.20	0.21	0.22	0.23	0.24	0.29				
	500	3-10					0.20	0.22	0.24	0.25	0.26	0.33	0.40			
Inorganic bonded-block	1000	10-15									0.33	0.38	0.45	0.55		
	1800	15-24									0.32	0.37	0.42	0.52	0.62	0.74
Pipe insulation slag or glass	1000	10-15									0.33	0.38	0.45	0.55		
MINERAL FIBER																
Resin binder		15			0.23	0.24	0.25	0.26	0.28	0.29						
RIGID POLYSTYRENE																
Extruded, Refrigerant 12 exp	170	3.5	0.16	0.16	0.15	0.16	0.16	0.17	0.18	0.19	0.20					
Extruded, Refrigerant 12 exp	170	2.2	0.16	0.16	0.17	0.16	0.17	0.18	0.19	0.20						
Extruded	170	1.8	0.17	0.18	0.19	0.20	0.21	0.23	0.24	0.25	0.27					
Molded beads	170	1	0.18	0.20	0.21	0.23	0.24	0.25	0.26	0.28						
POLYURETHANE••																
Refrigerant 11 exp	210	1.5-2.5	0.16	0.17	0.18	0.18	0.18	0.17	0.16	0.16	0.17					
RUBBER, Rigid Foamed	150	4.5						0.20	0.21	0.22	0.23					
VEGETABLE & ANIMAL FIBER																
Wool felt (pipe insulation)	180	20						0.28	0.30	0.31	0.33					
INSULATING CEMENTS																
MINERAL FIBER																
(Rock, slag, or glass)																
With colloidal clay binder	1800	24-30									0.49	0.55	0.61	0.73	0.85	
With hydraulic setting binder	1200	30-40									0.75	0.80	0.85	0.95		
LOOSE FILL																
Cellulose insulation (milled pulverized paper or wood pulp)		2.5-3							0.26	0.27	0.29					
Mineral fiber, slag, rock or glass		2-5			0.19	0.21	0.23	0.25	0.26	0.28	0.31					
Perlite (expanded)		5-8	0.25	0.27	0.29	0.30	0.32	0.34	0.35	0.37	0.39					
Silica aerogel		7.6			0.13	0.14	0.15	0.15	0.16	0.17	0.18					
Vermiculite (expanded)		7-8.2			0.39	0.40	0.42	0.44	0.45	0.47	0.49					
		4-6			0.34	0.35	0.38	0.40	0.42	0.44	0.46					

[a]Representative values for dry materials as selected by ASHRAE TC 4.4, Insulation and Moisture Barriers. They are intended as design (not specification) values for materials of building construction for normal use. For thermal resistance of a particular product, use the value supplied by the manufacturer or by unbiased tests.

•These temperatures are generally accepted as maximum. When operating temperature approaches these limits follow the manufacturer's recommendations.

••Values are for aged board stock. For change in conductivity with age of refrigerant-blown expanded urethane see section on Thermal Conductivity, Chapter 19.

Note: Some polyurethane foams are formed by means which produce a stable product (with respect to k), but most are blown with refrigerant and will change with time.

furnaces, the difficulty of blending available slags to achieve proper fiber properties, and the development of other types of insulants—rock and slag wool production and popularity has fallen off considerably.

Rock wool is still readily available and it is now principally used in insulating new construction and retrofitting. It is available in blanket-form, as standard-sized batts, or as loose-fill or blowing wool packed in bags. The batts are secured to a paper backing that includes stapling flanges and they are easy to install. The loose fill variety can be placed by hand in some applications, as between the ceiling joists in an open attic, but for most applications a much better installation is achieved by blowing the material into place with special equipment. Rock and slag wool is generally used to fill the voids within wall, ceiling, and floor sections.

Independent assessments show that rock or slag wool—virtually all that is produced in this country is actually slag wool—does indeed perform pretty much as advertised. The most important factor is the established R value. This differs for blanket type or loose-fill type. With loose-fill slag wool, which is often referred to as blowing/pouring wool, there are two critical thermal resistance criteria: a certain density and a certain thickness. Both are entirely dependent upon proper coverage and installation of the material. If these conditions are met a correct R value will result. With the batt type of slag wool, the situation is somewhat similar. When the batts are manufactured the fibers have comparatively low resilience. After cooling, they are sprayed with a phenolic resin as a binder, compressed somewhat to form the blanket, and then cured in ovens. When they are packaged, the batts are further compressed to a certain degree. Because of the inherent low resiliency and the presence of the binder, they might not recover their full thickness. The R value of the material might be variably diminished and the performance less than indicated by the established R value.

Note that slag and rock wool are included in the ASHRAE thermal properties table (Table 4-4) in combination with glass fiber material under the common-used generic heading of "mineral fiber insulating material." The R value is based upon a density of 0.3-2.0 pounds per cubic foot for all three kinds of material and is listed for specific thicknesses. The same is true of the loose-fill type of slag wool, which is included in the "mineral fiber" group, average density of 0.6-2.0, and R values listed for specific thicknesses. Actually, the density of slag wool insulation of either type is greater than that of fiberglass insulation in either blanket or loose form. The density of rock and slag wool, either blanket or loose-fill, ranges from 1.5 to 2.5 pounds per cubic foot. The R values of rock or slag wool blanket range from 3.2 to 3.7, while that for loose-fill is 2.9; both values are at 75 F, and for each 1-inch thickness.

Rock or slag wool is noncombustible. However, the binders used in the batts might be flammable and asphalt-coated or foil-faced kraft paper facing/backing *is* flammable. There is no danger of generation of toxic gases from the material; however, there could be from facings/backings.

When loose-fill is poured or blown into building sections, it can be considered as a fire-stop and its use is permissible under model building codes for that purpose.

Rock or slag wool has little moisture susceptibility. However, it can trap and hold a considerable amount of free water that might enter a building cavity through a leak. It is a very stable insulation. It is unaffected by aging except that the loose-fill type has a tendency to settle. This is especially true in walls if the wool is hand-placed, or is blown in and the cavity is not sufficiently or evenly packed. Because the material is virtually impervious, weathering or temperature or similar factors have no effect upon it. Various other characteristics are detailed in Table 3-3.

Fiberglass

Fiberglass insulation is similar in many respects to rock or slag wool. It is usually classified as a mineral wool insulation along with rock and slag wool. It is mineral-based and made from substances such as silica sand. The raw materials are melted in a furnace and then fiberized while in a molten state. A binder is added to the fibers. These are then collected and felted, cured, chopped and packaged as loose-fill or cut to size and packaged in blanket or batt form.

Since the 1950s, fiberglass insulation has been perhaps the most widely used of all types in residential insulation applications and it remains immensely popular today. This utilitarian insulant is available in numerous

Table 3-3. Properties of Rock and Slag Wool Insulation.

Material Property	Value	Test Method
Density	1.5-2.5 lbs/ft^3	
Thermal Conductivity (k factor) at 75F	0.31-0.27 Btu-in/ft^{2}hr^{o}F (batts) 0.34 Btu-in/ft^{2}hr^{o}F (loose fill)	ASTM C177
Thermal Resistance (R value) per 1" of thickness at 75F	3.2-3.7 hft^{2}F/Btu (batts) 2.9 hft^{2}F/Btu (loose fill)	ASTM C177
Water Vapor Permeability	>100 perm-in	
Water Absorption	2% by weight	
Capillarity	none	
Fire Resistance	non-combustible	ASTM E136
Flame Spread	15	
Fuel Contributed	0	ASTM E84
Smoke Developed	0	
Toxicity	none	
Effect of Age		
a) Dimensional Stability	none (batt settling (loose-fill)	
b) Thermal Performance	none	
c) Fire Resistance	none	
Degradation Due To		
Temperature	none	
Cycling	none	
Animal	none	
Moisture	transient	
Fugal/bacterial	does not support growth	
Weathering	none	
Corrosiveness	none	
Odor	none	

forms. It is most commonly seen in rolls either continuous or partially cut every 4 feet so that the roll can be easily separated into batt lengths. It is also available in bundles of precut batts and in various extra-wide rolls. The three principal forms are available in several standard thicknesses and associated nominal R values and in standard nominal widths of 16 and 24 inches for easy application between framing members spaced on 16- and 24-inch centers. All three forms are typically faced with asphalt-impregnated paper as a vapor barrier (Fig. 3-1) or foil-faced kraft paper (Fig. 3-2) which serves both as vapor barrier and reflective insulant.

So-called "friction-fit" or unfaced fiberglass insulation (Fig. 3-3) is also available in standard 4-foot batts either 16 or 24 inches wide (nominal). These batts have no facing and are installed by stuffing them between the framing members where they cling by friction alone. In addition, fiberglass insulation is available as loose-fill (Fig. 3-4) packed in bags for either pouring or blowing installations and as various kinds of semirigid and rigid fiberglass boards for various special applications. In one form or another, fiberglass insulation can be used for practically every purpose in residential construction.

The density of fiberglass wool insulants generally runs from 0.6 to 1.0 pounds per cubic foot and the k factor varies with the density of the material. In practice, the R value is often given as 3.16 per inch of thickness for blanket and batt fiberglass insulation and approximately 2.2 for loose-fill insulation. The R value of the material as installed depends upon the proper coverage in depth and density for loose-fill types and upon full loft or thickness for the blanket and batt types. The R value that is stamped upon the specific product is a nominal, rounded-off figure that can generally be relied upon. However, the actual accuracy might be off to a slight degree. In any event, the values closely follow those set forth in the ASHRAE table (Table 4-4). Glass-fiber board has an R of approximately 4 per inch of thickness.

Fiberglass wool insulants have excellent resiliency so that they generally regain their full loft or thickness after being compressed for packaging. Because it is made of inorganic materials, the insulant itself is incombustible, noncorrosive, and does not generate fumes; it is also odorless. However, combustible organic binders are used in the production of both blanket and loose-fill types and the kraft paper facings are also combustible (though flame-resistant types are available). The loose-fill type can be used as a fire-stop.

Fiberglass insulation absorbs very little moisture and no capillarity is apparent. However, it can retain sizeable quantities of free water for fairly long periods. If completely soaked, it can form a sodden mass that will not regain its loft and so becomes completely ineffective even after drying out. The material does not attract pests. However, certain insects might nest or lie dormant in it where it is exposed, mice like to nest in it and make runways through it, and squirrels and rats like to steak chunks of it for their nests. Aging apparently has no effect upon fiberglass insulants. The loose-fill type can settle and especially if improperly installed. Faced types should not be used in environments where the temperature is likely to approach 180 F or more. Details of this kind of insulation can be seen in Table 3-4.

Cellulose

Cellulose insulation is an old idea but a relative newcomer to the residential installation scene. There are a number of different ways to manufacture this material and the process requires relatively little equipment and not much cash outlay. The raw materials are so readily available that a good many dozens of small firms have set up shop all over the country. These materials must be properly processed to be fully effective—there are a couple of major considerations in that respect—and should only be purchased from reputable dealers/installers who have a proven track record. There are three variations on the manufacture of cellulose insulation.

The first method, which is the original one and still is by far the most popular, is to feed the raw cellulosic material into various sorts of grinding, shredding or chopping machinery in order to reduce it to a fibrous or

Fig. 3-1. Fiberglass insulation with kraft paper facing (courtesy of Johns-Manville).

Fig. 3-2. Fiberglass insulation with reflective aluminum foil facing (courtesy of Johns-Manville).

confetti-like bulk material of reasonable uniformity and of such consistency that it can be easily applied or installed. Typically, old newspapers and other paper materials make up the raw material. Other cellulosic materials such as virgin wood can also be used. Because of the inherent characteristics of the industry, the grade and quality—as well as other charactertistics of the end product—is neither uniform nor necessarily up to standard. In any event, once the material has been shredded or cut to a particular size, a dry chemical is mixed with the material as a fire retardant. Finally, the insulant is bagged for shipping and use.

There are several factors that influence the overall quality of the final product, such as homogeneity of the material, corrosiveness, and flammability. The latter factor is highly important. The raw cellulose is highly combustible and without a uniformly-distributed fire retardant in the material, it could easily be quite hazardous. Corrosiveness is also important. Many of the chemicals used as fire retardants have corrosive properties and when they are unevenly distributed through the material, excessive amounts of chemicals coming in contact with other building materials could cause difficulties.

The second method for manufacturing cellulose insulation is called the wet process. The basic insulating material is processed in much the same way as just described. Instead of a dry chemical fire retardant being added to the material, a liquid chemical solution is sprinkled or sprayed on during the manufacturing process. One of the critical points in the operation is the proper introduction and subsequent drying out of the liquid fire retardant. First, the proper solution must be made under just the right manufacturing conditions and then its application must be exact or else the end product will be either unusable or inferior.

A second type of wet process can be used. It is very much like the process employed for making paper. This reduces the raw materials to a slurry. The mass is "wrung out" by squeezing, then dried, and fluffed into final form. This method probably offers the best chance for quality control of the end product. This is particularly true with respect to dispersion of the fire retardant chemicals, a comparatively high degree of uniformity in fire retardancy throughout the material, lowered possibilities of corrosiveness, and an overall more homogeneous product of greater value to the consumer. Unfortunately, this is an expensive process and one that is not currently widespread.

Fig. 3-3. Unfaced or "friction-fit" fiberglass batts (courtesy of Johns-Manville).

Fig. 3-4. Typical fiberglass loose-fill insulation (courtesy of Johns-Manville).

A third method of making cellulosic insulation involves manufacturing a fibrous material in much the same manner as that for the dry-process material. However, a greater concentration of fire retardant chemicals is usually added to improve flame retardant properties. There are two principal differences in this material; it is applied by spraying, and it is usually left exposed and becomes a finish surface. There are numerous techniques for applying this insulation. One is to mix a polyvinyl acetate or an acrylic adhesive with water. In turn, this is sprayed over the insulating material as it emerges under air pressure from a special spraying nozzle. The whole mass adheres firmly to a prepared surface and can be built up to varying thicknesses in much the same way as certain mixes of concretes can be sprayed into place.

Perhaps the most serious problem with cellulosic insulants involves the fire retardant treatment. There must be a uniform dispersion through the material, but also a chemical combination that is fully effective. The combination of minimum cost and acceptable fire retardancy performance has been elusive and none have proven fully effective. Boric acid is the most commonly used fire retardant, but other chemicals such as zinc chloride, aluminum hydrate, ammonium phosphate, borax, and sodium carbonate have been tried alone, in combinations, and in various concentrations. It is these combinations that often prove to be of a corrosive nature.

Bulk dry cellulosic insulant can be applied by hand in one residential application—between the ceiling joists of an open attic floor—by simply pouring the material out and raking it to a uniform thickness. Note the importance of proper density in Table 3-5. However, the material is designed to be blown in place with special equipment and should be so installed for best results. This is the only way it should be installed in wall cavities. The spray-on insulant should be applied by qualified personnel who have the proper equipment and know-how to get the job done. For the most part, cellulose insulation installation cannot be satisfactorily handled by do-it-yourselfers—though doubtless there are exceptions.

The all-important resistance to heat transmission of loose-fill cellulosic insulation of either the milled paper or the wood pulp variety is

Table 3-4. Properties of Fiberglass Insulants.

Material Property	Value	Test Method
Density	0.6-1.0 lb/ft^3	
Thermal Conductivity (k factor)	varies with density	
Thermal Resistance (R value) per 1" of thickness* at 75F	3.16 hft^{2}F/Btu (batt) 2.2 hft^{2}F/Btu (loose-fill)	ASTM C518, C653
Water Vapor Permeability	>100 perm-in	
Water Absorption	<1% by weight	ASTM C553-70
Capillarity	none	
Fire Resistance	non-combustible	ASTM E136
Flame Spread	15-20	
Fuel Contributed	5-15	ASTM E84
Smoke Developed	0-20	
Toxicity	Some toxic fumes could develop due to combustion of binder.	
Effect of Age		
a) Dimensional Stability	none (batt)	
b) Thermal Performance	settling (loose-fill) none	
c) Fire Resistance	none	
Degradation Due To		
Temperature	none below 180°F	
Cycling	none	
Animal	none	
Moisture	none	
Fungal/Bacterial	does not promote growth	
Weathering	none	
Corrosiveness	non-corrosive	Federal HH-I-558D
Odor	none	ASTM C553 - Sec. 16

*Derived from R19 and R11 products for 6 and 3.5" thickness respectively.

Table 3-5. Compaction of Cellulose.

COMPACTION percent	THICKNESS inch	DENSITY lb/ft³	"K_app" BTU-in/hft²F	INSTALLED R	% REDUCTION in R
0	5.5	2.5	0.274	20.1	
10	5.0	2.75	0.277	18.1	10
20	4.5	3.06	0.280	16.1	20

listed in the ASHRAE table (Table 4-4) as R-3.13 to R-3.70 at a density of 2.3 to 3.2 pounds per cubic foot. Note the range of valuation; note also that these figures do not necessarily correspond to data provided by various manufacturers of the product nor to tests made by independent agencies. One such test series made by the U.S. Energy Research and Development Administration(ERDA) is typical of the results obtained (Fig. 3-5). Other samplings taken by Underwriter's Laboratories and other independent labs also show a wide divergence. In the ERDA results the value differences are greater than normally would be expected solely from differences in test densities of the material. In the other tests, as reported by the U.S. Department of Energy, the differences can be partly explained by the particular test methods and also by the material itself.

To sum up, it is apparent that in some cases a given cellulosic insulant might not live up to its performance claims. To avoid such difficulties, be sure to use only those products that are manufactured under and meet the requirements of standard industry specifications for the material. These would include the latest standards set forth by the *American Society for Testing and Materials (ASTM) C687, Federal Specification HH-I-515*, the *Cellulose Insulation Manufacturers Association (CIMA) Specification N-101*, and any others currently applicable to cellulosic insulation and its installation. As for the R value, the ASHRAE values are reasonable enough to use unless the manufacturers listed rating can be determined to be unquestionably accurate. Use the higher end of the range for insulation blown into an attic or other horizontal section and the lower R values for wall applications where the density is generally somewhat higher by virtue of the vertical building section.

Some cellulosic insulants might exhibit other problems besides variable R value. For example, in order to improve the fire-safety of the material, various fire-retardant chemicals are added to the material at some point during the manufacturing process. Independent tests have shown that the flame spread ratings of random samples of new material do agree with values reported by manufacturers, and the material is not excessively combustible. However, in many samples that have been tested the fire retardant chemical has shown a tendency to separate from the insulant. Of course this would reduce the fire retardancy. There is also some question about the stability of the fire retardant chemicals over a long period of time and whether or not they will indefinitely retain their effectiveness. There is a good possibility, too, that the chemicals can be leached out of the insulant over periods of time where high amounts of water vapor are present in the air or in a short period if the material becomes wet.

Cellulosic insulations of the type that would normally be used in residences can absorb relatively large quantities of moisture; I would also assume that the material has a high capillarity because it is essentially only paper. Data is not available to prove or disprove this supposition. If the material becomes soaked with water, the result would be about the same as using paper towels to mop up a spill of liquid. All that is left is a soggy mass of pulp that will eventually dry and harden into a clump that has little or no redeeming thermal value.

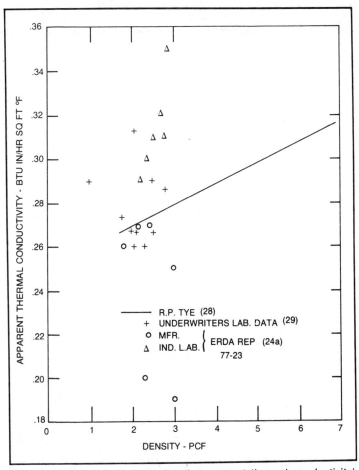

Fig. 3-5. Tests made to determine the apparent thermal conductivity/ density value of cellulosic insulation were somewhat inconclusive. The material has not always lived up to its advertised claims.

Paper will support the growth of fungus, bacteria, and molds; so will cellulosic insulation—depending upon the specific chemicals used as fire retardants. The cellulose might also attract certain kinds of insects—such as termites—that find starches, cellulose, and various organic materials very tasty indeed. At this point, it simply is not known whether or not this might be a consequential problem; no specific data has been developed.

The potential degrading effect of high temperature, temperature cycling, and general aging are not known. There is a tendency toward corrosiveness. This depends upon what chemicals are included in the material as fire retardant. Steel, aluminum, and copper might be attacked and degraded by certain of those chemicals.

It would appear that cellulosic insulants of the kind you would expect to be used in residences might, under certain conditions, have a few problems. Much depends on the individual application, the quality of the insulant itself, and the quality of the installation job. There seems little question that the material presents a certain degree of fire hazard (but so do others) and it does have a potential corrosion problem. The Consumer Product Safety Commission has been investigating the material and has initiated an amended CPSC standard for flame resistance and corrosiveness. At this time, a final safety standard has not been developed. Those who are interested in using cellulosic insulants might do well to first check with the CPSC. The general details of the material are listed in Table 3-6·

Polystyrene Foam

Polystyrene foam insulants have become increasingly popular over the past few years, especially since their use has become more economically attractive, and they are now in widespread use in the residential construction industry. Polystyrene is a derivative of styrene (a plastic familiar to many model-makers), and is a thermoplastic material produced by polymerization in the presence of a catalyst. Two kinds of polystyrene are manufactured: expanded and extruded.

The expanded type in light density is sometimes known as "beadboard" because of its characteristic of being made up of thousands of tiny beads of plastic all melted together; (Fig. 3-6); it is familiar as the plastic in which many delicate products such as radios and electronic gear are packaged for protection. This kind of polystyrene board or sheet insulation is made by placing quantities of tiny polystyrene beads, each contains a blowing agent (generally pentane gas) in a mold. The mold is then heated and the blowing agent expands. This causes the beads to also expand while the heat welds them together. The end result is a closed-cell rigid foam board, or for that matter, of any shape desired.

Extruded polystyrene stock is made somewhat differently, by forcing a mixture of hot polystyrene, solvent, and a fluorocarbon gas blowing agent under pressure through a slit and into the open air. As the mixture emerges, the blowing agent expands and results in an end product composed entirely of tiny closed cells. The manner in which the surface skin of extruded polystyrene insulating board is formed has an effect upon its R value. If the board is cut across the cells, which presents a somewhat roughened surface and also slices some of the cells open, density and R value are lower than if the material has a smooth unbroken surface skin and a somewhat higher density. In addition, the extruded polystyrene insulant generally has both a higher density and a higher R value per inch of thickness than does the expanded variety or beadboard.

Table 3-6. Properties of Cellulosic Insulants.

Material Property	Value	Test Method
Density	2.2-3.0 lb/ft^3	
Thermal Conductivity (k factor) at 75 F	0.27 to 0.31 Btu-in/ft^2	ASTM C177, C518
Thermal Resistance (R value) per 1" of thickness at 75 F	3.7 to 3.2 hft^{2}F/Btuhr°F	
Water Vapor Permeability	high	
Water Absorption	5 - 20% by weight	ASTM C739
Capillarity	not known	
Fire Resistance	Combustible	E-136
Flame Spread	15-40	
Fuel Contributed	0-40	ASTM E84
Smoke Developed	0-45	
Toxicity	develops CO when burned	
Effect of Age		
a) Dimensional Stability	settles 0-20%	
b) Thermal Performance	not known	
c) Fire Resistance	inconsistent information	
Degradation Due To		
Temperature	none	
Cycling	not known	
Animal	not known	
Moisture	not severe	
Fungal/Bacterial	may support growth	
Weathering	not known	
Corrosiveness	may corrode steel, aluminum, copper	ASTM C739
Odor	none	ASTM C739

Fig. 3-6. This broken-apart scrap of expanded (molded) polystyrene insulation board clearly shows the pellet-like cellular structure.

Either type is now being widely used to insulate concrete slab perimeters and foundation walls, to insulate exterior walls as exterior sheathing or backerboard for exterior siding, and as insulation in certain kinds of built-up roof assemblies. Incidentally, polystyrene beads themselves are sometimes used as a loose-fill or a movable insulation. An example of the former is as a pour-type, loose-fill insulant in the cores of concrete block. The best example of the movable bead insulation is in the window-wall concept developed by Zomeworks. Beads are blown into or sucked out of the space between two panes of a large window assembly. This creates a clear window expanse or an opaque, thermally efficient wall section.

Molded polystyrene insulant, or beadboard, is manufactured in densities ranging from 0.8 to 1.8 pounds per cubic foot and sometimes in higher densities as well. Because the thermal conductivity of beadboard is directly proportional to its density, the R value is also a variable range that runs from 3.85 to 4.35 per inch of thickness.

The ASHRAE table (Table 4-4), on the other hand, lists only one value of R-3.57 for material of a 1-pound per cubic foot density. This figure is on the low side and it might be best to use the manufacturer's listed rating for a given beadboard product—provided it is a reliable one. Further, molded polystyrene insulating board can vary around the average indicated density to an extent of about 10 percent because of quirks in the molding process. The R value does not change with age.

With extruded polystyrene insulating stock, the situation is somewhat different. The product is much more consistent in density; usually it is just about 2 pounds per cubic foot. The accepted R value in most cases is 5 per inch of thickness. However, ASHRAE lists R-5 only for the smooth-skin surface type in a density of 2.2 pounds per cubic foot and R-4 is listed for the same materials with a cut-cell surface.

The R value of extruded polystyrene foam is higher than that of the expanded type because the finished molded polystyrene cells or beads contain air. The cells of extruded polystyrene contain a mixture of fluorocarbon and air that has a lower k. While the R of extruded polystyrene diminishes over time from its highest point immediately after manufacture, that point is accounted for by establishing the R-value rating on a basis of a 5-year age of the material. In addition to having a greater resistance to transmission of heat, extruded polystyrene has a more uniform appearance and also is somewhat stronger.

Beadboard can be fairly easily fractured and broken. Some kinds actually can be crumbled as the beads separate at their joining faces. However, most have good compressive and tensile strength. Extruded polystyrene board stock has better tensile strength and can withstand a comparatively large amount of compression. Either type is suitable for use as slab perimeter insulation. Either type can be successfully strengthened into a tough board-stock by laminating on facing/backing of heavy kraft paper or similar material.

Polystyrene foam sheets are suitable for use on the exterior of a building frame and have the advantage of reducing heat transfer through the structural members. Additionally, the foam panels are much more effective in reducing air infiltration than are some other sheathings. These materials, however, do not have structural strength and cannot be used for that purpose; their nail-holding ability is almost nil.

Polystyrene insulants are combustible, develop a fair amount of smoke while burning, and also generate some carbon monoxide during combustion. For these reasons, they are not left exposed on building interiors (with the exception of some types of ceiling tiles), but are covered with a flame-resistant material such as plasterboard. Only the modified types of polystyrenes containing flame-retardant agents should be used in construction applications.

The material cannot be left permanently exposed outdoors because exposure to the ultraviolet segment of sunlight causes degradation over a period of time. The material has no odor and is completely noncorrosive. It will not attract insects or pests, mice do not favor it, and it will not support the growth of fungus or bacteria. It should not be used in ambient temperatures of 165 F or more (and preferably less), but is not affected by temperature cycling in the lower ranges. It will not shrink or otherwise change with age. It will, however, expand and contract somewhat during temperature changes at higher levels.

One of the advantages of polystyrene insulants is their versatility of shape and form. For example, expanded polystyrene sheathing board can be manufactured with an outside cover of heavy kraft paper topped with bright aluminum foil. This makes a stronger sheathing with greater resistance to weather, nailability, and durability, imparts greater strength to the material, and affords an extra *R-2* if installed in conjunction with an air space.

Not only can the material be produced as boards or slabs, but it can also be made in higher densities than normal to achieve a higher compressive strength such as might be required beneath a heavily loaded floor construction. Polystyrene can be made into siding backerboards, laminated panels of various sorts, with tongue-and-groove, shiplap or other edge or end joints for complete weather sealing, or in specially tapered plain or composite panels designed for various roofing applications. It can even be made in preformed shapes into which concrete can be poured. The polystyrene form is simply left in place as the insulant for the concrete. Table 3-7 shows the details of expanded polystyrene foam insulants.

Polyurethane and Polyisocyanurate Foams

Polyurethane and polyisocyanurate insulants are relatively new to the residential construction field. Both are plastics. Polyurethane is a product resulting from a reaction of isocyanates and alcohols. Polyisocyanurates are made from isocyanates in the presence of a catalyst. They can be made in either rigid or flexible form. For thermal insulations the rigid form is used.

Several different manufacturing processes are used, but basically they consist of mixing the required ingredients and then continuously metering the mix onto a moving conveyor system to produce a continuous strip of foam which can later be cut to size depending upon the desired end use. The end product can be either monolithic in numerous thicknesses or the process can be modified to produce laminates of various kinds. As with the polystyrenes, there is a considerable amount of flexibility in the form of the final product. This is advantageous for many particular building applications.

As residential insulation, polyurethanes and polyisocyanurates are primarily used as board or sheet stock of one sort or another and are suitable for application on interior or exterior walls as roof and ceiling insulation or as floor or foundation insulation. For residential purposes, the rigid type is almost always used. These plastics are also capable of being foamed in placed at the job site. This process has numerous advantages. However, this currently is not a common practice. There are two possibilities along these lines. The ingredients of the foam can be mixed and then dispensed and emplaced manually or automatically, or they can be sprayed onto practically any base or substrate that has been prepared if necessary.

For residential insulation work, polyurethane and polyisocyanurate insulating materials are available in several forms and under several trademarks. Typically, it is manufactured in sheet form with aluminum foil facing (Fig. 3-7). Several thicknesses from one-half inch on up are available and the sheets are usually either 2 or 4 feet wide and 8, 9, 10, or 12 feet long.

Even though these insulants are relatively expensive, they have caught on rapidly in the residential building field because of their high R value. Polyisocyanurate has the highest R value per inch of thickness of any insulant available on the market today. The ASHRAE table lists expanded polyurethane as having an average R value of 6.25 per inch of thickness at a density of 1.5 pounds per cubic foot; polyisocyanurate is not listed there.

The actual ratings of these insulants is a bit tricky. They might be variable to a certain degree depending upon the age of the stock. When the products are manufactured, a blowing agent (generally a fluorocarbon) is used to expand the raw-material mixture into its final state. Immediately after manufacture, the closed cells within the material are filled with the gas. The gas has a considerably lower conductivity than air does. The material at first has a very low k factor and a correspondingly high R value. However, as time passes the fluorocarbon vapor within the cells is replaced to some extent by air as the gas slowly escapes. The resulting mix

Table 3-7. Properties of Polystyrene Insulants.

Material Property	Value	Test Method
Density	0.8 to 2.0 lb/ft³	
Thermal Conductivity (k factor)	0.20 Btu-in/ft²hr°F (extruded) 0.23-0.26 Btu-in/ft²hr°F (molded)	ASTM C177, C518
Thermal Resistance (R value) per 1" of thickness at 75F	5 hft²F·Btu (extruded) 3.85 to 4.35 hft²F/Btu (molded)	
Water Vapor Permeability	0.6 perm-in extruded 1.2 to 3.0 perm-in molded	ASTM D2842-69 ASTM C355
Water Absorption	<0.7% by volume extruded	ASTM D2842-69
	<0.02% by volume extruded	ASTM C272
	<4% by volume molded	ASTM D2842-69
	<2% by volume molded	ASTM C272
Capillarity	none	
Fire Resistance	combustible	ASTM E136
Flame Spread	5-25	
Fuel Contributed	5-80	ASTM E84
Smoke Developed	10-400	
Toxicity	develops carbon monoxide when burned	
Effect of Age		
a) Dimensional Stability	none	
b) Thermal Performance	k increases to 0.20 after 5 years extruded none molded	
c) Fire Resistance	none	
Degradation Due To		
Temperature	above 165°F	
Cycling	none	
Animal	none	
Moisture	none	
Fungal/Bacterial	does not support	
Weathering	direct exposure to UV light degrades polystyrene	
Corrosiveness	none	
Odor	none	

85

Fig. 3-7. Polyurethane and polyisocyanurate insulants typically are manufactured in sheets covered with kraft paper and faced on one or both sides with foil. A portion of the paper backing can be seen at the lower left. Note the tiny, closed-cell construction.

of air and gas has a higher k factor and therefore a lower R value. One way to avoid this transmigration is to seal the surface of the material with an impervious skin. Then the degree of change in R value depends upon the effectiveness of the surface skin.

Most of these products now are rated in terms of "aged" values that range anywhere from R-5.8 to R-7.7. This depends upon the type of material and whether it is unfaced, has a spray-applied face, or is covered with an impermeable skin (the latter having the highest R value). Under the ASTM *Standard Specification for Rigid Preformed Cellular Urethane Thermal Insulation, C-591-69*, material with an initial value or R-8.33 to R-9.09 shows values of 5.88 to 6.25 when aged over 300 days.

At this point, little is known about actual long-term aging effects (say, 20 or 30 years), but it is assumed that once the material has reached the "aged" state, the rated R values will remain stable. You should always be guided by the "aged" rating, rather than an "as manufactured" rating. In practice, it is safe in the absence of a specific manufacturer's rating to assume R-6.25 for polyurethane. Typical values assumed for polyisocyanurate products range from R-7 to R-7.2. Both rate, in terms of R per inch of thickness, at 75 F. Both insulants are applied over the structural framework and minimize heat loss through the framing members. At the same time, they provide a substantially greater resistance to the passage of air through the building shell than do some other kinds of sheathing. They have the added attribute that they presently provide the highest possible R value for the least thickness of material. This can be very helpful in many applications and especially where space is a problem.

Both materials are combustible, and are best covered with a flame-retardant material such as plasterboard. However, notice that the flame spread rating of polyisocyanurate is considerably lower than that of polyurethane. Fuel contribution and smoke development are also substantially less. This means that while polyurethane insulants *must* be covered, certain products made with polyisocyanurate *can* be used in residential building construction without an additional gypsum fire barrier under certain building codes, such as ICBO, BOCA, and SBCC. This is because of the lower flame spread and the lower smoke emission ratings.

The dimensional stability of these insulants is somewhat less than perfect. It has been found that under certain conditions some dimensional changes will take place in the material. A volume change of up to 12 percent can occur in polyurethane under extreme conditions and up to 3 percent for polyisocyanurate. However, under normal operating conditions as installed in a residence, the initial aging has already taken place and further dimensional changes would doubtless not be of any great consequence. Here again, the long-term effects of aging, continual temperature cycling, weathering, and so on are now known.

Neither material will support bacterial or fungal growth. Neither attracts insects or pests and in fact will probably act as barriers to them. Water absorption and permeability of both materials is very low and free moisture is unlikely to harm them. One potential drawback is that they are so impermeable to the passage of water vapor that some manufacturers of polyisocyanurate sheathing products recommend that vent strips be installed to allow the escape of any water vapor that might manage to make its way through the inner face of the vapor barrier. This will partially negate the advantage of the low air infiltration factor that would otherwise be provided by the material. Complete details of these insulants can be found in Table 3-8.

Urea-formaldehyde Foam

Urea-formaldehyde (U-F) foam insulants are the newest to appear in the general residential marketplace and they are by far the most controversial. As usual there are several sides to the issue—actually there's more than one issue—and whether or not it is all a tempest in a teapot remains to be seen. I will delve into the controversy a bit later. First, a look at the material itself.

The principal use of urea-formaldehyde foam insulation is in retrofitting existing houses and there it is used almost entirely in filling wall cavities. It can be applied in new construction as well and can be employed for other insulating purposes than just wall cavities. It has also been applied to some extent in commercial/industrial buildings in both new and existing construction. U-F is one of the oldest cellular foam plastics (developed in 1933) and has been commercially available in this country since the early 1950s. It has been used in Europe for more than two decades, mostly as a masonry-wall cavity fill, but did not gain much recognition here until the energy crisis of the early 1970s.

Basically, a U-F foam insulant consists of a urea-formaldehyde based resin, a foaming agent containing a catalyst, or hardener, and air. Specific insulants are proprietary products and the exact compositions are closely-guarded secrets. The formula is varied with extenders, plasticizers, and assorted additives to improve certain characteristics of the

Table 3-8. Properties of Polyurethane and Polyisocyanurate Insulants.

Material Property	Value	Test Method
Density	2.0 lb/ft³	
Closed Cell Content	90%	ASTM C591-69
Thermal Conductivity (k factor)	0.16-0.17 Btu-in/ft²hr°F (aged & unfaced or spray applied) 0.13-0.14 Btu-in/ft²hr°F (impermeable skin faced)	ASTM C177, C518
Thermal Resistance (R value) per 1″ of thickness* at 75F	6.2-5.8 hft²(aged unfaced or spray applied) 7.7-7.1 hftF/Btu (impermeable skin faced)	
Water Vapor Permeability	2 to 3 perm in	
Water Absorption	Negligible	
Capillarity	none	
Fire Resistance	combustible	ASTM E136
Flame Spread	30-50 polyurethane 25 polyisocyanurate	
Fuel Contributed	10-25 polyurethane 5 polyisocyanrate	ASTM E84
Smoke Developed	155-500 polyurethane 55-200 polyisocyanurate	
Toxicity	produces CO when burned	
Effect of Age		
a) Dimensional Stability	0-12% change	ASTM D-2126
b) Thermal Performance	0.11 new	
c) Fire Resistance	0.17 aged 300 days none	
Degradation Due To		
Temperature	above 250°F	
Cycling	not known	
Animal	none	
Moisture	limited information available	
Fungal/Bacterial	does not promote growth	
Weathering	none	
Corrosiveness	none	
Odor	none	

finished product. Compressive strength is one example. The insulant is mixed at the job site and there are three somewhat different arrangements. The U-F resin can be premixed with water and transported from the factory to the job-site in 55-gallon drums, it can be delivered as a bulk dry powder and mixed into a solution at the job site, or it can be delivered as a concentrate and diluted with water at the site. The first method has been the most common in this country.

Special foaming and spraying equipment is used to apply the insulant. The U-F resin solution is withdrawn from the drum, the catalyst added, and the material is sprayed under pressure from a nozzle which aerates and foams it. At this point, the material is about 75 percent water by weight and the foam is composed of millions of tiny air bubbles coated with the U-F resin.

Curing begins immediately as the material leaves the foaming gun. The mix clings to the substrate surfaces against or into which it is being directed. Within 60 seconds or less it becomes self-supporting. It can be used not only to fill enclosed voids or cavities, but also open bays (as directly between the studs of a wall frame, for example).

Application in enclosed cavities is simple because the material is directed into place by squirting it through small holes drilled in the sheathing. Full chemical curing takes place over a period of several weeks and complete drying time varies with the nature of the installation. The end result is a solid foam composed of about 60 percent closed cells in a monolithic layer that seals off cracks and fissures and totally envelops the substrate (assuming correct installation).

When U-F foams started to be used in residences in the early 1970s, it was hailed as the best thing to come along since the legal right turn at a red light. It was relatively inexpensive and easy to apply and its apparently high thermal resistance made it ideal for retrofitting existing uninsulated house walls. Certainly it made possible a remarkable reduction in heating costs for such houses. There was no excessive hazard from combustion of the material, application cleanup could be made with water, and there was no apparent hazard from the material to the installers. The insulant was (and is) noncorrosive, inert, not subject to vermin attack and didn't attract pests or support the growth of mold or fungus. It cut down on air infiltration and was unaffected by mid-range temperature cycling. All in all, U-F foams had, and still has, some excellent properties (Table 3-9).

But it was not long before some problems began to surface. To take the least first, there seemed to be some discrepancy in the R values that manufacturers reported. The rang was anywhere from 3.5 to 5.5, quite a variance. But finally, by combining European experience with both Canadian and American testing (the latter by the National Bureau of Standards), it was determined that the usual density as applied and after curing is 0.7 to 0.8 pounds per cubic foot and that this density results in a reliable value of R-4.2 per inch of thickness. You can see the thermal worth of the material. The R of the insulation alone in a standard 3.5-inch frame wall cavity is 14.7 and the U for the full wall section is excellent.

However, other difficulties arose. Further investigation of the various U-F foam products disclosed that the range of rated maximum service temperature ran anywhere from 120 F to 320 F, hardly very conclusive. Further, it seemed that nobody knew much—or if they did they weren't saying—about such matters as what effects the foam might have on other building materials, effects of high temperature and humidity, effects of moisture on thermal conductivity, reactions to repeated freezing and thawing, susceptibility to water vapor transmission, and so on. Some preliminary formal testing uncovered two potentially serious defects;

Table 3-9. Properties of Urea-Formaldehyde Insulants.

Material Property	Value	Test Method
Density	Wet - Approximately 2.5 lb/ft³ Dry - 0.6 to 0.9 lb/ft³	Weigh a foam-filled plastic bag of known volume.
Closed Cell Content	0.7% - 80%	
Thermal Conductivity (k factor)	0.24 Btu-in/hrft²F	ASTM C177-76 Mean temperature 75 F
Thermal Resistance (R value) per 1" of thickness at 75 F	4.2 hft²F/Btu	
Water Vapor Permeability	4.5 to 100 perm in @ 50% rh 73 F	ASTM-C355
Water Absorption	32% by weight (0.35% volume) 95%rh 18% by weight (0.27% volume) 60%rh 68 F 180-3800% by weight (2-42% volume) immersion	
Capillarity	slight	
Fire Resistance	combustible	ASTM E-136
Flame Spread	0-25	
Fuel Contributed	0-30	ASTM E84
Smoke Developed	0-10	
Toxicity	No more toxic than fumes from burning wood.	
Effect of Age		
a) Dimensional Stability	1 to 4% shrinkage in 28 days due to curing. 4.6 to 10% shrinkage @ 100F 100% rh for 1 week 30 to 45% shrinkage @ 158F 90 to 100% rh -	ASTM D2126 proc C ASTM D2126-66
b) Thermal Performance	10 days	
c) Fire Resistance	No change	
Degradation Due To Temperature	Decomposes at 415 F	
Cycling	No damage after 25 freeze-thaw cycles.	
Animal	Not a feed for vermin.	
Moisture	Not established	
Fungal/Bacterial	Does not support growth.	ASTM G21-70 (1975)
Weathering		
Corrosiveness		
Odor	May exude formaldehyde until cured	

shrinkage with age and degradation under conditions of combined high temperature and humidity.

In general, the National Bureau of Standards was led to believe that the overall performance of U-F foams did not match up to the claims made for them. One test-house installation showed continuous shrinkage of the foam after 20 months, with no sign of stopping. The total shrinkage at that point was 7.3 percent. High temperature/humidity tests gave equally dismal results. In one test, three out of four different foams disintegrated after being exposed to a temperature of 122 F for only 7 weeks. In a retest at 102 F, the same three failed in 14 weeks. Both tests were made at 92 percent relative humidity. None of these conditions are hard to find within existing houses. Such performance renders an expensive insulating job worthless and does a great disservice to the public in general.

These and other findings subsequently led the U.S. Department of Housing and Urban Development to issue the following:

"If the average percent shrinkage of the foam expected to occur in building construction over a period of at least 2 years has not been established, then the average expected shrinkage of 6 percent shall be used to determine the effective thermal resistance. In this case, the effective thermal resistance of the foam is 72 percent of the thermal resistance that would be obtained on a laboratory specimen of the same thickness as that of the cavity." (*Use of Materials Bulletin No. 74.*)

The thermal resistance of U-F foams suddenly dropped from the accepted R-4.2 to R-3.02, a substantial reduction. HUD also established a table of reduction factors for other determinable shrinkage percentages, leaving the R value possibly as low as 2.52 (Table 3-10).

Canada conducted its own studies and subsequently the Canadian Government Specifications Board officially adopted a 60 percent correction factor, resulting in the same R-2.5.

But most of this got sidetracked by much more serious matters. Complaints from owners of U-F foam insulated houses began to be heard here and there around the land. Not about the relative effectiveness of the insulation, but because ever since the material had been installed in their homes, they hadn't felt physically well. Some remarked about a strange odor, all complained of various ailments including headaches and nausea, dizziness, irritation of eyes, nose and throat, difficulty in breathing, and persistent coughing. The degree of severity ranged from minimal to completely debilitating and seemed to have little rhyme or reason. Over 1600 active complaints, indicating the possibility of many more "inactive" ones, were made to the Consumer Product Safety Commission (CPSC). That agency launched an intensive investigation.

Meanwhile, the word put out by the disturbed homeowners was getting around. About 500,000 houses have been insulated with U-F foams. Yearly installations increased rapidly until 1977. Then there was an abrupt drop in 1978. Some companies—both manufacturers and installers—went out of business and some turned to other pursuits. Currently, there is but a handful of manufacturers of U-F foams and probably only 500 or so active installers. Adverse publicity probably did the greatest amount of damage. There were rumors of the possibility of a ban on the material. The rumors were not without foundation. In Colorado, the Office of the Attorney General issued a warning in 1978 about the material and the county of Denver adopted a prohibition of its use in new or existing buildings. In 1979, Massachusetts banned U-F foams and the ban is under litigation. Connecticut has taken an active role in the matter, New York and Rhode Island have adopted health and safety disclosure requirements,

**Table 3-10. *R*-Value Correction Factors
for Shrinkage of Urea-Formaldehyde Insulants**

ESTABLISHED AVERAGE PERCENT SHRINKAGE	REDUCTION FACTOR(%)
1	94
2	89
3	84
4	80
5	76
6	72
7	69
8	66
9	63
10	60

and Minnesota is investigating the health hazards. Virginia issued an alert in 1979 and other states have introduced legislation of various sorts that probably will affect the use of the material in one way or another. Canada has issued a temporary nationwide ban.

The CPSC investigation continued apace. The results to date have been less than charming. The proceedings and findings cover several hundred pages; I will go to the bottom lines. The problem is an outgassing of formaldehyde gas. Apparently the material releases the gas in different levels, depending upon the specific nature of the foam used and also the installation conditions, and evidence suggests that it might continue to do so for an indefinite period. This is the direct cause of the various ailments noted earlier. But worse, formaldehyde might be a carcinogen—a cancer-causing agent. From the *Federal Register*, Vol. 46, No. 24, Thursday, February 5, 1981:

"The CIIT [Chemical Industry Institute for Toxicology] study is a valid study that demonstrates that formaldehyde is carcinogenic to Fisher 344 laboratory rats when inhaled."

And there is more along these lines, "[t] here is no evidence demonstrating that there is a threshold for formaldehyde, or a dose level below which it is certain that formaldehyde will not induce cancer." Accordingly, the CPSC is pressing hard for an outright, nationwide ban on all U-F foam insulants.

There's another side to the story. The manufacturers of U-F foams recognize that the materials can, under certain circumstances, outgas formaldehyde. But they contend that the material is a safe, effective, and worthwhile insulant when properly manufactured under close control and when properly mixed and installed by qualified, trained personnel. And that situation is certainly no different than for many other products that we use daily, without a second thought. The manufacturers have proposed a set of industry standards which they feel will minimize, if not eliminate, any harmful side effects and they have confidence in their products. They also contend that past problems have been caused by poor materials and/or improper applications, and they might well be correct.

Apparently no one has yet proved that a properly-done U-F foam installation constitutes a health hazard or that there is a definite human cancer risk involved. Certainly not all of the 500,000-odd homeowners living with U-F foam insulation have officially complained. There must be a percentage of installations that are working out fine. In any event, no mention is made in the CPSC case of the other 498,400 residential U-F foam installations; surely the experiences of those homeowners is of some import.

As to the other problems with U-F foams, they can be, and are being, worked on and corrected by the manufacturers of the products. Like all other insulants, these foams are designed to be used in certain applications and under certain conditions. If properly compounded and installed, they will do what they are supposed to.

The use of U-F foams has not come to a halt and the material is still available in many places. There are certain applications where it is unlikely to pose any sort of health hazard. An example is within the cavity of a sealed masonry wall. In addition, the proposed CPSC ban contains provisions for exemptions so that development work of U-F foams can, and doubtless will, continue. Up-to-date information on the status of the proposed ban, or of the insulant, can be obtained free at any time from a number of sources. Local building department offices should be able to help at least with regards to local usage. Municipal, county, or state health departments should also have timely details. You can also contact the Formaldehyde Institute at 1075 Central Park Avenue, Scarsdale, NY 10583 (914-725-1492), and the Consumer Product Safety Commission at 1111 18th Street NW, Washington, DC 20207 (202-634-7780). Other contacts are the National Insulation Certification Institute, 803 King Street, Silver Springs, MD 20910 (800-638-2626, toll-free), and the National Association of Urea Foam Manufacturers, c/o RAPCO Foam, Inc., 22 Fifth Street, Stamford, CT 06904 (203-348-6418).

Perlite

Perlite (Fig. 3-8) is a naturally occuring substance that has been used as an insulant for a good many years. This is a siliceous volcanic glass that has a shell-like concentric structure. It is composed primarily of aluminum silicate and contains between 2 and 5 percent water as found. The material is mined or dug as an ore and then crushed. The particles are expanded to between 4 and 20 times their original volume by subjecting them to rapid heating at temperatures of up to 1000 C, depending upon the consistency desired of the end product. The heating process drives the moisture from the material and forms closed cells of vapor in the glass particles.

Perlite is not widely used as an insulant in residential construction. However, there are certain applications where it is useful. For the most

Fig. 3-8. Perlite is a naturally occurring glass-like mineral that can be easily processed to make this effective granular, poured insulant.

part, it is processed to make a relatively lightweight roof insulation board for commercial/industrial applications. It has a second principal use as an aggregate mixed with portland cement to make a lightweight insulating concrete that can be adjusted to practically any desired density.

In residential applications perlite can be used to fill the hollow cores of concrete or cinder blocks, spread as a crawlspace "floor" insulant, poured between the ceiling joists in an open attic, and so on. It can also be retrofitted in the wall cavities of existing houses. However, this is an unusual application. Perlite is presently manufactured in the United States by more than 30 companies, is readily available, and is also relatively inexpensive.

Perlite is manufactured in densities ranging from 2 to 11 pounds per cubic foot. The R value of the material is entirely dependent upon its density, as can be seen in Fig. 3-9. To gain the highest thermal resistance, use perlite of the lowest density. ASHRAE lists the R value of expanded perlite, of 5 to 8 pounds per cubic foot density, as 2.70 per inch of thickness (Table 4-4). The full R-value range, however, is from 2.5 to 3.7 per inch of thickness at 75 F.

When perlite is mixed with portland cement as a concrete, the density range is generally from 20 to 40 pounds per square foot and the R value of that material ranges form 1.08 to 2. Only in the higher density range does the concrete have sufficient mechanical strength to be of load-bearing or structural capability. In that case, the low R value should be assigned. If the material is nonstructural and lightweight with a density of around 20 pounds per cubic foot, then the higher R values can be assigned.

It is interesting to note that 40-pound perlite concrete has a R value 13.5 times greater than 140-pound ordinary concrete, per inch of thickness, and it also has 125 percent greater thermal resistance than lightweight cinder or pumice blocks of the same density.

Perlite is entirely noncombustible. It sometimes is treated with silicone to increase its resistance to water penetration—it is effectively water repellant and impervious to moisture—and the silicone is also noncombustible. Perlite is unaffected by temperatures up to 1200 F.

However, perlite concrete will begin to degrade at temperatures of 500 F and up. Both perlite and perlite concrete exhibit a high degree of water vapor permeability. Therefore, in many applications an external vapor barrier is essential. The material has no toxic or corrosive characteristics whatsoever, it will not attract or harbor insects or pests, and it is not affected by aging, temperature cycling or weathering. It will not sustain any sort of fungal or bacterial growth. It is also odorless and completely nontoxic. Table 3-11 lists the properties of both perlite and perlite concrete.

Vermiculite

Vermiculite is probably the most popular and commonly used of the pour-type loose-fill insulants. Like perlite, it is a mineral substance, but it is micaceous and composed of hydrous silicates of aluminum, iron, and magnesium in a laminar form. The insulant itself is manufactured from the raw mineral materials by subjecting them to high heat. This turns the entrapped moisture in the material to steam. The steam forcibly escapes and separates the laminae or "leaves." The "popped" material takes on various forms of particles such as flakes, feathery clumps and accordian-like lumps of very light weight (Fig. 3-10). The density of vermiculite, and consequently its R value as well as its pouring characteristics, can be varied considerably by controlling the heating process that governs the degree of expansion of the raw materials.

Vermiculite is commonly used in residential construction, mostly in retrofitting to fill the voids between ceiling joists in attics. But it has also been used to some extent in wall cavities and as a loose fill beneath a wood floor built on sleepers atop a concrete floor. It can be used in some instances to fill the hollow cores of concrete or cinder blocks and is also

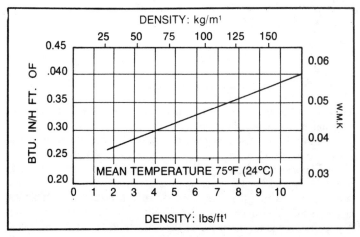

Fig. 3-9. As is largely true of all loose-fill and poured insulants, the as-installed R value of perlite is dependent upon its density.

95

Table 3-11. Properties of Perlite Insulation and Perlite Insulating Concrete.

Material Property	Value		Test Method
	Loose-Fill	Perlite Concrete	
Density	2-11 lb/ft³	20-40 lb/ft³	
Kapp at 75 F	0.27-0.40 Btu-in/ft²hr°F	0.50-0.93 Btu-in/ft²hr°F	ASTM C-177
Thermal Resistance (R value) per 1" thickness at 75 F	3.7-2.5 hft²F Btu	2.0-1.08 hft²F Btu	
Water Vapor Permeability	high	high	
Water Absorption	low		
Capillarity			
Fire Resistance	non-combustible	non-combustible	ASTM E136
Flame Spread	0	0	
Fuel Contributed	0	0	ASTM E84
Smoke Developed	0	0	
Toxicity	not toxic	not toxic	
Effect of Age			
a) Dimensional Stability	none	none	
b) Thermal Performance	none	none	
c) Fire Resistance	none	none	
Degradation Due To			
Temperature	none under 1200°F	none under 500°F	
Cycling	none	none	
Animal	none	none	
Moisture	none	none	
Fungal/Bacterial	does not promote growth	does not promote growth	
Weathering	none	none	
Corrosiveness	none	none	
Odor	none	none	

employed as an aggregate in lightweight insulating concrete for roof decks in commercial/industrial applications.

In today's manufacturing processes, the vermiculite is exfoliated during rapid heating to temperatures ranging from 700 C to 1000 C. This results in densities that range from 4 to 10 pounds per cubic foot. The lower-density material is made up of larger-sized particles and has the higher R value. It is the type to use as an attic insulant and in similar applications. The higher-density vermiculites are composed primarily of tiny particles and are mostly used as concrete and plaster aggregates, masonry fillers, and also in some industrial/commercial high-temperature applications.

ASHRAE lists vermiculite (Table 4-4) with a density of 4 to 6 pounds per cubic foot as having an R value of 2.27 per inch of thickness, and R-2.13 for densities of 7 to 8.2 pounds per cubic foot. The Department of Energy findings show that for the range of from 4 to 10 pounds per cubic foot density, the R value runs from 2.4 to 3.0 per inch of thickness at 75 F. In the absence of a manufacturer's rating to the contrary, you could assume that a value of R 3.0 would be acceptable for the lightest-density vermiculite and other densities could be interpolated for on the basis of the USDOE figures.

ASHRAE lists a range of R values of lightweight aggregate concrete (Table 4-4), which includes concretes made with vermiculite, of from 0.19 to 1.43 per inch of thickness at densities ranging from 20 to 120 pounds per cubic foot. The USDOE lists those figures in a range from 20 to 60 pounds per cubic foot as being R-1.0 to R-17. Again, there is some disparity in the numbers. However, the USDOE figures are particularly attributable to vermiculite concrete. The ASHRAE figures are general for aggregates that also include expanded shale, pumice and clay, among others. If possible, when using vermiculite or other lightweight aggregate concretes, it is well to assess the material on the basis of the supplier's R value rating, as tested.

Both vermiculite loose-fill and concrete are fully noncombustible and develop no smoke or fumes; they are completely nontoxic. Neither material is bothered by temperatures below 1000 F and temperature cycling has no effect. However, vermiculite concrete is susceptible to weathering and some forms of degradation when exposed to the outdoors for indefinite periods—just as are any concretes. Both materials have a high water vapor permeability, but they do not absorb water and show no capillarity. This does not mean, however, that vermiculite concrete is waterproof or even water-resistant without proper treatment. This is also true of other types of concrete. While vermiculite loose-fill does not absorb moisture, if penetrated by free water it becomes a slush that can easily compact to a much higher density. This negates its insulating value and also opening voids in the building section due to the compaction and settling process. Vermiculite loose-fill also has a tendency to settle when emplaced in

Fig. 3-10. Vermiculite is a hydrated laminar silicate that occurs naturally.

vertical sections. This is especially true if subjected to vibration (such as trucks rumbling by on the street outside), and it has a tendency to sift out of small cracks in building sections over a period of time. The material is odorless and wholly noncorrosive. It neither attracts nor harbors animals or insects and it will not support the growth of bacteria or fungus. The details of both vermiculite loose-fill and concrete are shown in Table 3-12.

Insulating Concrete

The two types of concrete previously discussed, perlite and vermiculite, are generically classed as insulating concrete, but they are specifically called lightweight aggregate concretes. Do not confuse them with insulating concrete. This material is not in widespread use and is generally found only in industrial/commercial applications. However, there is no reason that it cannot be used in residential constructions if there is a supply source close enough to the building site to make its purchase economically practical.

Insulating concrete is made by adding a foaming agent to the portland cement and aggregate mixture. One such foaming agent is aluminum dust. This causes a chemical reaction within the mix and evolves a gas that fills the mixture full of tiny bubbles. The result is a closed-cell, porous concrete. The density of the concrete can be varied simply by controlling the amount of gas produced within the mixture; the range normally produced runs from 12 to 88 pounds per cubic foot. The structural capability of the concrete is dependent upon its density. In order to be used for structural purposes where compressive loading is an important factor, the densities used might run from a minimum of 40 pounds per cubic foot and up. Below that figure, the concrete must be considered nonstructural.

On the other hand, the thermal insulating value of the material is also a function of its density. The lower the density, the higher the insulating value, and vice versa. Also, as the moisture content of the material increases, the R value decreases. This kind of insulant is generally used for roofing and decking applications where the material can be supported by a structural framing and decking system and the low-density concrete can be used for maximum thermal effectiveness. For walls, a higher density must be used. There are possibilities in residential design where insulating concrete might be employed to advantage in full basement walls. This is especially true if some of the load of the structure can be supported by steel posts or other structural members.

The R value of insulating concrete is about 0.85 at a 40-pound density and 1.2 at a 25-pound density. As the density increases and the R value decreases, at some point there might be a question of its usefulness because other kinds of insulants can be added to the wall after it is built to greatly increase the overall R value of the section at minimal cost. Therefore, some close calculating should be done to determine whether or not using insulating concrete is worth the effort.

It does have the advantage of being quite resistant to the penetration of moisture. However, it is susceptible to weathering and frost damage if

Table 3-12. Properties of Vermiculite Insulation and Vermiculite Insulating Concrete.

Material Property	Value		Test Method
	Loose-Fill	**Vermiculite Concrete**	
Density	4 to 10 lb/ft³	20 to 60 lb/ft³	
Kapp at 75 F	0.33-0.41 Btu-in/ft²hF	0.59-0.96 Btu-in/ft²hF	ASTM C177
Thermal Resistance (R value) per 1" thickness at 75 F	3.0-2.4 hrft²F/Btu	1.7-1.0 hft²F/Btu	
Water Vapor Permeability	high	high	
Water Absorption	none	none	
Capillarity	none	none	
Fire Resistance	non-combustible	non-combustible	ASTM E136
Flame Spread	0	0	
Fuel Contributed	0	0	ASTM E84
Smoke Developed	0	0	
Toxicity	none	none	
Effect of Age			
a) Dimensional Stability	none	none	
b) Thermal Performance	none	none	
c) Fire Resistance	none	none	
Degradation Due To			
Temperature	none below 1000 F	none below 1000 F	
Cycling	none	none	
Animal	none	none	
Moisture	none	none	
Fungal/Bacterial	does not promote growth	does not promote growth	
Weathering	none	none	
Corrosiveness	none	none	
Odor	none	none	

left unprotected in a permanent exterior environment. It is noncombustible and fireproof and can be exposed to high temperatures. Aging in no way affects it and under normal circumstances it will not degrade. It is impervious to pests and animals and will not support fungal or bacterial growth. Further details about insulating concrete are shown in Table 3-13.

Reflective

When is an insulant not an insulant? When it's reflective "insulation." These materials have virtually no bulk or mass and contain no tiny air cells. In and of themselves, they have no insulating value whatsoever. The key lies in the reflectivity; they work as isolators and heat shields. Incident radiant energy is reflected away from them to a very high degree so that a certain percentage of that energy cannot enter or exit the structure if the material is properly installed in conjunction with sizeable plane air spaces. They do not have universal effectiveness. Only in certain applications are they at their best. The reflective material can only turn away incident *radiant* energy and it is totally ineffective as a barrier against the transfer of heat by either conduction or convection. Reflective surfaces alone will work best wherever conductive and convective heat losses through a particular building section are relatively small and most of the heat transfer takes place by radiation. In a house, about 70 percent of the heat transfer through underfloor spaces takes place by radiation so this is an effective application for a reflective surface. On the other hand, the heat transfer through a vertical cavity is due about 60 percent to radiation and only about 50 percent through loft spaces.

Table 3-13. Properties of Insulating Concrete.

Material Property	Value	Test Method
Density	12 to 88 lb·ft³	
Thermal Conductivity (k factor) at 75 F	1.17 Btu-in·ft²·hr°F (40 lb ft³) 0.83 Btu-in/ft²·hr°F (25 lb ft³)	ASTM C177
Thermal Resistance (R value) per 1" of thickness at 75 F	0.85 hft²F Btu (40 lb ft³) 1.2 hft²F Btu (25 lb ft³)	
Water Vapor Permeability	varies with denisty	
Water Absorption		
Capillarity	none	
Fire Resistance	none-combustible	ASTM E-136
Flame Spread	0	
Fuel Contributed	0	ASTM E-84
Smoke Developed	0	
Toxicity	none	
Effect of Age		
a) Dimensional Stability	none	
b) Thermal Performance	none	
c) Fire Resistance	none	
Degradation Due To		
Temperature	none below 1000C	
Cycling	none	
Animal	none	
Moisture	none	
Fungal/Bacterial	does not support growth	
Weathering	below 30 lb/ft³ must be protected from frost	
Corrosiveness	none	
Odor	none	

The reflectivity can be accomplished in a number of ways. The material that is used for the purpose is bright and shiny aluminum foil. The foil can be applied in a very thin layer to the facing of fiberglass or rock wool insulating batts or blankets or to one or both sides of insulating sheathing sheets. When the insulant is installed, the reflective surface accompanies it and improves the overall R value of the material by barring the radiant component of the total heat transfer (assuming that the installation is properly done).

A common error is to apply the foil-faced material and then to cover it with another material without leaving an air space between the two. If the foil facing lies flat against another surface, its value is entirely negated. There must be a gap of at least three-eights of an inch in order for it to work effectively. In this situation, the R value of the foil facing is dependent upon the nature of the air space. The space can be foil faced on one or both of the major bounding surfaces. The R value gained is over and above the listed rating of the insulant to which it is attached and should be added in separately.

The value can be calculated by using the normal procedure for figuring plane air spaces and it is entirely dependent upon the depth and other controlling factors of the specific space. In practice, the usual assumption is that when a three-fourth inch air space that is reflective on one side (the insulation) is left by dishing mineral wool insulation into the framing cavity and stapling it along the sides of the framing members or by nailing three-fourth inch furring over the face of foil-covered insulating sheathing and then applying the exterior siding to the strips, the gained R value is 2.

In the past, aluminum foil alone was in fairly widespread use as a reflective heat barrier. The foil itself, plain and unbacked and much like the foil you buy at the grocery store, is installed by either securing it to the inside faces of structural members forming framing cavities or simply fastening it across the faces of the framing members. The foil is subsequently covered and enclosed by other building materials such as plasterboard. In the former instance, two separate air spaces, each reflective on one surface, are formed within the building cavity and the depth of each is variable depending upon just where the foil is placed. In the latter case, only one full-depth air space with one reflective surface is formed within the cavity. With either arrangement, much of the effectiveness of the insulation depends upon the absence of air currents within the cavities, which would have a diminishing effect. Reflective foil installations of this type are not now often being made because of several problems associated with them and the ready availability of other types of insulation that perform better and install more easily.

The multiple-layer type of aluminum foil insulation is a somewhat different story. Typical of this type of material is an insulation which consists of a double layer of heavy kraft paper, much like paper-bag stock, with a layer of unbacked aluminum foil attached to it at each side. This forms a stapling or attachment flange along the edges of the material.

When the material is properly stretched out for installation, the foil and the kraft paper layers separate in such a way that a three-eight inch air space is formed between the foil and paper (Fig. 3-11). When the material is properly installed, a second air space is formed between the foil and the building surface. This type of insulant is specifically designed to be attached to three-fourth inch-thick furring strips secured to masonry walls to provide two three-eighth inch air spaces. In this application, the foil insulation will provide a thermal resistance value of R-5.

Another type of multiple-layer aluminum foil insulation is made especially to be installed in an under-floor space, between the floor joists. The material consists of a single foil sheet and two foil-laminated kraft paper sheets. These are designed to go into a space between joists that is 9 ½ inches deep (though it can be used in other cavity depths as well). This material also expands as it is installed to provide two three-fourth inch air spaces within the material and a second, 8-inch air space in the building cavity when applied flush (Fig. 3-12), or will provide four plane air spaces in a recessed application (Fig. 3-13). This results in a thermal resistance of R-13 for downward heat flow. Both of these materials can be used as stand-alone insulants or they can be used in concert with other insulants.

Aluminum foil makes an excellent vapor barrier if properly applied and it will not absorb moisture nor does it exhibit any degree of capillarity. Water vapor will not adversely harm kraft paper backing; however a soaking will. The aluminum foil itself is not combustible, but an insulant to which it is attached might be and a kraft paper backing is combustible and will produce smoke and fumes. Aluminum is not subject to degration by temperatures of the kind normally found in residences or by temperature cycling. It has no corrosiveness, though it can be corroded, it is odorless, and it will not support fungal or bacterial growth. It attracts neither insects nor animals and is unaffected by aging. It is very delicate and can be easily

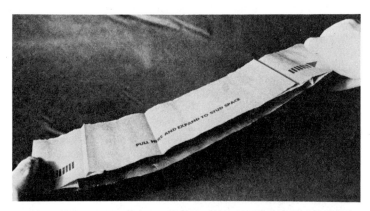

Fig. 3-11. A plane air space is created between the aluminum foil and the kraft paper facing when the facing of this reflective insulation is pulled taut.

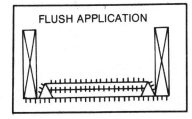

Fig. 3-12. This cross section of a pair of floor joists shows how expandable reflective insulation is installed flush with the lower edges of the joists (courtesy of Alfol Inc.).

damaged. It is also susceptible to dulling and some loss of reflectivity if improperly handled or installed. When applied as a facing to another insulant or building material or when used in combination with kraft paper, the overall installation must be considered on the basis of the characteristics of the supporting material and the presence of plane air spaces, as necessary.

Cellular Glass Foam

Cellular glass foam (Fig. 3-14) is fairly new to the insulation field (1946) and was developed primarily for commercial/industrial applications for use in roofs, core walls, wall linings, and floor and deck applications. Until now it has not often been promoted for use in residential applications, but its various attributes indicate that it could be very advantageous in several aspects of house construction. This rigid insulating material is lightweight and composed entirely of very tiny and fully sealed glass cells. No binders or fillers are used and the material is solid in that there are no open voids between the cells.

This insulant is manufactured somewhat along the lines of rigid foamed plastics. A chemical reaction is caused within the molten material which expands it into a foam. The expansion takes place in standard molds to shape the end products. Typically, cellular glass insulants are currently being manufactured in standard-sized blocks (generally 1 x 1½ or 1½ x 2 feet) in thicknesses from 2 to 5 inches in one-half inch increments and in tapered blocks of various sizes and degrees of taper for use in constructing self-draining roof systems. In addition, multiple blocks are laminated between kraft paper into 2-foot by 4-foot boards, in thicknesses from 1½ to 4 inches of one-half inch increments.

Though presently being used to little if any extent in residences, under certain conditions and in certain applications and depending upon the

Fig. 3-13. A recessed application of expandable reflective insulation between floor joists takes longer, but gives the material a bit of extra protection (courtesy of Alfol Inc.).

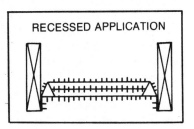

Fig. 3-14. Cellular glass foam insulation is typically manufactured in board, slab, block, and tapered block form (courtesy of the Pittsburgh Corning Corp.).

amount of thermal resistance needed and the cost-effectiveness involved, there are some applications where cellular glass insulants would be ideal. For example, this insulant could easily prove to be the best available for externally insulating the walls and floors, and probably roofs as well, of earth-sheltered houses. It is perfect for perimeter edge insulation for concrete slabs, as an upper basement wall insulant, or for use under a full concrete slab—whether at or below surface level. It is ideal for exterior use wherever ground moisture levels are high. It can be used as an interior insulant on walls or on ceilings or as part of a built-up roof construction where the insulant is outside the house shell. For flat roofs it is perfect; this is one of the specific applications for which it was developed.

Though cellular glass insulation by no means has as high an R value per inch of thickness as some insulants, nonetheless it does have relatively low conductivity and good thermal resistance. In combination with its other attributes, this makes it an outstanding material. Typical C and R values can be seen in Table 3-13. The values listed are for specific thicknesses; although ASHRAE lists the value as R-2.63 (Table 4-4) per inch of thickness, note that this product, at least, tests at 2.86 at a temperature of 75 F. At 50 F, the thermal resistance is a bit better (R-3.03) as opposed to the ASHRAE rating of R-2.777; as with other insulants, the R value increases as the temperature decreases. These values are based upon a density of 8.5 pounds per cubic foot. This is standard weight for these products.

The area where foam cellular glass insulation shines the brightest is in its compressive strength. No other insulant can compare favorably with it (see Table 3-15). Polystyrene board is commonly used as a foundation insulation in residences because of its lower susceptibility to crushing than other types. Note the tremendous difference between it and the cellular glass insulation.

The 100 pounds per square inch compressive strength of the material works out to the fact that it can withstand loads of greater than 7 tons per square foot of surface area if it is properly supported from beneath. For this reason, the insulant can be used beneath heavy foundation constructions without fear of crushing. It can also be used as the base for a floor which can then be covered with poured concrete or even with a relatively thin applied layer such as quarry tile, terrazzo, ceramic floor tile, or stone pavers or flags.

Another interesting characteristic is that the material is totally non-combustible and it need not be covered by any other material. Sparks or even open flames will not bother it at all. It cannot support combustion and will not catch fire and can only deform or degrade when temperatures become extremely high. Naturally, no smoke or fumes can be released and the material is also completely nontoxic. This insulant, unlike any of the others, is completely impervious to moisture and has a perm-inch rating of water vapor permeability of 0.0. It is equally proof against soaking in any way. Simply stated, no form of moisture can get through it. And this brings up an interesting point.

Other kinds of insulants, some more so than others, do have a certain degree of permeability. Water vapor or free moisture can work its way into

**Table 3-14. These R and C Values are Typical
of Cellular Glass Insulation (courtesy of the Pittsburgh Corning Corp.).**

FOAMGLAS®Thickness	R	C
1.50	4.41	.227
2.00	5.88	.170
2.50	7.35	.136
3.00	8.82	.113
3.50	10.29	.097
4.00	11.76	.085
4.50	13.23	.076
5.00	14.71	.068

Table 3-15. Cellular Glass Insulation (courtesy of the Pittsburgh Corning Corp.).

TYPE OF INSULATION	APPROXIMATE DENSITY: lb/cu ft	Compresive Strength psi @ % Consolidation*
FOAMGLAS Insulation	8.5	100 @ 0%
Perlite Board	10.0	35 @ 5%
Polystyrene	1.5-2.5	9-14 @ 5%
Polyurethane	1.5-2.5	33 @ 0%
Thermal-setting fill	18-22	33-39 psi

*Consolidation or deformation is the decrease in thickness produced in the original thickness of the test specimen under a compressive load.

the structure of the insulant. This has two effects. One is the potential degradation of the material itself. This can have an eventual deleterious effect upon its usefulness. The other is that the presence of any amount of water vapor, however slight, within an insulant at any given time diminishes to a certain extent its ability to retard the flow of heat. As insulants are applied in the field, there is almost always some degree of water vapor present and the insulating value is thereby diminished somewhat. With cellular glass insulation, however, this cannot happen. The insulating value, or the R value, of the material remains the same when it is submerged in a tub of water as it is when surrounded by air at 0 percent humidity. This is a unique characteristic, and points up the usefulness of cellular glass for roofing work as well as earth-sheltered house applications where keeping the externally-applied insulation absolutely dry is a critical factor.

Cellular glass insulation exhibits other plus factors as well. For example, it is perhaps the most dimensionally stable under all conditions of any insulants. The movement in inches of one cellular glass product per 100 feet of length per 100 F change in temperature is only 0.55. Contrast this with one polyurethane product that moves 6.0 inches under the same conditions.. When you install cellular glass insulation you can expect that it will remain stable and only extreme circumstances will lead to dimensional changes that might open seams between the sheets or blocks of the material. Unlike some insulants, this type will not degrade under severe temperature conditions.

In addition, aging has no effect upon the material. At least one manufacturer guarantees that it will not absorb **moisture,** will retain it original insulation efficiency, will keep its compressive strength, and will remain totally noncombustible for 20 years—if properly installed. Cellular glass insulation will slowly degrade under freeze/thaw cycles so its surface must be protected from standing water subject to freeze/thaw cycling.

But weathering has no effect, it will neither harbor nor support insect pests, and it will turn aside rodents as well. Typical properties details are set out in Table 3-16.

Other Insulants

The insulants just discussed are the major ones found in today's residential construction and for the most part are in common use and readily available—except perhaps for the concretes. But there are others as well. There are a few insulants that have been around for many years, that are still used to some extent, and are still easily obtainable. They are, however, slowly being superceded. Because the insulation industry is far from being a static one at this point, new types are being developed, tested, and evaluated for possible use. Some are specialized and others are not. The search continues for more and better products on a constant basis, so it always pays to check the latest developments before proceeding with your insulating projects.

Fiberboard. There are several kinds of fiberboard that are sometimes used as insulants—especially in a supplementary role. Mineral fiber that is bound together with a resin binder and formed into sheets is one such type. It is not often used in residential constructions. It does, however, have a relatively high R value of 3.45 per inch of thickness. Some of these products also have desirable physical characteristics that can make their consideration worthwhile in some special residential applications (such as ceiling tile).

Perhaps the most familiar and commonly used fiberboard is the wood composition fiber type used as an exterior sheathing in many wood-frame

Table 3-16. Properties of a Typical Cellular Glass Insulation Product (courtesy of the Pittsburgh Corning Corp.).

PHYSICAL PROPERTIES	ENGLISH	METRIC	ASTM TEST
Absorption of moisture (% by volume)	0.2	0.2	C 240
	Non-absorptive. (Only moisture retained is that adhering to surface cells after immersion.)		
Capillarity	None	None	
Combustibility	Noncombustible		E 136
Composition	Pure glass, totally inorganic, contains no binder		
Compressive strength, average	100psi	7.0 kg/cm²	C 165— Surfaces capped with hot asphalt per C 240-72
Density, average	8.5 lb/ft³	136 kg/m³	C 303
Linear coefficient of thermal expansion	4.6 x 10⁻⁶ °F	8.3 x 10⁻⁶ °C	
Water-vapor permeability	0.00 perm-in	0.00 perm-cm	C 355

houses. This material is generally installed as a sheathing rather than particularly as an insulant. The standard-density variety does have an R of 1.32 in the popular one-half inch thickness and 2.06 in the less widely used twenty-five-thirty-second inch thickness. This substantially exceeds the thermal resistance of plywood panels for exterior sheathing. Plywood has other physical characteristics that often dictate its use instead.

Acoustical tile is another familiar example of a fiberboard with good insulating qualities. The wet-molded mineral type has an R value of 2.38 per inch of thickness. Ordinary wood or cane fiberboard acoustical tile (Fig. 3-15) is listed as R-1.25 in the standard one-half inch thickness, and R-189 in the three-fourth inch thickness. The addition of acoustical tile to a residential ceiling has a relatively small, but nonetheless definite plus effect, upon the overall U of the ceiling assembly.

An interior finish fiberboard, available in both plank and tile varieties, has an R of 2.86. This material can be used on either walls or ceilings and has the advantage of easy retrofitting to an existing house without need for extensive renovation or refinishing. Obviously, there are instances when any of these materials might serve well in either new construction or retrofitting to provide a bit of extra thermal resistance with minimal cost and effort.

Decking Insulation. There is a wide variety of products made especially to serve as combined roof decking and insulation. While part of the intended purpose of these materials is an insulation, they are also designed to fill other needs as well so that they are compromise materials made for numerous different applications. There is a considerable range of thicknesses, sizes, and slab or panel types. Which one to choose depends entirely upon the specifics of the job conditions. ASHRAE lists a range of R-1.39 to R-8.33 for these materials (Table 4-4). However, it is best to obtain from the manufacturer exactly what the R value is for a given product before attempting to work out heat loss calculations. For a variety of reasons, these decking products are not often used in residences; but there is no reason at all why they cannot be if some advantage thereby accures.

Ceramic. Development of ceramic insulation was begun by one particular company some four years ago. The product has been developed and is now manufactured in a limited way. It is used primarily for test installations in houses built throughout a small, selected region, and for certain commercial purposes as well. Although it is not now generally available on a nationwide basis, one day it might be to every homeowner's advantage.

This ceramic insulation is a pouring, loose-fill type that comes bagged in granular form. It looks much like uniformly refined salt. It is designed to be placed between the ceiling joists in an attic by pouring in and then ranking it out to the desired depth. This can be as little as an inch or as much as 3 inches. Once in place, it eventually consolidates and bonds to the structural framework and becomes a monolithic reflector of radiant

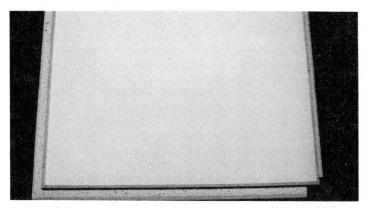

Fig. 3-15. Ordinary wood or cane fiberboard acoustic ceiling tile had good thermal properties, and will add a modest amount of thermal resistance to a ceiling assembly. Specially made thermal ceiling tiles have high R values.

energy. Because of its nature and the fact that it does not insulate against conductive and convective heat loss, its efficacy cannot be measured by conventional means. This, coupled with the apparently phenomenal performance of the material, has led to some difficulties in trying to determine just how it can and should be presented to the general public.

This material has been found to be particularly good in houses heated by electric radiant heat systems or heat pump installations. It has numerous advantages: ease of installation, excellent acoustic properties, being unaffected by temperature or temperature cycling, being nontoxic and odorless, and being completely impervious to moisture, insects, or animal pests. Its performance? An incredible "equivalent R" of 70 for a 3-inch thickness at 75 F. (That's not a misprint.) At higher temperatures, such as would be found in applications where the insulation is to be installed to minimize heat gain for cooling, the "equivalent R" rises right off the chart instead of dropping as is the case with other insulants. With performance of that sort, one would hope that the material will become generally available at some point in the not too distant future.

Foamed Asbestos. Foam asbestos is a good insulant insofar as its thermal characteristics are concerned and it is one that can be readily manufactured at a reasonable price. It has been used in Europe for some time, but it appears to do a relatively effective job. It has never gained a foothold in this country and the likelihood that it now will is very slim because of the potential health hazard of all materials containing asbestos.

Foamed Polyvinyl-chloride. There is a considerable similarity in both density and thermal performance, as well as assorted physical characteristics, between this type of foamed plastic and the polyurethane and polystyrene types. All are closed-cell plastic foams whose applications would be similar, if not identical. This being so, and given the fact that polyurethane and polystyrene foamed plastic insulants have gained a good

109

following in the marketplace, probably polyvinyl-chloride foams will not find widespread use. If a PVC foam can be found to fill some particular niche that other foams do not, it could see some limited use.

Foamed Gypsum. This is a relatively new material that is currently being developed and shows some promise. It is manufactured by combining gypsum, a common and inexpensive product and the principal constituent of ordinary plasterboard, with a blowing agent and glass fibers. The material has excellent fire resistance properties and can be manufactured in a low density with a correspondingly relatively high R value. This combination makes it an excellent interior wall and ceiling covering for residences. It incorporates a higher degree of fire safety than is now the norm and this is coupled with added thermal performance.

Dynamic Insulation. Dynamic insulation is not an insulant; it is a concept of house (or other structure) insulating. The concept originated in Sweden and is currently being developed and tested there. The idea is a relatively simple and logical one, but the system by which it is implemented is rather more difficult. An exceptionally tight and leak-free house of special construction is required.

The entire present theory and practical thrust of insulating a house built in this country depends upon preventing all air movement within confined spaces. The thermal effectiveness depends upon dead air space provided in one fashion or another, in the house, in the building sections, and within the insulant itself. The new concept of dynamic insulation is just the opposite. This system depends upon a closely controlled flow of air coming inward through the wall insulation of the structure, in exact opposition to the outward flow of heat. The outward-flowing heat never reaches the exterior of the building. It is picked up by the incoming air flow and returned to the building interior. With proper regulation that is uniform over the entire exterior surface, the total outflow of heat can theoretically be completely negated by the total inflow of air. The thermal performance of the building sections is exceptionally high and the heat loss is very low.

To accomplish this, some means must be built in to provide the necessary air flow and some way to accurately control that flow must be established. It must be fully automatic if it is to be successful.

Experimentation shows that the required air flow is low and the total incoming amount would represent approximately one-half an air change per hour in a typical residence. Besides the proper air input and control factors, there also is the problem that air cannot be introduced at other, random points in the building. This would diminish the overall thermal performance. Interestingly, the whole process can be reversed to limit or cancel solar gain from the outside during the summer months.

This would appear to be a high-technology system with a good many problems to be overcome. One major problem might be changes in the building structure because of aging. It also appears that it would be of benefit only in new construction; retrofitting does not seem possible.

Estimating Heat Losses

There is no simple rule of thumb for determining the heat loss of a given house and there is no "quick fix" for deciding upon how much and what kind of thermal insulation should be installed. In order to arrive at some satisfactory figures in support of developing a proper insulation envelope for a house, a series of heat loss calculations must be made. At first glance these calculations might seem terribly complex, but they really are not when considered bit by bit. Although making the calculations does take a certain amount of time, the chore is not a difficult one and it can be made relatively simple with the aid of a pocket calculator.

There are several good reasons for making these calculations instead of just following the "by guess and by gorry" course and hoping for the best. With new construction, the first object is to determine the overall heat loss under the given design conditions for the individual house and its particular environment—on an average hourly basis. This allows the designer to properly assess the thermal characteristics of the house and choose the type and thickness of insulation that will be best. In this context, the word "best" can involve one or several parameters and usually is a compromise situation. The thermal envelope could be designed specifically for absolute maximum effectiveness or might be based entirely on satisfactory initial cost to the builder. It could involve cost-effectiveness considerations for a certain mortgage period or the entire projected life span of the house. Other factors can enter into the picture as well. Seldom is any one factor considered alone. Compromise and a melding of various physical, thermal, acoustic, construction, and cost considerations are generally involved.

It is possible to simply follow local custom insofar as residential insulation applications are concerned. This often happens and it might not serve to the benefit of the house's occupants. Without making a series of comparative calculations, there really is no way to properly assess whether one insulation installation might be better or worse than another. From the standpoints of maximum occupant comfort and minimum heating expenses (not to mention the conservation of energy), making a series of heat loss calculations is essential.

Just as there is no simple way to figure out exactly what insulation should be used in a house, neither is there a quick method of determining the size of the heating plant or the details of the heat distribution system. Many years ago, a commonly used method of sizing the heating plant, where a central system was employed, was merely to install a very large unit that, based upon a few rudimentary calculations plus a knowledge of local custom and practice, the installer was more than sure would be plenty large enough. The unit was frequently grossly oversized and thoroughly inefficient as well.

Today, following this course is senseless; heating equipment is expensive and operating inefficiency cannot be tolerated. Once the heat loss calculations have been run for the house and a satisfactory level of thermal efficiency and effectiveness determined, these same figures can then be used to determine the heating load of the house. This is the second objective of making the calculations. The heating load is the total of all factors that combine to equal the amount of heat that the heating equipment must supply to the house in order to keep it heated to the desired temperature and provide the desired comfort level. The calculations are made on a room-by-room basis. The total heating load of the entire house is used to determine the size of a central heating system and the individual zone or room figures are used to determine the details of the heat distribution system or to work out the sizes of individual area heating units where a central system will not be installed.

The third objective of making heat loss calculations is to estimate the fuel or energy consumption and the operating costs of the heating system on a seasonal basis. This can easily be done by making a few simple calculations using the heating load figures as a basis. In many instances, it is also useful to compare these seasonal costs for two or more different fuels or energy sources—so that the least expensive source can be utilized—or the heating system can be arranged to run on two or more different fuels depending upon cost and availability at any given time.

For upgrading the thermal efficiency of existing houses, heat loss calculations are equally important. The homeowner can quickly determine the present heat loss of the house, the heat loss after various proposed improvements have been made to the thermal envelope, and also in lowering the rate of infiltration of outside air. These figures can be used to determine just which retrofitting projects are most cost-effective, which will do the most good, which will have the shortest paycheck periods, and which projects might best be undertaken first. When a homeowner sets out to improve the thermal efficiency and effectiveness of a house, the usual desire is to first undertake whatever projects will do the most good for the least cash outlay. Making heat loss calculations will quickly point out the most beneficial courses to follow.

Heat loss calculations can be made in a number of different ways. Despite the detail differences involved in the various procedures, they basically are but variations on a theme and all make use of the same fundamental data. Several organizations promulgate the use of information, procedures, and tabulated figures to achieve results that are, from a practical standpoint, very similar if not identical. There are five systems in particular that are in widespread use: those set forth by the American Society of Heating, Refrigerating and Air-Conditioning Engineers, Inc. (ASHRAE); the National Electrical Manufacturers Association (NEMA); the National Association of Home Builders (NAHB), the Air-Conditioning Contractors of America (ACCA); and The Hydronics Institute.

Any of these procedures can be successfully used to determine residential heat loss. The same organizations offer procedures for determining residential heat gain for house cooling applications. This information is covered in the next chapter. The information provided by NEMA is designed primarily for electric heat applications. The remaining four methods will serve for any type of heating equipment. With the exception of ASHRAE, the procedures offered are based upon certain formats and series of tabulated information that have been developed by the organizations involved. They all are somewhat different. However, the end results are approximately the same.

The information provided by ASHRAE is more basic and is broken down into its separate parts. Although the procedures and explanations are somewhat more involved and are a bit lengthier, they are no more complex. I will largely follow the ASHRAE procedures, as they are outlined in the *ASHRAE HANDBOOK & Product Directory*, in order to present a complete explanation of how the full calculations are actually done. By knowing how to make the fundamental calculations and by understanding what is involved in the determination of the calculation factors, you will then be able to develop relatively accurate heat loss assessments to cover any given situation by using only a few basic tables and formulas.

It's important to realize that the heat loss calculations usually made for residences are really not geared to pinpoint accuracy. There are a number of reasons for this. Residences are by and large relatively simple buildings by comparison with commercial and industrial designs, their use and occupancy is predictable, they are comparatively small in size, and the amount of dollars and energy involved is also small. Super-sophisticated, infinitely detailed procedures are widely used in determining heat losses from large buildings. This often involves hour-by-hour studies of great complexity that must be run on a computer for analysis. This degree of sophistication has been found to be unnecessary with residences. This is primarily because the extra effort and expense required to conduct such a study is impractical and unnecessary. Most designers and builders of residences do not have either the expertise or the equipment needed to do that kind of work. For do-it-yourself, owner-builders, this course would be impossible and fruitless.

Heating loss calculations of the type that are commonly made for residences are simplified and rather unsophisticated. The final results are an estimate that should be considered an approximation of what the heat losses and heating costs might be for an average heating season. The calculations cannot be made with a high degree of accuracy. On the other hand, residential heat loss calculations quite often prove to be surprisingly close to actuality when analyzed over a period of 10 or 20 years or more for any given house (provided that the calculations were carefully made in the first place). If all of the assessments involved in making the calculations for a given house could be arrived at under laboratory conditions and the house itself existed under carefully controlled conditions, we could hone the accuracy to the nth degree. The best that can be hoped for is a reasonable set of numbers upon which we can base our house design specifications and construction details.

There's no need to be discouraged about this seeming difficulty. If you make your calculations carefully (and avoid mistakes in the mathematics), you'll be able to develop a set of figures that will stand you in good stead. The unascertainable variables just have to be put up with because there's nothing you can do about them. It is the variables that make residential heat loss calculations relatively simplified and result in approximate - but workable - conclusions.

The weather is the biggest variable. There just is no way to tell on a weekly or monthly basis exactly what will happen in the way of the numbers and durations of storms, the length of time and sun will shine and how intense its radiation will be, how hard the wind will blow and from what direction, how many gyrations the outside temperature will go through each day, and so on. You can't assess ahead of time, with any degree of accuracy, what effects aging and weathering will have on your house and you usually have no control over the quality of workmanship that goes into its construction. Indeed, the materials and components that go into the house will themselves be of varying quality. The building materials will have slightly different thermal characteristics than those that are generally considered as average. There is no way at all to determine what the habits of the occupants of the house might be concerning the opening and closing of doors and windows, cooking habits, the way the heating system is controlled or adjusted, and so on.

All in all, there seem to be more variables than fixed values to work with and this means the decisions you make become very important. By closely following the procedures that I outline next and by maintaining as high a degree of accuracy in your calculations as you can, you will minimize the variables to a large extent. Even though your results will be an estimation, they will be close enough to the mark for you to live with comfortably.

114

THE GENERAL PROCEDURE

There are a good many different aspects to working heat loss calculations for a residence and during the first trip through them it's easy to get lost. Here is a brief examination of the general procedure:

☐ The first step is a critical one that depends to a substantial degree upon your judgment and a close examination of the climatic data at and around the building site. This involves selecting figures that will represent as closely as possible the prevailing weather conditions. An outdoor design temperature must be chosen and the average wind speed and direction evaluated. An indoor design temperature must also be selected, but this generally poses no problem. In addition, temperatures must be established for unheated space within the structure itself.

☐ The second step is to determine the heat transmission losses of the building. Coefficients must be established for each different building section: floors, walls, roofs, foundations, concrete slabs, windows, doors, and whatever other sections might be applicable. The transmission losses are computed section by section and room by room.

☐ The third step, which often is done concurrently with the second step, is to assess the infiltration losses of the house. This factor, which in some instances can be equal to or greater than the transmission heat loss totals, takes into account the flow of cold air that enters the structure by various means. This includes cracks in the construction or by virtue of doors and windows being opened and closed (mechanical ventilation is included if the volume is large, but disregarded when only one or two small vent fans are involved). As with the heat transmission losses, infiltration losses are developed on a room-by-room basis.

☐ Once all of these figures have been determined, they can be used to work out the total heat load of the structure. The validity of the results will depend largely upon the care with which you have developed all of the previous estimates.

☐ The last step consists of working out the seasonal figures. Here again, some judgement is needed in ascertaining just what constitutes a full heating season. There are several possible approaches to this problem. Once that has been determined, working out the seasonal heat load and consequent total fuel or energy requirements to operate the heating system are easily arrived at. From this follows the annual operating cost figure.

DESIGN CONDITIONS

There are two sets of design conditions that must be considered during the process of estimating heat losses. The first are the design conditions that are imposed by the physical layout and construction details of the house. These design data are generally a given set of conditions that are formulated before much, if any, consideration is given to the heating and cooling details. There might be a generalized choice of house design where the prospective owner selects, for instance, an earth-sheltered house in the knowledge that this type of design inherently offers lower heating and cooling costs than most other styles. You might choose a dome house for the same reasons. But even though the overall design details are a given situation, the thermal details should then be worked out to suit the individual building site. With very few exceptions, the structural design conditions are modified and altered as necessary to suit the thermal needs of the structure.

The second set of design data involves the weather conditions. This design data must be developed on the basis of personal preferences and judgment, published weather design data, and observation of conditions at the individual building site.

Indoor Design Temperature

The indoor design temperature of the house is by far the easiest factor to select. This temperature is the one at which the interior living spaces of the house will normally be kept. If a central heating system is to be installed, the same temperature is generally used for each room of the house. Two or more zones might be set at slightly different temperatures. Where area heating units will be installed, it is possible to vary the indoor design temperatures from room to room. For instance, you might choose 80 F for a bathroom temperature, 72 F for the living room, and 60 F for bedrooms.

There is a danger in selecting an unusually low design temperature for a room. During periods of extremely cold weather, the heating unit might have insufficient capacity to elevate the room temperature above the design temperature if that becomes necessary. For example, if a bedroom is being used as a sickroom in which a desirable air temperature might be 75 F, during a cold snap a heating unit designed to handle a 60 F temperature might not be able to do the job.

In settling upon an indoor design temperature, you naturally will first think about your preferences as to what constitutes an ideal level. Also consider the needs and desires of the remaining occupants of the household. People have widely varying ideas about what an indoor temperature should be and they also have diverse susceptibility to heat/cold discomfort. Generally, it's wise to select the highest temperature deemed comfortable by those who will regularly occupy the house. You should also keep in mind that you will not always occupy the house. Sooner or later someone else will move in and their judgment of bodily comfort will likely be different than yours. It's fine to be conservative in making your temperature selection, but if you settle upon 60 F, future occupants are likely to be unhappy.

If you choose a high indoor temperature, your heating equipment might operate inefficiently for at least part of the time. On the other hand, if you set the temperature too low there will be times when the equipment will have insufficient capacity to fully heat the house.

The common choice for an indoor design temperature is 70 F, but 72 F is probably as widely used. If you are of a conservative nature, 65 F would be a reasonable choice. This is especially true if an auxiliary heating unit such as a wood stove is planned. This would easily make up the difference during the few severe cold spells that are likely to occur during a heating season. If you aren't concerned much about conservation or if the house will be occupied by elderly or infirm persons, 75 F or even 78 F might be used.

Outdoor Design Temperature

Selecting an outdoor design temperature is considerably more difficult than selecting an indoor design temperature. Unless you live in one of the larger metropolitan areas of the country, the choice requires some careful thought, study of some published figures, and perhaps some personal observation at the building site. You might also try to find some local weather data that has been developed by interested parties.

The outside design temperature is based upon local winter extremes (the lowest temepratures). The record low temperature for your area should *not* be used, nor should such figures as the "normal lows" or the "average lows." But at the same time, worst-case conditions must form the basis for the selected temperature and the heating plant must also be designed to handle worst-case conditions. The starting point for determining this temperature level is to consult Table 4-1. This information is taken from the 1977 *Fundamentals Volume* of the *ASHRAE HANDBOOK & Product Directory*. It was abstracted from the more extensive tables in *Facility Design and Planning Engineering Weather Data*, published by the Departments of the Air Force, the Army, and the Navy. It is available from the U.S. Government Printing Office, Superintendent of Documents, Washington, DC 20402. These figures have been developed over long periods of time and have been found to be quite adequate for use in calculating residential heat losses. If your building site is in the immediate vicinity of one of these reporting stations, you can use the exact figures. I will explain a bit later why, when, and how the figures should be varied to better meet differing local conditions.

Using the table is not a difficult chore. For example, consider the first station on the list—Alexander City, Alabama. The first three columns of the table (reading from the left) give the latitude, longitude, and elevation of the city. Column 5 represents design-dry-bulb temperatures. One column is headed "99%" and the other "97.5%." The temperature figures are averages based upon hourly observations by trained observers and recorded over many years.

If there were a "100%" column here, the figure given would be the average low temperature for all of the total hours (2160) in the months of December, January and February. In other words, *on average* the temperature would not go below that listed figure for 100 percent of the three winter months (though it might at some times during some years). However, the 100 percent figure is not used as an outdoor design temperature.

Table 4-1. Climatic Conditions for the United States (Reprinted with Permission from the 1977 Fundamentals Volume, ASHRAE HANDBOOK & Product Directory).

Col. 1	Col. 2 Latitude		Col. 3 Longitude		Col. 4 Elevation (Ft)	Winter		Summer						
						Col. 5 Design Dry-Bulb		Col. 6 Design Dry-Bulb and Mean Coincident Wet-Bulb			Col. 7 Mean Daily Range	Col. 8 Design Wet-Bulb		
State and Station	°	'	°	'	Ft	99%	97.5%	1%	2.5%	5%		1%	2.5%	5%
ALABAMA														
Alexander City	33	0	86	0	660	18	22	96/77	93/76	91/76	21	79	78	78
Anniston AP	33	4	85	5	599	18	22	97/77	94/76	92/76	21	79	78	78
Auburn	32	4	85	3	730	18	22	96/77	93/76	91/76	21	79	78	78
Birmingham AP	33	3	86	5	610	17	21	96/74	94/75	92/74	21	78	77	76
Decatur	34	4	87	0	580	11	16	95/75	93/74	91/74	22	78	77	76
Dothan AP	31	2	85	2	321	23	27	94/76	92/76	91/76	20	80	79	78
Florence AP	34	5	87	4	528	17	21	97/74	97/74	92/74	22	78	77	76
Gadsden	34	0	86	0	570	16	20	96/75	94/75	92/74	22	78	77	76
Huntsville AP	34	4	86	4	619	11	16	95/75	93/74	91/74	23	78	77	76
Mobile AP	30	4	88	2	211	25	29	95/77	93/77	91/76	18	80	79	78
Mobile CO	30	4	88	1	119	25	29	95/77	93/77	91/77	16	80	79	78
Montgomery AP	32	2	86	2	195	22	25	96/76	95/76	93/76	21	79	79	78
Selma-Craig AFB	32	2	87	0	207	22	26	97/78	95/77	93/77	21	81	80	79
Talladega	33	3	86	1	565	18	22	97/77	94/76	92/76	21	79	78	78
Tuscaloosa AP	33	1	87	4	170r	20	23	98/75	96/76	94/76	22	79	78	77
ALASKA														
Anchorage AP	61	1	150	0	90	-23	-18	71/59	68/58	66/56	15	60	59	57
Barrow (S)	71	2	156	5	22	-45	-41	57/53	53/50	49/47	12	54	50	47
Fairbanks AP (S)	64	5	147	5	436	-51	-47	82/62	78/60	75/59	24	64	62	60
Juneau AP	58	2	134	4	17	-4	1	74/60	70/58	67/57	15	61	59	58
Kodiak	57	3	152	3	21	10	13	69/58	65/56	62/55	10	60	58	56
Nome AP	64	3	165	3	13	-31	-27	66/57	62/55	59/54	10	58	56	55
ARIZONA														
Douglas AP	31	3	109	3	4098	27	31	98/63	95/63	93/63	31	70	69	68

Station	Lat. °	Lat. '	Long. °	Long. '	Elev.	Winter 99%	Winter 97.5%	Summer 1%	Summer 2.5%	Summer 5%		
Fort Huachuca AP (S)	31	3	110	2	4664	24	28	95/62	92/62	90/62	69	68	67
Kingman AP	35	2	114	0	3446	18	25	103/65	100/64	97/64	70	69	69
Nogales	31	2	111	0	3800	28	32	99/64	96/64	94/64	71	70	69
Phoenix AP(S)	33	3	112	0	1117	31	34	109/71	107/71	105/71	76	75	75
Prescott AP	34	4	112	3	5014	4	9	96/61	94/60	92/60	66	65	64
Tuscon AP (S)	32	1	111	0	2584	28	32	104/66	102/66	100/66	72	71	71
Winslow AP	35	0	110	4	4880	5	10	97/61	95/60	93/60	66	65	64
Yuma AP	32	4	114	4	199	36	39	111/72	109/72	107/71	79	78	77
ARKANSAS													
Blytheville AFB	36	0	90	0	264	10	15	96/78	94/77	91/76	81	80	78
Camden	33	4	92	5	116	18	23	98/76	96/76	94/76	80	79	78
El Dorado AP	33	1	92	5	252	18	23	98/76	96/76	94/76	80	79	78
Fayetteville AP	36	0	94	1	1253	7	12	97/72	94/73	92/73	77	76	75
Fort Smith AP	35	2	94	2	449	12	17	101/75	98/76	95/76	80	79	78
Hot Springs	34	3	93	1	535	17	23	101/77	97/77	94/77	80	79	78
Jonesboro	35	5	90	4	345	10	15	96/78	94/77	91/76	81	80	78
Little Rock AP (S)	34	4	92	1	257	15	20	99/76	96/76	94/77	80	79	78
Pine Bluff AP	34	1	92	0	204	16	22	100/78	97/77	95/78	81	80	80
Texarkana AP	33	3	94	0	361	18	23	98/76	96/77	93/76	80	79	78
CALIFORNIA													
Bakersfield AP	35	2	119	0	495	30	32	104/70	101/69	98/68	73	71	70
Barstow AP	34	5	116	5	2142	26	29	106/68	104/68	102/67	73	71	70
Blythe AP	33	4	114	3	390	30	33	112/71	110/71	108/70	75	75	74
Burbank AP	34	1	118	2	699	37	39	95/68	91/68	88/67	71	70	69
Chico	39	5	121	5	205	28	30	103/69	101/68	98/67	71	70	68

a Table 1 was prepared by ASHRAE Technical Committee 4.2, Weather Data, from data compiled from official weather stations where hourly weather observations are made by trained observers.

b Latitude, for use in calculating solar loads, and longitude are given to the nearest 10 minutes. For example, the latitude and longitude for Anniston, Alabama are given as 33 34 and 85 55 respectively, or 33° 40, and 85° 50.

c Elevations are ground elevations for each station. Temperature readings are generally made at an elevation of 5 ft above ground, except for locations marked r, indicating roof exposure of thermometer.

d Percentage of winter design data shows the percent of the 3-month period, December through February.

e Percentage of summer design data shows the percent of 4-month period, June through September.

Table 4-1. Climatic Conditions for the United States (Reprinted with Permission from the 1977 Fundamentals Volume, ASHRAE HANDBOOK & Product Directory) (continued from page 119).

| Col. 1 | Col. 2 | | Col. 3 | | Col. 4 | Winter[d] | | Summer[e] | | | | | | |
| | Lati-tude[b] | | Longi-tude[b] | | Eleva-tion[c] | Col. 5 Design Dry-Bulb | | Col. 6 Design Dry-Bulb and Mean Coincident Wet-Bulb | | | Col. 7 Mean Daily | Col. 8 Design Wet-Bulb | | |
State and Station	°	'	°	'	Ft	99%	97.5%	1%	2.5%	5%	Range	1%	2.5%	5%
Concord	38	0	122	0	195	24	27	100/69	97/68	94/67	32	71	70	68
Covina	34	0	117	5	575	32	35	98/69	95/68	92/67	31	73	71	70
Crescent City AP	41	5	124	0	50	31	33	68/60	65/59	63/58	18	62	60	59
Downey	34	0	118	1	116	37	40	93/70	89/70	86/69	22	72	71	70
El Cajon	32	4	117	0	525	42	44	83/69	80/69	78/68	30	71	70	68
El Centro AP (S)	32	5	115	4	−30	35	38	112/74	110/74	108/74	34	81	80	78
Escondido	33	0	117	1	660	39	41	89/68	85/68	82/68	30	71	70	69
Eureka/Arcata AP	41	0	124	1	217	31	33	68/60	65/59	63/58	11	62	60	59
Fairfield-Travis AFB	38	2	122	0	72	29	32	99/68	95/67	91/66	34	70	68	67
Fresno AP (S)	36	5	119	4	326	28	30	102/70	100/69	97/68	34	72	71	70
Hamilton AFB	38	0	122	3	3	30	32	89/68	84/66	80/65	28	72	69	67
Laguna Beach	33	3	117	5	35	41	43	83/68	80/68	77/67	18	70	69	68
Livermore	37	4	122	0	545	24	27	100/69	97/68	93/67	24	71	70	68
Lompoc, Vandenburg AFB	34	4	120	3	552	35	38	75/61	70/61	67/60	20	63	61	60
Long Beach AP	33	5	118	1	34	41	43	83/68	80/68	77/67	22	70	69	68
Los Angeles AP (S)	34	0	118	2	99	41	43	83/68	80/68	77/67	15	70	69	68
Los Angeles CO (S)	34	0	118	1	312	37	40	93/70	89/70	86/69	20	72	71	70
Merced-Castle AFB	37	2	120	3	178	29	31	102/70	99/69	96/68	36	72	71	70
Modesto	37	4	121	0	91	28	30	101/69	98/68	95/67	36	71	70	69
Monterey	36	4	121	5	38	35	38	75/63	71/61	68/61	20	64	62	61
Napa	38	2	122	2	16	30	32	100/69	96/68	92/67	30	71	69	68
Needles AP	34	5	114	4	913	30	33	112/71	110/71	108/70	27	75	75	74
Oakland AP	37	4	122	1	3	34	36	85/64	80/63	75/62	19	66	64	63
Oceanside	33	1	117	2	30	41	43	83/68	80/68	77/67	13	70	69	68
Ontario	34	0	117	3	995	31	33	102/70	99/69	96/67	36	74	72	71
Oxnard	34	1	119	1	43	34	36	83/66	80/64	77/63	19	70	68	67

Palm Springs	33	5	116	4	411	33	35	112/71	110/70	108/70	76	74	73
Pasadena	34	1	118	—	864	32	35	98/69	95/68	92/67	73	71	70
Petaluma	38	1	122	4	27	26	29	94/68	90/66	87/65	72	70	68
Pomona CO	34	0	117	5	871	28	30	102/70	99/69	95/68	74	72	71
Redding AP	40	3	122	1	495	29	31	105/68	102/67	100/66	71	69	68
Redlands	34	0	117	1	1318	31	33	102/70	99/69	96/68	74	72	71
Richmond	38	0	122	2	55	34	36	85/64	80/63	75/62	66	64	63
Riverside-March AFB (S)	33	5	117	2	1511	29	32	100/68	98/68	95/67	72	71	70
Sacramento AP	38	3	121	3	17	30	32	101/70	98/70	94/69	72	71	70
Salinas AP	36	4	121	4	74	30	32	74/61	70/60	67/59	62	61	59
San Bernardino, Norton AFB	34	1	117	1	1125	31	33	102/70	99/69	96/68	74	72	71
San Diego AP	32	4	117	1	19	42	44	83/69	80/69	78/68	71	70	68
San Fernando	34	1	118	3	977	37	39	95/68	91/68	88/67	71	70	69
San Francisco AP	37	4	122	2	8	35	38	82/64	77/63	73/62	65	64	62
San Francisco CO	37	5	122	3	52	38	40	74/63	71/62	69/61	64	62	61
San Jose AP	37	2	121	5	70r	34	36	85/66	81/65	77/64	68	67	65
San Luis Obispo	35	2	120	4	315	33	35	92/69	88/70	84/69	73	71	70
Santa Ana AP	33	4	117	5	115r	37	39	89/69	85/68	82/68	71	70	69
Santa Barbara MAP	34	3	119	5	10	34	36	81/67	77/66	75/65	68	67	66
Santa Cruz	37	0	122	0	125	35	38	75/63	71/61	68/61	64	62	61
Santa Maria AP (S)	34	5	120	2	238	31	32	81/64	76/63	73/62	65	64	63
Santa Monica CO	34	0	118	2	57	41	43	83/68	80/68	77/67	70	69	68
Santa Paula	34	2	119	0	263	33	35	90/68	86/67	84/66	71	69	68
Santa Rosa	38	3	122	5	167	27	29	99/68	95/67	91/66	70	68	67
Stockton AP	37	5	121	2	28	28	30	100/69	97/68	94/67	71	70	68
Ukiah	39	1	123	1	620	27	29	99/69	95/68	91/67	71	70	68
Visalia	36	2	119	2	354	28	30	102/70	100/69	97/68	72	71	70
Yreka	41	4	122	4	2625	13	17	95/65	92/64	89/63	67	65	64
Yuba City	39	1	121	4	70	29	31	104/68	101/67	99/66	71	69	68
COLORADO													
Alamosa AP	37	3	105	5	7536	-11	-6	84/57	82/57	80/57	62	61	60
Boulder	40	0	105	5	5385	-6	0	93/59	91/59	89/59	64	63	62
Colorado Springs AP	38	5	104	4	6173	-3	2	91/58	88/57	86/57	63	62	61
Denver AP	39	5	104	5	5283	-5	-1	93/59	91/59	89/59	64	63	62
Durango	37	1	107	5	6550	-6	1	89/59	87/59	85/59	64	63	62

Table 4-1. Climatic Conditions for the United States (Reprinted with Permission from the 1977 Fundamentals Volume, ASHRAE HANDBOOK & Product Directory) (continued from page 121).

Col. 1	Col. 2 Latitude[b]		Col. 3 Longitude[b]		Col. 4 Elevation[c]	Winter[d] Col. 5 Design Dry-Bulb		Summer[e] Col. 6 Design Dry-Bulb and Mean Coincident Wet-Bulb			Col. 7 Mean Daily	Col. 8 Design Wet-Bulb		
State and Station	°	′	°	′	Ft	99%	97.5%	1%	2.5%	5%	Range	1%	2.5%	5%
Fort Collins	40	4	105	0	5001	-5	1	93/59	91/59	89/59	28	64	63	62
Grand Junction AP (S)	39	1	108	3	4849	-2	7	96/59	94/59	92/59	29	64	63	62
Greeley	40	3	104	4	4648	-2	4	96/60	94/60	92/60	29	65	64	63
La Junta AP	38	0	103	3	4188	-3	3	100/68	98/68	95/67	31	72	70	69
Leadville	39	2	106	2	10177	-18	-14	84/52	81/51	78/50	30	56	55	54
Pueblo AP	38	2	104	2	4639	-7	0	97/61	95/61	92/61	31	67	66	65
Sterling	40	4	103	1	3939	-7	-2	95/62	93/62	90/62	30	67	66	65
Trinidad AP	37	2	104	2	5746	-2	3	93/61	91/61	89/61	32	66	65	64
CONNECTICUT														
Bridgeport AP	41	1	73	1	7	6	9	86/73	84/71	81/70	18	75	74	73
Hartford														
Brainard Field	41	5	72	2	15	3	7	91/74	88/73	85/72	22	77	75	74
New Haven AP	41	2	73	3	6	3	7	88/75	84/73	82/72	17	76	75	74
New London	41	2	72	2	60	5	9	88/73	85/72	83/71	16	76	75	74
Norwalk	41	1	73	3	37	6	9	86/73	84/71	81/70	19	75	74	73
Norwich	41	3	72	2	20	3	7	89/75	86/73	83/72	18	76	75	74
Waterbury	41	3	73	3	605	-4	2	88/73	85/71	82/70	21	75	74	72
Windsor Locks, Bradley Field (S)	42	0	72	4	169	0	4	91/74	88/72	85/71	22	76	75	73
DELAWARE														
Dover AFB	39	0	75	3	38	11	15	92/75	90/75	87/74	18	79	77	76
Wilmington AP	39	4	75	3	78	10	14	92/74	89/74	87/73	20	77	76	75
DISTRICT OF COLUMBIA														
Andrews AFB	38	5	76	5	279	10	14	92/75	90/74	87/73	18	78	76	75
Washington National AP	38	5	77	0	14	14	17	93/75	91/74	89/74	18	78	77	76
FLORIDA														
Belle Glade	26	4	80	4	16	41	44	92/76	91/76	89/76	16	79	78	78
Cape Kennedy AP	28	3	80	3	16	35	38	90/78	88/78	87/78	15	80	79	79
Daytona Beach AP	29	1	81	0	31	32	35	92/78	90/77	88/77	15	80	79	78
Fort Lauderdale	26	0	80	0	13	42	46	92/78	91/78	90/78	15	80	79	79
Fort Myers AP	26	4	81	5	13	41	44	93/78	92/78	91/77	18	80	79	79

Fort Pierce	27	3	80	2	10	38	42	91/78	90/78	89/78	15	80	79	79
Gainesville AP (S)	29	4	82	2	155	28	31	95/77	93/77	92/77	18	80	79	79
Jacksonville AP	30	3	81	4	24	29	32	96/77	94/77	92/76	19	79	79	78
Key West AP	24	3	81	5	6	55	57	90/78	90/78	89/78	9	80	79	79
Lakeland CO (S)	28	0	82	0	214	39	41	93/76	91/76	89/76	17	79	78	78
Miami AP (S)	25	5	80	2	7	44	47	91/77	90/77	89/77	15	79	79	78
Miami Beach CO	25	5	80	1	9	45	48	90/77	89/77	88/77	10	79	79	78
Ocala	29	1	82	1	86	31	34	95/77	93/77	92/76	18	80	79	79
Orlando AP	28	3	81	2	106r	35	38	94/76	93/76	91/76	17	79	78	78
Panama City, Tyndall AFB	30	0	85	4	22	29	33	92/78	90/77	89/77	14	81	80	79
Pensacola CO	30	3	87	1	13	25	29	94/77	93/77	91/77	14	80	79	79
St. Augustine	29	5	81	2	15	31	35	92/78	89/78	87/78	16	80	79	79
St. Petersburg	28	0	82	4	35	36	40	92/77	91/77	90/76	16	79	79	78
Sanford	28	5	81	2	14	35	38	94/76	93/76	91/76	17	79	78	78
Sarasota	27	2	82	3	30	39	42	93/77	92/77	90/76	17	79	79	78
Tallahassee AP (S)	30	2	84	3	58	27	30	94/77	92/76	90/76	19	79	78	78
Tampa AP (S)	28	0	82	3	19	36	40	92/77	91/77	90/76	17	79	79	78
West Palm Beach AP	26	4	80	1	15	41	45	92/78	91/78	90/78	16	80	80	79
GEORGIA														
Albany, Turner AFB	31	3	84	1	224	25	29	97/77	95/76	93/76	20	80	79	78
Americus	32	0	84	1	476	21	25	97/77	94/76	92/75	20	79	78	77
Athens	34	0	83	2	700	18	22	94/74	92/74	90/74	21	78	77	76
Atlanta AP (S)	33	4	84	3	1005	17	22	94/74	92/74	90/73	19	77	76	75
Augusta AP	33	2	82	0	143	20	23	97/77	95/76	93/76	19	80	79	78
Brunswick	31	1	81	3	14	29	32	92/78	89/78	87/78	18	80	80	79
Columbus, Lawson AFB	32	3	85	0	242	21	24	95/76	93/76	91/75	21	79	78	77
Dalton	34	5	85	0	720	17	22	94/76	93/76	91/76	22	79	78	77
Dublin	32	3	83	0	215	21	25	96/77	93/76	91/75	20	79	78	77
Gainesville	34	2	83	5	1254	16	21	93/74	91/74	89/73	21	77	76	75
Griffin (S)	33	1	84	2	980	18	22	93/76	90/75	88/74	21	78	77	76

Table 4-1. Climatic Conditions for the United States (Reprinted with Permission from the 1977 Fundamentals Volume, ASHRAE HANDBOOK & Product Directory) (continued from page 123).

Col. 1	Col. 2 Latitude[b]		Col. 3 Longitude[b]		Col. 4 Elevation[c]	Col. 5 Winter[d] Design Dry-Bulb		Col. 6 Summer[e] Design Dry-Bulb and Mean Coincident Wet-Bulb			Col. 7 Mean Daily Range	Col. 8 Design Wet-Bulb		
State and Station	°	′	°	′	Ft	99%	97.5%	1%	2.5%	5%	Range	1%	2.5%	5%
La Grange	33	0	85	0	715	19	23	94/76	91/75	89/74	21	78	77	76
Macon AP	32	4	83	4	356	21	25	96/77	93/76	91/75	22	79	78	77
Marietta, Dobbins AFB	34	0	84	3	1016	17	21	94/74	92/74	90/74	21	78	77	76
Moultrie	31	1	83	4	340	27	30	97/77	95/77	92/76	20	80	79	78
Rome AP	34	2	85	1	637	17	22	94/76	93/76	91/76	23	79	78	77
Savannah-Travis AP	32	1	81	1	52	24	27	96/77	93/77	91/77	20	80	79	78
Valdosta-Moody AFB	31	0	83	1	239	28	31	96/77	94/77	92/76	20	80	79	78
Waycross	31	2	82	2	140	26	29	96/77	94/77	91/76	20	80	79	78
HAWAII														
Hilo AP (S)	19	4	155	0	31	61	62	84/73	83/72	82/72	15	75	74	74
Honolulu AP	21	2	158	0	7	62	63	87/73	86/73	85/72	12	76	75	74
Kaneohe Bay MCAS	21	2	157	5	18	65	66	85/75	84/74	83/74	12	76	76	75
Wahiawa	21	3	158	0	900	58	59	86/73	85/72	84/72	14	75	74	73
IDAHO														
Boise AP(S)	43	3	116	1	2842	-3	10	96/65	94/64	91/64	31	68	66	65
Burley	42	3	113	5	4180	-3	2	99/62	95/61	92/66	35	64	63	61
Coeur d'Alene AP	47	5	116	5	2973	-8	-1	89/62	86/61	83/60	31	64	63	61
Idaho Falls AP	43	3	112	0	4730r	-11	-6	89/61	87/61	84/59	38	65	63	61
Lewiston AP	46	2	117	0	1413	-1	6	96/65	93/64	90/63	32	67	66	64
Moscow	46	4	117	0	2660	-7	0	90/63	87/62	84/61	32	65	64	62
Mountain Home AFB	43	0	115	5	2992	6	12	99/64	97/63	94/62	36	66	65	63
Pocatello AP	43	0	112	4	4444	-8	-1	94/61	91/60	89/59	35	64	63	61
Twin Falls (AP) (S)	42	3	114	2	4148	-3	2	99/62	95/61	92/60	34	64	63	61
ILLINOIS														
Aurora	41	5	88	2	744	-6	-1	93/76	91/76	88/75	20	79	78	76
Belleville, Scott AFB	38	3	89	5	447	1	6	94/76	92/76	89/75	21	79	78	76
Bloomington	40	3	89	0	775	-6	-2	92/75	90/74	88/73	21	78	76	75
Carbondale	37	5	89	1	380	-2	7	95/77	93/77	90/76	21	80	79	77
Champaign/Urbana	40	0	88	2	743	-3	2	95/75	92/74	90/73	21	78	77	75

Chicago, Midway AP	41	5	87	5	610	-5	0	94/74	91/73	88/72	20	77	75	74
Chicago, O'Hare AP	42	0	87	5	658	-8	-4	91/75	89/74	86/72	20	77	76	74
Chicago CO	41	5	87	4	594	-3	2	94/75	91/74	88/73	15	79	77	75
Danville	40	1	87	4	558	-4	-1	93/75	90/74	88/73	21	78	77	75
Decatur	39	5	88	5	670	-3	2	94/75	91/74	88/73	21	78	77	75
Dixon	41	5	89	3	696	-7	-2	93/75	90/74	88/73	23	78	77	75
Elgin	42	0	88	2	820	-8	-2	91/75	88/74	86/73	21	78	77	75
Freeport	42	2	89	3	780	-9	-4	91/74	89/73	87/72	24	77	76	74
Galesburg	41	0	90	4	771	-7	-2	93/75	91/75	88/74	22	78	77	75
Greenville	39	0	89	2	563	-1	4	94/76	92/75	89/74	21	79	78	76
Joliet	41	3	88	1	588	-5	0	93/75	90/74	88/73	20	78	77	75
Kankakee	41	1	87	1	625	-4	0	93/75	90/74	88/73	21	78	77	75
La Salle/Peru	41	2	89	1	520	-7	-2	93/75	91/75	88/74	22	78	77	75
Macomb	40	3	90	4	702	-5	0	95/76	92/76	89/75	22	79	78	76
Moline AP	41	3	90	3	582	-9	-4	93/75	91/76	88/74	23	78	77	75
Mt Vernon	38	2	88	0	500	0	5	95/76	92/75	89/74	21	79	78	76
Peoria AP	40	4	89	4	652	-8	-4	91/75	89/73	87/73	22	78	76	75
Quincy AP	40	0	91	1	762	-2	3	96/76	93/76	90/76	22	80	78	77
Rantoul, Chanute AFB	40	2	88	1	740	-1	4	94/75	91/74	89/73	21	78	77	75
Rockford	42	1	89	0	724	-9	-4	91/74	89/73	87/72	24	77	76	74
Springfield AP	39	5	89	4	587	-3	1	94/75	92/74	89/74	21	79	77	76
Waukegan	42	2	87	5	680	-6	-2	92/76	89/74	87/73	21	78	76	75
INDIANA														
Anderson	40	0	85	3	847	0	6	95/76	92/75	89/74	22	79	78	76
Bedford	38	5	86	3	670	0	5	95/76	92/75	89/74	22	79	78	76
Bloomington	39	1	86	4	820	0	5	95/76	92/75	89/74	22	79	78	76
Columbus, Bakalar AFB	39	2	85	5	661	3	7	95/76	92/75	90/74	22	79	78	76
Crawfordsville	40	0	86	5	752	-2	3	94/75	91/74	88/73	22	79	77	76
Evansville AP	38	0	87	3	381	4	9	95/76	93/75	91/75	22	79	78	77
Fort Wayne AP	41	0	85	1	791	-4	-1	92/73	89/72	87/72	24	77	75	74
Goshen AP	41	3	85	5	823	-3	-1	91/73	89/73	86/72	23	77	75	74
Hobart	41	3	87	2	600	-4	2	91/73	88/73	85/72	21	77	75	74
Huntington	40	4	85	3	802	-4	-1	92/73	89/72	87/72	23	77	75	74
Indianapolis AP (S)	39	4	86	1	793	-2	2	92/74	90/74	87/73	22	78	76	75
Jeffersonville	38	2	85	4	455	5	10	95/74	93/74	90/74	23	79	77	76
Kokomo	40	3	86	2	790	-4	0	91/73	90/73	88/73	22	77	75	74
Lafayette	40	2	86	5	600	-3	3	94/74	91/73	88/73	22	78	76	75

Table 4-1. Climatic Conditions for the United States (Reprinted with Permission from the 1977 Fundamentals Volume, ASHRAE HANDBOOK & Product Directory) (continued from page 125).

Col. 1	Col. 2		Col. 3		Col. 4	Col. 5		Col. 6			Col. 7	Col. 8		
	Lati-tude[b]		Longi-tude[c]		Eleva-tion[c]	**Winter[d]** Design Dry-Bulb		**Summer[e]** Design Dry-Bulb and Mean Coincident Wet-Bulb			Mean Daily	Design Wet-Bulb		
State and Station	°	′	°	′	Ft	99%	97.5%	1%	2.5%	5%	Range	1%	2.5%	5%
La Porte	41	3	86	4	810	−3	3	93/73	90/74	87/73	22	78	76	75
Marion	40	3	85	4	791	−4	0	91/74	90/73	88/73	23	77	75	74
Muncie	40	1	85	2	955	−3	2	92/74	90/73	87/73	22	76	76	75
Peru,														
Bunker Hill AFB	40	4	86	1	804	−6	−1	90/74	88/73	86/73	22	77	75	74
Richmond AP	39	5	84	5	1138	−2	2	92/74	90/74	87/73	22	78	76	75
Shelbyville	39	3	85	3	765	−1	3	93/74	91/74	88/73	22	78	76	75
South Bend AP	41	4	86	2	773	−3	1	91/73	89/73	86/72	22	77	75	74
Terre Haute AP	39	3	87	2	601	−2	4	95/75	92/74	89/73	22	79	77	76
Valparaise	41	2	87	0	801	−3	3	93/74	90/74	87/73	22	78	76	75
Vincennes	38	4	87	3	420	−1	6	95/75	92/74	90/73	22	79	77	76
IOWA														
Ames (S)	42	0	93	4	1004	−11	−6	93/75	90/74	87/73	23	78	76	75
Burlington AP	40	5	91	1	694	−7	−3	94/74	91/75	88/73	22	78	77	75
Cedar Rapids AP	41	5	91	4	863	−10	−5	91/76	88/75	86/74	23	78	77	74
Clinton	41	5	90	1	595	−8	−3	92/75	90/75	87/74	23	78	77	76
Council Bluffs	41	2	95	5	1210	−8	−3	94/76	91/75	88/74	22	78	77	75
Des Moines AP	41	3	93	4	948r	−10	−5	94/75	91/74	88/73	23	78	77	75
Dubuque	42	2	90	4	1065	−12	−7	90/74	88/73	86/72	22	77	75	74
Fort Dodge	42	3	94	1	1111	−12	−7	91/74	88/74	86/72	23	77	75	74
Iowa City	41	4	91	3	645	−11	−6	92/76	89/76	87/74	23	80	78	76
Keokuk	40	2	91	2	526	−5	0	95/75	92/75	89/74	22	79	77	76
Marshalltown	42	0	92	5	898	−12	−7	92/76	90/75	88/74	23	78	77	75
Mason City AP	43	1	93	2	1194	−15	−11	90/74	88/74	85/72	24	77	75	74
Newton	41	4	93	0	946	−10	−5	94/75	91/74	88/73	23	78	77	75
Ottumwa AP	41	1	92	2	842	−8	−4	94/75	91/74	88/73	22	78	77	75
Sioux City AP	42	2	96	2	1095	−11	−7	95/74	92/74	89/73	24	78	77	75
Waterloo	42	3	92	2	868	−15	−10	91/76	89/75	86/74	23	78	77	75
KANSAS														
Atchison	39	3	95	1	945	−2	2	96/77	93/76	91/76	23	81	79	77
C... AP	39	3	95	1	1027	−2	2	100/74	98/74	94/74	23	79	78	77

Dodge City AP (S)	37	5	100	0	2594	0	5	100/69	97/69	95/69	25	74	73	71
El Dorado	37	5	96	5	1282	5	7	101/72	98/73	96/73	24	77	76	75
Emporia	38	2	96	1	1209	1	5	100/74	97/74	94/73	25	78	77	76
Garden City AP	38	0	101	0	2882	-1	4	99/69	96/69	94/69	28	74	73	71
Goodland AP	39	2	101	4	3645	-5	0	99/66	96/65	93/66	31	71	70	68
Great Bend	38	2	98	5	1940	0	4	101/73	98/73	95/73	28	78	76	75
Hutchinson AP	38	2	97	5	1524	4	8	102/72	99/72	97/72	28	77	75	74
Liberal	37	0	101	0	2838	2	7	99/68	96/68	94/68	28	73	72	71
Manhattan, Fort Riley (S)	39	0	96	5	1076	-1	3	99/75	95/75	92/74	24	78	77	76
Parsons	37	0	95	5	908	5	9	100/74	97/74	94/74	23	78	77	76
Russell AP	38	5	98	5	1864	0	4	101/73	98/73	95/73	29	78	76	75
Salina	38	5	97	4	1271	0	5	103/74	100/74	97/73	26	78	77	76
Topeka AP	39	0	95	4	877	0	4	99/75	96/75	93/74	24	79	78	76
Wichita AP	37	4	97	3	1321	3	7	101/72	98/73	96/73	23	77	76	75
KENTUCKY														
Ashland	38	3	82	4	551	5	10	94/76	91/74	89/73	22	78	77	75
Bowling Green AP	37	0	86	1	535	4	10	94/77	92/75	89/74	21	78	77	76
Corbin AP	37	0	84	3	1175	4	9	94/73	92/73	89/73	23	77	76	75
Covington AP	39	0	84	4	869	-1	6	92/73	90/72	88/72	22	77	76	74
Hopkinsville, Campbell AFB	36	4	87	3	540	4	10	94/77	92/75	89/74	21	79	77	76
Lexington AP (S)	38	0	84	4	979	3	8	93/73	91/73	88/72	22	77	76	75
Louisville AP	38	1	85	4	474	5	10	95/74	93/74	90/74	23	79	77	76
Madisonville	37	2	87	3	439	5	10	96/76	93/75	90/75	22	79	78	77
Owensboro	37	5	87	1	420	5	10	97/76	94/75	91/75	23	79	78	77
Paducah AP	37	0	88	4	398	7	12	98/76	95/75	92/75	20	79	78	77
LOUISIANA														
Alexandria AP	31	2	92	2	92	23	27	95/77	94/77	92/78	20	80	79	78
Baton Rouge AP	30	3	91	1	64	25	29	95/77	93/77	92/77	19	80	80	79
Bogalusa	30	3	89	5	103	24	28	95/77	93/77	92/77	19	80	80	79
Houma	29	3	90	4	13	31	35	95/78	93/78	92/77	15	81	80	79
Lafayette AP	30	1	92	0	38	26	30	95/78	94/78	92/78	18	81	80	79
Lake Charles AP (S)	30	1	93	1	14	27	31	95/77	93/77	92/77	17	80	79	79
Minden	32	4	93	2	250	20	25	99/77	96/76	94/76	20	79	79	78
Monroe AP	32	3	92	0	78	20	25	99/77	96/76	94/76	20	79	79	78
Natchitoches	31	5	93	0	120	22	26	97/77	95/77	93/77	20	79	79	78

Table 4-1. Climatic Conditions for the United States (Reprinted with Permission from the 1977 Fundamentals Volume, ASHRAE HANDBOOK & Product Directory) (continued from page 127).

Col. 1	Col. 2 Lati-tude[b] °	'	Col. 3 Longi-tude[c] °	'	Col. 4 Eleva-tion[c] Ft	Winter[d] Col. 5 Design Dry-Bulb 99%	97.5%	Summer[e] Col. 6 Design Dry-Bulb and Mean Coincident Wet-Bulb 1%	2.5%	5%	Col. 7 Mean Daily Range	Col. 8 Design Wet-Bulb 1%	2.5%	5%
State and Station														
New Orleans AP	30	0	90	2	3	29	33	93/78	92/78	90/77	16	81	80	79
Shreveport AP(S)	32	3	93	5	252	20	25	99/77	96/76	94/76	20	79	79	78
MAINE														
Augusta AP	44	2	69	5	350	-7	-3	88/73	85/70	82/68	22	74	72	70
Bangor, Dow AFB	44	5	68	5	162	-11	-6	86/70	83/68	80/67	22	73	71	69
Caribou AP (S)	46	5	68	0	624	-18	-13	84/69	81/67	78/66	21	71	69	67
Lewiston	44	0	70	1	182	-7	-2	88/73	85/70	82/68	22	74	72	70
Millinocket AP	45	4	68	4	405	-13	-9	87/69	83/68	80/66	22	72	70	68
Portland (S)	43	4	70	2	61	-6	-1	87/72	84/71	81/69	22	74	72	70
Waterville	44	3	69	4	89	-8	-4	87/72	84/69	81/68	22	74	72	70
MARYLAND														
Baltimore AP	39	1	76	4	146	10	13	94/75	91/75	89/74	21	78	77	76
Baltimore CO	39	2	76	3	14	14	17	92/77	89/76	87/75	17	80	78	76
Cumberland	39	3	78	5	945	6	10	92/75	89/74	87/74	22	77	76	75
Frederick AP	39	3	77	3	294	8	12	94/76	91/75	88/74	22	78	77	76
Hagerstown	39	4	77	4	660	8	12	94/75	91/74	89/74	22	77	76	75
Salisbury (S)	38	2	75	3	52	12	16	93/75	91/75	88/74	18	79	77	76
MASSACHUSETTS														
Boston AP (S)	42	2	71	0	15	6	9	91/73	88/71	85/70	16	75	74	72
Clinton	42	2	71	4	398	-2	2	90/72	87/71	84/69	17	75	73	72
Fall River	41	4	71	1	190	5	9	87/72	84/71	81/69	18	74	73	72
Framingham	42	2	71	3	170	3	6	89/72	86/71	83/69	17	74	73	71
Gloucester	42	3	70	4	10	2	5	89/73	86/71	83/70	15	75	74	72
Greenfield	42	4	72	4	205	-7	-2	88/72	85/71	82/69	23	74	73	71
Lawrence	42	4	71	1	57	-6	0	90/73	87/72	84/70	22	76	74	73
Lowell	42	3	71	2	90	-4	1	91/73	88/72	85/70	21	76	74	73
New Bedford	41	4	71	0	70	5	9	85/72	82/71	80/69	19	74	73	72
Pittsfield AP	42	3	73	2	1170	-8	-3	87/71	84/70	81/68	23	73	72	70
Springfield,														

Westover AFB	42	1	72	3	247	-5	0	90/72	87/71	84/69	19	75	73	72
Taunton	41	5	71	1	20	5	9	89/73	86/72	83/70	18	75	74	73
Worcester AP	42	2	71	5	986	0	4	87/71	84/70	81/68	18	73	72	70
MICHIGAN														
Adrian	41	5	84	0	754	-1	3	91/73	88/72	85/71	23	76	75	73
Alpena AP	45	0	83	3	689	-11	-6	89/70	85/70	83/69	27	73	72	70
Battle Creek AP	42	2	85	2	939	1	5	92/74	88/72	88/72	23	76	74	73
Benton Harbor AP	42	1	86	3	649	1	5	91/72	88/72	85/70	20	75	74	72
Detroit	42	2	83	0	633	3	6	91/73	88/72	86/71	20	76	74	73
Escanaba	45	4	87	4	594	-11	-7	87/70	83/69	80/68	17	73	71	69
Flint AP	42	0	83	4	766	-4	1	90/73	87/72	85/71	25	76	74	72
Grand Rapids AP	42	5	85	3	681	1	5	91/72	88/72	85/70	24	75	74	72
Holland	42	5	86	1	612	2	6	88/72	86/71	83/70	22	75	73	72
Jackson AP	42	2	84	2	1003	1	5	92/74	88/72	85/70	23	76	74	73
Kalamazoo	42	1	85	3	930	1	5	92/74	88/72	85/70	23	76	74	73
Lansing AP	42	5	84	4	852	-3	-3	90/73	87/72	84/70	24	75	74	72
Marquette CO	46	3	87	5	677	-12	-8	84/70	81/69	77/66	18	72	70	68
Mt Pleasant	43	4	84	5	796	0	4	91/73	87/72	84/71	24	76	74	72
Muskegon AP	43	1	86	1	627	2	6	86/72	84/70	82/70	21	75	73	72
Pontiac	42	4	83	2	974	0	4	90/73	87/72	85/71	21	76	74	73
Port Huron	43	0	82	2	586	0	4	90/73	87/72	83/71	21	76	74	73
Saginaw AP	43	3	84	1	662	0	4	91/73	87/72	84/71	23	76	74	72
Sault														
Ste. Marie AP (S)	46	3	84	2	721	-12	-8	84/70	81/69	77/66	23	72	70	68
Traverse City AP	44	4	85	4	618	-3	1	89/72	86/71	83/69	22	75	73	71
Yipsilanti	42	1	83	3	777	1	5	92/72	89/71	86/70	22	75	74	72
MINNESOTA														
Albert Lea	43	4	93	2	1235	-17	-12	90/74	87/72	84/71	24	77	75	73
Alexandria AP	45	5	95	2	1421	-22	-16	91/72	88/72	85/70	24	76	74	72
Bemidji AP	47	3	95	0	1392	-31	-26	88/69	85/69	81/67	24	73	71	69
Brainerd	46	2	94	2	1214	-20	-16	90/73	87/71	84/69	24	75	73	71
Duluth AP	46	5	92	1	1426	-21	-16	85/70	82/68	79/66	22	72	70	68
Fairbault	44	2	93	1	1190	-17	-12	91/74	88/72	85/71	24	77	75	73
Fergus Falls	46	1	96	0	1210	-21	-17	91/72	88/72	85/70	24	76	74	72
International														
Falls AP	48	3	93	2	1179	-29	-25	85/68	83/68	80/66	26	71	70	68

Table 4-1. Climatic Conditions for the United States (Reprinted with Permission from the 1977 Fundamentals Volume, ASHRAE HANDBOOK & Product Directory) (continued from page 129).

Col. 1	Col. 2		Col. 3		Col. 4	Col. 5		Col. 6			Col. 7	Col. 8		
	Lati-tude[b]		Longi-tude[c]		Eleva-tion[c]	Winter[d]		Summer[e]						
						Design Dry-Bulb		Design Dry-Bulb and Mean Coincident Wet-Bulb			Mean Daily	Design Wet-Bulb		
State and Station	°	'	°	'	Ft	99%	97.5%	1%	2.5%	5%	Range	1%	2.5%	5%
Mankato	44	1	94	0	785	-17	-12	91/72	88/72	85/70	24	77	75	73
Minneapolis/														
St Paul AP	44	5	93	1	822	-16	-12	92/75	89/73	86/71	22	77	75	73
Rochester AP	44	0	92	3	1297	-17	-12	90/74	87/72	84/71	24	77	75	73
St Cloud AP (S)	45	4	94	1	1034	-15	-11	91/74	88/72	85/70	24	76	74	72
Virginia	47	3	92	3	1435	-25	-21	85/69	83/68	80/66	23	71	70	68
Willmar	45	1	95	0	1133	-15	-11	91/74	88/72	85/71	24	76	74	72
Winona	44	1	91	4	652	-14	-10	91/75	88/73	85/72	24	77	75	74
MISSISSIPPI														
Biloxi,														
Keesler AFB	30	2	89	0	25	28	31	94/79	92/79	90/78	16	82	81	80
Clarksdale	34	1	90	3	178	14	19	96/77	94/77	92/76	21	80	79	78
Columbus AFB	33	4	88	3	224	15	20	95/77	94/77	91/76	22	80	79	78
Greenville AFB	33	3	91	1	139	15	20	95/77	93/77	91/76	21	80	79	78
Greenwood	33	3	90	1	128	15	20	95/77	93/77	91/76	21	80	79	78
Hattiesburg	31	2	89	2	200	24	27	96/78	94/77	92/77	21	81	80	79
Jackson AP	32	2	90	1	330	21	25	97/76	95/76	93/76	21	79	78	78
Laurel	31	4	89	1	264	24	27	96/78	94/77	92/77	21	81	80	79
McComb AP	31	2	90	3	458	21	26	96/77	94/76	92/76	18	80	79	78
Meridian AP	32	2	88	5	294	19	23	97/77	95/76	93/76	22	80	79	78
Natchez	31	4	91	3	168	23	27	96/78	94/78	92/77	21	81	80	79
Tupelo	34	2	88	3	289	14	19	96/77	94/77	92/76	22	80	79	78
Vicksburg CO	32	2	91	0	234	22	26	97/78	95/78	93/77	21	81	80	79
MISSOURI														
Cape Girardeau	37	1	89	3	330	8	13	98/76	95/75	92/75	21	79	78	77
Columbia AP (S)	39	0	92	2	778	-1	4	97/74	94/74	91/73	22	78	77	76
Farmington AP	37	5	90	3	928	3	8	96/76	93/75	90/74	22	78	77	75

Hannibal	39	4	91	2	489	−2	3	96/76	93/76	90/76	22	80	78	77
Jefferson City	38	4	92	1	640	2	7	98/75	95/74	92/74	23	78	77	76
Joplin AP	37	1	94	3	982	6	10	100/73	97/73	94/73	24	78	77	76
Kansas City AP	39	1	94	4	742		6	99/75	96/74	93/74	20	78	77	76
Kirksville AP	40	1	92	4	966	−5	0	96/74	93/74	90/73	22	78	77	76
Mexico	39	1	92	0	775	−1	4	97/74	94/74	91/73	23	78	77	76
Moberly	39	3	92	3	850	−2	3	97/74	94/74	91/73	22	78	77	76
Poplar Bluff	36	5	90	5	322	11	16	98/78	95/76	92/76	22	81	79	78
Rolla	38	0	91	0	1202	3	9	94/77	91/75	89/76	23	78	77	76
St Joseph AP	39	5	95	5	809	−3	2	96/77	93/76	91/76	21	81	79	77
St Louis AP	38	5	90	5	535	2	6	97/75	94/75	91/74	21	78	77	76
St Louis CO	38	4	90	2	465	3	8	98/75	94/75	91/74	18	78	77	76
Sedalia, Whiteman AFB	38	4	93	3	838	−1	4	95/76	92/76	90/75	22	79	78	77
Sikeston	36	5	89	3	318	9	15	98/77	95/76	92/75	21	80	78	77
Springfield AP	37	1	93	2	1265	3	9	96/73	93/74	91/74	23	78	77	75
MONTANA														
Billings AP	45	5	108	3	3567	−15	−10	94/64	91/64	88/63	31	67	66	64
Bozeman	45	5	111	0	4856	−20	−14	90/61	87/60	84/59	32	63	62	60
Butte AP	46	0	112	3	5526r	−24	−17	86/58	83/56	80/56	35	60	58	57
Cut Bank AP	48	4	112	2	3838r	−25	−20	88/61	85/61	82/60	35	64	62	61
Glasgow AP (S)	48	1	106	4	2277	−22	−18	92/64	89/63	85/62	29	68	66	64
Glendive	47	1	104	4	2076	−18	−13	95/66	92/64	89/62	29	69	67	65
Great Falls AP (S)	47	3	111	4	3664r	−21	−15	91/60	88/60	85/59	28	64	62	60
Havre	48	3	109	4	2488	−18	−11	94/65	90/64	87/63	33	68	66	65
Helena AP	46	4	112	0	3893	−21	−16	91/60	88/60	85/59	32	64	62	61
Kalispell AP	48	2	114	2	2965	−14	−7	91/62	87/61	84/60	34	65	63	62
Lewiston AP	47	0	109	3	4132	−22	−16	90/62	87/61	83/60	30	65	63	62
Livingston AP	45	4	110	3	4653	−20	−14	90/61	87/60	84/59	32	63	62	60
Miles City AP	46	3	105	5	2629	−20	−15	98/66	95/66	92/65	30	70	68	67
Missoula AP	46	5	114	1	3200	−13	−6	92/62	88/61	85/60	36	65	63	62
NEBRASKA														
Beatrice	40	2	96	5	1235	−5	−2	99/75	95/74	92/74	24	78	77	76
Chadron AP	42	5	103	0	3300	−8	−3	97/66	94/65	91/65	30	71	69	68
Columbus	41	3	97	3	1442	−6	−2	98/74	95/73	92/73	25	77	76	75
Fremont	41	3	96	3	1203	−6	−2	98/75	95/74	92/74	22	78	77	76

Table 4-1. Climatic Conditions for the United States (Reprinted with Permission from the 1977 Fundamentals Volume, ASHRAE HANDBOOK & Product Directory) (continued from page 131).

Col. 1	Col. 2		Col. 3		Col. 4	Winter[d] Col. 5		Summer[e] Col. 6			Col. 7	Col. 8		
State and Station	Lati-tude[b] °	'	Longi-tude[c] °	'	Eleva-tion[c] Ft	Design Dry-Bulb 99%	97.5%	Design Dry-Bulb and Mean Coincident Wet-Bulb 1%	2.5%	5%	Mean Daily Range	Design Wet-Bulb 1%	2.5%	5%
Grand Island AP	41	0	98	2	1841	−8	−3	97/72	94/71	91/71	28	75	74	73
Hastings	40	4	98	3	1932	−7	−3	97/72	94/71	91/71	27	75	74	73
Kearney	40	4	99	1	2146	−9	−4	96/71	93/70	90/70	28	74	73	72
Lincoln CO (S)	40	5	96	5	1150	−5	−2	99/75	95/74	92/74	24	78	77	76
McCook	40	1	100	4	2565	−6	−2	98/69	95/69	91/69	28	74	72	71
Norfolk	42	0	97	3	1532	−8	−4	97/74	93/74	90/73	30	78	77	75
North Platte AP (S)	41	1	100	4	2779	−8	−4	97/69	94/69	90/69	28	74	72	71
Omaha AP	41	2	95	5	978	−8	−3	94/76	91/75	88/74	22	78	77	75
Scottsbluff AP	41	5	103	3	3950	−8	−3	95/65	92/65	90/64	31	70	68	67
Sidney AP	41	1	103	0	4292	−8	−3	95/65	92/65	90/64	31	70	68	67
NEVADA														
Carson City	39	1	119	5	4675	4	9	94/60	91/59	89/58	42	63	61	60
Elko AP	40	5	115	5	5075	−8	−2	94/59	92/59	90/58	42	63	62	60
Ely AP (S)	39	1	114	5	6257	−10	−4	89/57	87/56	85/55	39	60	59	58
Las Vegas AP (S)	36	0	115	1	2162	25	28	108/66	106/65	104/65	30	71	70	69
Lovelock AP	40	0	118	3	3900	8	12	98/63	96/63	93/62	42	66	65	64
Reno AP (S)	39	3	119	5	4404	5	10	95/61	92/60	90/59	45	64	62	61
Reno CO	39	3	119	5	4490	6	11	96/61	93/60	91/59	45	64	62	61
Tonopah AP	38	0	117	1	5426	5	10	94/60	92/59	90/58	40	64	62	61
Winnemucca AP	40	0	117	5	4299	−1	3	96/60	94/60	92/60	42	64	62	61
NEW HAMPSHIRE														
Berlin	44	3	71	1	1110	−14	−9	87/71	84/69	81/68	22	73	71	70
Claremont	43	2	72	2	420	−9	−4	89/72	86/70	83/69	24	74	73	71
Concord AP	43	1	71	3	339	−8	−3	90/72	87/70	84/69	26	74	73	71
Keene	43	0	72	2	490	−12	−7	90/72	87/70	83/69	24	74	73	71
Laconia	43	3	71	3	505	−10	−5	89/72	86/70	83/69	25	74	73	71
Manchester, Grenier AFB	43	0	71	3	253	−8	−3	91/72	88/71	85/70	24	75	74	72
Portsmouth, Pease AFB	43	1	70	5	127	−2	2	89/73	85/71	83/70	22	75	74	72

	Lat °	′	Long °	′	Elev						MDR			
NEW JERSEY														
Atlantic City CO	39	3	74	3	11	10	13	92/74	89/74	86/72	18	78	77	75
Long Branch	40	2	74	0	20	10	13	93/74	90/73	87/72	18	78	77	75
Newark AP	40	4	74	—	11	6	14	94/74	91/73	88/72	20	77	76	75
New Brunswick	40	3	74	3	86	6	10	92/74	89/74	86/72	19	77	76	75
Paterson	40	5	74	1	100	6	10	94/74	91/73	88/72	21	77	76	75
Phillipsburg	40	4	75	1	180	1	6	92/73	89/72	86/71	21	76	75	74
Trenton CO	40	1	74	5	144	11	14	91/75	88/74	85/73	19	78	76	75
Vineland	39	3	75	0	95	8	11	91/75	89/74	86/73	19	78	76	75
NEW MEXICO														
Alamogordo, Holloman AFB	32	5	106	1	4070	14	19	98/64	96/64	94/64	30	69	68	67
Albuquerque AP (S)	35	0	106	0	5310	12	16	96/61	94/61	92/61	27	66	65	64
Artesia	35	5	104	4	3375	13	19	103/67	100/67	97/67	30	72	71	70
Carlsbad AP	32	2	104	2	3234	13	19	103/67	100/67	97/67	28	72	71	70
Clovis AP	34	1	103	1	4279	8	13	95/65	93/65	91/65	28	69	68	67
Farmington AP	36	5	108	1	5495	-1	6	95/63	93/62	91/61	30	67	65	64
Gallup	35	3	108	5	6465	0	5	90/59	89/58	86/58	32	64	62	61
Grants	35	1	107	5	6520	-1	4	89/59	88/58	85/57	32	64	62	61
Hobbs AP	32	4	103	4	3664	13	18	101/66	99/66	97/66	29	71	70	69
Las Cruces	32	2	107	2	3900	15	20	99/64	96/64	94/64	30	69	68	67
Los Alamos	35	5	106	2	7410	5	9	89/60	87/60	85/60	32	62	61	60
Raton AP	36	5	104	3	6379	-4	-1	91/60	89/60	87/60	34	65	64	63
Roswell, Walker AFB	33	2	104	3	3643	13	18	100/66	98/66	96/66	33	71	70	69
Santa Fe CO	35	4	106	0	7045	6	10	90/61	88/61	86/61	28	63	62	61
Silver City AP	32	4	108	2	5373	5	10	95/61	94/60	91/60	30	66	64	63
Socorro AP	34	0	106	5	4617	13	17	97/62	95/62	93/62	30	67	66	65
Tucumcari AP	35	1	103	4	4053	8	13	99/66	97/66	95/65	28	70	69	68
NEW YORK														
Albany AP (S)	42	5	73	5	277	-6	1	91/73	88/72	85/70	23	75	74	72
Albany CO	42	5	73	3	19	-4	1	91/73	88/72	85/70	20	75	74	72
Auburn	43	0	76	5	715	-3	2	90/73	87/71	84/70	22	75	73	72
Batavia	43	0	78	3	900	-3	5	90/72	87/71	84/70	22	75	73	72
Binghamton AP	42	1	76	1	1590	-2	1	86/71	83/69	81/68	20	73	72	70
Buffalo AP	43	0	78	4	705r	2	6	88/71	85/70	83/69	21	74	73	72
Cortland	42	4	76	1	1129	-5	0	88/71	85/71	82/70	23	74	73	71
Dunkirk	42	3	79	2	590	4	9	88/73	85/72	83/71	18	75	74	72
Elmira AP	42	1	76	5	860	-4	1	89/71	86/71	83/70	24	74	73	71
Geneva (S)	42	5	77	0	590	-3	2	90/73	87/71	84/70	22	75	73	72

Table 4-1. Climatic Conditions for the United States (Reprinted with Permission from the 1977 Fundamentals Volume, ASHRAE HANDBOOK & Product Directory) (continued from page 133).

Col. 1	Col. 2		Col. 3		Col. 4	Col. 5		Col. 6			Col. 7	Col. 8		
	Latitude[b]		Longitude[c]		Elevation[c]	Design Dry-Bulb		Design Dry-Bulb and Mean Coincident Wet-Bulb			Mean Daily Range	Design Wet-Bulb		
State and Station	°	'	°	'	Ft	99%	97.5%	1%	2.5%	5%		1%	2.5%	5%
Glen Falls	42	2	73	4	321	−11	−5	88/72	85/71	82/69	23	74	73	71
Gloversville	43	1	74	2	790	−8	−2	89/72	86/71	83/69	23	75	74	72
Hornell	42	2	77	4	1325	−4	0	88/71	85/70	82/69	24	74	73	72
Ithaca (S)	42	3	76	3	950	−5	0	88/71	85/71	82/70	24	74	73	71
Jamestown	42		79	2	1390	−1	3	88/70	86/70	83/69	20	74	72	71
Kingston	42	0	74	0	279	−3	3	91/73	88/72	85/70	22	76	74	73
Lockport	43	1	78	4	520	4	7	89/74	86/72	84/71	21	76	74	73
Massena AP	45	0	75	0	202r	−13	−8	86/70	83/69	80/68	20	73	72	70
Newburg- Stewart AFB	41	3	74	1	460	−1	4	90/73	88/72	85/70	21	76	74	73
NYC-Central Park (S)	40	5	74	0	132	11	15	92/74	89/73	87/72	17	76	75	74
NYC- Kennedy AP	40	4	73	5	16	12	15	90/73	87/72	84/71	16	76	75	74
NYC- La Guardia AP	40	5	73	5	19	11	15	92/74	89/73	87/72	16	76	75	74
Niagara Falls AP	43	1	79	0	596	4	7	89/74	86/72	84/71	20	76	74	73
Olean	42	1	78	3	1420	−2	2	87/71	84/71	81/70	23	74	73	71
Oneonta	42	3	75	0	1150	−7	−4	86/71	83/69	80/68	24	73	72	70
Oswego CO	43	3	76	3	300	1	7	86/73	83/71	80/70	20	75	73	72
Plattsburg AFB	44	4	73	3	165	−13	−8	86/70	83/69	80/68	22	73	72	70
Poughkeepsie	41	4	73	5	103	0	6	92/74	89/74	86/72	21	77	75	74
Rochester AP	43	1	77	4	543	1	5	91/73	88/71	85/70	22	75	73	72
Rome- Griffiss AFB	43	1	75	3	515	−11	−5	88/71	85/70	83/69	22	75	73	71
Schenectady (S)	42	5	74	0	217	−4	1	90/73	87/72	84/70	22	75	74	72
Suffolk County AFB	40	5			57	7	10	86/72	83/71	80/70	16	76	74	73
Syracuse AP	43	1	76	1	424	−3	2	90/73	87/71	84/70	20	75	73	72
Utica	43	1	75	2	714	−12	−6	88/73	85/71	82/70	22	75	73	71

Location	Lat °	′	Long °	′	Elev	Winter 99%	97.5%	Summer 1%	2.5%	5%	Range	WB 1%	2.5%	5%
NORTH CAROLINA														
Ashville AP	35	3	82	3	217r	10	14	89/73	87/72	85/71	21	75	74	72
Charlotte AP	35	0	81	0	735	18	22	95/74	93/74	91/74	20	77	76	76
Durham	36	0	78	5	406	16	20	94/75	92/75	90/75	20	78	77	76
Elizabeth City AP	36	2	76	1	10	12	19	93/78	91/77	89/76	18	80	78	78
Fayetteville, Pope AFB	35	1	79	0	95	17	20	95/76	92/76	90/75	20	79	78	77
Goldsboro, Seymour-Johnson AFB	35	2	78	0	88	18	21	94/77	91/76	89/75	18	79	78	77
Greensboro AP (S)	36	1	80	0	887	14	18	93/74	91/73	89/73	21	77	76	75
Greenville	35	4	77	2	25	18	21	93/77	91/76	89/75	19	79	78	77
Henderson	36	2	78	2	510	12	15	95/77	92/76	90/76	20	79	78	77
Hickory	35	4	81	2	1165	14	18	92/73	90/72	88/72	21	75	74	73
Jacksonville	34	5	77	3	24	20	24	92/78	90/78	88/77	18	80	79	78
Lumberton	34	4	79	0	132	18	21	95/76	92/76	90/75	20	79	78	77
New Bern AP	35	1	77	0	17	20	24	92/78	90/78	88/77	18	80	79	78
Raleigh/Durham AP (S)	35	5	78	5	433	16	20	94/75	92/75	90/75	20	78	77	76
Rocky Mount	36	0	77	0	81	18	21	94/77	91/76	89/75	19	79	78	77
Wilmington AP	34	2	78	0	30	23	26	93/79	91/78	89/77	18	81	80	79
Winston-Salem AP	36	1	80	1	967	16	20	94/74	91/73	89/73	20	76	75	74
NORTH DAKOTA														
Bismark AP (S)	46	5	100	5	1647	-23	-19	95/68	91/68	88/67	27	73	71	70
Devil's Lake	48	1	98	5	1471	-25	-21	91/69	88/68	85/66	25	73	71	69
Dickinson AP	46	5	102	5	2595	-21	-17	94/68	90/66	87/65	25	71	69	68
Fargo AP	46	5	96	5	900	-22	-18	92/73	89/71	85/69	25	76	74	72
Grands Forks AP	48	0	97	2	832	-26	-22	91/70	87/70	84/68	25	74	72	70
Jamestown AP	47	0	98	4	1492	-22	-18	94/70	90/69	87/68	26	74	74	71
Minot AP	48	2	101	2	1713	-24	-20	92/68	89/67	86/65	25	72	70	68
Williston	48	1	103	4	1877	-25	-21	91/68	88/67	85/65	25	72	70	68
OHIO														
Akron-Canton AP	41	0	81	3	1210	1	6	89/72	86/71	84/70	21	75	73	72
Ashtabula	42	0	80	5	690	4	9	88/73	85/72	83/71	18	75	74	72
Athens	39	2	82	1	700	0	6	95/75	92/74	90/73	22	78	76	74
Bowling Green	41	3	83	4	675	-2	2	92/73	89/73	86/71	23	76	75	73
Cambridge	40	0	81	4	800	1	7	93/75	90/74	87/73	23	78	76	75

Table 4-1. Climatic Conditions for the United States (Reprinted with Permission from the 1977 Fundamentals Volume, ASHRAE HANDBOOK & Product Directory) (continued from page 135).

Col. 1	Col. 2 Latitude		Col. 3 Longitude		Col. 4 Elevation (Ft)	Winter Col. 5 Design Dry-Bulb		Summer Col. 6 Design Dry-Bulb and Mean Coincident Wet-Bulb			Col. 7 Mean Daily Range	Col. 8 Design Wet-Bulb		
State and Station	°	'	°	'		99%	97.5%	1%	2.5%	5%		1%	2.5%	5%
Chillicothe CO	39	2	83	0	638	0	6	95/75	92/74	90/73	22	78	76	74
Cincinnati CO	39	1	84	4	761	1	6	92/73	90/72	88/72	21	77	75	74
Cleveland AP (S)	41	2	81	5	777r	1	5	91/73	88/72	86/71	22	76	74	73
Columbus AP (S)	40	0	82	5	812	0	5	92/73	90/73	87/72	24	77	75	73
Dayton AP	39	5	84	1	997	−1	4	91/73	89/72	86/71	20	76	75	74
Defiance	41	2	84	2	700	−1	4	94/74	91/73	88/72	24	77	76	74
Findlay AP	41	0	83	4	797	2	3	92/74	90/73	87/72	24	77	76	74
Fremont	41	2	83	3	600	−3	1	90/73	88/73	85/71	24	76	75	73
Hamilton	39	2	84	3	650	0	5	92/73	90/72	87/71	22	76	75	73
Lancaster	39	4	82	4	920	0	5	93/74	91/73	88/72	23	77	75	73
Lima	40	4	84	0	860	−1	4	94/74	91/73	88/72	24	77	76	74
Mansfield AP	40	5	82	3	1297	0	5	90/73	87/72	85/72	22	76	74	73
Marion	40	4	83	1	920	0	5	93/74	91/73	88/72	23	77	76	74
Middletown	39	3	84	4	635	0	5	92/73	90/72	87/71	22	76	75	73
Newark	40	1	82	3	825	−1	5	94/73	92/73	89/72	23	77	75	74
Norwalk	41	1	82	3	720	−3	1	90/73	88/73	85/71	22	76	75	73
Portsmouth	38	5	83	3	530	5	10	95/76	92/74	89/73	22	78	77	75
Sandusky CO	41	3	82	3	606	6	6	93/73	91/72	88/71	21	76	74	73
Springfield	40	0	83	5	1020	−1	3	91/74	89/73	87/72	21	77	76	74
Steubenville	40	2	80	4	992	1	5	89/72	86/71	84/70	22	74	73	72
Toledo AP	41	4	83	5	676r	−3	1	90/73	88/73	85/71	25	76	75	73
Warren	41	2	80	5	900	0	5	89/71	88/71	85/70	23	74	73	71
Wooster	40	5	82	0	1030	−1	6	89/72	87/71	84/70	22	75	73	72
Youngstown AP	41	2	80	4	1178	−1	4	88/71	86/71	84/70	23	74	73	71
Zanesville AP	40	0	81	5	881	1	7	93/75	90/74	87/73	23	78	76	75
OKLAHOMA														
Ada	34	5	96	4	1015	10	14	100/74	97/74	95/74	23	77	76	75
Altus AFB	34	4	99	2	1390	11	16	102/73	100/73	98/73	25	77	76	75
Ardmore	34	2	97	1	880	13	17	100/74	98/74	95/74	23	77	77	76
Bartlesville	36	5	96	0	715	6	10	101/73	98/74	95/74	23	77	77	76
Chickasha	35	0	98	0	1085	10	14	101/74	98/74	95/74	24	78	77	76

Enid-Vance AFB	36	2	98	2	1287	0	13	9	103/74	100/74	97/74	24	79	77	76
Lawton AP	34	3	98	3	1108	2	16	12	101/74	99/74	96/74	24	78	77	76
Mc Alester	34	5	95	5	760	5	19	14	99/74	96/74	93/74	23	77	76	75
Muskogee AP	35	4	95	4	610	2	15	10	101/74	98/75	95/75	23	79	78	77
Norman	35	1	97	1	1109	3	15	9	100/74	97/74	94/74	24	77	76	75
Oklahoma City AP (S)	35	2	97	2	1280	4	13	9	100/74	97/74	95/73	23	78	77	76
Ponca City	36	2	97	2	996	0	9	5	100/74	97/74	94/74	24	77	77	76
Seminole	35	2	96	1	865	4	15	11	99/74	96/74	94/73	23	77	76	75
Stillwater (S)	36	1	97	1	884	1	13	8	100/74	96/74	93/74	24	79	78	77
Tulsa AP	36	1	95	1	650	5	13	8	101/74	98/75	95/75	22	79	78	77
Woodward	36	3	99	3	1900	3	10	6	100/73	97/73	94/73	26	78	76	75
OREGON															
Albany	44	4	123	1	224	1	22	18	92/67	89/66	86/65	31	69	67	66
Astoria AP (S)	46	1	123	5	8	5	29	25	75/65	71/62	68/61	16	65	63	62
Baker AP	44	5	117	5	3368	5	6	-1	92/63	89/61	86/60	30	65	63	61
Bend	44	0	121	2	3599	2	4	-3	90/62	87/60	84/59	33	64	62	60
Corvallis (S)	44	3	123	2	221	2	22	18	92/67	89/66	86/65	31	69	67	66
Eugene AP	44	1	123	1	364	1	22	17	92/67	89/66	86/65	31	69	67	66
Grants Pass	42	3	123	2	925	2	24	20	99/69	96/68	93/67	33	71	69	68
Klamath Falls AP	42	1	121	4	4091	4	9	4	90/61	87/60	84/59	36	63	61	60
Medford AP (S)	42	2	122	5	1298	5	23	19	98/68	94/67	91/66	35	70	68	67
Pendleton AP (S)	45	4	118	5	1492	5	5	-2	97/65	93/64	90/62	29	66	65	63
Portland AP	45	4	122	4	21	4	23	17	89/68	85/67	81/65	23	69	67	66
Portland CO	45	3	122	2	57	2	24	18	90/68	86/67	82/65	21	69	67	66
Roseburg AP	43	1	123	3	505	0	23	18	93/67	90/66	87/65	30	69	67	66
Salem AP	45	0	123	0	195	0	23	18	92/68	88/66	84/65	31	69	68	66
The Dalles	45	4	121	1	102	1	19	13	93/69	89/68	85/66	28	70	68	67
PENNSYLVANIA															
Allentown AP	40	4	75	4	376	3	9	4	92/73	88/72	86/72	22	76	75	73
Altoona CO	40	2	78	2	1468	3	5	0	90/72	87/71	84/70	23	74	73	72
Butler	40	4	80	4	1100	0	6	-1	90/73	87/72	85/71	22	75	74	73
Chambersburg	40	0	77	0	640	4	8	4	91/75	88/73	87/73	23	77	76	75
Erie AP	42	1	80	1	732	1	9	4	88/73	85/72	83/71	18	75	74	72
Harrisburg AP	40	1	76	1	335	5	11	7	94/75	91/74	88/73	21	77	76	75
Johnstown	40	2	78	2	1214	5	2	-3	86/70	83/70	80/68	23	72	71	70
Lancaster	40	1	76	1	255	5	8	4	92/75	90/74	87/73	22	77	76	75
Meadville	41	4	80	4	1065	1	4	0	93/75	88/71	83/69	21	73	72	71
New Castle	41	0	80	0	825	2	7	2	91/73	88/72	86/71	23	75	74	73

Table 4-1. Climatic Conditions for the United States (Reprinted with Permission from the 1977 Fundamentals Volume, ASHRAE HANDBOOK & Product Directory) (continued from page 137).

Col. 1	Col. 2 Latitude° '	Col. 3 Longitude° '	Col. 4 Elevation Ft	Winter Col. 5 Design Dry-Bulb 99%	97.5%	Summer Col. 6 Design Dry-Bulb and Mean Coincident Wet-Bulb 1%	2.5%	5%	Col. 7 Mean Daily Range	Col. 8 Design Wet-Bulb 1%	2.5%	5%
State and Station												
Philadelphia AP	39 5	75 2	7	10	14	93/75	90/74	87/72	21	77	76	75
Pittsburgh AP	40 3	80 1	1137	2	5	89/73	86/71	84/70	22	74	73	72
Pittsburgh CO	40 3	80 0	749r	3	7	91/72	88/71	86/70	19	74	73	73
Reading CO	40 2	76 0	226	9	13	92/73	89/72	86/72	19	76	75	73
Scranton/ Wilkes-Barre	41 2	75 4	940	1	5	90/72	87/71	84/70	19	74	73	72
State College (S)	40 5	77 5	1175	3	7	90/72	87/71	84/70	23	74	73	72
Sunbury	40 5	76 5	480	2	7	92/73	89/72	86/70	22	75	74	73
Uniontown	39 5	79 4	1040	5	9	91/74	88/73	85/72	22	76	75	74
Warren	41 1	79 1	1280	-2	4	89/71	86/71	83/70	24	74	73	72
West Chester	40 0	75 4	440	9	13	92/75	89/74	86/72	20	77	76	75
Williamsport AP	41 1	77 0	527	2	7	92/73	89/72	86/70	23	75	74	73
York	40 0	76 4	390	8	12	94/75	91/74	88/73	22	77	76	75
RHODE ISLAND												
Newport (S)	41 3	71 2	20	5	9	88/73	85/72	82/70	16	76	75	73
Providence AP	41 4	71 3	55	5	9	89/73	86/72	83/70	19	75	74	73
SOUTH CAROLINA												
Anderson	34 3	82 4	764	19	23	94/74	92/74	90/74	21	77	76	75
Charleston AFB (S)	32 5	80 0	41	24	27	93/78	91/78	89/77	18	81	80	79
Charleston CO	32 5	80 0	9	25	28	94/78	92/78	90/77	13	81	80	79
Columbia AP	34 0	81 1	217	20	24	97/76	95/75	93/75	22	79	78	77
Florence AP	34 1	79 4	146	22	25	94/77	92/77	90/76	21	80	79	78
Georgetown	33 2	79 2	14	23	26	92/79	90/78	88/77	18	81	80	79
Greenville AP	34 5	82 1	957	18	22	93/74	91/74	89/74	21	78	77	76
Greenwood	34 1	82 1	671	18	22	95/75	93/74	91/74	21	79	78	77
Orangeburg	33 3	80 5	244	20	24	97/76	95/75	93/75	20	78	77	76
Rock Hill	35 0	81 0	470	19	23	96/75	94/74	92/74	20	79	78	77
Spartanburg AP	35 0	82 0	816	18	22	93/74	91/74	89/74	20	77	76	75
Sumter-Shaw AFB	34 0	80 3	291	22	25	95/77	92/76	90/75	21	79	78	77

Station	Lat °	Lat ′	Long °	Long ′	Elev									
Huron AP	44	3	98	1	1282	−18	−14	96/73	93/72	90/71	28	77	75	73
Mitchel	43	5	98	0	1346	−15	−10	96/72	93/71	90/70	28	76	75	73
Pierre AP	44	2	100	2	1718r	−15	−10	99/71	95/71	92/69	29	75	74	72
Rapid City AP (S)	44	0	103	0	3165	−11	−7	95/66	92/65	89/65	28	71	69	67
Sioux Falls AP	43	4	96	4	1420	−15	−11	94/73	91/72	88/71	24	76	75	73
Watertown AP	45	0	97	0	1746	−19	−15	94/73	91/72	88/71	26	76	75	73
Yankton	43	0	97	2	1280	−13	−7	94/73	91/72	88/71	25	77	76	74
TENNESSEE														
Athens	33	3	84	4	940	13	18	95/74	92/73	90/73	22	77	76	75
Bristol-														
Tri City AP	36	3	82	2	1519	9	14	91/72	89/72	87/71	22	75	75	73
Chattanooga AP	35	0	85	1	670	13	18	96/75	93/74	91/74	22	78	77	76
Clarksville	36	4	87	2	470	6	12	95/76	93/74	90/74	21	78	77	76
Columbia	35	4	87	0	690	10	15	97/75	94/74	91/74	21	78	77	76
Dyersburg	36	0	89	3	334	10	15	96/78	94/77	91/76	21	81	80	78
Greenville	35	5	82	5	1320	11	16	92/73	90/72	88/72	22	76	75	74
Jackson AP	35	4	88	5	413	11	16	98/76	95/75	92/75	21	79	78	77
Knoxville AP	35	5	84	5	980	13	19	94/74	92/73	90/73	21	77	76	75
Memphis AP	35	0	90	0	263	13	18	98/77	95/76	93/76	21	80	79	78
Murfreesboro	35	5	86	2	608	9	14	97/75	94/74	91/74	22	78	77	76
Nashville AP (S)	36	1	86	4	577	9	14	97/75	94/74	91/74	21	78	77	76
Tullahoma	35	2	86	1	1075	8	13	96/74	93/73	91/73	22	77	76	75
TEXAS														
Abilene AP	32	3	99	4	1759	15	20	101/71	99/71	97/71	22	75	74	74
Alice AP	27	4	98	0	180	31	34	100/78	98/77	95/77	20	82	81	79
Amarillo AP	35	1	101	4	3607	6	11	98/67	95/67	93/67	26	71	70	70
Austin AP	30	2	97	4	597	24	28	100/74	98/74	97/74	22	78	77	77
Bay City	29	0	96	0	52	29	33	96/77	94/77	92/77	16	80	79	79
Beaumont	30	0	94	0	18	27	31	95/79	93/78	91/78	19	81	80	80
Beeville	28	2	97	2	225	30	33	99/78	97/77	95/77	18	82	81	79
Big Spring AP (S)	32	2	101	2	2537	16	20	100/69	100/69	95/69	26	74	73	72
Brownsville AP (S)	25	5	97	3	16	35	39	94/77	93/77	92/77	18	80	79	79
Brownwood	31	1	99	0	1435	18	22	101/73	99/73	96/73	22	77	76	75
Bryan AP	30	2	96	2	275	24	29	98/76	96/76	94/76	20	79	78	78

Table 4-1. Climatic Conditions for the United States (Reprinted with Permission from the 1977 Fundamentals Volume, ASHRAE HANDBOOK & Product Directory) (continued from page 139).

Col. 1	Col. 2 Latitude		Col. 3 Longitude		Col. 4 Elevation	Winter Col. 5 Design Dry-Bulb		Summer Col. 6 Design Dry-Bulb and Mean Coincident Wet-Bulb			Col. 7 Mean Daily	Col. 8 Design Wet-Bulb		
State and Station	°	'	°	'	Ft	99%	97.5%	1%	2.5%	5%	Range	1%	2.5%	5%
Corpus Christi AP	27	5	97	3	43	31	35	95/78	94/78	92/78	19	80	80	79
Corsicana	32	0	96	3	425	20	25	100/75	98/75	96/75	21	79	78	77
Dallas AP	32	5	96	5	481	18	22	102/75	100/75	97/75	20	78	78	77
Del Rio, Laughlin AFB	29	2	101	0	1072	26	31	100/73	98/73	97/73	24	79	77	76
Denton	33	1	97	1	655	17	22	101/74	99/74	97/74	22	78	77	76
Eagle Pass	28	5	100	3	743	27	32	101/73	99/73	98/73	24	78	78	77
El Paso AP (S)	31	5	106	2	3918	20	24	100/64	98/64	96/64	27	69	68	68
Fort Worth AP (S)	32	5	97	0	544r	17	22	101/74	99/74	97/74	22	78	77	76
Galveston AP	29	2	94	5	5	31	36	90/79	89/79	88/78	10	81	80	80
Greenville	33	0	96	1	575	17	22	101/74	99/74	97/74	21	78	77	76
Harlingen	26	1	97	4	37	35	39	96/77	94/77	93/77	19	80	79	79
Houston AP	29	4	95	2	50	27	32	96/77	94/77	92/77	18	80	79	79
Houston CO	29	5	95	2	158r	28	33	97/77	95/77	93/77	18	80	79	79
Huntsville	30	4	95	3	494	22	27	100/75	98/75	96/75	20	78	78	77
Killeen-Gray AFB	31	1	97	4	1021	20	25	99/73	97/73	95/73	22	77	76	75
Lamesa	32	5	102	0	2965	13	17	99/69	96/69	94/69	26	73	72	71
Laredo AFB	27	3	99	4	503	32	36	102/73	101/73	99/74	23	78	78	77
Longview	32	2	94	4	345	19	24	99/76	97/76	95/76	20	80	79	78
Lubbock AP	33	4	101	5	3243	10	15	98/69	96/69	94/69	26	73	72	71
Lufkin AP	31	1	94	4	286	25	29	99/76	97/76	94/76	20	80	79	78
Mc Allen	26	1	98	1	122	35	39	97/77	95/77	94/77	21	80	79	79
Midland AP (S)	32	0	102	1	2815r	16	21	100/69	98/69	96/69	26	73	72	71
Mineral Wells AP	32	5	98	0	934	17	22	101/74	99/74	97/74	22	78	78	77
Palestine CO	31	5	95	4	580	23	27	100/76	98/76	96/76	20	79	79	78
Pampa	35	3	101	0	3230	7	12	99/67	96/67	94/67	26	71	70	70

San Angelo, Goodfellow AFB	31	2	100	2	1878	18	22	101/71	99/71	97/70	24	75	74	73
San Antonio AP (S)	29	3	98	3	792	25	30	99/72	97/73	96/73	19	77	76	76
Sherman														
Perrin AFB	33	4	96	1	763	15	20	100/75	98/75	95/74	22	78	77	76
Snyder	32	4	101	5	2325	13	18	100/70	98/70	96/70	26	74	73	72
Temple	31	1	97	3	675	22	27	100/74	99/74	97/74	22	78	77	77
Tyler AP	32	2	95	2	527	19	24	99/76	97/76	95/76	21	80	79	78
Vernon	34	1	99	2	1225	13	17	102/73	100/73	97/73	24	77	76	75
Victoria AP	28	5	97	0	104	29	32	98/78	96/77	94/77	18	82	81	79
Waco AP	31	4	97	0	500	21	26	101/75	99/75	97/75	22	78	78	77
Wichita Falls AP	34	0	98	3	994	14	18	103/73	101/73	98/73	24	77	76	75
UTAH														
Cedar City AP	37	4	113	1	5613	-2	5	93/60	91/60	89/59	32	65	63	62
Logan	41	4	111	5	4775	-3	2	93/62	91/61	88/60	33	65	64	63
Moab	38	5	109	3	3965	6	11	100/60	98/60	96/60	30	65	64	63
Ogden AP	41	1	112	0	4455	1	5	93/63	91/61	88/61	33	66	65	64
Price	39	4	110	5	5580	-2	5	93/60	91/60	89/59	33	65	63	62
Provo	40	1	111	4	4470	1	6	98/62	96/62	94/61	32	66	65	64
Richfield	38	5	112	0	5300	-2	5	93/60	91/60	89/59	34	65	63	62
St George CO	37	4	113	4	2899	14	21	103/65	101/65	99/64	33	70	68	67
Salt Lake City AP (S)	40	5	112	0	4220	3	8	97/62	95/62	92/61	32	66	65	64
Vernal AP	40	3	109	3	5280	-5	0	91/61	89/60	86/59	32	64	63	62
VERMONT														
Barre	44	1	72	3	1120	-16	-11	84/71	81/69	78/68	23	73	71	70
Burlington AP (S)	44	3	73	1	331	-12	-7	88/72	85/70	82/69	23	74	72	71
Rutland	43	3	73	0	620	-13	-8	87/72	84/70	81/69	23	74	72	71
VIRGINIA														
Charlottesville	38	1	78	3	870	14	18	94/74	91/74	88/73	23	77	76	75
Danville AP	36	3	79	2	590	14	16	94/74	92/73	90/73	21	77	76	75
Fredericksburg	38	2	77	3	50	10	14	96/76	93/75	90/74	21	78	77	76
Harrisonburg	38	3	78	5	1340	12	16	93/72	91/72	88/71	23	75	74	73
Lynchburg AP	37	2	79	1	947	12	16	93/74	90/74	88/73	21	77	76	75
Norfolk AP	36	5	76	1	26	20	22	93/77	91/76	89/76	18	79	78	77
Petersburg	37	1	77	3	194	14	17	95/76	92/76	90/75	20	79	78	77

Table 4-1. Climatic Conditions for the United States (Reprinted with Permission from the 1977 Fundamentals Volume, ASHRAE HANDBOOK & Product Directory) (continued from page 141).

Col. 1	Col. 2		Col. 3		Col. 4	Col. 5		Col. 6			Col. 7	Col. 8		
	Latitude[b]		Longitude[c]		Elevation[c]	Winter[d] Design Dry-Bulb		Summer[e] Design Dry-Bulb and Mean Coincident Wet-Bulb			Mean Daily	Design Wet-Bulb		
State and Station	°	′	°	′	Ft	99%	97.5%	1%	2.5%	5%	Range	1%	2.5%	5%
Richmond AP	37	3	77	2	162	14	17	95/76	92/76	90/75	21	79	78	77
Roanoke AP	37	2	80	0	1174r	12	16	93/72	91/72	88/71	23	75	74	73
Staunton	38	2	78	5	1480	12	16	93/72	91/72	88/71	23	75	74	73
Winchester	39	1	78	1	750	6	10	93/75	90/74	88/74	21	77	76	75
WASHINGTON														
Aberdeen	47	0	123	5	12	25	28	80/65	77/62	73/61	16	65	63	62
Bellingham AP	48	5	122	3	150	10	15	81/67	77/65	74/63	19	68	65	63
Bremerton	47	3	122	4	162	21	25	82/65	78/64	75/62	20	66	64	63
Ellensburg AP	47	0	120	3	1729	2	6	94/65	91/64	87/62	34	66	65	63
Everett-Paine AFB	47	5	122	2	598	21	25	80/65	76/64	73/62	20	67	64	63
Kennewick	46	0	119	1	392	5	11	99/68	96/67	92/66	30	70	68	67
Longview	46	1	123	0	12	19	24	88/68	85/67	81/65	30	69	67	66
Moses Lake, Larson AFB	47	1	119	1	1183	1	7	97/66	94/65	90/63	32	67	66	64
Olympia AP	47	0	122	5	190	16	22	87/66	83/65	79/64	32	67	66	64
Port Angeles	48	1	123	3	99	24	27	72/62	69/61	67/60	18	64	62	61
Seattle-Boeing Fld	47	3	122	2	14	21	26	84/68	81/66	77/65	24	69	67	65
Seattle CO (S)	47	4	122	2	14	22	27	85/68	82/66	78/65	19	69	67	65
Seattle-Tacoma AP (S)	47	3	122	2	386	21	26	84/65	80/64	76/62	22	66	64	63
Spokane AP (S)	47	4	117	3	2357	-6	2	93/64	90/63	87/62	28	65	64	62
Tacoma-Mc Chord AFB	47	1	122	3	350	19	24	86/66	82/65	79/63	22	68	66	64
Walla Walla AP	46	1	118	2	1185	0	7	97/67	94/66	90/65	27	69	67	66
Wenatchee	47	2	120	2	634	7	11	99/67	96/66	92/64	32	68	67	65
Yakima AP	46	3	120	3	1061	-2	5	96/65	93/65	89/63	36	68	66	65
WEST VIRGINIA														
Beckley	37	5	81	1	2330	-2	4	83/71	81/69	79/69	22	71	71	70

142

State and Station	Lat. °	′	Long. °	′	Elev., ft	—	Winter 99%	97.5%	Summer 1%	2.5%	5%	D.R.	WB 1%	2.5%	5%
Clarksburg	39	2	80	2	977	2	6	10	92/74	90/73	87/72	21	76	75	74
Elkins AP	38	5	79	5	1970	5	1	6	86/72	84/70	82/70	22	74	72	71
Huntington CO	38	2	82	2	565r	3	5	10	94/76	91/74	89/73	22	78	77	75
Martinsburg AP	39	2	78	2	537	0	6	10	93/75	90/74	88/74	21	77	76	75
Morgantown AP	39	4	80	4	1245	0	4	8	90/74	87/73	85/73	22	76	75	74
Parkersburg CO	39	2	81	2	615r	3	7	11	93/75	90/74	88/73	21	77	76	75
Wheeling	40	1	80	1	659	4	1	5	89/72	86/71	84/70	21	74	73	72
WISCONSIN															
Appleton	44	2	88	2	742	2	−14	−9	89/74	86/72	83/71	23	76	74	72
Ashland	46	3	90	3	650	5	−21	−16	85/70	82/68	79/66	23	72	70	68
Beloit	42	3	89	3	780	0	−7	−3	92/75	90/75	88/74	24	78	77	75
Eau Claire AP	44	5	91	5	888	3	−15	−11	92/75	89/73	86/71	23	77	75	73
Fond du Lac	43	5	88	5	760	3	−12	−8	89/74	86/72	84/71	23	76	74	72
Green Bay AP	44	3	88	3	683	1	−13	−9	88/74	85/72	83/71	23	76	74	72
La Crosse AP	43	5	91	5	652	2	−13	−9	91/75	88/73	85/72	22	77	75	74
Madison AP (S)	43	1	89	1	858	2	−11	−7	91/74	88/73	85/71	22	77	75	73
Manitowoc	44	1	87	2	660	4	−11	−7	89/74	86/72	83/71	21	76	74	72
Marinette	45	0	87	4	605		−15	−11	87/73	84/71	82/70	20	75	73	71
Milwaukee AP	43	0	87	5	672	5	−8	−4	90/74	87/73	84/71	21	76	74	73
Racine	42	4	87	4	640	4	−6	−2	91/75	88/73	85/72	21	77	75	74
Sheboygan	43	4	87	4	648	4	−10	−6	89/75	86/73	83/72	20	77	75	74
Stevens Point	43	0	89	1	1079	3	−15	−11	92/75	89/73	86/71	23	77	75	73
Waukesha	43	0	88	0	860	1	−9	−5	90/74	87/73	84/71	22	76	74	73
Wausau AP	44	6	89	6	1196	4	−16	−12	91/74	88/72	85/70	23	76	74	72
WYOMING															
Casper AP	42	5	106	5	5319	3	−11	−5	92/58	90/57	87/57	31	63	61	60
Cheyene AP	41	1	104	1	6126	5	−9	−1	89/58	86/58	84/57	30	63	62	60
Cody AP	44	3	109	3	5090	0	−19	−13	89/60	86/60	83/59	32	64	63	61
Evanston	41	2	111	0	6860	0	−9	−3	86/55	84/55	82/54	32	59	58	57
Lander AP (S)	42	5	108	5	5563	4	−16	−11	91/61	88/61	85/60	32	64	63	61
Laramie AP (S)	41	2	105	2	7266	3	−14	−6	84/56	81/56	79/55	28	61	60	59
Newcastle	43	5	104	5	4480	1	−17	−12	91/64	87/63	84/63	30	69	68	66
Rawlins	41	5	107	5	6736	1	−12	−4	86/57	83/57	81/56	40	62	61	60
Rock Springs AP	41	4	109	4	6741	0	−9	−3	86/55	84/55	82/54	32	59	58	57
Sheridan AP	44	5	107	5	3942	0	−14	−8	94/62	91/62	88/61	32	66	65	63
Torrington	42	0	104	0	4098	1	−14	−8	94/62	91/62	88/61	30	66	65	63

The "99%" column means that for 99 percent of 2160 hours during the three months, the temperature either equalled or was above the figure given. To turn that around, for 1 percent of that period (about 22 hours) in Alexander City, the temperature was below 18 F. For 2.5 percent of the time (approximately 54 hours), the temperature was at or below 22 F.

Which column should you use and what is the practical difference between the two beyond the obvious differences in figures? To take the last question first, consider again the figures for Alexander City. If you were to design your heating system to cope with 18 F temperatures, that means for about 22 hours over the period of the three winter months your heating system might not have quite enough capacity to meet the heating demands (on the other hand, it might; most heating systems cannot be tailored exactly to an individual house heating load, and there is usually both some overage in capacity as well as a built-in safety factor).

If you design a heating system for 22 F, for about 54 hours during that three-month period the heating plant output might fall behind the heating demand. Chances are that those short periods of time would not come all in one block. They would occur as an hour or two here and an hour or two there. You might not even notice the difference. The slight underage could easily be made up with a small auxiliary heating unit in the event of a drastic cold snap.

The question of which figure to use (18 F or 22 F) becomes a matter of judgment. A 100 percent figure is not used because it has been found to be unnecessary. There remains the choice between chancing insufficient heating capacity for your house for about 22 hours or for about 54 hours. Choosing some temperature level below the 97.5 percent mark is not recommended because of the possibility of more domestic discomfort than we are accustomed to or willing to put up with. The usual recommendation is that if the structure is relatively lightweight, but reasonably well insulated (true of most modern frame houses), the 99 percent value is a good choice. If the structure has a high thermal mass and a workable flywheel effect, the 97.5 percent value would be a reasonable selection. However, any unusual design features of the house that might involve excessive heat transmission or infiltration of cold air must be taken into consideration. An example is unusually large expanses of glass.

The problem with using a table of this sort is that your building site quite possibly is somewhere else. It frequently happens that a site even just a few miles from a reporting station can have considerably different weather conditions and be a part of a quite dissimilar microclimate.

In such cases, the first step is to try to find some local weather records that will be of more concrete value. Some possible sources are an airport, weather station or observatory, newspaper office, or a heating fuels dealer. There might be someone in the neighborhood who has made a hobby of recording weather data. Ski areas, agricultural organizations, or forest service offices might have information available. Check every possible lead to find the average low temperature for your immediate locale covering the 2160 hours of December, January and February. If you have the opportunity, you might even be able to record those temperatures over one winter at your own building site. Although by no means conclusive, your figures can be used in conjunction with others in making a final determination.

Bear in mind, too, that the terrain surrounding your building site can make an appreciable difference in weather activity. In plains areas, for instance, the climate might well be essentially the same for a radius of many miles—including the nearest town. In mountainous country, there can be remarkable differences from one valley or ridge to the next.

If you don't live near one of the reporting stations listed in Table 4-1, the information might still be of some help to you in verifying or corroborating information that you have obtained from other sources. You can successfully do a certain amount of interpolating with the tabulated figures. For instance, notice that Alexander City is located at 33 degrees north latitude. A quick check of other cities located at approximately the same latitude shows that the design dry-bulb temperatures are much the same. There are some exceptions such as Tucson, Arizona. There both temperatures are a full 10 F higher—doubtless a desert influence. Even so, if your building site happens to be located at approximately 33 degrees north, you might realistically assume that the design dry-bulb temperatures would be approximately the same as for those stations listed at that latitude. If a check of the listings shows that there is some variation from station to station despite the latitude being the same, an average of all of the stations could give you a workable figure that would not be too far off of the mark. By interpolating and tempering the results with judgement, then relating that to local information, you can eventually settle upon a suitable outdoor design temperature.

Another possibility is to interpolate the elevation figures. This can be done by first locating a reporting station closest to your building site. Note its elevation. Find the elevation of your building site and either add or subtract 1 F for every 200 feet of difference in elevation. This should be done only if the site is relatively close to the reporting station. Elevation itself is not a governing factor on a country-wide basis. Compare, for example, Fort Huachuca, Arizona with Greeley, Colorado. Though the elevations are almost the same, the design dry-bulb temperatures are considerably different. Note, too, that these adjustments do not apply if the site is subject to cold air drainage (which occurs mainly in mountainous country) or where substantial radiational cooling frequently takes place at night.

There are other adjustments that can be made. Large bodies of water tend to temper the temperature and can cause variations of as much as 4 F. Check local records or common knowledge to determine the specifics. In many areas, a hilltop site will be warmer than a nearby deep valley that forms a cold-air pocket. These specifics can also be determined on a local basis. Heavily vegetated areas can modify local temperatures. If the countryside is dry and relatively barren, a site located upwind can be as much as 2 F higher than if the countryside is densely vegetated.

Design Temperature Difference

Once you have determined the indoor and the outdoor design temperatures, the design temperature difference follows automatically. This figure is merely the difference between the indoor and outdoor temperatures and is widely used in making heat loss calculations. You will see it variously referred to as the formula $(t_i - t_o)$, or as the abbreviation DTD, and frequently as delta t, which is symbolized as Δt. If you have chosen 70 F as your indoor temperature and have decided that 10 F is a suitable outdoor temperature, then the Δt is 60. If the indoor temperature is 70 F and the outdoor temperature is -15 F, the Δt is 85.

Wind

The prevailing direction of the wind during the winter months and its average speed have an important influence upon the potential heat loss of a house. If one house is located on an exposed, windy hilltop and another indentical house is located in a sheltered spot—and weather conditions are otherwise equal—the operating costs for the heating system in the sheltered house will be less to some degree. Wind speed and direction should be carefully considered during the sitting and orientation of a house. This might well play a part in the design of the house as regards the detailing of roofs, overhangs, fenestration, and so on in order to reduce adverse wind effects. The house is best positioned to present the least amount of exposed exterior surface to the prevailing wind flow and it should be sheltered as much as possible by windbreaks (natural or otherwise).

Taking the specifics of wind speed and direction into account in heat loss calculations is a difficult proposition. The speed factor is just as variable as outdoor temperatures. There really is no formula factor to account for direction (though wind forces come under much closer scrutiny when large buildings are analyzed for heat loss). As far as residential heat loss calculations are concerned, wind velocity is employed in two regards. Because air movement affects surface conductance from exposed exterior building surfaces, the factor is made a part of surface conductance and resistance computations. A rule of thumb used here is the assumption that moving air under winter conditions travels at an average 15 miles per hour. Obviously, this figure does not hold true for all building sites. Conversion factors have been developed for use in situations where the wind volocity is on average a different value than 15 mph. These factors are listed in the Table 4-2. They should only be used if you are absolutely sure that the actual wind velocity on average at your building site is more or less than the standard factor. This is particularly true if the result will lower the estimated total heating load.

The second aspect of wind velocity has to do with heat loss that is caused by infiltration of cold air into the house—a process that is greatly aided by wind.

Unheated Spaces

Temperature differences in living spaces are not sufficient to cause problems in making heat loss calculations. It will not matter if one or two unused rooms are closed off during the heating season unless this is done on a regular and consistent basis for long periods of time. Any spaces within the building envelope that are enclosed and remain at a permanent lower temperature by 20 F or more, whether actually heated or not, from the remainder of the normally-heated living space are treated as separate entities and must be accounted for in the heat loss calculations.

An unheated attic or an attached garage are typical examples where temperatures are somewhere between indoor and outdoor design temperatures. Each of these spaces must be assigned an intermediate design temperature. This is used in conjunction with the indoor design temperature to develop a design temperature difference needed for the heat loss calculations. If the space is actually *heated* to a lower temperature, then that specific temperature becomes the intermediate design temperature—simple enough. But if the space is unheated, a problem arises in deciding just what that temperature might be because it is influenced by factors such as the relative positions of the adjacent heated and unheated spaces, the thermal resistance of boundary building sections, the amount of surface area exposed to the different temperature levels, and so on. There are several possibilities in selecting this intermediate design temperature.

Sometimes it is possible to select an arithmetic mean temperature. This is the simplest way, but unfortunately the conditions are seldom right. This will only work when the surface area in the unheated space, and adjacent to the heated area, and the surface area of the unheated space exposed to the outdoors are the same and also have identical thermal transmission coefficients.

For example, consider the attached garage (or workshop, storage area, etc.) As shown in Fig. 4-1. The wall surface area separating the unheated garage from the heated living space is the same as the wall

Table 4-2. Factors for use in Converting Wall U to Compensate for Prevailing Wind Velocities other than the Assumed 15 mph (Reprinted with Permission from the 1977 Fundamentals Volume, ASHRAE HANDBOOK & Product Directory).

U for 15 mph	U for 0 to 30 mph Wind Velocities						U for 15 mph	U for 0 to 30 mph Wind Velocities					
	0	5	10	20	25	30		0	5	10	20	25	30
0.050	0.049	0.050	0.050	0.050	0.050	0.050	0.290	0.257	0.278	0.286	0.293	0.295	0.296
0.060	0.059	0.059	0.060	0.060	0.060	0.060	0.310	0.273	0.296	0.305	0.313	0.315	0.317
0.070	0.068	0.069	0.070	0.070	0.070	0.070	0.330	0.288	0.314	0.324	0.333	0.336	0.338
0.080	0.078	0.079	0.080	0.080	0.080	0.080	0.350	0.303	0.332	0.344	0.354	0.357	0.359
0.090	0.087	0.089	0.090	0.090	0.091	0.091	0.370	0.318	0.350	0.363	0.375	0.378	0.380
0.100	0.096	0.099	0.100	0.100	0.101	0.101	0.390	0.333	0.368	0.382	0.395	0.399	0.401
0.110	0.105	0.108	0.109	0.110	0.111	0.111	0.410	0.347	0.385	0.402	0.416	0.420	0.422
0.130	0.123	0.127	0.129	0.131	0.131	0.131	0.430	0.362	0.403	0.421	0.436	0.441	0.444
0.150	0.141	0.147	0.149	0.151	0.151	0.152	0.450	0.376	0.420	0.439	0.457	0.462	0.465
0.170	0.158	0.166	0.169	0.171	0.172	0.172	0.500	0.410	0.464	0.487	0.509	0.514	0.518
0.190	0.175	0.184	0.188	0.191	0.192	0.193	0.600	0.474	0.548	0.581	0.612	0.620	0.626
0.210	0.192	0.203	0.208	0.212	0.213	0.213	0.700	0.535	0.631	0.675	0.716	0.728	0.736
0.230	0.209	0.222	0.227	0.232	0.233	0.234	0.800	0.592	0.711	0.766	0.821	0.836	0.847
0.250	0.226	0.241	0.247	0.252	0.253	0.254	0.900	0.645	0.789	0.858	0.927	0.946	0.960
0.270	0.241	0.259	0.266	0.273	0.274	0.275	1.000	0.695	0.865	0.949	1.034	1.058	1.075

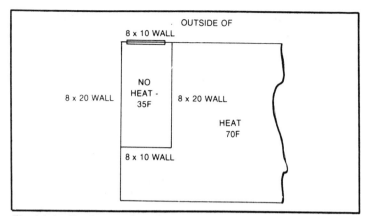

Fig. 4-1. In situations such as the one shown, where the exposed and the intermediate wall surfaces have the same area and the same U factor, the intermediate design temperature of the unheated space can be taken to be the mean of the inside and the outside design temperatures.

surface area separating the garage from the outdoors. If you assume that the garage doors are the insulated bulkhead type and that the heat transfer coefficient of the outside wall is the same as that of the intermediate wall, then the design intermediate temperature of the unheated garage is the arithmetic mean of the outside and inside design temperatures. If the inside design temperature of the house is 70 F and the outside design temperature is 0 F, the intermediate design temperature is the arithmetic mean of those two temperatures (35 F).

In practice, though, the above situation seldom occurs. The National Electrical Manufacturers Association suggests using a rule of thumb approach that works adequately in almost all instances and avoids a series of calculations.

If the bounding building sections are walls, you can assume that the temperature of the unheated space is one-third as much above the outside design temperature as the heated living space is above the outside design temperature. To illustrate, assume an inside design temperature of 70 F and an outside design temperature of 20 F. The inside temperature is therefore 50 F above the outside temperature. The intermediate temperature can be assumed to be one-third as much above 20 F as the inside temperature is above 20 F; one-third of 50 is 16.7, plus 20, equals an intermediate design temperature of 36.7 F.

If the calculations are for a floor over an unheated space, the situation is slightly different. Here the intermediate temperature of the unheated space can be assumed to be one-half as much above the outside design temperature as the inside design temperature is above the outside design temperature. Using the same figures as in the wall example, one-half of the temperature difference is 25, plus 20 (outside temperature), equals an intermediate design temperature of 45 F.

This is a simple enough method and perfectly workable. But the problem with rules of thumb is that they are not always as accurate as you might hope for. If greater accuracy is desired, the following formula from the *1977 Fundamentals Volume* of the *ASHRAE HANDBOOK* can be used:

$$t_u = \frac{\begin{array}{l} T_i\,(A_1U_1 + A_2U_2 + A_3U_3 + \text{etc.}) \\ + t_0(2.16V_o + A_aU_a + A_bU_b + A_cU_c + \text{etc.}) \end{array}}{\begin{array}{l} A_1U_1 + A_2U_2 + A_3U_3 + \text{etc.} \\ + 2.16V_o + A_aU_a + A_bU_b + A_cU_c + \text{etc.} \end{array}}$$

where

t_u = temperature in unheated space, degrees F.

t = indoor design temperature of heated room, degrees F.

t_o = outdoor design temperature, degrees F.

A_1, etc. = areas of surface of unheated space adjacent to heated space, square feet.

A_a, etc. = areas of surface of unheated space exposed to outdoors, square feet.

U_1, etc. = heat transfer coefficients of surfaces of A_1, etc.

U_a, etc. = heat transfer coefficients of surfaces of a_a, etc.

V_o = rate of introduction of outside air into the unheated space by infiltration and/or ventilation, cubic feet per minute.

This formula only looks very complex. By simply substituting the necessary numbers for the formula symbols and working out the arithmetic, you can easily arrive at a satisfactory answer. When making residential heat loss calculations, the areas being considered are generally fairly small. For that reason, you can usually disregard the final element of the formula, V_o. On the other hand, including it will certainly do no harm. Similarly, you can disregard unheated ground surface area such as the concrete floor of an unheated storage area.

Establishing an intermediate design temperature for an unheated attic space is usually considered as a special case. When making separate calculations of this sort, the attic is generally assumed to be one of at least fairly substantial volume—such as a pitched-roof attic. Attics that consist essentially of only a shallow space between ceiling and roof assembly can be considered as a building section without an intermediate unheated space. As you might expect, there are both rules of thumb and explicit formulas for determining attic intermediate design temperatures.

The simplest approach, and the one perhaps most often used, it just to proceed as though the space were not there at all. In other words, the ceiling of the living space is regarded as though it were actually the roof and the roof itself does not enter into the actual calculations. This works relatively well provided the attic is well-ventilated and that the ceiling is heavily insulated. The only change that is made in the calculation is in the

149

surface conductance factor. If you calculate heat loss through a roof, the exposed rooftop would be considered as an outside surface when assessing its conductance. With the ceiling, however, the attic floor or the upper face of the insulation is actually indoors and must be treated as having the conductance attributable to an inside surface.

Although the above method will introduce an error factor into the heat loss calculations of probably no more than 2 to 3 percent, some prefer to employ the more involved formula method of determing an attic intermediate design temperature. This formula is as follows:

$$t_a = \frac{A_c U_c t_c + t_o(2.16 \ A_c V_c + A_r U_r + A_w U_w + A_g U_g)}{A_c \ (U_c + 2.16 \ V_c) + A_r U_r + A_w U_w + A_g U_g}$$

where

t_a = attic temperature, Fahrenheit.

t_c = indoor temperature near top floor ceiling, Fahrenheit.

t_o = outdoor temperature, Fahrenheit.

A_c = area of ceiling, square feet.

A_r = area of roof, square feet.

A_w = area of net vertical attic wall surface, square feet.

A_g = area of attic glass, square feet.

U_c = heat transfer coefficient of ceiling, based on surface conductance of 2.20 Btu per (hour) (square foot) (degree Fahrenheit) (upper surface).

U_r = heat transfer coefficient of roof, Btu per (hour) (square foot) (degree Fahrenheit), based on surface conductance of 2.2 Btu per (hour) (square foot) (degree Fahrenheit) (lower surface).

U_w = heat transfer coefficient of vertical wall surface, Btu per (hour) (square foot) (degree Fahrenheit).

U_g = heat transfer coefficient of glass, Btu per (hour) (square foot) (degree Fahrenheit).

V_c = rate of introduction of outside air into the attic space by ventilation per square foot of ceiling area (cubic feet per minute per square foot).

Note that this equation takes into account the effect of air interchange that normally takes place through attic vents or louvers that are installed to prevent condensation formation. If the louvers happen to be substantially larger than would normally be called for, an effective approach is simply to assume that the attic temperature is the average of the outdoor and the indoor temperature. Otherwise, using the above formula is simply a matter of substituting the proper numeric values for the formula symbols and working out the mathematics. Two further points should be noted. The area of the roof is that portion that lies within the perimeter of the structure and does not include overhangs. If there are no windows in the attic, those factors can be dropped from the formula.

150

There sometimes are circumstances where an unheated space is not considered as having an intermediate design temperature. Instead, the interior building sections that bound these unheated spaces are treated as though they were fully exposed to the outdoor design temperature. This would be the case with attached rooms having at least two surfaces exposed to the outdoors and fitted with large expanses of glass. Examples are sun porches, solariums, or enclosed patio areas.

HEAT LOSS CALCULATIONS

Calculating the heat loss of residences basically involves first ascertaining individual building section heat losses and then tallying them up. This is done on a room-by-room basis and considers every building section through which heat is lost to the outdoors or to an area of intermediate temperature. There are two main categories of heat loss that must be considered: transmission losses and infiltration losses. The transmission losses consists of heat that is transferred through the various building sections—doors, windows, walls, roofs, and floors—by means of conduction, convection, and radiation. Infiltration losses are comprised of the additional heat required to elevate to room temperature the cold air that filters into the house through cracks, doors, and windows, and also to replace the heat that is transferred out of the house via chimney flues, ventilating fans, doors and windows being opened and closed, and the like.

Calculation Worksheets

As you go about making the heat loss calculations for your house, you will be dealing with a great many individual numbers. They can easily become confusing and the simplest way to keep track of things is to make up a worksheet similar to the one shown in Table 4-3. Each room or space to be heated is considered individually and is listed under the "Room" heading. Under the "Section" heading, list the various building sections for which calculations will be made—including infiltration. The "Area" column represents the net exposed surface area of each of the building sections except on the infiltration line. Infiltration is expressed as air volume in cubic feet per hour. The U column is for the coefficients of heat transmission that you will develop for each section.

The next three columns can be combined into one. Sometimes, however, it is easier to separately list the indoor and outdoor design temperatures and the consequent design temperature difference so that there are no slip-ups in the calculations. The figures entered in "#1 Loss, Btuh" results from multiplying area x U x Δt for the first set of design transmission coefficients that you run. The next two columns (which can be deleted or expanded as you prefer) are for subsequent trial runs to develop comparative figures for heat loss through building sections composed of different materials and having different U values. The last column is for the total heat loss of the room or space.

In the next few sections of the book, I will discuss the details of determining U values for the various building sections. As I do so, you can

Table 4-3. A Worksheet for Heat Loss Calculations.

ROOM	SECTION	AREA	U	U # 2	t_i	t_0	Δt	#1 LOSS Btuh	#2 LOSS Btuh	TOTAL LOSS Btuh
Living	Wall	183	0.075		72	8	80	1098	1098	
	Ceiling	400	0.053	0.026	72	8	80	1696	832	
	Floor	400	0.046		72	8	80	1472	1472	
	Windows	74	0.58		72	8	80	3434	3434	
	Band Joist	48	0.043		72	8	80	165	165	
	Header	15	0.132		72	8	80	158	158	
	Wall	80	0.083		72	32	40	266	266	
	Infil. (1)	2560	0.018		72	8	80	3686	3686	
										#1 - 11975
										#2 - 11111
Kitchen										
Bed #1										
Bed #2										
Etc.										

follow along and enter the specific figures that apply to your own calculations.

Transmission Losses

The bulk of the heat loss calculations involve determining the correct design heat transmission coefficients for the different parts of the structure. After the areas of the sections have also been computed and the Δt has been developed, the coefficients are then used to determine the section heat loss on an hourly basis by multiplying the three factors together. In a modern, well-insulated house, the transmission losses will usually account for the larger portion of the total heat loss of the building.

Walls

The easiest place to start the heat loss calculations is with the walls of the building. The process for determining the U of a wall section is the same as discussed in Chapter 2 and the process is illustrated in Fig. 4-2. For an ordinary frame wall, you would list, in order, the outside surface with an applicable wind speed, the exterior siding, the exterior sheathing, the insulation, the interior wall covering, and the inside surface—with the respective R values for each. For wall constructions of a different nature than shown, simply substitute the correct R values taken from Table 4-4.

In the example shown, the total R value of this wall section is 14.43. Note that this value is for the wall sections between the studs and does not include the insulating value of the studs themselves. Their presence means that a certain portion of the wall area has a somewhat different R value; at each stud, there is actually a different construction. Here you have two courses open to you. You can disregard the effect of the studs, as is sometimes done, or you can include them in your calculations to find an average U for the wall section that takes into account the presence of the studs. The latter course results in a more accurate assessment.

To use this method, set up another list of the wall components. This time omit the insulation value and include the R of the stud thickness (Fig.

4-3). In the case of 2 x 4 studs, the value is 4.38. This changes the total R value of the wall section at the studs to 7.81. Now you have two different wall values: 14.43 between the studs and 7.81 at the studs. The next step is to find the average U of the whole wall. The formula for that is as follows:

$$U_{av} = \frac{S}{100}(U_s) + 1 - \frac{S}{100}(U_i)$$

where
U_{av} = average U value for building section.
U_i = U value for area between framing members.
U_s = U value for area backed by framing members.
S = percentage of area backed by framing members.

The most difficult part of this formula lies in determining S, the actual percentage of area that is backed by framing members. Here it is important to note that in making the calculations the true size of the framing members is used, rather than the nominal size. For example, a two-by-four is not actually 2 inches by 4 inches. That is nominal or trade size (in the old days it was an actual size as well). Today, a two-by-four actually measures approximatley 1½ by 3½ inches. The 1½-inch thickness of the stud is the dimension to use.

Table 4-5 shows the nominal and actual dimensions for common building construction members. Note that the $S/100$ portion of the formula is actually a percentage. In practice, the framing of walls (or other building sections), if of nominal 2-inch thickness, is generally considered to be 20 percent of the total wall area when placed on 16-inch centers and 15 percent of the total wall area when placed on 24-inch centers. (For other spacings or sizes of structural numbers, the percentage should be worked

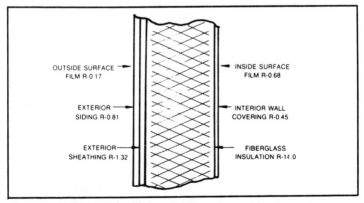

OUTSIDE SURFACE FILM R-0.17

EXTERIOR SIDING R-0.81

EXTERIOR SHEATHING R-1.32

INSIDE SURFACE FILM R-0.68

INTERIOR WALL COVERING R-0.45

FIBERGLASS INSULATION R-14.0

Fig. 4-2. This cross section of a typical exterior wall construction shows the various wall components and their respective R values. The section is taken through the insulation-filled cavity area. The components are added to find the total R and then converted to U.

153

out using the actual dimensions involved.) This reduces the formula to U_{av} equals % (U_s) + (1 - %) (U_i).

Now, let's complete the calculations for the wall sections shown in Tables 4-4 and 4-5. To convert the R values to U values, you must find the reciprocals. The U value of the between-studs wall section is the reciprocal of 14.43 (or 0.0693). The U value of the wall area at the studs is the reciprocal of 7.81, or 0.128. If the area of wall at the studs is assumed to be 20 percent, then obviously the remaining area comprises 80 percent of the wall. Thus, U_{av} equals 0.2 (0.128) plus 0.8(0.0693) (which equals 0.081).

This exercise points up an interesting fact that is frequently overlooked during the process of deciding what insulation to use and where to put it in house walls. Note the substantial difference between the heat loss through the insulated wall sections and through the area backed by stud framing. The heat loss at the studs is relatively substantial and serves to diminish the overall thermal effectiveness of the wall by a fair amount. To counter this, a fairly common current practice is to substitute a high-R-value rigid insulation sheathing board for ordinary exterior sheathing. This covers the stud framing on the outside and substantially improves the heat loss situation through them. The insulating sheathing improves the thermal characteristics of the between-studs wall area as well. The differential is still proportionate. The U_{av}, however, is substantially improved.

Now we can relate this figure to the heat loss worksheet. Following the general procedure just discussed, you can work out an appropriate U_{av} for each exposed wall section of your house, room by room. Where the construction of the wall sections differs in one room (the front wall of a living room might be brick veneered, while the side wall might be wood-sided), you can list the different wall sections separately and call them wall A and wall B (or whatever). Or you can use the formula for determining overall U given in Chapter 2 and enter a single U_o that accounts for the two (or more) wall sections.

The next step is to determine the net wall area. Measure the gross wall area first—multiply its overall length by its overall height—and make a note of the figure. Then measure the sizes of all of the openings in the wall, such as doors, windows, or vent ports, and tally them all up. Subtract the square footage of non-wall sections from the gross wall area and the result is the net wall area. Enter that figure in the proper column. Enter the correct Δt in its column and multiply the three figures to arrive at the Btuh loss.

If you want to assess the transmission loss of a wall section constructed in a different way or perhaps insulated to a higher R value, run through the same series of calculations using the new figures and enter the result in the second Btuh loss column. This will give you an easy reference for comparing the cost-effectiveness of sections built with different materials or fitted with more or less insulation.

There is also another method, somewhat faster and easier, to determine the result of adding insulation to a given building section. This

Table 4-4. Thermal Properties of Various Common Building Materials (Reprinted with Permission from the 1977 Fundamentals Volume, ASHRAE HANDBOOK & Product Directory).

Description	Density (lb/ft³)	Customary Unit				Specific Heat, Btu/(lb)(deg F)	SI Unit	
		Conductivity (k)	Conductance (C)	Resistance[b] (R) Per inch thickness (1/k)	Resistance[b] (R) For thickness listed (1/C)		Resistance[b] (R) (m·K)/W	Resistance[b] (R) (m²·K)/W
BUILDING BOARD								
Boards, Panels, Subflooring, Sheathing								
Woodboard Panel Products								
Asbestos-cement board	120	4.0	—	0.25	—	0.24	1.73	
Asbestos-cement board ....0.125 in.	120	—	33.00	—	0.03			0.005
Asbestos-cement board ....0.25 in.	120	—	16.50	—	0.06			0.01
Gypsum or plaster board ....0.375 in.	50	—	3.10	—	0.32	0.26		0.06
Gypsum or plaster board ....0.5 in.	50	—	2.22	—	0.45			0.08
Gypsum or plaster board ....0.625 in.	50	—	1.78	—	0.56			0.10
Plywood (Douglas Fir)	34	0.80	—	1.25	—	0.29	8.66	
Plywood (Douglas Fir) ....0.25 in.	34	—	3.20	—	0.31			0.05
Plywood (Douglas Fir) ....0.375 in.	34	—	2.13	—	0.47			0.08
Plywood (Douglas Fir) ....0.5 in.	34	—	1.60	—	0.62			0.11
Plywood (Douglas Fir) ....0.625 in.	34	—	1.29	—	0.77			0.19

155

Table 4-4. Thermal Properties of Various Common Building Materials (Reprinted with Permission from the 1977 Fundamentals Volume, ASHRAE HANDBOOK & Produce Directory) (continued from page 155).

Description	Density (lb/ft³)	Conductivity (k)	Conductance (C)	Resistance (R) Per inch thickness (1/k)	Resistance (R) For thickness listed (1/C)	Specific Heat, Btu/(lb)(deg F)	SI Resistance (R) (m·K)/W	SI Resistance (R) (m²·K)/W
Plywood or wood panels .... 0.75 in.	34	—	1.07	—	0.93	0.29		0.16
Vegetable Fiber Board								
Sheathing, regular density .... 0.5 in.	18	—	0.76	—	1.32	0.31		0.23
.... 0.78125 in.	18	—	0.49	—	2.06	0.31		0.36
Sheathing intermediate density ...... 0.5 in.	22	—	0.82	—	1.22	0.31		0.21
Nail-base sheathing .... 0.5 in.	25	—	0.88	—	1.14	0.31		0.20
Shingle backer .... 0.375 in.	18	—	1.06	—	0.94	0.31		0.17
Shingle backer .... 0.3125 in.	18	—	1.28	—	0.78			0.14
Sound deadening board .... 0.5 in.	15	—	0.74	—	1.35	0.30		0.24
Tile and lay-in panels, plain or acoustic	18	0.40	—	2.50	—	0.14	17.33	
.... 0.5 in.	18	—	0.80	—	1.25			0.22
.... 0.75 in.	18	—	0.53	—	1.89			0.33
Laminated paperboard	30	0.50	—	2.00	—	0.33	13.86	
Homogeneous board from repulped paper	30	0.50	—	2.00	—	0.28	13.86	
Hardboard								
Medium density	50	0.73	—	1.37	—	0.31	9.49	
High density, service temp. service underlay	55	0.82	—	1.22	—	0.32	8.46	
High density, std. tempered	63	1.00	—	1.00	—	0.32	6.93	
Particleboard								
Low density	37	0.54	—	1.85	—	0.31	12.82	
Medium density	50	0.94	—	1.06	—	0.31	7.35	
High density	62.5	1.18	—	0.85	—	0.31	5.89	
Underlayment .... 0.625 in.	40	—	1.22	—	0.82	0.29		0.14
Wood subfloor .... 0.75 in.		—	1.06	—	0.94	0.33		0.17

Vapor—permeable felt	—	—	16.70	—	0.06	—	0.01
Vapor—seal, 2 layers of mopped 15-lb felt	—	—	8.35	—	0.12	—	0.02
Vapor—seal, plastic film	—	—	—	—	Negl.	—	
FINISH FLOORING MATERIALS							
Carpet and fibrous pad	—	—	0.48	—	2.08	0.34	0.37
Carpet and rubber pad	—	—	0.81	—	1.23	0.33	0.22
Cork tile . . . . 0.125 in.	—	—	3.60	—	0.28	0.48	0.05
Terrazzo . . . . 1 in.	—	—	12.50	—	0.08	0.19	0.01
Tile—asphalt, linoleum, vinyl, rubber	—	—	20.00	—	0.05	0.30	0.01
vinyl asbestos						0.24	
ceramic						0.19	
Wood, hardwood finish . . . . . . 0.75 in.	—	—	1.47	—	0.68	—	0.12
INSULATING MATERIALS							
Blanket and Batt							
Mineral Fiber, fibrous form processed from rock, slag, or glass						0.17–0.23	
approx.[c] 2–2.75 in.	0.3–2.0	—	0.143	—	7[d]		1.23
approx.[c] 3–3.5 in.	0.3–2.0	—	0.091	—	11[d]		1.94
approx.[c] 5.50–6.5	0.3–2.0	—	0.053	—	19[d]		3.35
approx.[d] 6–7 in.	0.3–2.0	—	0.045	—	22[d]		3.87
approx.[d] 8.5 in.	0.3–2.0	—	0.033	—	30[d]		5.28
Board and Slabs							
Cellular glass	8.5	0.38	—	2.63	—	0.24	18.23
Glass fiber, organic bonded	4–9	0.25	—	4.00	—	0.23	27.72
Expanded rubber (rigid)	4.5	0.22	—	4.55	—	0.40	31.53
Expanded polystyrene extruded Cut cell surface	1.8	0.25	—	4.00	—	0.29	27.72
Expanded polystyrene extruded Smooth skin surface	2.2	0.20	—	5.00	—	0.29	34.65
Expanded polystyrene extruded	3.5	0.19	—	5.26	—	0.29	36.45
Expanded polystyrene, molded beads	1.0	0.28	—	3.57	—		24.74
Expanded polyurethane[f] (R-11 exp.) (Thickness 1 in. or greater)	1.5, 2.5	0.16	—	6.25	—	0.38	43.82

Table 4-4. Thermal Properties of Various Common Building Materials (Reprinted with Permission from the 1977 Fundamentals Volume, ASHRAE HANDBOOK & Produce Directory) (continued from page 157).

Description	Density (lb/ft³)	Customary Unit						SI Unit	
		Conductivity (k)	Conductance (C)	Resistance (R)		Specific Heat, Btu/(lb·deg F)		Resistance (R)	
				Per inch thickness (1/k)	For thickness listed (1/C)			(m·K)/W	(m²·K)/W
Mineral fiber with resin binder	15	0.29	—	3.45	—	0.17		23.91	
Mineral fiberboard, wet felted									
Core or roof insulation	16-17	0.34	—	2.94	—	0.19		20.38	
Acoustical tile	18	0.35	—	2.86	—			19.82	
Acoustical tile	21	0.37	—	2.70	—			18.71	
Mineral fiberboard, wet molded									
Acoustical tile	23	0.42	—	2.38	—	0.14		16.49	
Wood or cane fiberboard									
Acoustical tile .... 0.5 in.	—	—	0.80	—	1.25	• 0.31			0.22
Acoustical tile .... 0.75 in.	—	—	0.53	—	1.89				0.33
Interior finish (plank, tile)	15	0.35	—	2.86	—	0.32		19.82	
Wood shredded (cemented in preformed slabs)	22	0.60	—	1.67	—	0.31		11.57	
LOOSE FILL									
Cellulosic insulation (milled paper or wood pulp)	2.3-3.2	0.27-0.32	—	3.13-3.70	—	0.33		21.69-25.64	
Sawdust or shavings	8.0-15.0	0.45	—	2.22	—	0.33		15.39	
Wood fiber, softwoods	2.0-3.5	0.30	—	3.33	—	0.33		23.08	
Perlite, expanded	5.0-8.0	0.37	—	2.70	—	0.26		18.71	
Mineral fiber (rock, slag or glass)									
approx. 3.75-5 in.	0.6-2.0	—	—	—	11	0.17			1.94
approx. 6.5-8.75 in.	0.6-2.0	—	—	—	19				3.35
approx. 7.5-10 in.	0.6-2.0	—	—	—	22				3.87
approx. 10.25-13.75 in.	0.6-2.0	—	—	—	30				5.28

ROOF INSULATION[b]

Preformed, for use above deck

Different roof insulations are available in different thicknesses to provide the design C values listed.[h] Consult individual manufacturers for actual *thickness of their material.*

MASONRY MATERIALS

Description	Density, lb/ft³	Conductivity (k)	Conductance (C)	Resistance 1/k	Resistance 1/C	Specific Heat
ROOF INSULATION[b] (preformed, above deck)	—	—	0.72 to 0.12	—	1.39 to 8.33	0.24 to 1.47
CONCRETES						
Cement mortar	116	5.0	—	0.20	1.39	0.21
Gypsum-fiber concrete 87.5% gypsum, 12.5% wood chips	51	1.66	—	0.60	4.16	
Lightweight aggregates including expanded shale, clay or slate; expanded slags; cinders; pumice; vermiculite; also cellular concretes	120	5.2	—	0.19	1.32	
	100	3.6	—	0.28	1.94	
	80	2.5	—	0.40	2.77	
	60	1.7	—	0.59	4.09	
	40	1.15	—	0.86	5.96	
	30	0.90	—	1.11	7.69	
	20	0.70	—	1.43	9.91	
Perlite, expanded	40	0.93	—	1.08	7.48	0.32
	30	0.71	—	1.41	9.77	
	20	0.50	—	2.00	13.86	
Sand and gravel or stone aggregate (oven dried)	140	9.0	—	0.11	0.76	0.22
Sand and gravel or stone aggregate (not dried)	140	12.0	—	0.08	0.55	
Stucco	116	5.0	—	0.20	1.39	
MASONRY UNITS						
Brick, common[i]	120	5.0	—	0.20	1.39	0.19
Brick, face[i]	130	9.0	—	0.11	0.76	
Clay tile, hollow:						
1 cell deep .... 3 in.	—	—	1.25	—	0.80	0.21
1 cell deep .... 4 in.	—	—	0.90	—	1.11	
2 cells deep .... 6 in.	—	—	0.66	—	1.52	
2 cells deep .... 8 in.	—	—	0.54	—	1.85	
2 cells deep .... 10 in.	—	—	0.45	—	2.22	
3 cells deep .... 12 in.	—	—	0.40	—	2.50	

159

Description	Customary Unit						SI Unit	
	Density (lb/ft³)	Conductivity (k)	Conductance (C)	Resistance[b](R)		Specific Heat, Btu/(lb) (deg F)	Resistance[b] (R)	
				Per inch thickness (1/k)	For thickness listed (1/C)		(m·K)/W	(m²·K)/W
Concrete blocks, three oval core:								
Sand and gravel aggregate .... 4 in.	—	—	1.40	—	0.71	0.22		0.13
.... 8 in.	—	—	0.90	—	1.11			0.20
.... 12 in.	—	—	0.78	—	1.28			0.23
Cinder aggregate .... 3 in.	—	—	1.16	—	0.86	0.21		0.15
.... 4 in.	—	—	0.90	—	1.11			0.20
.... 8 in.	—	—	0.58	—	1.72			0.30
.... 12 in.	—	—	0.53	—	1.89			0.33
Lightweight aggregate .... 3 in.	—	—	0.79	—	1.27	0.21		0.22
(expanded shale, clay, slate .... 4 in.	—	—	0.67	—	1.50			0.26
or slag; pumice) .... 8 in.	—	—	0.50	—	2.00			0.35
.... 12 in.	—	—	0.44	—	2.27			0.40
Concrete blocks, rectangular core.*ʲ								
Sand and gravel aggregate								
2 core, 8 in. 36 lb. k*·;	—	—	0.96	—	1.04	0.22		0.18
Same with filled cores]*	—	—	0.52	—	1.93	0.22		0.34
Lightweight aggregate (expanded shale, clay, slate or slag; pumice):								
3 core, 6 in. 19 lb. k*	—	—	0.61	—	1.65	0.21		0.29
Same with filled cores]*	—	—	0.33	—	2.99			0.53
2 core, 8 in. 24 lb. k*·	—	—	0.46	—	2.18			0.38
Same with filled cores]*	—	—	0.20	—	5.03			0.89
3 core, 12 in. 38 lb. k*	—	—	0.40	—	2.48			0.44
Same with filled cores]*	—	—	0.17	—	5.82			1.02
Stone, lime or sand.	—	12.50	—	0.08	—	0.19	0.55	
Gypsum partition tile:								
3 × 12 × 30 in. solid	—	—	0.79	—	1.26	0.19		0.22

PLASTERING MATERIALS

Material	Density							
Cement plaster, sand aggregate	116	5.0	—	0.20	—	0.20	1.39	0.01
Sand aggregate .... 0.375 in.	—	—	13.3	—	0.08	0.20		0.03
Sand aggregate .... 0.75 in.	—	—	6.66	—	0.15	0.20		
Gypsum plaster:								
Lightweight aggregate .... 0.5 in.	45	—	3.12	—	0.32	0.32		0.06
Lightweight aggregate .... 0.625 in.	45	—	2.67	—	0.39			0.07
Lightweight agg. on metal lath ..... 0.75 in.	—	—	2.13	—	0.47			0.08
Perlite aggregate	45	1.5	—	0.67	—		4.64	
Sand aggregate .... 0.5 in.	105	5.6	11.10	0.18	0.09	0.20	1.25	0.02
Sand aggregate .... 0.625 in.	105	—	9.10	—	0.11			0.02
Sand aggregate on metal lath ...... 0.75 in.	105	—	7.70	—	0.13			0.02
Vermiculite aggregate	45	1.7	—	0.59	—		4.09	

ROOFING

Material	Density							
Asbestos-cement shingles	120	—	4.76	—	0.21	0.24		0.04
Asphalt roll roofing	70	—	6.50	—	0.15	0.36		0.03
Asphalt shingles	70	—	2.27	—	0.44	0.30		0.08
Built-up roofing .... 0.375 in.	70	—	3.00	—	0.33	0.35		0.06
Slate .... 0.5 in.	—	—	20.00	—	0.05	0.30		0.01
Wood shingles, plain and plastic film faced	—	—	1.06	—	0.94	0.31		0.17

SIDING MATERIALS (On Flat Surface)

Shingles

Material	Density							
Asbestos-cement	120	—	4.75	—	0.21			0.04
Wood, 16 in., 7.5 exposure	—	—	1.15	—	0.87	0.31		0.15
Wood, double, 16-in., 12-in. exposure	—	—	0.84	—	1.19	0.28		0.21
Wood, plus insul. backer board, 0.3125 in.	—	—	0.71	—	1.40	0.31		0.25

Siding

Material	Density							
Asbestos-cement, 0.25 in., lapped	—	—	4.76	—	0.21	0.24		0.04
Asphalt roll siding	—	—	6.50	—	0.15	0.35		0.03
Asphalt insulating siding (0.5 in. bed.)	—	—	0.69	—	1.46	0.35		0.26
Hardboard siding, 0.4375 in.	40	1.49	—	0.67	—	0.28	4.65	
Wood, drop, 1 × 8 in.	—	—	1.27	—	0.79	0.28		0.14
Wood, bevel, 0.5 × 8 in., lapped	—	—	1.23	—	0.81	0.28		0.14
Wood, bevel, 0.75 × 10 in., lapped	—	—	0.95	—	1.05	0.28		0.18
Wood, plywood, 0.375 in., lapped	—	—	1.59	—	0.59	0.29		0.10

Table 4-4. Thermal Properties of Various Common Building Materials (Reprinted with Permission from the 1977 Fundamentals Volume, ASHRAE HANDBOOK & Produce Directory) (continued from page 161).

Description	Customary Unit						SI Unit	
	Density (lb/ft³)	Conductivity (k)	Conductance (C)	Resistance[b] (R)		Specific Heat, Btu/(lb) (deg F)	Resistance[b] (R)	
				Per inch thickness (1/k)	For thickness listed (1/C)		(m·K)/W	(m²·K)/W
Aluminum or Steel[m], over sheathing								
Hollow-backed	—	—	1.61	—	0.61	0.29		0.11
Insulating-board backed nominal 0.375 in.	—	—	0.55	—	1.82	0.32		0.32
Insulating-board backed nominal 0.375 in., foil backed	—	—	0.34	—	2.96			0.52
Architectural glass	—	—	10.00	—	0.10	0.20		0.02
WOODS								
Maple, oak, and similar hardwoods	45	1.10	—	0.91	—	0.30	6.31	
Fir, pine, and similar softwoods	32	0.80	—	1.25	—	0.33	8.66	
Fir, pine, and similar softwoods . . . 0.75 in.	32	—	1.06	—	0.94	0.33		0.17
. . . 1.5 in.		—	0.53	—	1.89			0.33
. . . 2.5 in.		—	0.32	—	3.12			0.60
. . . 3.5 in.		—	0.23	—	4.35			0.75

Notes for Table

a Representative values for dry materials were selected by ASHRAE TC4.4, Insulation and Moisture Barriers. They are intended as design (not specification) values for materials in normal use. For properties of a particular product, use the value supplied by the manufacturer or by unbiased tests

b Resistance values are the reciprocals of C before rounding off C to two decimal places.

c Also see Insulating Materials, Board.

d Does not include paper backing and facing, if any. Where insulation forms a boundary (reflective or otherwise) of an air space, see Tables 1 and 2 for the insulating value of air space for the appropriate effective emittance and temperature conditions of the space.   Insulation is produced by different densities; therefore, there

e Conductivity varies with fiber diameter.   is a wide variation in thickness for the same R-value among manufacturers. No effort should be made to relate any specific R-value to any specific thickness. Commercial thicknesses generally available range from 2 to 8.5.

f Values are for aged board stock.

g Insulating values of acoustical tile vary, depending on density of the board and on type, size, and depth of perforations.

h The U. S. Department of Commerce, *Simplified Practice Recommendation for Thermal Conductance Factors for Preformed Above-Deck Roof Insulation*, No. R 257-55, recognizes the specification of roof insulation on the basis of the C-values shown. Roof insulation is made in thicknesses to meet these values.

i Face brick and common brick do not always have these specific densities. When density is different from that shown, there will be a change in thermal conductivity.

j Data on rectangular core concrete blocks differ from the above data on oval core blocks, due to core configuration, different mean temperatures, and possibly differences in unit weights. Weight data on the oval core blocks tested are not available.

k Weights of units approximately 7.625 in. high and 15.75 in. long. These weights are given as a means of describing the blocks tested, but conductance values are all for 1 ft² of area.

l Vermiculite, perlite, or mineral wool insulation. Where insulation is used, vapor barriers or other precautions must be considered to keep insulation dry.

m Values for metal siding applied over flat surfaces vary widely, depending on amount of ventilation of air space beneath the siding; whether airspace is reflective or nonreflective; and on thickness, type, and application of insulating backing-board used. Values given are averages for use as design guides, and were obtained from several guarded hotbox tests (ASTM C236) or calibrated hotbox (BSS 77) on hollow-backed types and types made using backing-boards of wood fiber, foamed plastic, and glass fiber. Departures of ±50% or more from the values given may occur.

163

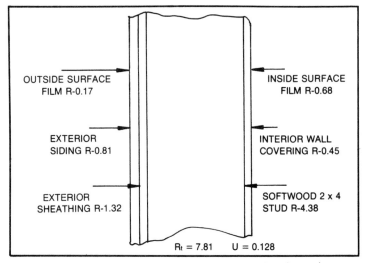

Fig. 4-3. This cross section of a typical wall construction shows the same wall as in Fig. 4-2, but is taken through a stud. Note the difference in thermal performance of the two parts of the same wall.

method makes use of the values listed in Table 4-6 but has its greatest use where the U of the given building section is no less than the lowest value listed. That value, in the lower left hand corner, is 0.08. Notice that the figures progressing from left to right across the bottom line diminish only slightly in value as the amount of added insulation increases greatly. This points up another important fact. As you add increasing amounts of thermal insulation to a building section that already has a good U value, the benefits derived in the form of an even better U value become less and less pronounced (Fig. 4-4) until finally you reach a point where the U value can be lowered no further regardless of how much the R value is increased. Of course, there is a practical point of diminishing returns long before that state is reached. But for building sections with a relatively high U value (relatively low R value), the table works very well.

For example, if you know the U value of a given building section to be 0.20 or the R value to be 5.00, you can quickly determine what the new U value would be with the addition of certain R values of insulation. Read down the left-hand column until you find 0.20 and then read across the line to the right. The addition of insulation with an R value of 4 results in a U of 0.11, R-6 results in 0.09, and so on. Conversely, if you want specifically to raise the value of an existing U-0.20 wall to 0.06, you can readily see that supplimentary insulation to the value of R-12 would be required.

It is also possible to do a certain amount of interpolating within the table. More definitive figures could be arrived at by actually making the calculations. To illustrate, suppose that you want a quick comparison of the U value of the wall construction shown in Tables 4-4 and 4-5 with another wall made the same way but with the addition of a layer of R-4 isocyanurate rigid insulating sheathing.

The between-studs U of the original wall is 0.0693 (approximately 0.07). That figure first appears in the table in the "$R = 12$" column (on the 0.70 line). You want to add R-4; adding that to R-12 equals R-16 (the next column to the right). There you see that the resulting U would be on the order of 0.06. Following the same process for the U-0.128 stud-backed wall area, you can use the U-0.10 line of the table. This shows that an addition of R-4 would result in U-0.07. Working out the U_{av} would result in 0.062 (a substantial improvement).

Actually, calculating the two U values separately is not necessary. The U_{av} of the original wall is .081. Using the table again, the U-0.08 line shows that the addition of R-4 results in a U of 0.06.

The U values developed in the previous examples are predicated on an outside average wind velocity of 15 mph. But suppose that the average velocity at your site is 25 mph? In that case, the U of the wall (or other) sections should be modified to reflect that fact. Use an appropriate figure from Table 4-2.

First work out the overall U of the section on the basis of 15 mph wind. Let's say it is 0.081. Find the closest U in the left-hand column of the table, 0.080, and read across to the 25 mph column. The figure listed is still 0.080 (no change). There's no change for any wind velocity between 10 and 30 mph.

If you'll examine the table, you'll notice that the changes are very minor for U values below 0.100 and below 0.050 they are so infinitesimal

Table 4-5. The Nominal or Trade Sizes of Building Framing Members.

TYPE	NOMINAL	ACTUAL
Dimension	2 x 2	1 ½ x 1 ½
Lumber	2 x 3	1 ½ x 2 ½
	2 x 4	1 ½ x 3 ½
	2 x 6	1 ½ x 5 ½
	2 x 8	1 ½ x 7 ¼
	2 x 10	1 ½ x 9 ¼
	2 x 12	1 ½ x 11 ¼
	Over 12	1 ½ x Off ¾
	3 x —	2 ½ x As above
	4 x —	3 ½ x As above
Timbers	5 x —	Off ½ x Off ½
	and up	
Decking	2 x 6	1 ½ x 5
	2 x 8	1 ½ x 6 ¾
	2 x 10	1 ½ x 8 ¾
	2 x 12	1 ½ x 10 ¾
	3 x 6	2 ½ x 5 ¼
	4 x 6	3 ½ x 5 ¼

Table 4-6. Determination of U-Value Resulting from Addition of Insulation to the Total Area[e] of a Given Building Section (Reprinted with Permission from the 1977 Fundamentals Volume, ASHRAE HANDBOOK & Product Directory).

Given Building Section Property[a,b]		Added R[c,d,e]						
		$R = 4$	$R = 6$	$R = 8$	$R = 12$	$R = 16$	$R = 20$	$R = 24$
U	R	U	U	U	U	U	U	U
1.00	1.00	0.20	0.14	0.11	0.08	0.06	0.05	0.04
0.90	1.11	0.20	0.14	0.11	0.08	0.06	0.05	0.04
0.80	1.25	0.19	0.14	0.11	0.08	0.06	0.05	0.04
0.70	1.43	0.18	0.13	0.11	0.07	0.06	0.05	0.04
0.60	1.67	0.18	0.13	0.10	0.07	0.06	0.05	0.04
0.50	2.00	0.17	0.13	0.10	0.07	0.06	0.05	0.04
0.40	2.50	0.15	0.12	0.10	0.07	0.05	0.04	0.04
0.30	3.33	0.14	0.11	0.09	0.07	0.05	0.04	0.04
0.20	5.00	0.11	0.09	0.08	0.06	0.05	0.04	0.03
0.10	10.00	0.07	0.06	0.06	0.05	0.04	0.03	0.03
0.08	12.50	0.06	0.05	0.05	0.04	0.04	0.03	0.03

[a] For U- or R-values not shown in the table, interpolate as necessary.
[b] Enter column 1 with U or R of the design building section.
[c] Under appropriate column heading for added R, find U-value of resulting design section.
[d] If the insulation occupies previously considered air space, an adjustment must be made in the given building section R-value.

that no entries are made. This is because sections with high thermal resistance are not subject to conductive and convective heat losses. They are also less prone to infiltration of outside air than are poorly insulated sections with low thermal performance. For all practical purposes, wind velocities of anywhere from 0 to 30 mph have no effect upon well constructed building sections with U values of 0.100 or better. Below that value, the effects of wind are of increasingly important consequence. Building sections constructed in cold climates today invariably have U values of greater than 0.100. Elsewhere, the possibility of modification should be considered.

Doors

If the exterior doors of your house approximate those in Table 4-7, you can use the U values given. Enter the appropriate value on your worksheet. Compute the total door area by multiplying height times width and rounding off to the next highest square foot. Note that the door thicknesses are nominal and not actual. Except as specified in Note b, the doors do not contain panes of glass. The inside and outside surface resistances have been computed into the listed figures.

There are a great many different varieties of exterior doors and a more accurate figure can be obtained by making calculations for each individual type of door. This can be done for wood doors by using the R value of hardwood or softwood (see Table 4-4). A solid pine door 2 inches thick would be R-2.50, plus the inside and outside surface resistances of 0.17 and 0.68 respectively, for a total R of 3.35. The reciprocal equals U-0.299. A 2-inch oak door has a lesser R value of 1.82 and its U value would be 0.375. If the door is a panel type where the stiles and rails are thicker than the panels, you can assess the U value first of the door frame and then of the average thickness of the panels, and find U_{av} for the door as a whole. Accuracy in figuring the respective surface areas is important.

Perhaps you've heard this old child's riddle. When is a door not a door? The answer—when its ajar. But in making heat loss calculations, a door is not a door when it contains more than 50 percent glass—then it is a window. If the total area of an exterior door—whether an entry door or a storm door—is less than half glass, calculate the two elements separately and then compute for U_{av}, and be sure to include the inside and outside surface resistances.

If the door area is more than half glass, treat it as though it were a window. Exterior doors are frequently considered as being all glass if they contain any glass at all. If the exterior door—whether it contains glass or not—is fitted with a storm door, treat both doors as though they comprise one building section.

The total R would then consist of the following elements (working from the outside to the inside): outside surface resistance; storm door

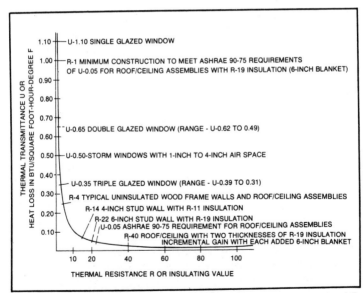

Fig. 4-4. As this graph shows, the addition of increasing amounts of R value—whether insulation or other materials—results in ever-diminishing practical thermal effectiveness.

Table 4-7. Coefficients of Transmission (Reprinted with Permission from the 1977 Fundamentals Volume, ASHRAE HANDBOOK & Product Directory).

	Btu per (hr· ft² · F)			
	Winter			Summer
	Solid Wood, No Storm Door	Storm Door[b]		No Storm Door
Thickness[a]		Wood	Metal	
1-in.	0.64	0.30	0.39	0.61
1.25-in.	0.55	0.28	0.34	0.53
1.5-in.	0.49	0.27	0.33	0.47
2-in.	0.43	0.24	0.29	0.42
	Steel Door[14]			
1.75 in.				
A[c]	0.59	—	—	0.58
B[d]	0.19	—	—	0.18
C[e]	0.47	—	—	0.46

[a]Nominal thickness.
[b]Values for wood storm doors are for approximately 50% glass; for metal storm door values apply for any percent of glass.
[c]A = Mineral fiber core (2 lb/ft³).
[d]B = Solid urethane foam core with thermal break.
[e]C = Solid polystyrene core with thermal break.

material; inside surface resistance; nonreflective air space (the space between the two doors); inside surface resistance; entry door material; and inside surface resistance (Fig. 4-5). Both inside and outside surfaces are vertical with horizontal heat loss. The inside surfaces would all be in still air. The outside surface would be subject to moving air at an appropriate wind velocity (commonly 15 mph).

Windows

Of all of the elements found in residential construction, panes of glass are by far the least effective barriers to heat. As you can see in Fig. 4-5, the U of a vertical pane of single-thickness glass is a dismal 1.10. Horizontal glass is even worse. It has a U of 1.23 (both figures for winter conditions). All glazed areas—whether fitted with glass, plastic, or glass block—should be carefully calculated for heat loss. In some cases, you might be able to use specific values for thermal transmission that have been developed by actual tests by the manufacturer of the window units you plan to use. When such figures are available, they are the best ones to base your calculations upon. Failing that, you can take the figures for your calculations directly from Table 4-8. Inside and outside surface film resistances are included in these values. The values are given in Btu per hour per square foot per degree F.

When using the table, first choose the kinds of glazing that best approximate the types you will actually use or that presently exist in the house. If your glazing is somewhat different, you can safely interpolate or select the next highest appropriate value to give yourself a slight safety margin. Calculate the glass area on the basis of the gross size of the window opening rather than the area of the glass itself. In other words, include the sash if there is any.

As necessary, use the adjustment factors in Part C of Table 4-8 to compensate for the sash. If the glazing is at an angle instead of either vertical or horizontal, as is usually the case with skylights and roof windows, you have a couple of choices. You can consider the glazing as being horizontal and use the higher values as a safety margin or you can interpolate between the vertical and horizontal values. A single-glazed roof window in a 45-degree roof section could be reasonably assessed at 1.165. That is the average of the vertical and horizontal values.

As with the previous construction sections, the window U should be set down in the appropriate column of the worksheet. If there are two or more different kinds of glazing in a particular room, you can either list them individually or lump all of the window calculations together in the form of U_{av}. Generally, the former course is the easiest. Figure the window area, and multiply by the U and Δt to find the total Btuh loss.

There's a temptation here to make some informal adjustments to window heat losses by making allowances for certain factors that might apply to a given house design. For instance, it's obvious that a great deal of solar heat gain can be realized, even during the winter, if several large windows are installed in a south-facing wall. It is also possible to fit the windows with one or another of the new varieties of thermal insulating shutters, insulating drapes or some other similar heat-saving device. Some of these devices work remarkably well and substantial savings in heat loss can be realized. However, they only work when they are in place and they never are on a 24-hour-a-day basis during the heating season.

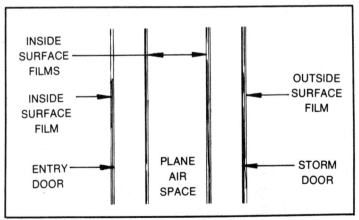

Fig. 4-5. Cross section through a typical entry door/storm door arrangement showing the elements that should be considered in developing a U value for the section.

Table 4-8. Coefficients of Transmission and Adjustment Factors for Various Types of Vertical and Horizontal Glazing Panels and Windows (Reprinted with Permission from the 1977 Fundamentals Volume, ASHRAE HANDBOOK & Product Directory).

These values are for heat transfer from air to air, Btu/(hr · ft² · F).

PART A—VERTICAL PANELS (EXTERIOR WINDOWS, SLIDING PATIO DOORS, AND PARTITIONS)—FLAT GLASS, GLASS BLOCK, AND PLASTIC SHEET

Description	Exterior[a] Winter	Exterior[a] Summer	Interior
Flat Glass[b]			
single glass	1.10	1.04	0.73
insulating glass—double[c]			
0.1875-in. air space[d]	0.62	0.65	0.51
0.25-in. air space[d]	0.58	0.61	0.49
0.5-in. air space[e]	0.49	0.56	0.46
0.5-in. air space, low emittance coating[f]			
$e = 0.20$	0.32	0.38	0.32
$e = 0.40$	0.38	0.45	0.38
$e = 0.60$	0.43	0.51	0.42
insulating glass—triple[c]			
0.25-in. air spaces[d]	0.39	0.44	0.38
0.5-in. air spaces[g]	0.31	0.39	0.30
storm windows			
1-in. to 4-in. air space[d]	0.50	0.50	0.44

PART B—HORIZONTAL PANELS (SKYLIGHTS)—FLAT GLASS, GLASS BLOCK, AND PLASTIC DOMES

Description	Exterior[a] Winter[i]	Exterior[a] Summer[j]	Interior[f]
Flat Glass[e]			
single glass	1.23	0.83	0.96
insulating glass—double[c]			
0.1875-in. air space[d]	0.70	0.57	0.62
0.25-in. air space[d]	0.65	0.54	0.59
0.5-in. air space[e]	0.59	0.49	0.56
0.5-in. air space, low emittance coating[f]			
$e = 0.20$	0.48	0.36	0.39
$e = 0.40$	0.52	0.42	0.45
$e = 0.60$	0.56	0.46	0.50
Glass Block[h]			
11 × 11 × 3 in. thick with cavity divider	0.53	0.35	0.44
12 × 12 × 4 in. thick with cavity divider	0.51	0.34	0.42

Plastic Sheet

Description			
single glazed			
0.125-in. thick	1.06	0.98	—
0.25-in. thick	0.96	0.89	—
0.5-in. thick	0.81	0.76	—
insulating unit—double^c			
0.25-in. air space^d	0.55	0.56	—
0.5-in. air space^c	0.43	0.45	—
Glass Block^h			
6 × 6 × 4 in. thick	0.60	0.57	0.46
8 × 8 × 4 in. thick	0.56	0.54	0.44
—with cavity divider	0.48	0.46	0.38
12 × 12 × 4 in. thick	0.52	0.50	0.41
—with cavity divider	0.44	0.42	0.36
12 × 12 × 2 in. thick	0.60	0.57	0.46
Plastic Domes^k			
single-walled	1.15	0.80	—
double-walled	0.70	0.46	—

PART C—ADJUSTMENT FACTORS FOR VARIOUS WINDOW AND SLIDING PATIO DOOR TYPES (MULTIPLY U VALUES IN PARTS A AND B BY THESE FACTORS)

Description	Single Glass	Double or Triple Glass	Storm Windows
Windows			
All Glass^l	1.00	1.00	1.00
Wood Sash—80% Glass	0.90	0.95	0.90
Wood Sash—60% Glass	0.80	0.85	0.80
Metal Sash—80% Glass	1.00	1.20^m	1.20^m
Sliding Patio Doors			
Wood Frame	0.95	1.00	—
Metal Frame	1.00	1.10^m	—

a See Part C for adjustment for various window and sliding patio door types.
b Emittance of uncooled glass surface = 0.84.
c Double and triple refer to the number of lights of glass.
d 0.125-in. glass.
e 0.25-in. glass.
f Coating on either glass surface facing air space; all other glass surfaces uncoated.
g Window design: 0.25-in. glass—0.125-in. glass—0.25-in. glass.
h Dimensions are nominal.
i For heat flow up.
j For heat flow down.
k Based on area of opening, not total surface area.
l Refers to windows with negligible opaque area.
m Values will be less than these when metal sash and frame incorporate thermal breaks. In some thermal break designs, U-values will be equal to or less than those for the glass. Window manufacturers should be consulted for specific data.

Even those that operate automatically don't continuously reduce the heat loss; if they did, you'd be living in a cave all winter. And of course solar radiation gain through windows in an otherwise conventional house is a fickle and chancy gain that is difficult to compute. The best bet is to calculate window areas in the normal way and rely upon solar heat gain and thermal window protectors to provide whatever savings they might (unless you're specifically designing for passive solar heat input). Remember that the values you work out or take from tables can be only approximate. It is assumed that the window is in a normal location and is uneffected by any unusual influences. Often as not there *are* some influences. It is common practice to locate heat units or outlets directly below large windows. In that case, every time the heat is on there can be a flow of warm air across the glass. This changes the heat loss characteristics. Wherever there is an unusual window situation and the thermal effectiveness of the glazing may be affected by unusual heat, cold, or air movement, the calculations for the particular window might have to be modified to suit the circumstances. This is a judgment that should be approached with some caution.

Floors

For purposes of heat loss calculations, floors are considered to be of the conventional wood frame construction. Concrete slab floors are considered separately because their thermal characteristics are entirely different. As far as the building section itself is concerned, the U value is developed for the section in the same way as for walls. The surface resistances, however, are different because the floor is horizontal rather than vertical and the heat flow is downward.

To determine the heat loss of a floor section over a crawlspace or a basement, several factors must be considered. If the basement or crawlspace is heated to the same temperature as the living space above the floor, there is no appreciable net exchange of heat and no calculations need be made. If the basement or crawlspace is heated to a lower temperature than the space above, there is no need for calculations if the temperature differential is less than 10 degrees or so. But when the difference approaches 15 F or more, the heat loss is worth considering. In that case, the only difference in the calculations lies in Δt, which must be adjusted to suit the conditions. If the basement or crawlspace is unheated, then an intermediate Δt must be determined as was previously explained. In the case of a fully open or very well-ventilated crawlspace, generally the temperature is considered to be the same as the outdoor design temperature. If the space is partially ventilated or unventilated, you *can* use the outside design temperature if you prefer. However, this will introduce an error on the high side in your figuring. If you want to be more accurate, calculate an intermediate design temperature for the unheated space.

To determine the heat loss of a floor over a basement or crawlspace, first work out the R values of the floor components for the floor area between the joists—and also for the area including the joists—and then find U_{av}. Be sure to include the finish flooring. This is especially important if that includes carpeting and padding—both of which have relatively high R values. The surface resistances are calculated on the assumption of still air, horizontal surfaces, and downward heat flow (R-0.92).

An upper floor of a house separating two levels of living quarters that generally are heated to the same temperature is usually neither insulated nor figured into the heat loss calculations. However, there are some exceptions to that. Sometimes an upper-level floor is insulated and particularly if there is reason to believe the upper floor will be periodically closed off during the heating season or if zoned or electric heat units are installed. The theory is that the insulation between the two living space levels will prevent upward heat flow through the floor from the lower to the upper level. This might otherwise disturb the proper functioning of the upper heat zone. If the upper level might be closed off during the heating season, a considerable amount of heat would escape the lower level and move into the presumably much cooler upper level to no good effect. If the upper level will at times be much cooler or unheated, then the floor separating the two levels should be well insulated. Heat loss calculations should be run on the basis of an unheated or a cooler heated space above the fully heated space. Use an intermediate design temperature. In some instances, the upper level is considered an unheated attic space for purposes of calculations. This arrangement is considered as a ceiling calculation.

Band Joists

There are areas of heat loss in wood-frame houses frequently neglected in the calculations. These are the band joist areas that can occur at the first-floor level between the foundation top and the floor itself or between the first-floor ceiling and the second-floor flooring. Typically, this consists of a band around the perimeter of the house that is formed by the end joists and the header joists to which the common floor joists are attached (Figs. 4-6A and 4-6B). The cross section of this area is different than the other building sections and consequently it has different and usually less effective thermal characteristics. Because of the fairly awkward and out-of-sight location, band joist areas often get little consideration when it comes to insulation.

The cross section of band joist construction varies depending upon the construction specifications of the house. To take a typical example, the component R values must be determined as follows; from the inside to the outside: inside surface resistance; end or header joist thickness (typically 1½ inches actual); one-half inch exterior sheathing; three-eighth inch exterior plywood siding; exterior surface resistance (Fig. 4-7). The R-values for these components are, respectively: 0.68; 1.875; 0.62; 0.47; and 0.17 (assuming wind speed at 15 mph). Rounded off, this results in a total R of 3.82, or a U of 0.262. No insulation was included in the cross section in this particular example. In cold climates, insulation should be installed in the band joist areas because the U value is not very substantial.

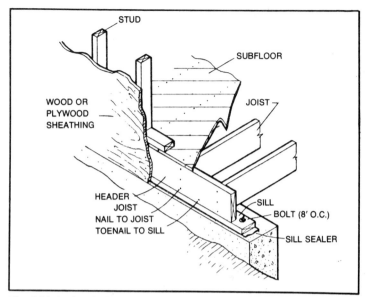

Fig. 4-6A. In the platform framing method of construction, the header and end joist areas lie between the sill and the subflooring.

There is actually a slight difference in the *U* value of the band joist area located just atop a foundation wall and the band joist area located at upper floor levels (even though the construction cross section may be the same). This is because of the influence of the masonry foundation, the presence of a joint between the sill upon which the band joist rides and the foundation wall, and also because of the exposed lower edges of the

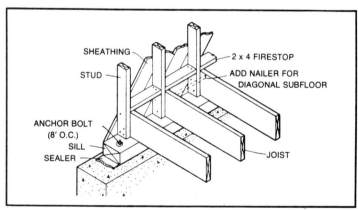

Fig. 4-6B. In balloon framing, they are between the sill and the firestop. Note that there is no actual header joist but there are end joists (not shown).

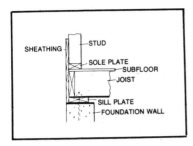

Fig. 4-7. Cross section of header joist area as constructed in the platform framing method of building.

exterior sheathing and siding. The overall effect is a chilling one. The foundation band joist area will generally have a somewhat less effective U value. Just how much less depends upon the components of the wall construction.

You have three choices in making your calculations. The first choice is to ignore the difference between the two types of band joist areas and simply make the calculations as previously described. The second choice is to use standard calculations for an upper floor level band joist area and modify the result for a foundation band joist area by decreasing the U value a bit with a correction factor. The factor itself will only be a rule of thumb, but it will more closely approximate the heat loss (on average). An addition of 0.006 to the resulting U factor in a relatively mild climate or 0.008 in a more severe one would not be unreasonable. The third and most accurate alternative would be to consult tables that have been developed by the NAHB for both kinds of band joist areas with various different construction cross sections.

The square footage of the band joist areas is found by multiplying the height of the joists by the total running length. Use the actual joist height rather than the nominal size. There are two kinds of joists and they must be treated differently. End joists are those that lie parallel with the common floor joists and they are found at each end of each rank of common joists. Header joists run at right angles to the common floor joists, which butt up against the headers. The end joist areas should be calculated at 100 percent of their actual surface areas. But the surface area of the header joists that is occupied by the ends of the abutting common joists should be subtracted from the total.

This is best done by actual computation. For example, the end face of a nominal 2 x 8 common floor joist (actual about 1.5 x 7.25 inches) equals 10.875 square inches. If there were 20 common joists secured to a header joist length, they would occupy 217.5 square inches of the header joist surface area (or approximately 1.5 square feet). This area would be subtracted from the gross band joist area to arrive at the net area.

The U, area, and Δt for band joist areas should be entered on the worksheet. The foundation band joist areas would be part of the basement. Upper-level band joist areas would be attributable to the appropriate first or second floor living spaces.

175

Header Areas

Another kind of construction section that is often ignored in making residential heat loss calculations is the header or lintel areas. Although their total area is relatively small, the heat loss through them is of some consequence. You might want to include them in your calculations in the interest of making as accurate an assessment as possible of total heat loss. Above each door and window there is a structural member called a header (Fig. 4-8). The purpose of this member is to add extra strength to the wall frame and compensate for the lack of studs in the window or door rough-opening areas.

Headers are typically constructed in either of two ways and in cross section they are somewhat variable. The first method is to stand two parallel lengths of 2-inch stock on edge and secure them to the studs at each end. These members are typically made of 2 x 8s or 2 x 10s. In order to fill out the full depth of the wall thickness, the two members might have a one-half inch air space between them, or the space can be filled with a scrap of one-half inch plywood (Fig. 4-9).

The second method is to construct a box header using dimension stock and plywood as shown in Fig. 4-10. This kind of header is generally hollow. In either case, the interior surface of the headers is generally covered with gypsum board or a similar interior wall covering and the outsides are covered by exterior sheathing and siding or whatever other combination is used to cover the wall frames.

Determining the heat loss from these areas is done in exactly the same way as for any wall section. First, tally up the total R of all of the individual components of the header sections—including both inside and outside surface films—and convert them to the U value. Then figure out the actual area of each header and tally them all up. Multiply the header area times the U times the Δt to find the total loss in Btuh. If you ignore the header areas, they will of course be a part of the U_{av} wall heat loss. But if you do calculate them separately, be sure to subtract the header area from the total wall area—just as is done with windows and doors—when you make the wall heat loss calculations.

Slab Floors

Slab floors that are in direct contact with the earth surface have their own peculiar thermal characteristics. There are two kinds of slab floors that must be considered: those that are unheated, and those that are heated by virtue of having perimeter heat ducts embedded in the concrete (a common residential heating system arrangement). Either type, but especially the heated slab, must be well insulated if the total heat loss from the slab is to remain reasonable.

The heat loss from an unheated concrete slab actually constitutes only about 10 percent or less of the total heat loss from a typical wood-frame house. However, that relatively small amount of loss becomes disproportionately important because of the comfort factor. If a substantial loss is allowed, the slab will remain uncomfortably cold.

176

This is especially true around the perimeter in severe winter weather. Unheated concrete slabs are not recommended for use in harsh winter climates unless the heating system can deliver sufficient heat to overcome the combined effects of heat transmission through the floor and downdrafts of cool air slipping down the inside of the exterior walls. Without this additional heat (which is relatively costly to provide), an unheated concrete slab—even if well insulated—might frequently be below the comfort level because of cold-air cooling at the slightly above floor level.

One way to calculate the heat loss from an unheated concrete slab, where the loss takes place primarily from the slab edges, is to consult Table 4-9. The values shown are directly expressed in terms of heat loss per linear foot of slab edge in Btu per hour. These values are also predicated upon the fact that the edge insulation extends back under the floor horizontally for a minimum of 2 feet or vertically along the outside of the foundation and extending to a depth of 2 feet or more below floor level.

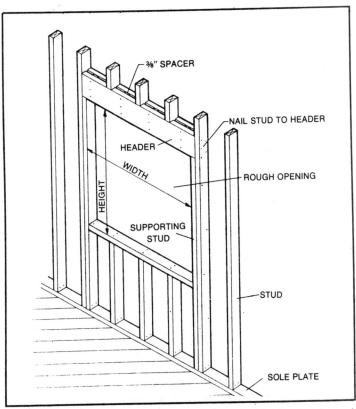

Fig. 4-8. The location and typical construction of a window header and framing arrangement. A typical door framing arrangement would be the same as far as the header is concerned.

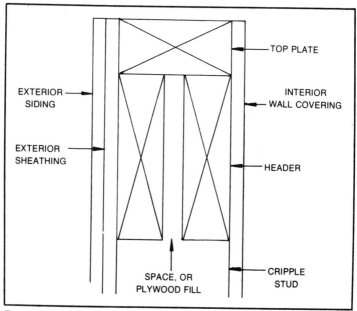

Fig. 4-9. Cross section of a typical two-piece door or window header construction.

All that you need do is choose the appropriate value for your outdoor design temperature and enter the figure in the U column of your worksheet. Then determine the length in linear feet of the slab edge and enter that in the area column. Multiply the two figures to find the total Btuh loss. In this instance, Δt is not used on the worksheet.

This method for finding slab perimeter heat loss involves the use of the basic formula:

$$q = F_2 P(t_i - t_o)$$

where

q = heat loss of floor, Btu per hour.

F_2 = heat loss coefficient, Btu per hour per linear foot of exposed edge per degree F temperature difference between the indoor air and the outdoor air.

P = perimeter for exposed edge of floor, linear feet.

t_i = indoor air temperature, degrees F.

t_o = outdoor air temperature, degrees F.

The various values for F_2 (shown in Fig. 4-11) for slab perimeters insulated to differing R values can be interpolated, or extrapolated if you do not go too far. Note that this formula accomplishes the same purpose as if you entered F_2 on your worksheet in the U column, P in the area column, t_i and t_o in the Δt column, and then multiplied the figures as usual to find the total Btuh loss.

178

Insulation is a critical factor in reducing heat loss through the edges of a heated slab. With a perimeter type of heating system, the ductwork is of a special type that is embedded directly in the concrete all the way around the perimeter of the slab and only a few inches from the edge (Table 4-10). The potential for substantial heat loss is great. This heat loss, which travels both downward into the ground and outward around the perimeter of the slab, is called *reverse loss*.

As with losses from unheated slabs, there are two methods that you can use to make your calculations. The first is to be guided by the values listed in Fig. 4-10. For example, if your Δ *t* is 0 F and you plan to install 2-inch, L-type insulation, the heat loss is 65 Btu per linear foot of slab perimeter for every degree of temperature difference between the inside and the outside temperatures, per hour.

Neither a specific type of insulation nor a particular *R* value is noted in Table 4-10. The assumption is that one of the standard bead-board or foam-board rigid insulations that is normally used for this purpose will be employed. However, there are now several types of such insulations with varying *R* values vis-a-vis thickness. Use the second method for a more accurate assessment that will better suit your particular conditions. Follow the formula provided previously for calculating the edge heat loss of unheated slabs.

You probably noticed that, unlike in the previous heat calculations, no consideration has been given here to the floor surface area itself or to the portions of the concrete slab within the perimeter. This is because experimentation has shown that the total heat loss from a concrete slab is

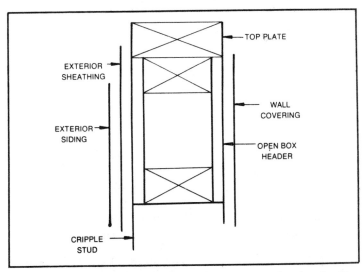

Fig. 4-10. Cross section of a typical box-type window or door header. The void should be filled with insulation during construction.

Table 4-9. Heat Loss Through Concrete Slab Edges (Printed with Permission from the 1977 Fundamentals Volume, ASHRAE HANDBOOK & Product Directory).

Outdoor Design Temperature, F	Heat Loss per Foot of Exposed Edge, Btuh	
	Recommended 2-in. Edge Insulation	1-in. Edge Insulation
−20 to −30	50	55
−10 to −20	45	50
0 to −10	40	45
Outdoor Design Temperature, F	**1-in. Edge Insulation**	**No Edge Insulation[a]**
−20 to −30	60	75
−10 to −20	55	65
0 to −10	50	60

[a]This construction not recommended; shown for comparison only.

more directly proportional to the perimeter in linear feet than to the surface area in square feet. In a sense the interior portions, or field, of the concrete slab is included in the calculation methods discussed previously. But there is heat loss through the slab surface at all points. This is true because the ground beneath the slab is always at a lower temperature than the heated space above the slab.

The tables and formula just cited are based upon the assumption of an average ground temperature that one would normally find throughout the United States. As long as there is no reason to believe that the ground temperature is markedly below the average (as it might be in Alaska permafrost country), these methods will prove quite satisfactory. Making explicit calculations on the basis of actual ground temperatures at each individual building site would be a sizable challenge. Because of the peculiar and variable way in which heat flow lines are likely to travel through the ground beneath a concrete slab—whether integrally heated or not—the loss is relatively small and the calculations would not be worth the effort.

Foundations

Of the several different kinds of house foundations, only three need have heat loss calculations made for them. The first, concrete slabs, have already been discussed. Pier and similar open foundations are disregarded and so are fully ventilated and many partially ventilated crawlspace foundations, and unheated basements. These are treated either as unheated spaces or ignored. That leaves only heated basements and heated unventilated crawlspaces to consider.

The heat losses from heated basements are calculated in three steps; first, the above-grade wall section; second, the below-grade wall section; and third, the basement floor.

The above-grade wall section is the easiest to calculate and is done in the same way as any wall section. The wall is generally either concrete block or poured concrete, and there might or might not be insulating material applied to either the inside or outside of the wall. Whatever the case, just find the R values of the wall components and convert their sum to U. When working out the area of the above-ground wall surface, the easiest method is to determine the average height (this can be done in sections if the terrain slopes markedly) of the foundation wall top above grade level and then round off to the nearest half-foot below grade level.

If the exposed wall height is 1 foot 7 inches, round off to 2 feet. If it is 1 foot 5 inches, round off to 1½ feet. Window or door areas should be subtracted from the gross wall area and the windows and doors separately calculated. The resulting figures are entered in the worksheet in the usual way.

Figuring the heat loss from the below-grade sections of the wall is a bit more complex. The pattern of radial isotherms and heat flow lines from a basement wall is shown in Fig. 4-12. The rate of heat flow from the wall at any given point depends upon factors such as wall thickness, presence or absence of inside or outside insulation, the depth below grade, the soil characteristics, the ground temperature at any given point, and the material from which the foundation wall is made. Accounting for all of these factors is a difficult chore and virtually impossible to do with great accuracy without engineering studies and computerized calculations for each individual site and indeed for each individual section of the underground basement wall. From a practical standpoint, about the best that can be done is to make some assumptions and use some averages and rules of thumb in making approximate calculations. This method does generally provide satisfactory results.

One possibility for making the calculations is to use Table 4-11. This table is for 8-inch poured concrete walls that are typically used in residential construction. For an uninsulated basement wall, there is a fair difference in heat loss between a poured concrete wall and one made of either

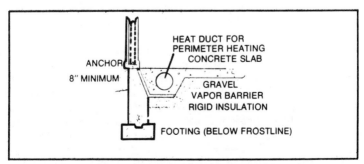

Fig. 4-11. A cross section of a perimeter heating duct embedded in a slab-on-grade foundation. Note the positioning of the rigid insulation. This is a critical part of this type of installation.

**Table 4-10. Heat Losses From the Perimeter
of a Heated Slab-on-Grade Foundation (Reprinted with Permission from
the 1977 Fundamentals Volume, ASHRAE HANDBOOK & Product Directory).**

Floor Heat Loss to be Used When Warm
Air Perimeter Heating Ducts Are Embedded in Slabs[a]
Btuh per (linear foot of heated edge)

Outdoor Design Temperature, F	Edge Insulation		
	1-in. Vertical Extending Down 18 in. Below Floor Surface	1-in. L-Type Extending at Least 12 in. Deep and 12 in. Under	2-in. L-Type Extending Down and 12 in. Under
−20	105	100	85
−10	95	90	75
0	85	80	65
10	75	70	55
20	62	57	45

[a] Factors include loss downward through inner area of slab.

standard concrete block, cinder block, or a lightweight aggregate block. All three have progressively higher R values. However, when insulation is added to the wall, even in only a 1-inch thickness (at a k of 0.24), the difference in heat loss between the four different constructions diminishes to only a very slight amount. The more insulation is added the less the difference becomes. On the assumption that in this day and age every heated-basement wall will be insulated to at least some degree, Table 4-11 is usable for most common basement wall constructions.

To use Table 4-11, first choose the appropriate insulation column for your construction. Then add all of the values shown in that column for each 1-foot height increment of foundation wall that lies below grade level. If you have 3 feet of below-ground foundation wall covered by 1 inch of insulation, you would add 0.152, 0.116, and 0.094. The total of 0.362 represents the heat loss in Btu per linear foot of foundation wall that is below grade to that extent. In other words, each chunk of basement wall 1 foot wide, 3 feet high, and 8 inches thick will lose 0.362 Btu per hour into the ground for every degree F of temperature difference between the inside air and, in this case, the ground beyond the wall.

You've perhaps just remembered that the ground temperature beyond the foundation wall is obviously not the same as the above-grade air temperature, so your basic outdoor design temperature will be of no value in arriving at Δt. Furthermore, the ground temperature is variable. It changes less as the depth increases. Short of actually taking a series of temperature measurements, how then do you arrive at a suitable intermediate design temperature? Theoretically this is very difficult. It has been made simple by generalizing. Figure 4-13 shows a map of North and Central America. Lines of constant amplitude have been superimposed. The temperature at the surface of the ground fluctuates around a mean value to the extent of a certain amplitude (symbolized as A). The value A

varies with geographic location and also with surface cover. The mean annual air temperature is symbolized as t_a and can be obtained from local meterological records for the site location or its reasonably close vicinity. Find your approximate geographic location on the map in Fig. 4-13—you can interpolate as required—and determine a reasonable value for A. Then subtract A for t_a to find your intermediate design temperature.

On the worksheet, enter the new Δt in its column, the Btuh heat loss per linear foot of the foundation in the U column, and the total length of the foundation wall in the area column. Multiply the values to find the total Btuh loss.

It is possible to compute heat losses through a basement floor in much the same manner as below-grade basement walls. Use the heat flow lines and the path lengths through the soil. The total heat loss through the basement floor is only a very small part of the total basement heat loss. Therefore, going through such gyrations is hardly worth the effort. Instead, consult the Table 4-12 and choose a value that is most appropriate for your purposes.

The width of the house is the narrow dimension. The shallower and narrower the basement, the greater is the heat loss through the basement floor. If the basement is irregular, such as an L-shape, break the total area up into rectangular sections. You can interpolate the figures in the table to a certain degree (if necessary). Enter the value in the U column of the worksheet and the total floor area in the area column. The Δt is the same as for the basement walls. Then multiply to find the total Btuh loss through the basement floor.

There is another method for determining basement heat loss values. This method makes use of special tables and correction factors published in the NAHB *Insulation Manual*. Values are listed for poured concrete, standard concrete block, and lightweight concrete block foundation walls in three thicknesses—with and without various values of insulation and different interior finishes. The values are presented for both above-grade and below-grade walls and are modified by means of a special temperature

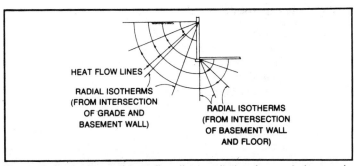

Fig. 4-12. Isotherms and heat flow lines radiating from a below-grade foundation wall (Reprinted with Permission from the 1977 Fundamentals Volume, ASHRAE HANDBOOK & Product Directory).

183

		Heat Loss			
Depth	Path Length through Soil		Insulation		
(ft)	(ft)	Uninsulated	1-in.	2-in.	3-in.
0-1 (1st)	0.68	0.410	0.152	0.093	0.067
1-2 (2nd)	2.27	0.222	0.116	0.079	0.059
2-3 (3rd)	3.88	0.155	0.094	0.068	0.053
3-4 (4th)	5.52	0.119	0.079	0.060	0.048
4-5 (5th)	7.05	0.096	0.069	0.053	0.044
5-6 (6th)	8.65	0.079	0.060	0.048	0.040
6-7 (7th)	10.28	0.069	0.054	0.044	0.037

[a] k_{soil} = 9.6(Btuh)(in.)/(ft^2)(F); $k_{insulation}$ = 0.24(Btuh)(in.)/(ft^2)(F).

difference multiplying factor. The tables allow somewhat more flexibility of choice in computations than are given here, but the results are not appreciably different in most cases. The heat loss through the basement floor slab is included in the calculations rather than being separately computed.

The heat loss calculations for heated crawlspaces are made in exactly the same way as for basements. You must assess the above-grade portion of the walls, then the below-grade portions, and finally the crawlspace floor. In some cases, this floor is a concrete slab and it is calculated the same way as a basement floor. In other situations the floor might be packed earth or the ground might be covered with a layer of insulating board, tar paper, or vapor barrier material. If no insulation is present, make the calculations as though the floor were concrete. The R of concrete is so low that the presence or absence of the thin floor layer makes little appreciable difference. Where a layer of insulation is in place, for all practical purposes the heat loss through the surface area can be ignored.

Ceilings

There are two occasions in particular when ceiling sections are calculated for heat loss. The first is when the ceiling area is surmounted by a shallow-pitched roof enclosing a relatively small unheated attic or crawlway area. In this example, it is easier and almost as accurate to consider the ceiling section as actually being the roof. The second circumstance is when there is a relatively large unheated space above the ceiling such as a full attic or perhaps unused living space that is kept closed off most of the time and heated by unit heaters only when the area is in use. The two situations are calculated somewhat differently.

Where the roof assembly is to be disregarded and the ceiling assumed to be the roof, the way the calculations are made depends upon the amount of insulation included in the ceiling assembly. If there is no insulation or only a minimal amount (an unhappy situation today), the first step is to determine the intermediate design temperature of the attic area.

Use the special formula, provided earlier, for finding the unheated attic temperature. Then determine the U value of the ceiling assembly in much the same way as you would for a wall or floor. Include the underside ceiling surface film resistance under upward heat flow conditions, as well as the topside surface film resistance, on the basis of still air.

If the unheated attic space is exceptionally well ventilated, you might even choose to consider the upper surface film resistance on a basis of a 5 mph wind. Tally the R values for all of the component parts of the ceiling assembly and then convert to find the U value. Enter this figure in the U column of the worksheet, along with the net area of the ceiling and the Δt that has been derived from the intermediate design temperature of the unheated attic space. Multiply the three factors to determine total loss in Btuh.

If the ceiling assembly is well insulated, has a relatively high R value and the attic space is well ventilated, make your calculations in the same way, but instead of finding an intermediate design temperature for the unheated attic space, use the normal outside design temperature to arrive at Δt. For purposes of calculations, the roof assembly doesn't exist. If the upper living space is kept at 40 F (or some other temperature) regularly, use that temperature to find Δt and proceed with the calculations as usual. If the space is unheated, first determine the intermediate design temperature of the space by using either the formula for estimating temperatures of adjacent unheated spaces or the special formula for estimating the temperature of unheated attic space. This depends upon the nature of the unheated area.

Whatever the circumstances, openings that lead from the heated space through the ceiling into the upper space—scuttle, access hatch, closed stairwell, or whatever—should be treated separately unless their construction closely approximates that of the ceiling assembly itself. A small access hatch of approximately the same U value as the ceiling assembly itself can be ignored and made a part of the net ceiling area. A

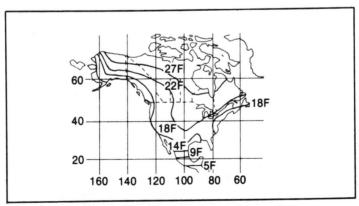

Fig. 4-13. Map of amplitude lines crossing the North American Continent (Reprinted with Permission from the 1977 Fundamentals Volume, ASHRAE HANDBOOK & Product Directory).

Table 4-12. Heat Loss through Basement Floors
[Btu/(h)(ft²)(F)] (Reprinted with Permission from the 1977
Fundamentals Volume, ASHRAE HANDBOOK & Product Directory).

Depth of Foundation Wall below Grade (ft)	Width of House			
	20 (ft)	24 (ft)	28 (ft)	32 (ft)
5	0.032	0.029	0.026	0.023
6	0.030	0.027	0.025	0.022
7	0.029	0.026	0.023	0.021

large, uninsulated pull-down stairway or a stairwell with an ordinary interior door might well be separately calculated.

Roofs

Roof calculations are made for flat, slightly pitched, and shed roofs that are of monolithic construction; roofs having only minimal access or crawlway area between ceiling and roof decking or roof frame; vaulted roofs of the type that are found in open-plan houses with cathedral ceilings; and pitched roofs that enclose heated living space (such as the "expanded attic" arrangement often found in Cape Code and similar house styles).

In all of these cases, the calculations are made in much the same way as for wall constructions. Add up all of the R values of the roof section components. Start with the inside surface film resistance (still air, horizontal or sloping surface position, upward heat flow) and end with the outside surface film resistance figured on the basis of moving air.

When computing the area of the roof, consider the gross area as that portion of the roof which actually lies over the heated living space. The part that extends beyond the house walls or lies over an unheated area enclosed by knee walls should not be considered. Skylights, roof windows, and access hatches should be calculated separately and their area deducted from the gross roof area to arrive at a net roof area. Once you have arrived at the net area, the roof U, and the Δt, you can enter them on your worksheet and multiply to determine the total heat loss in Btuh. Note that dormers should be treated separately by calculating the roof, wall and window sections that are attributable to them.

Infiltration Losses

In older houses, or even new ones that are not particularly well-built and "tight," infiltration losses can be dismayingly high. This is usually a correctable situation and these losses are relatively low in the modern, well-built house. If a house is designed and constructed to minimize infiltration heat losses to the greatest possible extent, the results can be surprisingly good and the losses kept within very reasonable bounds.

Infiltration heat losses occur through both natural and mechanical ventilation of the structure. In older houses, the losses due to natural ventilation are apt to be the greatest. In new, ultra-tight houses the greatest losses can occur from mechanical ventilation. Though usually referred to only as infiltration, actually two processes are at work—the second is exfiltration. Whatever *amount* of air comes into the house from outside must also return to the outside at the same time, but at diverse points of exit. The air pressure within the house shell remains roughly the same as it is outside. There are always minor pressure differentials, otherwise there wouldn't be any natural airflow at all.

Because the infiltrating air is cold, a certain amount of heat is lost in warming it to room temperature. On the other hand, the exfiltrating air is warm and so a certain amount of heat is lost when it is carried outside. In addition, there are two components involved in heat loss by infiltration: the loss of sensible heat, and the loss of latent heat. In years past, common practice has been to consider only the sensible component in assessing infiltration heat losses of residences. These days, however, the desire to refine heat loss calculations to the greatest practical degree sometimes leads to an inclusion of the latent component as well. This is especially true for super-insulated, ultra-efficient houses.

The critical factor in assessing heat loss due to infiltration in a house is the volume of outside air that enters the house over a period of time. The accepted time interval for calculations is 1 hour. Because a certain amount of air enters the house every hour, in due course the entire volume of air inside the house will be replaced by an equal volume that comes in from the outside. The actual amount of cubic feet of air that enters and leaves the house during any given hour depends primarily upon outside influences such as wind velocity and direction, the extent and kind of crackage, the number of times doors are opened and closed, and so forth. The first step is to assess the total volume of air that enters and leaves the house per hour.

There are two principal methods of calculating heat loss due to infiltration in a house. One is called the *crack length method*. The cracks in the house, particularly around doors and windows, are measured for length and then tables are used to determine the actual volume of air per hour that enters through the crackage—depending upon the specific nature of the crack.

The second procedure is called the *air change method* or *ACH* (air changes per hour). This is a commonly used way of calculating infiltration heat losses in residences. Instead of attempting to determine the actual volume of outside air that is likely to infiltrate the house per hour through various cracks, the ACH method simply assumes that the volume of air within the structure will replace itself, or change, on a regular average basis of so many times per hour. Long experience has shown these factors to be suitably workable if a logical choice is made concerning which specific factor to use. Table 4-13 lists ACH values that can be used in residences on a room by room basis. You can also use a generalized figure for the entire house.

It is generally assumed that older houses that are not particularly tight have an ACH of 1. Those that are notably loose in construction and

**Table 4-13. Air Changes Occurring Under Average
Conditions in Residences, Exclusive of Air Provided for
Ventilation[a] (Reprinted with Permission from the 1977
Fundamentals Volume, ASHRAE HANDBOOK & Product Directory).**

Kind of room	Number of Air Changes per hour
Rooms with no windows or exterior doors	0.5
Rooms with windows or exterior doors on one side	1
Rooms with windows or exterior doors on two sides	1.5
Rooms with windows or exterior doors on three sides	2
Entrance halls	2

[a] For rooms with weatherstripped windows or with storm sash, use two-thirds these values.

have rattly windows and ill-fitting doors might have an ACH of 1.5 or even higher. NEMA recommends assuming an air change of 0.5 to 0.75 for well-constructed modern houses with average insulation and set up for electric heat. Modern houses that are very carefully constructed and heavily insulated might well have an ACH of 0.5 or below. Super-efficient houses might range as low as 0.25. When the natural ventilation becomes this low, usually it is necessary to introduce mechanical ventilation in order to avoid a close, stuffy atmosphere, to expel odors, and to properly circulate warm air. However, atmosphere is still healthful even below 0.25 ACH.

In order to minimize the introduction of cold outside air through ordinary kinds of mechanical ventilation, some experimentation is now going on with special heat-exchanger venting systems in super-efficient houses. Much will be heard about these systems in the near future.

Note that the ACH method does not provide for the introduction of outside air by mechanical ventilating means. This can be separately figured, if necessary, by determining the actual volume of air flow that will, on average, be introduced into the building. However, with most conventional houses this is unnecessary because the total intake of air by this means is usually proportionately quite low.

The initial step in making the calculations is to determine the sensible heat loss and the first necessary factor is the U value of the infiltrating air. This is a given value, obtained by multiplying the specific heat of air (which is 0.24) by the standard density of air (0.075). This results in a U of 0.018. The formula to find the amount of heat (in Btuh) needed to raise the temperature of the air infiltrating the house from the outside temperature to the inside temperature (Q_s) equals 0.018 $(t_i - t_0)$.

Select your ACH, then determine the volume of each heated room or space by multiplying height times width times length. Then multiply the volume by the ACH. This will give you the volume of air that must be raised from the outside to the inside temperature and the figure can be entered in the area column of the worksheet. Enter 0.018 (the U of air) in the U column and the Δt in its column. Multiply the three values to find the total loss in Btuh of sensible heat. To illustrate, assume that a room is 10 feet wide, 14 feet long, and has a ceiling 7 feet 6 inches high. The volume is therefore 1050 cubic feet. If the ACH is 0.75, the volume of infiltrating air that must be heated to room temperature is 787.5 cubic feet. Then, $0_s = 0.018 \, (787.5) \, (t_i - t_0)$. If the Δt is 80, for instance, the result is 1134 Btuh heat loss for that room.

Latent heat loss due to infiltration is generally ignored in residential heat loss calculations. This is primarily because that loss is not of great consequence and also because the factors needed to make the calculations are not easily determined. There is a lack of readily obtainable and easily understandable information on the subject. Bypass the whole exercise, don't be concerned-because your overall heat loss calculations won't suffer. Using Table 4-14, you can easily calculate, heat loss due to infiltration in a house. It is a generalization, but it works. All you need do is select an appropriate value from the table—you can interpolate for unlisted temperature differences—and multiply that by the volume of each room or of the entire house. The answer will be the total heat loss in Btuh.

TOTAL HEATING LOAD

Once you have worked out all of the room-by-room details and entered the values on your worksheet, the hard work is all done. All that remains is to determine the total heating load of the house. The next step is to make up a summary work sheet (Table 4-15). This lists all of the heated rooms or areas on the left. The various building section categories are listed to the right. Transpose the figures from your worksheet to the summary sheet and add up all of the individual heat losses. The totals for each heated room or space appear in the far right-hand column and each column should be added at the bottom to provide the design totals.

On the line below, enter the values for the operating totals. For each of the building sections, the design heat loss total in Btuh will be the same as the operating total—with one exception. On the operating total line in the infiltration column, enter a value that is one-half of the design total. The reason for this is that in theory the exfiltration from the house equals the infiltration. However, the infiltration was initially calculated for all sides of the house. At any given time, it will actually take place through only half the sides or approximately one-half of the total exposed surface area. Hence, the infiltration totals should logically be only approximately 0.5 of the computed total value.

The final value in the lower right hand corner of the summary work sheet is the total heat loss of the entire house in terms of Btu per hour. This figure represents the total heating load of the house. The heating system that you install, whatever its type, must be capable of delivering

The tabulated factors, when multiplied by room or building volume (ft³), will result in estimated heat loss (Btu/hr) due to infiltration and does not include the heat needed to warm ventilating air

Room or Building Type	No. of Walls with Windows	Temp. Difference, deg F				Room or Building Type	No. of Walls with Windows	Temp. Difference, deg F			
		25	50	75	100			25	50	75	100
	None	0.23	0.45	0.68	0.90	B	Any	1.35	2.70	4.05	5.40
	1	0.34	0.68	1.02	1.36	C	Any	0.90-1.35	1.80-2.70	2.70-4.05	3.60-5.40
A	2	0.68	1.35	2.02	2.70	D	Any	0.45-0.68	0.90-1.35	1.35-2.02	1.80-2.70
	3 or 4	0.90	1.80	2.70	3.60	E	Any	0.68-1.35	1.35-2.70	2.03-4.05	2.70-5.40

A = Offices, apartments, hotels, multistory buildings in general.
B = Entrance halls or vestibules.
C = Industrial buildings.
D = Houses, all types, all rooms except vestibules.
E = Public or institutional buildings.

this amount of heat into the living space on an hourly basis. The total in the right-hand column for each heated room or space represents its heat loss in Btu per hour and the total heating load for that room. If you plan to install a central heating system, the heat distribution system must be designed to deliver at least the specified amount of heat to each room. If you plan to install unit or area heaters, such as electric baseboard units, the capacity of the units installed in each room must be equal to or greater than the listed total heat loss for that room.

SEASONAL HEATING REQUIREMENTS

The last task is to determine the total seasonal heating requirements and the cost of heating the house. This process is once again one that requires a bit of judgment. In making residential calculations, the traditional method for developing the seasonal heating requirements has been to use the degree-day method. Although this standard procedure is now recognized to be not as valid or effective as it was formerly thought to be, nonetheless it is still in widespread use and results in an adequate, if not always entirely accurate, assessment.

One degree-day of heating occurs for every degree F that the average outside temperature, during a 24-hour period, is below an arbitrary base of 65 F. The value of 65 F is commonly used because it has been determined that until the outside temperature falls below that figure, no additional mechanically-generated heat is needed inside an average house. The heat that is retained and also generated within the house from sources other than the heating system is sufficient to maintain a comfort level of about 70 F. Once the outside temperature falls below 65 F, then additional heat is needed within the structure.

Suppose, for example, that in one 24-hour period the high temperature was 42 F and the low temperature was 6 F. The total is 48 degrees; divide by 2 to get the average of 24 F. This figure subtracted from 65 equals 41. For that 24-hour period, 41 degree-days of heat were required. Note that this can also be done on an hourly basis, by using degree-hours and calculating the high, low, and average temperature every hour, for a more accurate assessment. In practice, this is infrequently done for residential calculations.

In order to find your total seasonal heating requirement, you first must determine the average number of degree-days of heat that will be required at your building site. This is usually done by consulting a table of degree-days for cities (See Table 4-16). If you live in or near any of these cities, you can simply choose the listed yearly total of degree days as the value for your calculations. Similar information can be found in the *Facility Design And Planning Engineering Weather Data* manual or from the National Climatic Center, Federal Building, Asheville, NC 28801, in the form of data for individual states as published by the U.S. Department of Commerce. Temperature records that are applicable to the immediate vicinity of the building site are always better than generalized values, if you can locate them. A heating fuels dealer is a likely source for this information and especially if the company bases its automatic fuel delivery program upon heating degree-days.

The formula for finding seasonal heating load is a simple one that is found in a number of slight variations.

This one is typical:

$$F = \frac{HL \times 24 \times DD}{T \times Eff}$$

Where

HL = heating load Btu per hour.

24 = hours per day.

DD = number of degree-days per heating season.

T = design temperature difference, degrees F.

Eff = seasonal efficiency factor of heating equipment.

The factor *Eff* varies from 45 to 50 percent to as high as 80 to 85 percent for most kinds of heating equipment. There are two exceptions. One is electric resistance heating equipment, which as an *Eff* of 100 percent, and the second is the heat pump, which can have an *Eff* (although it is called a COP, or coefficient of performance) of 300 percent or more.

Table 4-15. Typical Heating Load Summary Sheet.

ROOM	WALLS	CEIL.	FLOOR	WINDOW	DOOR	BAND	HEAD.	INFIL	TOTAL
Living	1364	832	1472	3434		165	158	3686	11111
Kitchen									
Bed #									
Bed #2									
Etc.									
Design Totals									
Operating Totals									

Table 4-16. Average Monthly and Yearly Degree Days for Cities in the United States and Canada[a,b,c]

(Base 65 F) (Reprinted with Permission from the 1976 Systems Volume, ASHRAE HANDBOOK & Product Directory).

State	Station	Avg. Winter Temp[d]	July	Aug.	Sept.	Oct.	Nov.	Dec.	Jan.	Feb.	Mar.	Apr.	May	June	Yearly Total
Ala.	Birmingham .... A	54.2	0	0	6	93	363	555	592	462	363	108	9	0	2551
	Huntsville............... A	51.3	0	0	12	127	426	663	694	557	434	138	19	0	3070
	Mobile.................. A	59.9	0	0	0	22	213	357	415	300	211	42	0	0	1560
	Montgomery.............. A	55.4	0	0	0	68	330	527	543	417	316	90	0	0	2291
Alaska	Anchorage .... A	23.0	245	291	516	930	1284	1572	1631	1316	1293	879	592	315	10864
	Fairbanks .... A	6.7	171	332	642	1203	1833	2254	2359	1901	1739	1068	555	222	14279
	Juneau................. A	32.1	301	338	483	725	921	1135	1237	1070	1073	810	601	381	9075
	Nome .... A	13.1	481	496	693	1094	1455	1820	1879	1666	1770	1314	930	573	14171
Ariz.	Flagstaff .... A	35.6	46	68	201	558	867	1073	1169	991	911	651	437	180	7152
	Phoenix .... A	58.5	0	0	0	22	234	415	474	328	217	75	0	0	1765
	Tucson .... A	58.1	0	0	0	25	231	406	471	344	242	75	6	0	1800
	Winslow .... A	43.0	0	0	6	245	711	1008	1054	770	601	291	96	0	4782
	Yuma .... A	64.2	0	0	0	0	108	264	307	190	90	15	0	0	974
Ark.	Fort Smith .... A	50.3	0	0	12	127	450	704	781	596	456	144	22	0	3292
	Little Rock .... A	50.5	0	0	9	127	465	716	756	577	434	126	9	0	3219
	Texarkana .... A	54.2	0	0	0	78	345	561	626	468	350	105	0	0	2533
Calif.	Bakersfield .... A	55.4	0	0	0	37	282	502	546	364	267	105	19	0	2122
	Bishop.................. A	46.0	0	0	48	260	576	797	874	680	555	306	143	36	4275
	Blue Canyon .... A	42.2	28	37	108	347	594	781	896	795	806	597	412	195	5596
	Burbank .... A	58.6	0	0	6	43	177	301	366	277	239	138	81	18	1646
	Eureka C	49.9	270	257	258	329	414	499	546	470	505	438	372	285	4643
	Fresno.................. A	53.3	0	0	0	84	354	577	605	426	335	162	62	6	2611
	Long Beach .... A	57.8	0	0	9	47	171	316	397	311	264	171	93	24	1803
	Los Angeles .... A	57.4	28	28	42	78	180	291	372	302	288	219	158	81	2061
	Los Angeles C	60.3	0	0	6	31	132	229	310	230	202	123	68	18	1349
	Mt. Shasta C	41.2	25	34	123	406	696	902	983	784	738	525	347	159	5722

	Station		Temp.													Annual
	Red Bluff	A	53.8	0	0	0	53	318	555	605	428	341	168	47	0	2515
	Sacramento	A	53.9	0	0	0	56	321	546	583	414	332	178	72	0	2502
	Sacramento	C	54.4	0	0	0	62	312	533	561	392	310	173	76	0	2419
	Sandberg	C	46.8	0	0	30	202	480	691	778	661	620	426	264	57	4209
	San Diego	A	59.5	9	0	21	43	135	236	298	235	214	135	90	42	1458
	San Francisco	A	53.4	81	78	60	143	306	462	508	395	363	279	214	126	3015
	San Francisco	C	55.1	192	174	102	118	231	388	443	336	319	279	239	180	3001
	Santa Maria	A	54.3	99	93	96	146	270	391	459	370	363	282	233	165	2967
Colo.	Alamosa	A	29.7	65	99	279	639	1065	1420	1476	1162	1020	696	440	168	8529
	Colorado Springs	A	37.3	9	25	132	456	825	1032	1128	938	893	582	319	84	6423
	Denver	A	37.6	6	9	117	428	819	1035	1132	938	887	558	288	66	6283
	Denver	C	40.8	0	0	90	366	714	905	1004	851	800	492	254	48	5524
	Grand Junction	A	39.3	0	0	30	313	786	1113	1209	907	729	387	146	21	5641
	Pueblo	A	40.4	0	0	54	326	750	986	1085	871	772	429	174	15	5462
Conn.	Bridgeport	A	39.9	0	0	66	307	615	986	1079	966	853	510	208	27	5617
	Hartford	A	37.3	0	12	117	394	714	1101	1190	1042	908	519	205	33	6235
	New Haven	A	39.0	0	12	87	347	648	1011	1097	991	871	543	245	45	5897
Del.	Wilmington	A	42.5	0	0	51	270	588	927	980	874	735	387	112	6	4930*
D.C.	Washington	A	45.7	0	0	33	217	519	834	871	762	626	288	74	0	4224
Fla.	Apalachicola	C	61.2	0	0	0	16	153	319	347	260	180	33	0	0	1308
	Daytona Beach	C	64.5	0	0	0	0	75	211	248	190	140	15	0	0	879
	Fort Myers	A	68.6	0	0	0	0	24	109	146	101	62	0	0	0	442
	Jacksonville	A	61.9	0	0	0	12	144	310	332	246	174	21	0	0	1239
	Key West	C	73.1	0	0	0	0	0	28	40	31	9	0	0	0	108
	Lakeland	C	66.7	0	0	0	0	57	164	195	146	99	0	0	0	661
	Miami	A	71.1	0	0	0	0	0	65	74	56	19	0	0	0	214

Data for United States cities from a publication of the United States Weather Bureau, *Monthly Normals of Temperature, Precipitation and Heating Degree Days,* 1962, are for the period 1931 to 1960 inclusive. These data also include information from the 1963 revisions to this publication, where available.

b Data for airport stations, A, and city stations, C, are both given where available.

c Data for Canadian cities were computed by the Climatology Division, Department of Transport from normal monthly mean temperatures, and the monthly values of heating degree days data were obtained using the National Research Council computer and a method devised by H. C. S. Thom of the United States Weather Bureau. The heating degree days are based on the period from 1931 to 1960.

d For period October to April, inclusive.

Table 4-16. Average Monthly and Yearly Degree Days for Cities in the United States and Canada[a,b,c] (Base 65 F)
(Reprinted with Permission from the 1976 Systems Volume, ASHRAE HANDBOOK & Product Directory) (continued from page 193).

State	Station		Avg. Winter Temp[d]	July	Aug.	Sept.	Oct.	Nov.	Dec.	Jan.	Feb.	Mar.	Apr.	May	June	Yearly Total
Fla. (Cont'd)	Miami Beach	C	72.5	0	0	0	0	0	40	56	36	9	0	0	0	141
	Orlando	A	65.7	0	0	0	0	72	198	220	165	105	6	0	0	766
	Pensacola	A	60.4	0	0	0	19	195	353	400	277	183	36	0	0	1463
	Tallahassee	A	60.1	0	0	0	28	198	360	375	286	202	36	0	0	1485
	Tampa	A	66.4	0	0	0	0	60	171	202	148	102	0	0	0	683
	West Palm Beach	A	68.4	0	0	0	0	6	65	87	64	31	0	0	0	253
Ga.	Athens	A	51.8	0	0	12	115	405	632	642	529	431	141	22	0	2929
	Atlanta	A	51.7	0	0	18	124	417	648	636	518	428	147	25	0	2961
	Augusta	A	54.5	0	0	0	78	333	552	549	445	350	90	0	0	2397
	Columbus	A	54.8	0	0	0	87	333	543	552	434	338	96	0	0	2383
	Macon	A	56.2	0	0	0	71	297	502	505	403	295	63	0	0	2136
	Rome	A	49.9	0	0	24	161	474	701	710	577	468	177	34	0	3326
	Savannah	A	57.8	0	0	0	47	246	437	437	353	254	45	0	0	1819
	Thomasville	C	60.0	0	0	0	25	198	366	394	305	208	33	0	0	1529
Hawaii	Lihue	A	72.7	0	0	0	0	0	0	0	0	0	0	0	0	0
	Honolulu	A	74.2	0	0	0	0	0	0	0	0	0	0	0	0	0
	Hilo	A	71.9	0	0	0	0	0	0	0	0	0	0	0	0	0
Idaho	Boise	A	39.7	0	0	132	415	792	1017	1113	854	722	438	245	81	5809
	Lewiston	A	41.0	0	0	123	403	756	933	1063	815	694	426	239	90	5542
	Pocatello	A	34.8	0	0	172	493	900	1166	1324	1058	905	555	319	141	7033
Ill.	Cairo (O'Hare)	C	47.9	0	0	36	164	513	791	856	680	539	195	47	0	3821
	Chicago (O'Hare)	A	35.8	0	12	117	381	807	1166	1265	1086	939	534	260	72	6639
	Chicago (Midway)	A	37.5	0	0	81	326	753	1113	1209	1044	890	480	211	48	6155
	Chicago	C	38.9	0	0	66	279	705	1051	1150	1000	868	489	226	48	5882
	Moline	A	36.4	0	9	99	335	774	1181	1314	1100	918	450	189	39	6408
	Peoria	A	38.1	0	6	87	326	759	1113	1218	1025	849	426	183	33	6025
	Rockford	A	34.8	0	9	114	400	837	1221	1333	1137	961	516	236	60	6830
	Springfield	A	40.6	6	6	72	301	696	1023	1135	935	761	354	135	18	5429

194

State	Station														
Ind.	Evansville	A	45.0	0	0	66	220	606	896	955	767	620	237	68	0	4435
	Fort Wayne	A	37.3	0	9	105	378	783	1135	1178	1028	890	471	189	39	6205
	Indianapolis	A	39.6	0	0	90	316	723	1051	1113	949	809	432	177	39	5699
	South Bend	A	36.6	0	6	111	372	777	1125	1221	1070	933	525	239	60	6439
Iowa	Burlington	A	37.6	0	0	93	322	768	1135	1259	1042	859	426	177	33	6114
	Des Moines	A	35.5	0	6	96	363	828	1225	1370	1137	915	438	180	30	6588
	Dubuque	A	32.7	12	31	156	450	906	1287	1420	1204	1026	546	260	78	7376
	Sioux City	A	34.0	0	9	108	369	867	1240	1435	1198	989	483	214	39	6951
	Waterloo	A	32.6	12	19	138	428	909	1296	1460	1221	1023	531	229	54	7320
Kans.	Concordia	A	40.4	0	0	57	276	705	1023	1163	935	781	372	149	18	5479
	Dodge City	A	42.5	0	0	33	251	666	939	1051	840	719	354	124	9	4986
	Goodland	A	37.8	0	6	81	381	810	1073	1166	955	884	507	236	42	6141
	Topeka	A	41.7	0	0	57	270	672	980	1122	893	722	330	124	12	5182
	Wichita	A	44.2	0	0	33	229	618	905	1023	804	645	270	87	6	4620
Ky.	Covington	A	41.4	0	0	75	291	669	983	1035	893	756	390	149	24	5265
	Lexington	A	43.8	0	0	54	239	609	902	946	818	685	325	105	0	4683
	Louisville	A	44.0	0	0	54	248	609	890	930	818	682	315	105	9	4660
La.	Alexandria	A	57.5	0	0	0	56	273	431	471	361	260	69	0	0	1921
	Baton Rouge	A	59.8	0	0	0	31	216	369	409	294	208	33	0	0	1560
	Lake Charles	A	60.5	0	0	0	19	210	341	381	274	195	39	0	0	1459
	New Orleans	A	61.0	0	0	0	19	192	322	363	258	192	39	0	0	1385
	New Orleans	C	61.8	0	0	0	12	165	291	344	241	177	24	0	0	1254
	Shreveport	A	56.2	0	0	0	47	297	477	552	426	304	81	0	0	2184
Me.	Caribou	A	24.4	78	115	336	682	1044	1535	1690	1470	1308	858	468	183	9767
	Portland	A	33.0	12	53	195	508	807	1215	1339	1182	1042	675	372	111	7511
Md.	Baltimore	A	43.7	0	0	48	264	585	905	936	820	679	327	90	0	4654
	Baltimore	C	46.2	0	0	27	189	486	806	859	762	629	288	65	0	4111
	Frederick	A	42.0	0	0	66	307	624	955	995	876	741	384	127	12	5087
Mass.	Boston	A	40.0	0	9	60	316	603	983	1088	972	846	513	208	36	5634
	Nantucket	A	40.2	12	22	93	332	573	896	992	941	896	621	384	129	5891
	Pittsfield	A	32.6	25	59	219	524	831	1231	1339	1196	1063	660	326	105	7578
	Worcester	A	34.7	6	34	147	450	774	1172	1271	1123	998	612	304	78	6969

Table 4-16. Average Monthly and Yearly Degree Days for Cities in the United States and Canada[a,b,c] (Base 65 F)
(Reprinted with Permission from the 1976 Systems Volume, ASHRAE HANDBOOK & Product Directory) (continued from page 195).

State	Station		Avg. Winter Temp	July	Aug.	Sept.	Oct.	Nov.	Dec.	Jan.	Feb.	Mar.	Apr.	May	June	Yearly Total
Mich.	Alpena	A	29.7	68	105	273	580	912	1268	1404	1299	1218	777	446	156	8506
	Detroit (City)	A	37.2	0	0	87	360	738	1088	1181	1058	936	522	220	42	6232
	Detroit (Wayne)	A	37.1	0	0	96	353	738	1088	1194	1061	933	534	239	57	6293
	Detroit (Willow Run)	A	37.2	0	0	90	357	750	1104	1190	1053	921	519	229	45	6258
	Escanaba	C	29.6	59	87	243	539	924	1293	1445	1296	1203	777	456	159	8481
	Flint	A	33.1	16	40	159	465	843	1212	1330	1198	1066	639	319	90	7377
	Grand Rapids	A	34.9	9	28	135	434	804	1147	1259	1134	1011	579	279	75	6894
	Lansing	A	34.8	6	22	138	431	813	1163	1262	1142	1011	579	273	69	6909
	Marquette	C	30.2	59	81	240	527	936	1268	1411	1268	1187	771	468	177	8393
	Muskegon	A	36.0	12	28	120	400	762	1088	1209	1100	995	594	310	78	6696
	Sault Ste. Marie	A	27.7	96	105	279	580	951	1367	1525	1380	1277	810	477	201	9048
Minn.	Duluth	A	23.4	71	109	330	632	1131	1581	1745	1518	1355	840	490	198	10000
	Minneapolis	A	28.3	22	31	189	505	1014	1454	1631	1380	1166	621	288	81	8382
	Rochester	A	28.8	25	34	186	474	1005	1438	1593	1366	1150	630	301	93	8295
Miss.	Jackson	A	55.7	0	0	0	65	315	502	546	414	310	87	0	0	2239
	Meridian	A	55.4	0	0	0	81	339	518	543	417	310	81	0	0	2289
	Vicksburg	C	56.9	0	0	0	53	279	462	512	384	282	69	0	0	2041
Mo.	Columbia	A	42.3	0	0	54	251	651	967	1076	874	716	324	121	12	5046
	Kansas City	A	43.9	0	0	39	220	612	905	1032	818	682	294	109	0	4711
	St. Joseph	A	40.3	0	6	60	285	708	1039	1172	949	769	348	133	15	5484
	St. Louis	A	43.1	0	0	60	251	627	936	1026	848	704	312	121	15	4900
	St. Louis	C	44.8	0	0	36	202	576	884	977	801	651	270	87	0	4484
	Springfield	A	44.5	0	0	45	223	600	877	973	781	660	291	105	6	4900
Mont.	Billings	A	34.5	6	15	186	487	897	1135	1296	1100	970	570	285	102	7049
	Glasgow	A	26.4	31	47	270	608	1104	1466	1711	1439	1187	648	335	150	8996
	Great Falls	A	32.8	28	53	258	543	921	1169	1349	1154	1063	642	384	186	7750
	Havre	A	28.1	28	53	306	595	1065	1367	1584	1364	1181	657	338	162	8700
	Havre	C	29.8	19	37	252	539	1014	1321	1528	1305	1116	612	304	115	8182

State	Station															
	Helena	A	31.1	31	59	294	601	1002	1265	1438	1170	1042	651	381	195	8129
	Kalispell	A	31.4	50	99	321	654	1020	1240	1401	1134	1029	639	397	207	8191
	Miles City	A	31.2	6	6	174	502	972	1296	1504	1252	1057	579	276	99	7723
	Missoula	A	31.5	34	74	303	651	1035	1287	1420	1120	970	621	391	219	8125
Neb.	Grand Island	C	36.0	0	6	108	381	834	1172	1314	1089	908	462	211	45	6530
	Lincoln	A	38.8	0	6	75	301	726	1066	1237	1016	834	402	171	30	5864
	Norfolk	A	34.0	9	0	111	397	873	1234	1414	1179	983	498	233	48	6979
	North Platte	A	35.5	0	6	123	440	885	1166	1271	1039	930	519	248	57	6684
	Omaha	A	35.6	0	12	105	357	828	1175	1355	1126	939	465	208	42	6612
	Scottsbluff	A	35.9	0	0	138	459	876	1128	1231	1008	921	552	285	75	6673
	Valentine	A	32.6	9	12	165	493	942	1237	1395	1176	1045	579	288	84	7425
Nev.	Elko	A	34.0	9	34	225	561	924	1197	1314	1036	911	621	409	192	7433
	Ely	A	33.1	28	43	234	592	939	1184	1308	1075	977	672	456	225	7733
	Las Vegas	A	53.5	0	0	0	78	387	617	688	487	335	111	6	0	2709
	Reno	A	39.3	43	87	204	490	801	1026	1073	823	729	510	357	189	6332
	Winnemucca	A	36.7	0	34	210	536	876	1091	1172	916	837	573	363	153	6761
N.H.	Concord	A	33.0	6	50	177	505	822	1240	1358	1184	1032	636	298	75	7383
	Mt. Washington Obsv.		15.2	493	536	720	1057	1341	1742	1820	1663	1652	1260	930	603	13817
N.J.	Atlantic City	A	43.2	0	0	39	251	549	880	936	848	741	420	133	15	4812
	Newark	A	42.8	0	0	30	248	573	921	983	876	729	381	118	0	4589
	Trenton	C	42.4	0	0	57	264	576	924	989	885	753	399	121	12	4980
N. M.	Albuquerque	A	45.0	0	0	12	229	642	868	930	703	595	288	81	0	4348
	Clayton	A	42.0	0	6	66	310	699	899	986	812	747	429	183	21	5158
	Raton	A	38.1	9	28	126	431	825	1048	1116	904	834	543	301	63	6228
	Roswell	A	47.5	0	0	18	202	573	806	840	641	481	201	31	0	3793
	Silver City	A	48.0	0	0	6	183	525	729	791	605	518	261	87	0	3705
N.Y.	Albany	A	34.6	0	19	138	440	777	1194	1311	1156	992	564	239	45	6875
	Albany	C	37.2	0	9	102	375	699	1104	1218	1072	908	498	186	30	6201
	Binghamton	A	33.9	22	65	201	471	810	1184	1277	1154	1045	645	313	99	7286
	Binghamton	C	36.6	0	28	141	406	732	1107	1190	1081	949	543	229	45	6451
	Buffalo	A	34.5	19	37	141	440	777	1156	1256	1145	1039	645	329	78	7062
	New York (Cent. Park)	C	42.8	0	0	30	233	540	902	986	885	760	408	118	9	4871
	New York (La Guardia)	A	43.1	0	0	27	223	528	887	973	879	750	414	124	6	4811

Table 4-16. Average Monthly and Yearly Degree Days for Cities in the United States and Canada[a,b,c] (Base 65F)
(Reprinted with Permission from the 1976 Systems Volume, ASHRAE HANDBOOK & Product Directory) (continued from page 197).

State	Station		Avg. Winter Temp[d]	July	Aug.	Sept.	Oct.	Nov.	Dec.	Jan.	Feb.	Mar.	Apr.	May	June	Yearly Total
	New York (Kennedy)	A	41.4	0	0	36	248	564	933	1029	935	815	480	167	12	5219
	Rochester	A	35.4	9	31	126	415	747	1125	1234	1123	1014	597	279	48	6748
	Schenectady	C	35.4	0	22	123	422	756	1159	1283	1131	970	543	211	30	6650
	Syracuse	A	35.2	6	28	132	415	744	1153	1271	1140	1004	570	248	45	6756
N. C.	Asheville	C	46.7	0	0	48	245	555	775	784	683	592	273	87	0	4042
	Cape Hatteras	A	53.3	0	0	0	78	273	521	580	518	440	177	25	0	2612
	Charlotte	A	50.4	0	0	6	124	438	691	691	582	481	156	22	0	3191
	Greensboro	A	47.5	0	0	33	192	513	778	784	672	552	234	47	0	3805
	Raleigh	A	49.4	0	0	21	164	450	716	725	616	487	180	34	0	3393
	Wilmington	A	54.6	0	0	0	74	291	521	546	462	357	96	0	0	2347
	Winston-Salem	A	48.4	0	0	21	171	483	747	753	652	524	207	37	0	3595
N. D.	Bismarck	A	26.6	34	28	222	577	1083	1463	1708	1442	1203	645	329	117	8851
	Devils Lake	C	22.4	40	53	273	642	1191	1634	1872	1579	1345	753	381	138	9901
	Fargo	A	24.8	28	37	219	574	1107	1569	1789	1520	1262	690	332	99	9226
	Williston	A	25.2	31	43	261	601	1122	1513	1758	1473	1262	681	357	141	9243
Ohio	Akron-Canton	A	38.1	0	0	96	381	726	1070	1138	1016	871	489	202	39	6037
	Cincinnati	C	45.1	0	0	39	208	558	862	915	790	642	294	96	6	4410
	Cleveland	A	37.2	9	25	105	384	738	1088	1159	1047	918	552	260	66	6351
	Columbus	A	39.7	0	6	84	347	714	1039	1088	949	809	426	171	27	5660
	Columbus	C	41.5	0	0	57	285	651	977	1032	902	760	396	136	15	5211
	Dayton	A	39.8	0	6	78	310	696	1045	1097	955	809	429	167	30	5622
	Mansfield	A	36.9	0	22	114	397	768	1110	1169	1042	924	543	245	60	6403
	Sandusky	C	39.1	0	6	66	313	684	1032	1107	991	868	495	198	36	5796
	Toledo	A	36.4	0	16	117	406	792	1138	1200	1056	924	543	242	60	6494
	Youngstown	A	36.8	6	19	120	412	771	1104	1169	1047	921	540	248	60	6417
Okla.	Oklahoma City	A	48.3	0	0	15	164	498	766	868	664	527	189	34	0	3725
	Tulsa	A	47.7	0	0	18	158	522	787	893	683	539	213	47	0	3860
Ore.	Astoria	A	45.6	146	130	210	375	561	679	753	622	636	480	363	231	5186

State	City		Temp														Total
	Eugene	A	45.6	34	34	129	366	585	719	803	627	589	426	279	135	4726
	Meacham	A	34.2	84	124	288	580	918	1091	1209	1005	983	726	527	339	7874
	Medford	A	43.2	0	0	78	372	678	871	918	697	642	432	242	78	5008
	Pendleton	A	42.6	0	0	111	350	711	884	1017	773	617	396	205	63	5127
	Portland	A	45.6	25	28	114	335	597	735	825	644	586	396	245	105	4635
	Portland	C	47.4	12	16	75	267	534	679	769	594	536	351	198	78	4109
	Roseburg	A	46.3	22	16	105	329	567	713	766	608	570	405	267	123	4491
	Salem	A	45.4	37	31	111	338	594	729	822	647	611	417	273	144	4754
Pa.	Allentown	A	38.9	0	0	90	353	693	1045	1116	1002	849	471	167	24	5810
	Erie	A	36.8	0	25	102	391	714	1063	1169	1081	973	585	288	60	6451
	Harrisburg	A	41.2	0	0	63	298	648	992	1045	907	766	396	124	12	5251
	Philadelphia	A	41.8	0	0	60	297	620	965	1016	889	747	392	118	40	5144
	Philadelphia	C	44.5	0	0	30	205	513	856	924	823	691	351	93	0	4486
	Pittsburgh	A	38.4	0	9	105	375	726	1063	1119	1002	874	480	195	39	5987
	Pittsburgh	C	42.2	0	0	60	291	615	930	983	885	763	390	124	12	5053
	Reading	C	42.4	0	0	54	257	597	939	1001	885	735	372	105	0	4945
	Scranton	A	37.2	0	19	132	434	762	1104	1156	1028	893	498	195	33	6254
	Williamsport	A	38.5	0	9	111	375	717	1073	1122	1002	856	468	177	24	5934
R. I.	Block Island	A	40.1	0	16	78	307	594	902	1020	955	877	612	344	99	5804
	Providence	A	38.8	0	16	96	372	660	1023	1110	988	868	534	236	51	5954
S. C.	Charleston	A	56.6	0	0	0	59	282	471	487	389	291	54	0	0	2033
	Charleston	C	57.9	0	0	0	34	210	425	443	367	273	42	0	0	1794
	Columbia	A	54.0	0	0	0	84	345	577	570	470	357	81	0	0	2484
	Florence	A	54.5	0	0	0	78	315	552	552	459	347	84	0	0	2387
	Greenville-Spartenburg	A	51.6	0	0	6	121	399	651	660	546	446	132	19	0	2980
S. D.	Huron	A	28.8	9	12	165	508	1014	1432	1628	1355	1125	600	288	87	8223
	Rapid City	A	33.4	22	12	165	481	897	1172	1333	1145	1051	615	326	126	7345
	Sioux Falls	A	30.6	19	25	168	462	972	1361	1544	1285	1082	573	270	78	7839
Tenn.	Bristol	A	46.2	0	0	51	236	573	828	828	700	598	261	68	0	4143
	Chattanooga	A	50.3	0	0	18	143	468	698	722	577	453	150	25	0	3254
	Knoxville	A	49.2	0	0	30	171	489	725	732	613	493	198	43	0	3494
	Memphis	A	50.5	0	0	18	130	447	698	729	585	456	147	22	0	3232

Table 4-16. Average Monthly and Yearly Degree Days for Cities in the United States and Canada[a,b,c] (Base 65 F)
(Reprinted with Permission from the 1976 Systems Volume, ASHRAE HANDBOOK & Product Directory) (continued from page 199).

State or Prov.	Station		Avg. Winter Temp[d]	July	Aug.	Sept.	Oct.	Nov.	Dec.	Jan.	Feb.	Mar.	Apr.	May	June	Yearly Total
Tex.	Memphis	C	51.6	0	0	12	102	396	648	710	568	434	129	16	0	3015
	Nashville	A	48.9	0	0	30	158	495	732	778	644	512	189	40	0	3578
	Oak Ridge	C	47.7	0	0	39	192	531	772	778	669	552	228	56	0	3817
	Abilene	A	53.9	0	0	0	99	366	586	642	470	347	114	0	0	2624
	Amarillo	A	47.0	0	0	18	205	570	797	877	664	546	252	56	0	3985
	Austin	A	59.1	0	0	0	31	225	388	468	325	223	51	0	0	1711
	Brownsville	A	67.7	0	0	0	0	66	149	205	106	74	0	0	0	600
	Corpus Christi	A	64.6	0	0	0	0	120	220	291	174	109	0	0	0	914
	Dallas	A	55.3	0	0	0	62	321	524	601	440	319	90	6	0	2363
	El Paso	A	52.9	0	0	0	84	414	648	685	445	319	105	0	0	2700
	Fort Worth	A	55.1	0	0	0	65	324	536	614	448	319	99	0	0	2405
	Galveston	A	62.2	0	0	0	6	147	276	360	263	189	33	0	0	1274
	Galveston	C	62.0	0	0	0	0	138	270	350	258	189	30	0	0	1235
	Houston	A	61.0	0	0	0	6	183	307	384	288	192	36	0	0	1396
	Houston	C	62.0	0	0	0	0	165	288	363	258	174	30	0	0	1278
	Laredo	C	66.0	0	0	0	0	105	217	267	134	74	0	0	0	797
	Lubbock	A	48.8	0	0	18	174	513	744	800	613	484	201	31	0	3578
	Midland	A	53.8	0	0	0	87	381	592	651	468	322	90	0	0	2591
	Port Arthur	A	60.5	0	0	0	22	207	329	384	274	192	39	0	0	1447
	San Angelo	A	56.0	0	0	0	68	318	536	567	412	288	66	0	0	2255
	San Antonio	A	60.1	0	0	0	31	204	363	428	286	195	39	0	0	1546
	Victoria	A	62.7	0	0	0	6	150	270	344	230	152	21	0	0	1173
	Waco	A	57.2	0	0	0	43	270	456	536	389	270	66	0	0	2030
	Wichita Falls	A	53.0	0	0	0	99	381	632	698	518	378	120	6	0	2832
Utah	Milford	A	36.5	0	0	99	443	867	1141	1252	988	822	519	279	87	6497
	Salt Lake City	A	38.4	0	0	81	419	849	1082	1172	910	763	459	233	84	6052
	Wendover	A	39.1	0	0	48	372	822	1091	1178	902	729	408	177	51	5778
Vt.	Burlington	A	29.4	28	65	207	539	891	1349	1513	1333	1187	714	353	90	8269

Va.	Cape Henry	C	50.0	0	0	0	112	360	645	694	633	536	246	53	0	3279
	Lynchburg	A	46.0	0	0	51	223	540	822	849	731	605	267	78	0	4166
	Norfolk	A	49.2	0	0	0	136	408	698	738	655	533	216	37	0	3421
	Richmond	A	47.3	0	0	36	214	495	784	815	703	546	219	53	0	3865
	Roanoke	A	46.1	0	0	51	229	549	825	834	722	614	261	65	0	4150
Wash.	Olympia	A	44.2	68	71	198	422	636	753	834	675	645	450	307	177	5236
	Seattle-Tacoma	A	44.2	56	62	162	391	633	750	828	678	657	474	295	159	5145
	Seattle	C	46.9	50	47	129	329	543	657	738	599	577	396	242	117	4424
	Spokane	A	36.5	9	25	168	493	879	1082	1231	980	834	531	288	135	6655
	Walla Walla	C	43.8	0	0	87	310	681	843	986	745	589	342	177	45	4805
	Yakima	A	39.1	0	12	144	450	828	1039	1163	868	713	435	220	69	5941
W. Va.	Charleston	A	44.8	0	0	63	254	591	865	880	770	648	300	96	9	4476
	Elkins	A	40.1	9	25	135	400	729	992	1008	896	791	444	198	48	5675
	Huntington	A	45.0	0	0	63	257	585	856	880	764	636	294	99	12	4446
	Parkersburg	C	43.5	0	0	60	264	606	905	942	826	691	339	115	6	4754
Wisc.	Green Bay	A	30.3	28	50	174	484	924	1333	1494	1313	1141	654	335	99	8029
	La Crosse	A	31.5	12	19	153	437	924	1339	1504	1277	1070	540	245	69	7589
	Madison	A	30.9	25	40	174	474	930	1330	1473	1274	1113	618	310	102	7863
	Milwaukee	A	32.6	43	47	174	471	876	1252	1376	1193	1054	642	372	135	7635
Wyo.	Casper	A	33.4	6	16	192	524	942	1169	1290	1084	1020	657	381	129	7410
	Cheyenne	A	34.2	28	37	219	543	909	1085	1212	1042	1026	702	428	150	7381
	Lander	A	31.4	6	19	204	555	1020	1299	1417	1145	1017	654	381	153	7870
	Sheridan	A	32.5	25	31	219	539	948	1200	1355	1154	1051	642	366	150	7680
Alta.	Banff	C	—	220	295	498	797	1185	1485	1624	1364	1237	855	589	402	10551
	Calgary	A	—	109	186	402	719	1110	1389	1575	1379	1268	798	477	291	9703
	Edmonton	A	—	74	180	411	738	1215	1603	1810	1520	1330	765	400	222	10268
	Lethbridge	A	—	56	112	318	611	1011	1277	1497	1291	1159	696	403	213	8644
B. C.	Kamloops	A	—	22	40	189	546	894	1138	1314	1057	818	462	217	102	6799
	Prince George*	A	—	236	251	444	747	1110	1420	1612	1319	1122	747	468	279	9755
	Prince Rupert*	C	—	273	248	339	539	708	868	936	808	812	648	493	357	7029
	Vancouver*	A	—	81	87	219	456	657	787	862	723	676	501	310	156	5515
	Victoria*	A	—	136	140	225	462	663	775	840	718	691	504	341	204	5699
	Victoria	C	—	172	184	243	426	607	723	805	668	660	487	354	250	5579

Table 4-16. Average Monthly and Yearly Degree Days for Cities in the United States and Canada[a,b,c] (Base 65 F)
(Reprinted with Permission from the 1976 Systems Volume, ASHRAE HANDBOOK & Product Directory) (Continued from page 201).

State or Prov.	Station		Avg. Winter Temp[d]	July	Aug.	Sept.	Oct.	Nov.	Dec.	Jan.	Feb.	Mar.	Apr.	May	June	Yearly Total
Man.	Brandon*	A	—	47	90	357	747	1290	1792	2034	1737	1476	837	431	198	11036
	Churchill	A	—	360	375	681	1082	1620	2248	2558	2277	2130	1569	1153	675	16728
	The Pas	C	—	59	127	429	831	1440	1981	2232	1853	1624	969	508	228	12281
	Winnipeg	A	—	38	71	322	683	1251	1757	2008	1719	1465	813	405	147	10679
N. B.	Fredericton*	A	—	78	68	234	592	915	1392	1541	1379	1172	753	406	141	8671
	Moncton	C	—	62	105	276	611	891	1342	1482	1336	1194	789	468	171	8727
	St. John	C	—	109	102	246	527	807	1194	1370	1229	1097	756	490	249	8219
Nfld.	Argentia	A	—	260	167	294	564	750	1001	1159	1085	1091	879	707	483	8440
	Corner Brook	C	—	102	133	324	642	873	1194	1358	1283	1212	885	639	333	8978
	Gander	A	—	121	152	330	670	909	1231	1370	1266	1243	939	657	366	9254
	Goose*	A	—	130	205	444	843	1227	1745	1947	1689	1494	1074	741	348	11887
	St. John's*	A	—	186	180	342	651	831	1113	1262	1170	1187	927	710	432	8991
N. W. T.	Aklavik	C	—	273	459	807	1414	2064	2530	2632	2336	2282	1674	1063	483	18017
	Fort Norman	C	—	164	341	666	1234	1959	2474	2592	2209	2058	1386	732	294	16109
	Resolution Island	C	—	843	831	900	1113	1311	1724	2021	1850	1817	1488	1181	942	16021
N. S.	Halifax	C	—	58	51	180	457	710	1074	1213	1122	1030	742	487	237	7361
	Sydney	A	—	62	71	219	518	765	1113	1262	1206	1150	840	567	276	8049
	Yarmouth	A	—	102	115	225	471	696	1029	1156	1065	1004	726	493	258	7340

	Station															Annual
Ont.	Cochrane	C	—	96	180	405	760	1233	1776	1978	1701	1528	963	570	222	11412
	Fort William	A	—	90	133	366	694	1140	1597	1792	1557	1380	876	543	237	10405
	Kapuskasing	C	—	74	171	405	756	1245	1807	2037	1735	1562	978	580	222	11572
	Kitchener	C	—	16	59	177	505	837	1234	1342	1226	1101	663	322	66	7566
	London	A	—	12	43	159	477	855	1206	1305	1198	1066	648	332	66	7349
	North Bay	C	—	37	90	267	608	990	1507	1680	1463	1277	780	400	120	9219
	Ottawa	C	—	25	81	222	567	936	1469	1624	1441	1231	708	341	90	8735
	Toronto	C	—	7	18	151	439	760	1111	1233	1119	1013	616	298	62	6827
P.E.I.	Charlottetown	C	—	40	53	198	518	804	1215	1380	1274	1169	813	496	204	8164
	Summerside	C	—	47	84	216	546	840	1246	1438	1291	1206	841	518	216	8488
Que.	Arvida	C	—	102	136	327	682	1074	1659	1879	1619	1407	891	521	231	10528
	Montreal*	A	—	9	43	165	521	882	1392	1566	1381	1175	684	316	69	8203
	Montreal	C	—	16	28	165	496	864	1355	1510	1328	1138	657	288	54	7899
	Quebec*	A	—	56	84	273	636	996	1516	1665	1477	1296	819	428	126	9372
	Quebec	C	—	40	68	243	592	972	1473	1612	1418	1228	780	400	111	8937
Sasks	Prince Albert	A	—	81	136	414	797	1368	1872	2108	1763	1559	867	446	219	11630
	Regina	A	—	78	93	360	741	1284	1711	1965	1687	1473	804	409	201	10806
	Saskatoon	C	—	56	87	372	750	1302	1758	2006	1689	1463	798	403	186	10870
Y. T.	Dawson	C	—	164	326	645	1197	1875	2415	2561	2150	1838	1068	570	258	15067
	Mayo Landing	C	—	208	366	648	1135	1794	2325	2427	1992	1665	1020	580	294	14454

*The data for these normals were from the full ten-year period 1951-1960, adjusted to the standard normal period 1931-1960.

203

When a heat pump installation is involved, a number of additional variable factors enter into the picture and the calculations are best made by the heating engineer specifying the equipment (based upon the particularities of that equipment). For all other types of heating equipment, the formula on page 189 works nicely.

The *Eff*, which might also be called a performance factor or have some other name, is generally noted on a disclosure plate attached to the equipment. However, this is not true of wood-burning stoves. If you plan to heat by this means, you will have to judge the efficiency of your stove either by figures obtained from the manufacturer that show an average efficiency as tested or simply by making a guess. For want of a better figure, you can reasonably assume that the efficiency of a good airtight wood stove is 50 percent on average.

The principle problem with using the above formula to determine seasonal heating load is that the results are often a bit cockeyed. This is particularly true for electric resistance heating installed in a tight house. The estimates can be off as much as 50 percent. Though the formula worked well enough three and four decades ago, houses today tend to be tighter and more heavily insulated and the method often leaves something to be desired. A considerable amount of study is under way to find a new formula with substantially greater accuracy. In the meantime, the ASH-RAE suggests using a modified degree-day method that solves the equation for the *probable* energy consumption of the heating system. This formula is as follows:

$$E = \frac{H_L \times D \times 24}{\Delta \tau \times \eta \times V \; (C_D) \; (C_F)}$$

Where

E = fuel for energy consumption for the estimate period.

H_L = design heat loss, including infiltration, Btu per hour.

D = number of 65 F degree-days for the estimate period.

Δt = design temperature difference, degrees F.

η = rated full load efficiency, decimal.

V = heating value of fuel, consistent with H_L and E.

C_D = interim correction factor for heating effect versus degree-days.

C_F = interim part-load correction factor for fueled systems only; equals 1.0 for electric resistance heating.

The factor H_L is the total heating load in Btuh that you developed on your worksheet. A value for V can be found in Table 4-17. Take the factor C_D from Table 4-18 and the factor C_F from Table 4-19.

Let's assume that your log cabin has a total Btuh heat loss of 20,000 and that the number of degree-days at your site is 5500. We'll assume a Δt of 65 F and that you have installed a new wood furnace with an efficiency of 60 percent. For fuel, you're going to use equal parts of paper birch and sugar maple with heating values of 23.1 million Btu (or MBtu) per cord, and 27.0 MBtu per cord, respectively. So, 20,000 (H_L) times 5500 (D) times 24 (hours per day) equals 2,640,000,000. Then, 65 (Δt) times 0.60

(efficiency times 25,000,000 (average heating value of the wood) equals 975,000,000.

All but one of the zeros cancel themselves out and dividing the first figure by the second equals 2.708 cords of birch and maple evenly mixed. Now, multiply 2.708 times 0.75 (C_D, interpolated from Table 4-18 from an outside design temperature of +6 F) times 1.36 (C_F, from Table 4-19, assumed), for a total of 2.76. Lay in three cords and you'll be all set. Calculating for other fuels is done in the same way and the answer is obtained in whatever fuel units are applicable (gallons, cubic feet, etc.).

Estimating the seasonal heating cost now becomes a simple chore of multiplying the amount of fuel that presumably will be needed by its unit cost. And when projecting ahead, it's not a bad idea to plug in an inflation factor on the rather good assumption that fuel cost probably will rise from time to time in the future. If you have made two or more trial runs on your worksheet for different U values of building sections, now you can perform the same calculations for the various combinations to see exactly what their cost-effectiveness will be. Comparing fuel costs for the different combinations will give you the seasonal savings of one over another. The cost figures can be divided into the added cost of one construction method over another to determine the number of heating seasons that would be required before the initial outlay will be returned to you in fuel-cost savings. When making such calculations, it's wise to include external operative factors such as potential increases in fuel cost, inflationary diminishing of the dollar value, interest costs of the added material by virtue of the mortgage, and so on.

CALCULATIONS FOR SPECIAL DESIGNS

All of the foregoing relates specifically to conventional styles of houses constructed in more or less conventional ways. There are, how-

Table 4-17. Fuel or Heating Values (V Factors) of Various Kinds of Fuels and Energy.

FUEL	Btu	UNIT
Natural gas	1,035	cu. ft.
Methane gas	1,000	cu. ft.
Liquid propane	91,500	gal.
Liquid butane	102,000	gal.
No. 2 fuel oil	140,000	gal.
Diesel oil	138,000	gal.
Kerosene	135,000	gal.
Shale oil (kerogen)	138,000	gal.
Crude oil	138,000	gal.
Electricity	3,413	kwh
Anthracite coal	25,400,000	ton
Bituminous coal	26,200,000	ton
Lignite coal	13,800,000	ton
Wood, dry average	9,000	lb.
Quaking aspen	16,000,000	cord
Paper birch	23,100,000	cord
Red maple	23,200,000	cord
Sugar maple	27,000,000	cord
Northern red oak	26,800,000	cord
Eastern white pine	15,000,000	cord
White spruce	17,100,000	cord
Ponderosa pine	17,100,000	cord
Douglas fir	21,400,000	cord

**Table 4-18. Interim Correction Factors in Compensation of
Heating Effect Versus Degree-Days (Reprinted with Permission
from the 1976 Systems Volume, ASHRAE HANDBOOK & Product Directory).**

Heat Loss vs Degree Days Interim Factor C$_D$					
Outdoor Design Temp. F	−20	−10	0	+10	+20
Factor C$_D$	0.57	0.64	0.71	0.79	0.89

ever, three new house designs that are now gaining increasing popularity. Calculations are made in somewhat different fashions and touch upon different areas. These are the dome, earth-sheltered, and solar designs. In all of these cases, the fundamentals of heat loss remain identical to those just discussed.

Dome houses are calculated using the same principles, but the formulas vary somewhat for ease of determining section areas, volumes, and so on. The differences are in methodology and not basic factors. As to earth-sheltered houses, the study of their particular thermal characteris-

**Table 4-19. Part-Load Correction Factors for
Fuel Heating Systems (Reprinted with Permission from the
1976 Systems Volume, ASHRAE HANDBOOK & Product Directory).**

Percent oversizing	0	20	40	60	80
Factor C$_F$	1.36	1.56	1.79	2.04	2.32

tics continues. Making some of the calculations for the below-ground portions of such structures can be tricky and each should be calculated with some factors developed on an individual basis. Rules of thumb are best supplanted by more accurate data.

Making loss calculations for houses specifically designed to utilize passive, active, or hybrid solar heating systems is done in exactly the same fashion as I have just discussed. However, there are numerous added considerations that must be factored in and these upon the specifics of the design. Such matters as flywheel effect, thermal mass, average insolation at the building site, solar incidence, orientation, and similar elements become extremely important.

In some cases, the house is actually the heating system and many of these calculations must be made on the basis of specific factors pertinent to the particular site. The usual methods of making heat loss calculations can serve as a basis. Those who are interested in these special designs must usually go several steps further in specialized calculations to complete the process.

Estimating Heat Gains

5

Calculating heat gains and figuring out the cooling load for a house (or other building) is a complicated affair. The same variables that are considered in calculating heat losses are involved—plus a few more. With winter conditions, where the object is to conserve mechanically generated or entrapped solar heat within the building, the exterior of the building is surrounded by air at a relatively uniform lower temperature and the heat inside the house is trying to get out. Humidity in the house, which has a direct bearing upon bodily comfort, presents no problems in heat generation except that moisture often has to be added to the interior atmosphere for optimum comfort.

During summer, maintaining a satisfactorily low and comfortable temperature and relative humidity within a house by keeping warm air and moisture out is much more problematical than is keeping them in during winter. Under summer conditions, the house is surrounded by warmer air of varying temperatures at different points. Excessive humidity is commonplace in most areas of the country during the summer months. There are a number of outside influences that bear upon structural heat gain and make adequate control difficult. While there are two principal factors when making heat loss calculations (infiltration losses and transmission losses), there are five to consider in calculating cooling loads.

HEAT GAIN FACTORS

Houses that are well insulated and have an effective and efficient thermal design for comfortable, economical heating can also perform well under hot-weather conditions. Because of the innate differences between heating loads and cooling loads, houses can be made to perform much better where cooling—either natural or mechanical—is desirable by giving due consideration to some additional elements of thermal design. This in no way interferes with thermal performances during a heating mode and it will sometimes serve to somewhat improve it. The only way to determine exactly what the cooling load will be under various design conditions is to work out a series of calculations that include the five main elements of heat gains and to consider some of the lesser factors that influence those elements.

Transmission Heat Gains

A substantial portion of the cooling load of a house is due to transmission heat gains through the building sections. The mechanisms of heat transfer are the same as for transmission heat losses and the coefficients of transmission are determined in just the same way as those used in calculating heat losses. However, there is one notable difference. Under summer conditions, the heat flow is reversed from that of winter conditions. The warmer outside air is transferred through the building sections into the cooler interior of the house. This leads to some slight changes in the details of determining heat transmission coefficients. For example, the heat flow through floors is upward instead of downward and the heat flow through ceilings and roofs is downward rather than upward. Factors for summer conditions must be used for determining the U value of glazing and the R value of exterior surface films.

An additional difference in making the overall calculations lies in the fact that the heat transmission coefficients are not multiplied by a fixed Δt (design temperature difference) as they are for heat loss calculations. Instead, special tabulated design equivalent temperature differences (DETD) are substituted for Δt. The DETD values vary with the different kinds of building sections and the conditions to which they are subject.

Infiltration Heat Gains

As with the infiltration factor that is considered while calculating heat losses, infiltration under summer conditions is comprised of two components: natural ventilation and mechanical ventilation. Summer infiltration flows into the house and brings warm air inside the exfiltrate cooler air at various natural escape points. The total amount of natural air leakage in a house that is normally kept well closed up to allow mechanical cooling equipment to do its job properly is substantially less than cold air infiltration during the winter heating season.

Wind velocities, which have such a drastic effect upon infiltration under winter conditions, are generally much lower during the summer months. Also, the wind directions are generally different and more variable and the total wind impact on a residence is substantially lower. In addition, the winter "stack effect" is absent. The stack effect is caused by considerably colder temperatures outside than inside which, along with the influence of the wind, forces the warm air to migrate to the outside. When exterior temperatures are *higher* than the interior and the warm air is trying to get in rather than out, the stack effect disappears. Despite this the relatively small sensible cooling load due to infiltration must be made a part of the heat gain calculations.

The mechanical-ventilation component of infiltration is in some houses considerably more important than natural air leakage because it is likely to impose a greater load on the cooling equipment. This is true for two reasons. First, the actual volume of air likely to be introduced into a house by mechanical means is far greater than that of natural air leakage and consequently a much larger quantity of outside heat is brought into the building. Second, introducing outside warm air under positive pressure by mechanical means just about eliminates any natural air leakage in the meantime.

Many central air-conditioning systems include provision for mechanical ventilation so that the equipment can be operated in a ventilating mode rather than in a full cooling mode. When conditions are right, this can provide comfort cooling at lower cost because only the blower of the air-conditioning unit is actually in operation.

In other instances, mechanical cooling and ventilation might be carried on simultaneously. Small houses most often are not equipped with a ventilation system, either integral with or separate from an air-conditioning system, and mechanical ventilation is not a requirement of building codes in most locales.

However, large houses should be fitted with positive ventilation systems and so should any houses where the occupants anticipate a substantial amount of indoor activity during hot weather. A positive ventilation factor should be included in the heat gain calculations for any such house. This can be done on the basis of a tabulated experiential value that will work satisfactorily in most installations. If the volume of outside air that will be regularly introduced into the house will obviously be substantially greater than a tabulated average, that value should be substituted. For smaller houses, natural leakage provides sufficient fresh air for a healthful interior environment. However, each design should be individually assessed.

Solar Heat Gains

Heat transfer through building sections under winter conditions is relatively uniform over an entire structure. At certain times, the wind will influence heat transfer through certain areas, but this factor is made a part of the heat loss calculations. At certain other times, sunshine striking surface areas of the house or shining in through windows can help to minimize heat losses and perhaps add a certain amount of useful heat. But in that instance the sun is working with the heating system and only serves to periodically reduce the heating load somewhat. Under summer conditions the situation changes. The wind, when it has any effect at all, might simply serve to slightly increase the cooling load. The impact of sunshine adds heat to the building. In this case, it is a hindrance because it further increases the cooling load. The solar impact is an adverse, worst-case factor, and cooling capacity to remove these peak loads of heat must be provided if a satisfactory level of comfort cooling is to be maintained.

Solar heat gain is developed in two ways. One occurs when sunshine strikes windows and glass doors. A certain portion of the radiant energy is reflected from the glass. This is variable depending upon the type of glass and the angle of the sun's rays. A part of the remaining radiant energy is immediately converted into heat within and on the surfaces of the glass itself. The remainder is transmitted into the house. When the transmitted radiant energy strikes floors, walls, furniture, etc., it too is converted to heat. Eventually, and through diverse complex paths, most or all of this heat will appear as a part of the overall cooling load of the house. The load segments and the time intervals are almost impossible to determine. The effects upon the cooling load begin to take place soon after the introduction of the radiant energy. They are dependent upon the amount of radiant energy admitted and they tend to diminish fairly soon after the radiant energy has been excluded.

The other way in which the impact of solar heat occurs is through sunlight striking upon opaque building sections (primarily walls and roofs). Part of the incident radiation is reflected away. The exact amount depends upon the angle of incidence and the reflectivity of the surfaces. The remaining energy is absorbed by the building surface. This raises its temperature and causes heat to flow into the building faster (to a variable degree) than would be the case if the surface temperature were equal to the ambient outside air temperature.

The thermal resistance of the building section determines the rate of heat transfer into the section and the heat storage capacity of the materials from which the section is constructed delays the heat transfer from outside to inside. The flywheel effect influences the time span over which heat developing on the exterior surface becomes a part of the interior cooling load. In very lightweight, low-mass construction, especially if little or no insulation is included, the time difference can be as short as half an hour. In an average frame house construction, that time lag might well be 3 to 4 hours. And in heavy, massive construction the lag could easily reach 8 to 12 hours or more. That is why a thick-walled adobe house built in desert country, where the days are very hot and dry and the nights are cold, works so well. By the time the day's heat buildup has managed to reach the inner surface of the walls, outside temperatures have cooled markedly and the heat transfer reverses direction before the heat becomes a part of the interior cooling load.

Occupancy Heat Gains

Not all of the heat that becomes a part of a cooling load comes from outside the house. People living in the house and pursuing their daily activities—and some of the mechanical equipment that they use in the process—generate a certain amount of heat that remains within the house and adds to the cooling load. Certain experiential values are assigned to these heat gains and included in the calculations. The values are approximate only because of the tremendous variability and unpredictability of actual loads in any given instance.

Latent Heat Gains

Heat is composed of two separate components, sensible and latent, and that in making residential heat loss calculations the latent component is generally ignored. This is because of the problems involved in properly assessing the necessary values with which the calculations are made, the difficulties of the calculations themselves, and the fact that in most residential heating applications the latent heat loss doesn't amount to much anyway. The amount of moisture vapor in the interior atmosphere of houses in most locales during winter conditions is not very great. They must often be added to by humidification of one sort or another in order to increase comfort levels and decrease ambient dry-bulb air temperature for lower operating costs.

That situation does not hold true under summer conditions. With the exception of the few hot-dry areas of the country, outdoor relative humidity quite consistently ranges anywhere from moderately high to very high and indoor relative humidities follow closely along. To make matters worse, the numerous sources of additional moisture within the house contribute greatly to water vapor in the interior atmosphere. In the interest of comfort, however, interior relative humidity must be decreased substantially in order to maintain a comfortable environment. This is part of the chore faced by the cooling equipment. The latent heat within the conditioned space is a part of the cooling load.

THE GENERAL PROCEDURE

Making heat gain calculations to determine the total cooling load of a residence or other building can range from relatively simple to incredibly complex. As with heat loss calculations under many circumstances, super-sophisticated programs are computer-run and analysed to arrive at the final design data. Except in very unusual circumstances, that sort of sophistication is usually unnecessary for residence cooling data. The same organizations mentioned in Chapter 4 that offer various methods for determining residential heating loads also can supply full information on methods for determining cooling loads.

There are some differences in methodology, but you can use any of these systems with complete assurance that the results will be satisfactory. Of them, the NAHB system found in the *Insulation Manual* is well detailed and affords great flexibility of choice amongst construction specifics. The ASHRAE goes into considerable basic detail in the *HANDBOOK & Product Directory, 1977 Fundamentals Volume*, Chapter 25, "Air-Conditioning Cooling Load." This chapter contains a wealth of basic information on determining cooling loads for all kinds of buildings. In the same chapter, ASHRAE presents a simplified method, using experiential averages, for determining cooling load in residences only. In most situations, this method will serve quite adequately and it is the one that I shall outline here.

Given the obvious complexity of most methods of calculating cooling loads, and given also the incredibly complicated nature of the subject, how is it that a simple procedure for residential cooling load calculations can be workable? There are several reasons, and they can best be expressed by quoting from the ASHRAE manual.

"1. Residences, unlike many other structures, are assumed to be occupied, and usually conditioned, for 24 hours a day, every day of the cooling season.

"2. Residential cooling system loads are primarily imposed by heat flow through structural components and by air leakage or ventilation. Internal loads, particularly those imposed by occupants and lights, are small in comparison to those in commercial or industrial installations.

"3. Most residences are cooled as a single zone, since there is no means to redistribute cooling unit capacity from one area to another as loads change from hour to hour.

"4. Most residential systems employ units of relatively small capacity (from about 20,000 to 60,000 Btuh) which have no means for controlling capacity, except by cycling the condensing unit. Since cooling load is largely affected by outside conditions, and few days each season are *design* days, a partial load situation exists during most of the season. An oversized unit with no capacity control is detrimental to good system performance under these circumstances.

"5. Dehumidification is achieved only during periods of cooling unit operation, since there is only very limited use of reheat or by-pass systems to directly control humidity under conditions of relatively light sensible load. Space condition control is usually restricted to use of room thermostats, essentially sensible heat-actuated devices.

"6. Many residential systems are operated 24 hours a day, thus permitting full advantage to be taken of thermal *flywheel* effects of structural members and furnishings within the structure."

Even though this procedure is classed as a simplified one, there still are a good many facts and figures that must be kept track of. It's easy to get lost and take a wrong turn somewhere during the process. Here are the steps that must be taken.

☐ The first step is very similar to that of making heat loss calculations. You must evolve a reasonably accurate estimation of the climatic data at and around the building site. Using this information, you must select an outdoor design temperature and also estimate the mean daily temperature range.

☐ Indoor design conditions must also be selected. In residential applications, this involves choosing an indoor design temperature, determining an allowable temperature swing, and establishing a mechanical ventilation rate if that is called for.

212

☐ Next it is necessary to determine the coefficients of heat transfer for all of the various building sections. This is done in much the same way as when making heat loss calculations. There are some variations that I will explain shortly.

☐ The next step consists of finding the combined transmission and solar gains for the various building sections through the use of entabulated average values. These figures are then related to the building section areas in order to determine the hourly heat gains through them.

☐ Assess the heat gain by infiltration and/or ventilation air.

☐ Estimate the heat gain from occupancy factors.

☐ Calculate the latent heat gain.

☐ Find the total cooling load of the house, the seasonal cooling load, and the approximate operating costs. From these figures, the details of both the cooling equipment and the cool-air distribution system can be developed.

HEAT GAIN CALCULATIONS

Making the heat gain calculations under the simplified ASHRAE procedure is not a difficult chore. I will proceed on the assumption that you have already gone through the process of making heat loss calculations. Much of the work is similar and in some instances many of those basic values can be used in these calculations as well.

The Worksheet

As with heat loss calculations, the room-by-room method of calculating should be used to determine heat gains and consequent cooling load for each conditioned space. Table 5-1 shows a representative worksheet that you can use as it is or modify to better suit your purposes. In the "Room" column, enter the different rooms or spaces that will be cooled. Don't include bathrooms, walk-in utility closets, or other spaces that will not be directly cooled. Add the cooling load of such spaces, equally divided, to those of the immediately adjacent cooled rooms.

In the "Section" column, list the various building sections for which a coefficient of transmission must be found. The net exposed area in square feet of each section should be entered in the "Area" column. The "U" heading is for the coefficients of transmission and the "DETD" column is for the appropriate design equivalent temperature differences that will be taken from a table. The "GF" heading will be used to enter the applicable values for the glass factors. This includes design transmitted and absorbed solar energy and air-to-air temperature differences, as well as shade line factors where required. The "I&V" column is for the infiltration and ventilation heat gains. Multiplying the appropriate factors results in the gain in Btu per hour. Those entries are added together to find the total Btuh heat gain for each room or space.

Outdoor Design Factors

The next step is to select the outdoor design factors. This exercise is carried out in much the same way as for determining outdoor design factors

Table 5-1. Worksheet for Heat Gain Calculations.

ROOM	SECTION	AREA	U	DETD	GF	I&V	GAIN Btuh	TOTAL GAIN
Living	Wall	183	0.075	18.6			255	
	Ceiling	400	0.051	31.0			657	
	Floor	400	0.047	10.0			188	
	Windows	74	0.610		22		993	
	Band Joist	48	0.043	18.6			38	
	Header	15	0.132	18.6			37	
	Partition	80	0.083	10.0			66	
	Infil.	320				1.1	352	
	Occupancy						338	
	Latent						731	
								3655
Kitchen								
Etc.								

for heat loss calculations. Much of the general information contained in that section in Chapter 4 is applicable. If you live in or near one of the reporting stations listed in Table 4-1, you will be able to use the summer condition figures that are listed. Otherwise, you will have to modify those figures with others obtained locally or perhaps rely entirely upon local averaged figures obtained from as many different sources as you can find. Additional weather data can be obtained from the National Climatic Center, Asheville, NC 28801, and a considerable amount of tabulated data is contained in *Facility Design and Planning Engineering Weather Data*.

There are two outside design factors that you must determine: the outside design temperature and the mean daily temperature range. Referring to Table 4-1, you'll see that column 6 lists both design dry-bulb and mean coincident wet-bulb temperatures in three value sets for each reporting station. For example, Alexander City, Alabama, is listed as 96/77, 93/76, and 91/76 in the "1%", "2.5%", and "5%" columns respectively. The first figure of each pair is the dry-bulb temperature and the second figure is the coincident wet-bulb temperature. The wet-bulb temperature in this case is the mean of all wet-bulb temperatures that occurred at the specific dry-bulb design temperature with which it is associated. For our purposes, the dry-bulb temperature is the one of principal interest.

These figures represent values that have been equalled or exceeded by 1, 2.5, or 5 percent of the total of 2928 hours during the summer months of June, July, August, and September. In other words, during those four months on average there would be about 29 hours at or above the listed value in the "1%" column, about 73 hours at "2.5%", and about 146 hours at "5%." Selecting a design dry-bulb temperature from the "1%" column will mean that there will be, during an average cooling season, about 29 hours of time during which the cooling system will be working at peak capacity. You might not be able to hold the interior temperature at the desired design set-point. In most cases, a value from the "2.5%" column would be a reasonable choice for residential cooling applications.

Column 7 of the table lists the values for the mean daily temperature range (or "swing"). These figures represent the difference between the average daily maximum and the average daily minimum temperatures during the warmest month at each reporting station. Column 8, the design wet-bulb temperatures, were compiled independently of the figures listed in column 6, and should not be considered as coincident with those dry-bulb temperatures. These values are to be used when sizing cooling equipment that depends primarily upon wet-bulb temperature assessments. They need not be considered here.

Select an appropriate dry-bulb design temperature and a mean daily temperature range from this table, from other sources, or from a combination of sources. You can adjust, interpolate, extrapolate, or perhaps make actual observations at your own building site to arrive at your final figures. It's a good idea to obtain values or corroborate those that you have developed with a local heating/cooling engineer or equipment dealer. Make a not of your final chosen values on your worksheet so that they'll be handy for later use.

Indoor Design Factors

There are four indoor design factors to be determined. The first factor is the indoor design temperature. There are a number of possibilities. A value of 75 F is most commonly used. Because the subsequent calculations will be based upon this assumption, I suggest that you select that value. Other values sometimes chosen are 72 F and 78 F.

An indoor temperature swing must also be determined. This is the allowable variation in degrees F from the indoor design temperature. A swing of 3 F is most commonly used and is the generally recommended value. However, there is some argument over just what a maximum acceptable temperature swing should be and swings of 4.5 F and 6 F have been responsibly recommended. Because 3 F appears to be a very workable practical minimum, I will use that recommendation.

The third factor to be determined is the temperature difference (or Δt). Subtract the indoor design temperature of 75 F from whatever outdoor design temperature you have selected and the result is the Δt. If your outdoor design temperature is 95 F, the Δt is 20.

The last indoor design factor to be developed might or might not be necessary in your case. If your house design calls for a substantial amount of mechanical ventilation—markedly greater than the average values that we shall use a bit later on—those details can be worked out now. Make a note of all of these factors on the worksheet for ready reference during the calculation process.

Transmission Heat Gains

With the preliminaries out of the way, you can start making the heat gain calculations. The first step in doing so is to assess the transmission heat gains attributable to the various building sections. Much of this process is the same as for determining transmission heat losses. I will go through the different building sections step by step.

Walls. First determine the net wall areas of the cooled rooms or spaces that are exposed to the outdoors or to unconditioned spaces. Enter the total in the "Area" column. Then find the U of each wall section. You can use separate U values for different kinds of wall sections or you can combine them to find an overall U. This is done in exactly the same way as for calculating heat transmission losses except that the exterior surface film resistance is calculated on the basis of a 7.5 mph average wind. The value is R-0.25. No correctional factors are used for other wind speeds. The relative position of the exposed surface does not matter. Enter the appropriate U values in that column on the worksheet.

Next, consult Fig. 5-2. Locate your design temperature at the top of the table. Then determine if your daily temperature range is low (L - less than 15 degrees F), medium (M - 15 to 25 degrees F), or high (H - more than 25 degrees F). Locate the type of wall construction in the left-hand column that best approximates yours and follow across the line to the appropriate value column.

For example, if your design temperature is 95 F and your outdoor mean daily temperature range is 18 F or medium, the DETD for a frame wall is 23.6. Enter that value in the DETD column on your worksheet. Then multiply the area times the U times the DETD to find the gain in Btuh for the wall sections.

If the wall sections are not actually exposed to the outdoors, but rather are partition walls separating a conditioned surface from an unconditioned one; calculate the wall area and the wall U as usual. But in determining the DETD, use the "Partitions" line in the Table 5-5.

In using the design equivalent temperature differences table, if the outdoor design temperature that you have selected is not an even increment of 5 F you can make adjustments to suit. Just correct the DETD 1 F for each 1 F difference between your design temperature and the tabulated one.

For example, if your design temperature is 97 F, your mean daily temperature range is medium, and you need the DETD for a frame wall, you could look in the "95" column, medium swing, and find a value of 23.6. Because your design temperature is 2 F higher than the tabulated value of 95, you would then add 2 to that for a corrected DETD of 25.6.

Similarly, you could look in the "100" column to find a DETD of 28.6. In this case, the design temperature is 3 F lower than the tabulated value. You would subtract 3 from 28.6 for a corrected DETD of 25.6.

Doors. Find the total area in square feet of the exterior doors exposed to the outdoors or to unconditioned spaces. If the doors are of different construction, it will probably be easiest to list them separately. Then determine the U value of the doors in the same way as for making heat loss calculations except that the outside surface film resistance will be assessed under summer conditions. Enter the figures on the work-

216

Table 5-2. Design Equivalent Temperature Differences (Reprinted with Permission from the 1977 Fundamentals Volume, ASHRAE HANDBOOK & Product Directory).

Design Temperature, °F	85		90			95			100		105	110
Daily Temperature Range [a]	L	M	L	M	H	L	M	H	M	H	H	H
WALLS AND DOORS												
1. Frame and veneer-on-frame	17.6	13.6	22.6	18.6	13.6	27.6	23.6	18.6	28.6	23.6	28.6	33.6
2. Masonry walls, 8-in. block or brick	10.3	6.3	15.3	11.3	6.3	20.3	16.3	11.3	21.3	16.3	21.3	26.3
3. Partitions, frame	9.0	5.0	14.0	10.0	5.0	19.0	15.0	10.0	20.0	15.0	20.0	25.0
masonry	2.5	0	7.5	3.5	0	12.5	8.5	3.5	13.5	8.5	13.5	18.5
4. Wood doors	17.6	13.6	22.6	18.6	13.6	27.6	23.6	18.6	28.6	23.6	28.6	33.6
CEILINGS AND ROOFS [b]												
1. Ceilings under naturally vented attic or vented flat roof—dark	38.0	34.0	43.0	39.0	34.0	48.0	44.0	39.0	49.0	44.0	49.0	54.0
—light	30.0	26.0	35.0	31.0	26.0	40.0	36.0	31.0	41.0	36.0	41.0	46.0
2. Built-up roof, no ceiling—dark	38.0	34.0	43.0	39.0	34.0	48.0	44.0	39.0	49.0	44.0	49.0	54.0
—light	30.0	26.0	35.0	31.0	26.0	40.0	36.0	31.0	41.0	36.0	41.0	46.0
3. Ceilings under unconditioned rooms	9.0	5.0	14.0	10.0	5.0	19.0	15.0	10.0	20.0	15.0	20.0	25.0
FLOORS												
1. Over unconditioned rooms	9.0	5.0	14.0	10.0	5.0	19.0	15.0	10.0	20.0	15.0	20.0	25.0
2. Over basement, enclosed crawl space or concrete slab on ground	0	0	0	0	0	0	0	0	0	0	0	0
3. Over open crawl space	9.0	5.0	14.0	10.0	5.0	19.0	15.0	10.0	20.0	15.0	20.0	25.0

[a] Daily Tmperature Range
L (Low) Calculation Value: 12 deg F.
   Applicable Range: Less than 15 deg F.
M(Medium) Calculation Value: 20 deg F.
   Applicable Range: 15 to 25 deg F.
H (High) Calculation Value: 30 deg F.
   Applicable Range: More than 25 deg F.

[b] Ceilings and Roofs: For roofs in shade, 18-hr average = 11 deg temperature differential. At 90 F design and medium daily range, equivalent temperature differential for light-colored roof equals $11 + (0.71)(39 - 11) = 31$ deg F.

sheet. Consult Table 5-2 to determine the DETD, just as you did for the wall sections.

Note that only wood doors are listed here. If you have insulated metal doors with built in thermal breaks, you can safely cut the listed value in half. If a wood entryway door is fitted with a metal storm door, use 75 percent of the listed value. If a metal entryway door is fitted with a metal storm door, reduce the listed value by 10 percent. Enter the values on your worksheet and multiply the area times the U times the DEDT to find the total heat gain in Btuh.

Windows. Under this procedure for calculating heat gains, it is unnecessary to work out U values for windows. Instead, a special table (see Table 5-3) that reads out directly in Btu gain per square foot per hour under varying conditions is employed.

The first step is to find the area of each window. Do this separately as necessary for each of the three different kinds of glass listed, for each of the four different shading conditions, and for each of the five different compass directions listed. You might have entries in the "Section" column for a single-glazed window facing east with no shading, a double-glazed window with an awning facing southeast, and so on. Include glass block sections, plastic glazing, windows that are inserted in doors, exterior doors that are more than 50 percent glass and glass sliding doors.

Find the area of each individual window type (two or more of the same kind can be added) and enter the figures on the worksheet. Then go to the Table 5-3 and locate the glass factor. For example, a double-glazed window facing north with roller shades half-drawn at an outside design temperature of 95 F has a factor of 20. Enter the factors in the "GF" column on the worksheet and multiply area times GF to find the heat gain in Btuh. If your outside design temperature is not a 5-degree increment, interpolate the listed values as necessary.

Table 5-3 takes care of the effects of shading device quite satisfactorily—with one exception. If permanent shading devices such as fixed overhangs, fixed awnings, or architectural projections are incorporated in the house design and serve to effectively shade the windows on a permanent basis, their effects must be separately considered. This is done by making use of the shade line factors set forth in Table 5-4. These factors are based upon a solar declination of 18°N (August 1) and are the averages of the shade line values for the 5 hours of maximum solar intensity for each different wall orientation listed.

Notice that neither northeast nor northwest compass directions are included. This is because overhangs do not adequately protect windows facing in those directions and shading credit for them should not be taken. Likewise, north-facing glass is not included. It needs no shading and is unaffected by sunlight. In addition, if a window is permanently shaded by a massive projection such as a porch roof—whereby sunlight never reaches the glass under any circumstances—the window is also considered as north-facing regardless of its actual orientation.

218

Table 5-3. Design Transmitted and Absorbed Solar Energy and to Air-to-Air Temperature Difference,
Btu/(h · ft²) (Reprinted with Permission from the 1977 Fundamentals Volume, ASHRAE HANDBOOK & Product Directory).

Outdoor	Regular Single Glass						Regular Double Glass						Heat Absorbing Double Glass					
Design Temp.	85	90	95	100	105	110	85	90	95	100	105	110	85	90	95	100	105	110
No Awnings or Inside Shading																		
North	23	27	31	35	38	44	19	21	24	26	28	30	12	14	17	19	21	23
NE and NW	56	60	64	68	71	77	46	48	51	53	55	57	27	29	32	34	36	38
East and West	81	85	89	93	96	102	68	70	73	75	77	79	42	44	47	49	51	53
SE and SW	70	74	78	82	85	91	59	61	64	66	68	70	35	37	40	42	44	46
South	40	44	48	52	55	61	33	35	38	40	42	44	19	21	24	26	28	30
Draperies or Venetian Blinds																		
North	15	19	23	27	30	36	12	14	17	19	21	23	9	11	14	16	18	20
NE and NW	32	36	40	44	47	53	27	29	32	34	36	38	20	22	25	27	29	31
East and West	48	52	56	60	63	69	42	44	47	49	51	53	30	32	35	37	39	41
SE and SW	40	44	48	52	55	61	35	37	40	42	44	46	24	26	29	31	33	35
South	23	27	31	35	38	44	20	22	25	27	29	31	15	17	20	22	24	26
Roller Shades Half-Drawn																		
North	18	22	26	30	33	39	15	17	20	22	24	26	10	12	15	17	19	21
NE and NW	40	44	48	52	55	61	38	40	43	45	47	49	24	26	29	31	33	35
East and West	61	65	69	73	76	82	54	56	59	61	63	65	35	37	40	42	44	46
SE and SW	52	56	60	64	67	73	46	48	51	53	55	57	30	32	35	37	39	41
South	29	33	37	41	44	50	27	29	32	34	36	38	18	20	23	25	27	29
Awnings																		
North	20	24	28	32	35	41	13	15	18	20	22	24	10	12	15	17	19	21
NE and NW	21	25	29	33	36	42	14	16	19	21	23	25	11	13	16	18	20	22
East and West	22	26	30	34	37	43	14	16	19	21	23	25	12	14	17	19	21	23
SE and SW	21	25	29	33	36	42	14	16	19	21	23	25	11	13	16	18	20	22
South	21	24	28	32	35	41	13	15	18	20	22	24	11	13	16	18	20	22

Here's how the table works. Assume a south-facing window with single glazing and no awnings or inside shading. Further assume an outdoor design temperature of 100 F. This window is shaded a certain part of the time by a permanent overhang on the building. However, not all of it is in shade all of the time because the sun's position continually changes. The portion of the window that is on seasonal average shaded by the projection is considered as north-facing glass. The portion that is on seasonal average struck by sunlight is considered as south-facing glass with no awnings or inside shading. It's necessary to find the level of the shade line that lies across the window in order to determine how many square feet of glass is north-facing for calculation purposes and how many square feet are south-facing.

In Table 5-4, choose the column for the latitude that most closely approximates your own; you can interpolate as necessary. Next, measure the width of the overhang on the house. Let's say that the width is 2 feet and the latitude is 40 degrees. In the "S" line, under the "40" heading there is a shade line factor of 2.6. When multiplied by 2 (width of overhang), it equals 5.2. That is the distance in feet below the edge of the overhang that the shade line falls. Whatever part of the window lies above that shade line will be treated as north-facing and whatever portion lies below that point will be considered as south-facing. Once those two different window areas have been determined, their values can then be found in Table 5-3.

Floors. Only certain kinds of floors are considered in making heat gain calculations. Those over a basement, an unventilated crawlspace, a normally ventilated crawlspace, or comprised of a concrete slab-on-grade are not considered. They are invariably cooler than their surroundings and serve to absorb heat rather than add heat to a cooling load. Floors over hyperventilated or entirely open crawlspaces are considered and so are those that lie over unconditioned rooms (except for normally-cool basement rooms).

Calculate the U value of floors in the usual fashion. Remember that in this situation the surface resistances must be calculated on a basis of upward heat flow rather than downward as when making heat loss calculations. Determine the floor areas and enter the square footage and the U values on the worksheet. Then turn to Table 5-2 to determine the DETD and enter that value. Multiply the three figures to find the total heat gain in Btuh.

Band Joist Areas. Just as in making heat loss calculations, band joist areas are frequently ignored while making assessments of heat gains. However, it is just as well to include them. Determine the U-values and areas in the same way as when making heat loss calculations—but under summer conditions. Note the values on the worksheet. Select an appropriate DETD from the frame wall line of Table 5-2. Multiply the three figures to find the Btuh heat gain.

If a basement space is to be conditioned, a first-floor band joist area heat gain is attributable to that space. If the basement remains unconditioned there is no need to include that band joist area in the calculation. First-floor band joist area heat gains are attributable to the appropriate first-floor conditioned spaces or rooms. In either case, be sure to subtract the gross areas from the gross wall areas, along with the windows and doors.

Header Areas. The situation for header areas is exactly the same as for the band joist areas. Assess them in the same way as when making heat loss calculations—but using summer conditions. Find the appropriate DETD value from the frame wall line of Table 5-2 and work out the total heat gain on your worksheet.

Foundations. The only part of a foundation that needs to be assessed for heat gain is the portion of the masonry walls that lies above ground and any windows or doors that might be included in them. The only time foundation walls need to be figured at all is when they enclose a space that will be conditioned. An example would be a basement recreation room. The coefficient of transmission of the sections are determined just as for heat loss calculations—except under summer conditions. Find the U values and the areas of the sections involved and then select appropriate DETD values from Table 5-2. The commonly-used poured concrete masonry wall is not mentioned, but it can be considered to be the same as either brick or 8-inch block.

Ceiling/Roofs. For the purposes of making heat gain calculations under this procedure, ceiling and roof assemblies are lumped together in the DETD table. Select the type of assembly from the table that most closely approximates the one for which you are making calculations and work out the coefficient of heat transmission for the section. If this involves a ceiling under a naturally vented attic or beneath a vented flat roof, use the combined U-value for the roof, vented space, and the ceiling. Remember that the U values should be determined on the basis of summer conditions and downward heat flow—rather than upward. Then select an appropriate DETD from the table, work out the section areas, and enter

Table 5-4. Shade Line Factors (Reprinted with Permission from the 1977 Fundamentals Volume, ASHRAE HANDBOOK & Product Directory).

Direction	Latitude, Degrees						
Window Faces	25	30	35	40	45	50	55
E	0.8	0.8	0.8	0.8	0.8	0.8	0.8
SE	1.9	1.6	1.4	1.3	1.1	1.0	0.9
S	10.1	5.4	3.6	2.6	2.0	1.7	1.4
SW	1.9	1.6	1.4	1.3	1.1	1.0	0.9
W	0.8	0.8	0.8	0.8	0.8	0.8	0.8

• Note: Distance shadow line falls below the edge of the overhand equals shade line factor multiplied by width of overhang. Values are averages for 5 hr of greatest solar intensity on August 1.

Design Temperature, F	85	90	95	100	105	110
Infiltration, Btuh/ft^2 of gross exposed wall area	0.7	1.1	1.5	1.9	2.2	2.6
Mechanical ventilation, Btuh/cfm	11.0	16.0	22.0	27.0	32.0	38.0

the values on the worksheet. Multiply the three figures to find the total heat gain in Btuh.

Infiltration Heat Gains

Determining the heat gains from infiltration under summer conditions is easier than that for winter conditions. Natural infiltration calculations are commonly based on a leakage rate of one-half air change per hour. That is, it is assumed that once every two hours the air within the residence will be replaced by air leaking in from the outside. The necessary factors are directly entabulated in terms of Btu per square foot of gross exposed wall area in Table 5-5.

First determine the gross exposed wall area of the house. This includes all windows and doors, but does not include partition walls separating conditioned from unconditioned spaces. Enter the gross area figure for each room or space on the worksheet. Then find an appropriate infiltration factor in the table based upon your outside design temperature. Interpolate if necessary. Enter the value in the I&V column of the worksheet and multiply the two figures to find the total Btuh heat gain from natural infiltration.

If no mechanical ventilation will be included in the house, you can ignore that part of the calculations. Incidentally, this does not include small vent fans such as those that are found in bathrooms and kitchens. If ventilation is a part of the design, it probably will be based upon a total ventilating rate of about one air change per hour. In this case, select an appropriate value for mechanical ventilation from Table 5-5, and enter it in the I&V column of the worksheet. Determine, in cubic feet, the volume of the conditioned space in the house. Multiply the two figures to find the mechanical ventilation heat gain in Btuh.

Occupancy Heat Gains

Although the heat gains due to various kinds of occupancy are very difficult to figure in commercial and industrial buildings, they are simplicity itself in residences. The first step is to estimate as accurately as possible what the actual number of occupants will be in the house on a regular basis. If large groups of people will be entertained or recreating in the house fairly regularly, that fact needs to be considered. If a solid determination can be made of the number of regular occupants, multiply

**Table 5-6. Estimated Equivalent Rated Full-Load Hours
of Operation for Properly Sized Equipment During Normal
Cooling Season (Reprinted with Permission from the 1977
Fundamentals Volume, ASHRAE HANDBOOK & Produce Directory).**

Albuquerque, NM	800–2200
Atlantic City, NJ	500–800
Birmingham, AL	1200–2200
Boston, MA	400–1200
Burlington, VT	200–600
Charlotte, NC	700–1100
Chicago, IL	500–1000
Cleveland, OH	400–800
Cincinnati, OH	1000–1500
Columbia, SC	1200–1400
Corpus Christi, TX	2000–2500
Dallas, TX	1200–1600
Denver, CO	400–800
Des Moines, IA	600–1000
Detroit, MI	700–1000
Duluth, MN	300–500
El Paso, TX	1000–1400
Honolulu, HI	1500–3500
Indianapolis, IN	600–1000
Little Rock, AR	1400–2400
Minneapolis, MN	400–800
New Orleans, LA	1400–2800
New York, NY	500–1000
Newark, NJ	400–900
Oklahoma City, OK	1100–2000
Pittsburgh, PA	900–1200
Rapid City, SD	800–1000
St. Joseph, MO	1000–1600
St. Petersburg, FL	1500–2700
San Diego, CA	800–1700
Savannah, GA	1200–1400
Seattle, WA	400–1200
Syracuse, NY	200–1000
Trenton, NJ	800–1000
Tulsa, OK	1500–2200
Washington, DC	700–1200

that number times 225 Btuh. If the number of occupants is uncertain, multiply the number of bedrooms in the house by 2 and then multiply that by 225 Btuh. Do not grossly overestimate the number of occupants. Once you've arrived at a total Btuh, divide the result equally between the living rooms of the house (as opposed to the sleeping and utility rooms) and enter the figures on the worksheet.

A flat value is also used to cover the sensible heat that is released within the house by appliances and equipment. Various figures have been used in the past (ranging from 1200 to 1600 Btuh). That being so, it seems reasonable to split the difference and assume this portion of the occupancy heat gain to be 1400 Btuh. Note, however, that in some circumstances it might be necessary to include specific appliance loads attributable to particular equipment. This might be the case, for instance, where a residence kitchen is used for extensive cooking several hours per day every day or where laundry equipment is in constant use. Heat gains from such equipment can be taken from special tables that list values for numbers of different kinds of equipment. Once a suitable figure has been settled upon, it should be entered on the worksheet as a part of the kitchen cooling load.

Latent Heat Gains

As you might expect, latent heat gains can be calculated with a fair amount of accuracy by employing the same methodology and formulas as are used during heat loss calculations. The same problems and complexities are involved and the job is just a bit more difficult. For that reason, among others, an approximation of the latent heat gains is generally used (with quite satisfactory results) when making residential cooling load calculations.

All of the Btuh heat gains that you've calculated so far have been sensible heat gains. For each room or space on your worksheet, tally up all of the individual Btuh heat gains for each building section and make a note of them. The latent heat gain is a proportion of the sensible heat gain and is usually taken to be from 20 percent to 30 percent. The difference lies in the normal outdoor relative humidity range of the area in which the house is located.

Most areas of the country normally experience moderately high relative humidity during the summer months. In such cases factor of 25 percent is about right. If the humidity consistently runs quite high, as along the seacoast, near large lakes, or in any other particularly damp areas, use the 30 percent factor. Only if you live in a definitely arid area like the lower-altitude parts of the Southwest, where relative humidities consistently range from 5 to 15 percent or so, should you use the 20 percent value. For each room total heat gain, find an appropriate percentage of the amount and add it to each room total.

Cooling Load

The simplest part of the entire calculation is determining the total cooling load. Just add up all of the individual heat gains in Btuh. That's the total cooling load or the amount of heat that must be extracted per hour from the house by the cooling equipment.

OPERATING COSTS

Determining the operating costs of a cooling system is not a difficult chore, but I can only show you generally how it is done. The equivalent number of hours that the cooling equipment will operate under full load must be estimated (as opposed to the total number of hours during which the equipment operates under varying loads) and these figures must be estimated on a basis of local conditions. There are no tabulated experiential or average figures that can be used on a general, nationwide basis.

Also, the specific distribution system must be designed and the particular cooling equipment must be selected in concert with one another.

Then the performance of both the system and the equipment must be related to the cooling load. The result is equipment capacity multipliers that must be applied as correcting factors. This can't be done on a generalized basis either. It must be computed for each individual installation. Additional factors such as water-usage for water-cooled equipment, the electrical requirements for fans or other associated equipment, and the total hourly power requirements of the cooling equipment itself must be known so that these figures can be plugged into the calculations. Averages or rough estimates of these requirements simply are not suitable.

Seasonal cooling load costs can only be estimated on a broad basis and for any given cooling season the estimate and the actuality are not likely to be very close to one another. Over a long period of one or two decades they will, in many instances, be relatively close.

First determine the number of equivalent rated full-load hours of operation for the cooling equipment.

Table 5-6 shows some representative numbers of this sort. Residential hours are likely to be close to the lower figure of each entry range rather than the higher one. If none of these figures are applicable in your case, your best bet is to contact your local electric utility and ask them for help in developing some reasonable estimates. Find the total power requirements of the cooling system and multiply times the number of equivalent rated full-load hours of operation. Multiply the total requirement in kilowatt-hours by the appropriate power rate in your area. Note that in many areas you must assess the approximate kwh usage for each month and then relate that to the proper step on the electric utility's rate schedule. Exceptions are those few areas of the country where all power is rated the same regardless of the amount used. The result is a general estimate of seasonal operating costs for the cooling equipment.

6

Design for Heating/Cooling

Thermal insulations are special materials developed for the primary purpose of retarding heat flow. They are used everywhere today in residential construction. Without them, we'd be in a world of trouble nowadays in trying to construct tight, comfortable houses that can be efficiently heated and cooled at an affordable cost. Many folks who are struggling with old, uninsulated houses can attest to that fact. Building a new house in almost any section of the country without the inclusion of special thermal insulation materials in the building sections is nothing short of sheer lunacy. There are ways that this can be done and still achieve descent performance. But except in rare instances, the completed project is more expensive than need be and it will not be as efficient.

But thermal insulation materials are not the whole answer. You can't build a house out of those materials alone, and thermal insulations should never be expected—much less relied upon—to carry the full load of providing superior thermal efficiency in a house. Nor should they be used in compensation for poor design, shoddy construction, bad location or orientation, or similar faulty factors. Thermal insulation materials are not a crutch. They are an aid—albeit a very important one—to the overall development of a housing unit.

HOUSE DESIGN

In the past, it has been common practice to build the house according to whatever structural design was easiest and handiest for the builder. Little or no thought was usually given to the effects of either structural or architectural design insofar as thermal efficiency was concerned. After all, fuel was cheap and you simply installed a heating system of some kind big enough to handle any sort of weather conditions and fed the fuel into it as required.

226

In some areas a modicum of attention was paid to the possibility of natural cooling as affected by design, but mechanical cooling was virtually unknown (in the practical sense) until after World War II. Special thermal insulation materials are a relative newcomer to the housing scene. Early houses had to depend almost entirely upon their inherent thermal resistance—which generally was minimal—for conservation of or protection against heat. One common practice was to pour sawdust into the wall cavities and beneath the attic floor. That was of some help, but it was relatively ineffective. Even after thermal insulations began to appear in the marketplace, little use was made of them until comparatively recently.

Research has shown that either structural design or architectural design, and usually both, can have a notable effect upon the thermal efficiency of a house. Bear in mind that there are no blanket rules for this. Everything depends upon the sum total of the conditions and characteristics of the house and its immediate environment. For example, consider an ordinary typical Cape Cod style. This has been found to be a practical, comfortable, and livable style of house in the Northeast (when properly constructed).

The same style of house built in the desert Southwest is, by modern-day standards, a housing disaster. Why? Because for a variety of architectural and structural reasons, the Cape Cod style is not well suited to economical comfort in hot-dry conditions. By the same token, a Spanish-style adobe house—which is so effective in the desert country—is a poor choice for the winters of upper Minnesota. Now this is not to say that either house could not be altered, modified and redesigned to make it workable, it's just that they are not inherently suitable. There would be more work and expense involved than is generally worth the effort.

Certain architectural styles are better for some conditions than they are for others. The same can be true of structural designs. Perhaps the best example is the dome house. The geodesic dome is a peculiar-looking affair to many people. We're just not accustomed to the style because it is so different from the conventional houses. The geodesic dome has perhaps more going for it than any other above-ground structural design as far as heating-cooling efficiency is concerned. A dome structure encloses the same living space area (in terms of square footage) as a conventional rectangular wood-frame house but uses about 30 percent less material (Fig. 6-1). It also has about 30 percent less exterior surface exposed to the weather. This simply means that weather has less effect upon a dome than upon a conventional house of identical living space.

This translates into, among other things, less susceptibility to outside air infiltration. This is a very important factor to consider in both heating and cooling. Because less surface area is exposed, less heat is radiated away from the structure or a less heat is gained by radiation from the sun on the exposed surfaces. The result is that heating/cooling costs average from 30 percent to 40 percent less in a dome structure than for a conventional house of comparable living-space size.

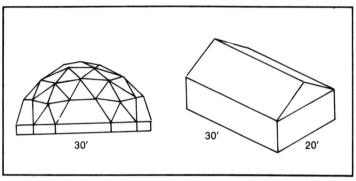

Fig. 6-1. A geodesic dome style of house can enclose the same amount of living space in square footage as a conventional house does.

In addition, the shape of the dome (a hemisphere) affords a certain pattern of natural air circulation and ventilation—unobtainable in a conventional style of house—that for more even, efficient and effective use of the warm/cool air introduced into the structure by either mechanical or natural means. The dome has other attributes such as an unusually high degree of seismic resistance, a particularly low susceptibility to wind damage because of the rounded shape and the minimized exposed surface area, and the ability to shed snow and rain very rapidly. It also is the strongest known structure for its weight.

The earth-sheltered house is a good example of how both architectural and structural design can have a definite effect upon heating/cooling cost and efficiency. The earth-sheltering aspect can run from simple berming of earth against one or two exposed walls all the way to complete burial at considerable depth of the entire structure. The degree of earth sheltering, and the attendant variables in both structural and architectural design, influence to a large degree the thermal efficiency of the house.

Consider a properly constructed earth-sheltered house that has only one south-facing wall exposed—a common general design. Three walls and the roof are completely buried in earth to varying depths. The earth itself acts as a buffer between most of the house and the outside atmosphere, and serves to greatly dampen normal outside temperature swings. At the same time, the average temperature to which the buried wall surfaces are subjected can be considerably higher or lower than those at surface level. The result is substantially lowered heat loss during cold weather, a substantially lowered heat gain during hot weather, and a long-term evening-out of heating/cooling requirements for any given time interval. This means a smaller heating/cooling system can be used, at lower initial cost, and the operating expenses can be considerably less than for a comparable size of house built entirely aboveground. In short, the thermal characteristics of earth-sheltered houses are more favorable, other things being equal.

DESIGN DETAILS

Architectural/structural design factors often bear upon lesser aspects than the complete house as a unit. Various facets of a given design can have definite effects upon thermal efficiency. Conversely, the addition of certain design fillips can often serve to enhance thermal efficiency.

Fenestration

Fenestration (the design and placement of windows and doors in a house) can be a very important factor. Vast expanses of glass on the north side of a house located where winter conditions are extremely harsh is not a good idea from a thermal standpoint. The heat loss in winter would be horrendous and there would be no compensating heat gain from sunshine. On the other hand, properly positioned windows on the south face of a house could be beneficial. If the house is located in desert country those large north windows would be fine. The south windows should be small or protected to prevent the entry of heat during the particularly hot summer months.

Glass Area

The amount of glass used in the building also plays a part. The ratio of exposed glass area to the interior heated or cooled volume of the house affects the heating and cooling load—though not necessarily in direct proportion. For example, a 10,000 cubic foot house containing 1000 square feet of glass area will obviously be less affected by heat loss through the glass than will an otherwise identical one containing 2000 square feet of glass. When the heat loss calculations are made, the difference will be proportional (assuming the same R value for all the glass) because all of it will be figured on the same basis. But in practice, if the locations of the various glass units differ (more expanse facing to the north than to the south, for instance), the net effect will vary. Therefore both placement and relative amounts of glass are important. But by and large, one can assume that the less glass area a house has, of whatever type, the better the thermal performance will be. If large areas of glass are to be a part of the design, the deficit in thermal performance should be compensated for elsewhere (if possible).

Surface Area

The amount of exposed surface area of a house is also important. The more area there is the greater the opportunity for heat transfer. A dome house has less exposed surface area than a conventional rectangular house for the same inside square footage of living area and therefore has better thermal performance. Compare a traditional Victorian single-story house containing 10-foot walls and ceilings with a modern ranch house having 8-foot walls. If the perimeter of each house is 160 feet, the ranch house will have 320 square feet less of exposed surface through which heat can transfer, but still have the same amount of usable interior living space. Standard wall height today, in most houses, is 8 feet. Some new houses are being built with 7-foot-6-inch walls and sometimes even a bit less. For a house with a 160-foot perimeter, this takes away another 80 square feet of unnecessary outside wall through which heat can be gained or lost. That is not a great deal, but every little bit helps. And besides, construction costs are also lowered a little bit.

Many houses are built upon concrete foundations that extend substantially above grade. This is often done to save a bit of initial excavating cost. However, masonry walls that are below grade have better thermal performance and are less subject to infiltration and outside temperature swings than those above grade level. This is due to the buffering effect of the earth. If the foundation can't be set deep, at least earth can be graded up around them, or bermed, to provide much the same thermal protection. The best arrangement is for the entire foundation to be sunk as deep into the earth as is possible. This reduces heat loss and gain to the minimum and this is especially true with the addition of suitable insulation.

Another example involving foundations is that of the hyperventilated crawlspace or a fully open pier arrangement. This leaves the underside of the house floor exposed to low temperatures and perhaps wind as well. There is a consequent increased potential for heat loss (the heat gain problem is not quite as serious, but can also be important in some climates). Covering the underside of the floor joists with a sheathing, preferably of the insulating variety, does help. Better yet, an enclosed foundation design means that the house floor is subjected to an intermediate design temperature instead of the lower outside design temperature and the thermal performance will be correspondingly improved.

Volume

Outside surface area is not the only important aspect of diminished size; interior volume is equally significant. When surface area is diminished so is volume. That is the critical factor in infiltration/exfiltration heating/cooling losses. The less volume you can manage for a given square-foot expanse of usable living space, the lower will be the heating/cooling load. Consider a house that is 30 x 50 feet in size with 8-foot walls. That is 1500 square feet and the volume is 12,000 cubic feet. If the infiltration rate is pegged at one air change per hour, 12,000 cubic feet of air (disregarding the volume taken up by partition, etc.) have to be constantly reheated/recooled. Lower the walls and ceiling to 7 feet 6 inches and the volume is reduced to 11,250 cubic feet that have to be processed. The usable living space remains the same (Fig. 6-2). That is another small gain, to be sure, but they all add up.

Roof Design

Exposed surface areas of roofs can have a pronounced effect upon the thermal performance of a house. When a roof encloses an unheated attic space above a heavily insulated ceiling, the size and shape of the roof—as well as its orientation with respect to sun, wind, and storm tracks—is not usually of great consequence to heating or cooling. In those situations, the effects of added heat gain are more likely to be noticeable than those of heat loss. But if the roof itself is insulated and encloses part of the living space of the house, its physical characteristics do sometimes play a part in thermal performance.

The amount of surface area of the roof matters. The smaller the area for a given amount of living space enclosed, the less opportunity there is for heat to transfer in or out. A flat roof covers a given living space area with the least amount of exposed surface area. The steeper the pitch of a gable or shed roof, the greater the total exposed surface area required to cover the same interior space (Fig. 6-3). A steep cathedral ceiling over a living room, for instance, will have a markedly greater heat loss or gain. A shallow-pitched one will exhibit only somewhat more than a flat roof or a shallow-shed roof. Both types will also increase the volume of interior air that must be conditioned, by comparison with a flat roof or insulated ceiling.

The orientation of the roof also has an impact on solar gain. A fairly steep shed roof (the breakpoint angle varies with the geographical latitude of the building site) oriented east-west and with its high edge facing south will receive minimal insolation (Fig. 6-4) and can be engineered to receive none. Turn that roof around 180 degrees and it will receive a great deal. A gable roof oriented with its long axis north-south will be hit by sunlight early and late in the day. However, the impact of strong midday sun will be minimized. Turn that roof 90 degrees and one surface will get the full brunt of daylong sunshine. The other surface will gain little if any heat. Any pitched roof section that faces anywhere up to about 15 degrees to either side of due south will receive the greatest amount of solar radiation available at the site. A flat roof will receive sunshine all the time regardless of its orientation. Pitched, or multiple-section roofs will receive varying amounts depending upon their orientation.

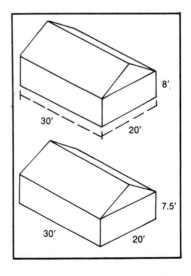

Fig. 6-2. Both of these houses enclose 600 square feet of living space. The one with 8-foot sidewalls has a first-floor volume of 4800 cubic feet and an exterior wall surface area of 800 square feet. But the house with 7.5-foot sidewalls has a volume of 4500 cubic feet and a sidewall area of 750 square feet. While the resulting heat loss/gain savings are not great, they are well worth considering in a cold climate.

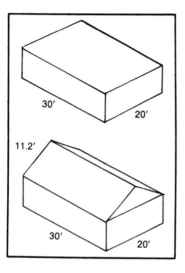

Fig. 6-3. A pitched roof has a greater exposed surface area than does a flat roof on a house of identical perimeter. The flat roof has a surface area of 600 square feet (no overhangs are included). The pitched roof is pitched at 6 inches per foot of run and has a surface area of 671 square feet. While this is of no consequence in many designs and especially where the ceiling of the house is very heavily insulated, in other designs it can lead to higher heat losses/gains.

The pitch of a roof makes a difference. If the angle of a roof section facing south (or nearly so) is just right—the specific figure depends upon the geographical latitude of the site and the time of year—the roof surface will be subjected to maximum insolation and potential heat gain from the sun. Substantially changing the angle from that optimum point (or shifting it to another compass direction, or both) reduces the solar load correspondingly. A roof pitch can be chosen (some compromise in angle is inevitable) for minimum insolation during the hot summer months. This will be a slight aid in reducing potential heat gain. That optimum angle is just what's needed to make the solar collectors tied to solar heating systems fully effective. But that calculation is made for the winter sun and not summer. Pitching and orienting an ordinary roof section in the hope of utilizing some possible heat gain in winter to help counteract heat losses in futile. It doesn't work.

Section Thickness

Roof and wall thicknesses in particular—floor thicknesses don't make so much difference—can be selected with an eye toward increased comfort and livability. Most homeowners are most familiar with the conventional 2 × 4 stud frame wall construction and relatively lightweight roof constructions.

There are other possibilities as well. Two-by-six wall construction is becoming popular in some regions. This is solely for the purpose of increasing wall U. Two-by-eight and even up to 2 × 14 wall sections are also being built. Heavy log wall construction is enjoying a resurgence and so is solid timber wall construction of both single and double thickness. Double-stud walls offer another possibility. The walls could be made 2 feet thick if you prefer. Massive masonry construction, heavily insulated on the outside, offers some advantages and existing masonry buildings can also be retrofitted with insulation.

There are several gains that can be realized from thick rather than lightweight building sections. A decision to build in such a fashion must be based on a good many additional factors as well. The thermal resistance properties are enhanced. The R value of a 14-inch wall section could be worked up to 60 (U-0.017) or more without much trouble (or could be as low as R-1.12 for unadorned concrete!).

The heat capacity of the structure would be increased even with the extra-thick frame type of construction. Massive masonry would have fine thermal lag and flywheel effect if properly designed as well as immense heat storage capacity. Houses built with thick sections, especially if heavy, are also practically soundproof. Little if any outside noise intrudes into the living space. This is a factor often noted by the occupants of heavy log houses and the silence and lack of vibration encountered in earth-sheltered houses is phenomenal. In addition, sound generated within such houses is invariably more muted, less harsh, and music played on a stereo system has more presence. Stability and the ability to withstand the impact of storms and rough weather is another attribute of heavy-section houses.

The point is that conventional lightweight framing is not the only possibility. The thermal properties of a house can be enhanced by employ-

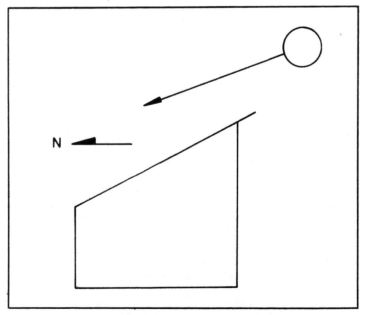

Fig. 6-4. A north-facing pitched roof section if angled sharply enough will never be impacted by the sun's rays.

ing thick sections if there are good and sufficient overlying reasons to do so. The main drawback is cost. Heavy construction, especially if combined with super-insulation, *is* generally more expensive.

Shading Projections

The design treatments given to the eaves and rakes, or to any building projections, of a house located in a hot climate have far more importance than mere architectural emphasis. However, that can be, and frequently is, one of the reasons for lavishing a good deal of attention upon them. One of the best ways to reduce heat gain through windows, and to a lesser degree through opaque wall sections, is to build in eave and rake overhangs or other types of architectural projections that block the sun's rays not only from entering the building, but from even touching the glass surface. At the same time, these projections are generally made so that they will also throw a substantial part of the adjacent wall section in shade (Fig. 6-5).

The details of sunshade projection design are critical if they are to be fully effective. Each projection must be of just the right width, just the right height, and cocked at the proper angle to block the greatest amount of sun throughout the hottest part of the summer during the hottest part of each day, but yet admit the greatest amount of sunshine and light during the winter.

The design factors are variable with the geographical latitude of the site and the ideal factors change daily. A satisfactory compromise has to be reached.

Tha main concern is with windows facing approximately south. West-facing windows might receive treatment suitable for low, late-afternoon sun. East-facing windows might or might not be considered and it's unnecessary for north windows. The degree of shading required for windows facing in the various compass directions changes with geographical latitude. The projections have to be coordinated and intergrated with the overall house design, too, not just tacked on any old how. All in all, it's a good challenge, but a worthwhile one, especially in hot-dry climates at the higher altitudes where solar radiation can be so intense.

BUILDING MATERIALS

As you might expect, building materials that are specifically designed and intended for use as thermal insulations are the most important of all in house construction insofar as heating/cooling and comfortable, economical living is concerned.

Building materials should be coordinated with the type of thermal insulation, overall thermal resistance factors, and suitability for the specific job conditions. This includes esthetics, decorative impact, price and similar factors.

For example, consider a floor over an open crawlspace. If you cover the floor joists with a layer of one-half inch plywood subflooring, you'll have an R value of 0.62. The overall U will be more effective because of

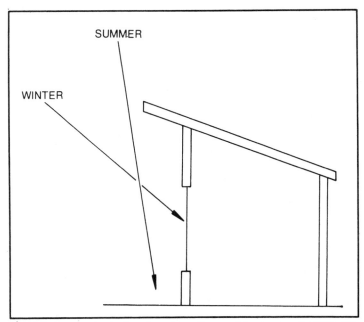

SUMMER

WINTER

Fig. 6-5. A properly designed roof or other architectural projection can permanently block the rays of the summer sun from entering south-facing (and a few other directions as well) windows, yet allow full admittance during the winter for additional heat.

the surface resistances and any added insulation. The average U of the floor section would have to take into account the floor joists themselves, but I will set those details aside for purposes of this example.

If you were to cover the subflooring with a layer of one-half inch medium-density particle board, you would add another R-0.50. A layer of sheet vinyl finish floor covering would add about R-0.05. So the total R for the floor (only) thickness would be 1.27 (U-0.787). If you were in a warm climate, that might be perfectly adequate. But if you were to lay nominal 2 x 6 tongue-and-groove pine decking on the joists, you would have an R of 1.89 (U-0.529). You'd have a strong, stiff floor laid in one operation instead of three—a surface that can be treated as a finish floor—and a higher thermal resistance at the same time. You might lay a combination subflooring/underlayment of three-fourth inch tongue-and-groove plywood, with an R of 0.94 and then cover that with a layer of sheet vinyl floor covering. The total thermal resistance would be about 1.00 (U-1.0). If you were to lay carpet on the subflooring, you would improve both comfort and thermal resistance. A fairly thick carpet with a fibrous pad beneath it could easily add R-2.00 or more (rubber pads are less effective). As you can see, there are a number of approaches and the details can be coordinated to achieve whatever overall effect is desired.

The usual course, and generally the easiest one, is to rely upon thermal insulating materials wherever low thermal transmission is required. But, the ordinary building materials, both structural and finish, should not be ignored as the building specifications are worked out. Sometimes added value (both thermal and otherwise) is easily gained and especially when the various characteristics and potential advantages of the materials are considered as well. This is particularly true in areas where heating or cooling needs are not very stringent, if situations where an existing structure needs to be thermally upgraded a bit, or in marginal situations where it might be desirable to have just a little more thermal resistance than a given set of specifications allows without taking the trouble to add another thermal insulation layer.

CONSTRUCTIONS

Just as some combinations of building materials provide greater thermal resistance than others, so do certain construction methods and procedures aid in increasing the overall thermal efficiency of a house. This can be true of the thermal resistance of the sections, but it is perhaps more notable insofar as potential infiltration of outside air is concerned. Infiltration is a major reason for high heating bills in older houses that have many air leaks. Within reason, the lower the infiltration the easier and more economical it is to heat and cool a house.

The traditional method for applying exterior sheathing to house walls, for instance, is to nail boards either horizontally or diagonally to the outsides of the wall studs. If the boards are square-edged, no matter how tightly they are fitted together during construction they eventually will shrink and perhaps warp to some degree. This will open sizable cracks between them.

If the boards are tongue-and-groove, the situation is considerably better. However, even those joints will open up to some extent with time. The net result is a substantial amount of crackage where outside air has an opportunity to infiltrate the structure. In older constructions, the board sheathing was generally covered with sheets of building paper in an attempt to reduce this infiltration possibility. Then the exterior siding, often boards or clapboards that also offered plenty of joints and cracks for more infiltration possibilities, was applied. But even with the building paper, this type of construction is subject to relatively high infiltration. This usually increases as the house ages, shifts and settles.

By comparison, if the exterior sheathing consists of plywood panels, the number of joints is greatly reduced and so is the possibility of infiltration. In the case of boards, the R-value of the sheathing is about 0.95 (assuming a three-fourth inch thickness). If a similar thickness of plywood is used, the R would be about the same. For this purpose, one-half inch plywood is much more commonly applied. This has an R of only 0.62 so there is a slight loss in thermal resistance. Because of the substantial reduction in infiltration potential, the one-half inch plywood is likely to be a better bet from a heating/cooling standpoint than the boards. Plywood is much stiffer and stronger as well and can be installed much more rapidly with less waste. The exterior siding can be practically any suitable material and the building paper is unnecessary.

This idea can also be taken a step further. Instead of just nailing the plywood panels in place as is usually done, they can be secured with both construction adhesive and nails. This seals off the few joints that do exist and reduces the possibility of infiltration even further. The construction is also stronger.

This procedure is widely used in the manufactured house industry and especially for the so-called panelized and modular/sectional types. In some cases, the industry carries the idea even farther by utilizing special factory equipment and processes that cannot be matched in the field. It is possible to make complete wall sections 8 feet high and 40 feet or more long that are entirely seamless and with both inside and outside covering glue-bonded to the framework in presses under heat and pressure. Not only is the construction extremely strong, it is also virtually infiltration-proof.

Whether a house is to be constructed for maximum thermal efficiency in a harsh climate (either hot or cold) or simply designed to be adequate and reasonable for moderate conditions, investigating various constructions is a good idea. This includes not only constructions that reduce infiltration to an absolute minimum, while providing either the maximum or the most cost-effective thermal resistance for cold conditions, but also those that will allow beneficial ventilation, shading, heat-shielding, reflectivity, and low thermal conductance in both hot-dry and hot-humid climates. For example, a roof construction that includes a free-flow air space from eave to peak of 2 inches or so in depth beneath a bright and shiny aluminum finish roofing can greatly decrease the interior solar load. On the other hand, three-eighth inch plywood sheathing topped with black asphalt roofing felt and ordinary black asphalt shingles will absorb a tremendous amount of solar heat.

There are any number of ways to go about building a particular house wall to achieve a certain U value. If the wall includes large areas of glass, the remainder might be of solid, 4-inch-thick timber and the windows might be double-glazed. Or it might be of standard 2 x 4 stud-frame construction filled with fiberglass insulation with the windows single-glazed to achieve approximately the same results. A 2 x 6 stud-frame wall might be filled with heavier fiberglass insulation and fitted with single-glazed windows. The proportions of glazed areas could be balanced against the opaque wall area. A roof section containing skylights might be constructed differently and use different materials in order to preserve a certain thermal integrity. The time spent in mulling over numerous possibilities can often pay dividends.

ENVIRONMENTAL INTEGRATION

Wherever possible, a house should be as fully integrated with its environment as is possible and practical. Sometimes there is little opportunity to do so, but more often than not some careful thought uncovers a number of ways in which at least some beneficial integration can be accomplished. Good environmental integration is not something that can be plugged into a series of heat loss/gain calculations in order to find out whether it's worth the trouble. There are too many variables and intangibles involved. A successfully integrated house not only has a more attractive appearance (and a higher salability), but is also very likely to be more comfortable to live in and more economical to maintain and operate.

Environmental integration simply means taking advantage of all of the plus factors that a particular building lot or ground parcel has to offer and doing whatever can be done to diminish any negative aspects that exist. This includes working with not only the natural features of the site itself, but also with the prevailing climatic conditions on and around the building site.

All of the characteristics should be assessed before the house is built, and through all four seasons (if possible). The house can be designed around these conditions and to suit them.

Environmental integration of a house has no added effect upon the specifications for its thermal efficiency or effectiveness for either heating or cooling. These calculations are made in the usual way, as discussed in Chapters 4 and 5. There are no changes made in the way the heating or cooling systems are sized or installed. You can't practically determine ahead of time, in most cases, what reductions in operating costs there might be or what increases in comfort or livability might occur. There is no reasonable way to make comparisons between the house as integrated and the same house as nonintegrated. All you can really do is proceed in good faith that the process is worthwhile and will be beneficial over the years. To give you an idea of how the process works, the following are a few examples.

Temperature

The effects of outside temperature on the inside environment can be somewhat mitigated in several ways. You can choose a site with plenty of shrubbery and tall trees to break wind blasts or one that is sheltered from the prevailing wind by a hill or ridge. A location atop a nob is likely to be very exposed, while one in a deep hollow might never get much breeze and might also be a collector of cold air. You can locate near a body of water, which tends to even out extremes of temperature and often can be cooler in summer weather, but if wrongly exposed the house can be chilly and damp. Some lakeside or streamside locations might actually be colder in winter than surrounding, somewhat higher areas. Proper orientation of the house in a cold climate will allow maximum sun through windows in winter, but minimum in summer or vice versa in desert country. Doors and operable windows can be located so that they are protected against winter winds, but are open to cooling summer breezes.

The layout and design of the house itself should be made compatible with temperature conditions. For instance, a hot climate suggests an open, airy plan that takes maximum advantage of natural ventilation and shading. For cold climates, a compact design with minimum exterior surface exposure is best. Room arrangement can be made so that those least used are on the most exposed sides of the house while the living areas face protected areas.

In cold climates, north-facing exposures should have minimum window and door area and be as protected as possible. In hot climates, protection from the sun in south and west directions is desirable. In cold climates, construction should include full insulation, weatherstripping, double glazing or triple glazing, thermal shutters, complete sealing and caulking, and other protective measures. Warm climates require the inclusion of special sun-control devices, roof overhangs, adequate ventilation means, heat-blocking glazing, and other items that will help reduce heat gain.

A good landscaping plan might include broadleaf trees for summer shade and winter sunlight, or evergreens for year-round shade and/or as wind breaks. Lawns and gardens tend to reduce exterior air temperatures in the immediate vicinity of the house and so does shrubbery. Vines and climbers can be planted for shade or sun shields. Drives and walks should be arranged to minimize or eliminate reflection of radiant heat against the structure.

Humidity

Humidity effects can be tempered. The site should be high and dry, away from swampy ground, not in a hollow, and away from areas where fog is likely to develop readily. Air motion is important for drying and the site should not have a high water table or be subject to runoff of rainwater or snowmelt. The house should be oriented to take best advantage of summer breezes, but be protected from winter winds. The layout and design of the house should make the fullest use of natural ventilation year-round and should be constructed with full vapor barriers to prevent moisture damage within the building sections. Stoves, laundry equipment and the like must be vented and the area or rooms in which any moisture-producing equipment is used, especially baths and laundries, should be fitted with ventilation systems. Attic ventilation might also be required.

Tight construction employing full caulking, weatherstripping, and double-glazed windows or triple-glazed windows is usually necessary. Landscaping should be arranged so that there is plenty of air circulation space around the house itself so that there can be no buildup of dampness. Mechanical ventilation equipment, humidifiers, and dehumidifiers, can be used as necessary to help maintain a proper humidity balance.

House design should include roof overhangs, roof guttering systems and drainaway runs, and proper roof drainage. There should be no possibility for snow to drift or pocket on a roof and no chance for rainwater to stand in place. Construction must be fully weatherproof and as tight as possible. Use top-grade flashing, caulking and sealing materials. Landscaping can be planned to afford protection against storms. Sod or very low, thick plantings near the foundation will serve to minimize potential seepage into the house and proper grading away from the house will also help.

Insolation

Depending upon your location, it might be advisable to either take advantage of the free sun's heat or to minimize its effects as much as possible. This can be done by choosing a site that has whatever degree of sun exposure, day by day and season by season, is most desirable. Then the house should be oriented on the site in such a way as to take best advantage of the sun's rays for maximum solar assist in heating, minimum solar load in cooling, or some combination of the two. The house can be designed to either receive or reject sunlight and the room plan can likewise be arranged to suit sun conditions.

In hot climates, the living quarters might be on the north side away from the sun and a kitchen might face east to take advantage of early morning sun and be protected from the hot afternoon sun. In cold and harsh climates, the layout could be just the opposite. The construction of the house should include elements that deflect the sun's rays. Examples are special roof construction or deep roof overhang, or to gain fullest entry of sunshine with large, south-facing glass expanses. Landscaping can be arranged to either minimize or maximize the sun's rays.

Air Motion

A site can be chosen that is protected to at least some degree from cold winter blasts, but open to the summer breezes. Winter winds and storms and summer breezes frequently flow from different directions. Attention must also be paid to air flow reversal in canyon or mountainous areas. Warm air can flow in one direction during the day and then in the opposite direction as cold air during the night. Air motion within the house can be controlled by various mechanical means such as openable windows, vent ports, vent fans, cooling fans, and air conditioning.

Sound Control

Planning the house layout involves segregating quiet areas from noisy areas within the house and placing those rooms that require the most quiet farthest away from outdoor or indoor noisy areas. Where necessary, construction should include features such as double-glazed windows, heavy structural cross sections, acoustic insulation and perhaps extra layers of thermal insulation, and any other measures that might be indicated to control or reduce sound transmission.

SOLAR INTEGRATION

Simple solar integration is a procedure that should be used during the construction of an ordinary, conventional house. *Full solar integration* means to construct houses that are particularly designed to make fullest possible use of solar energy for heating or cooling (whether the use of solar is passive, active, or hybrid). Solar integration is absolutely essential if the solar systems are to function correctly.

All of the elements involved in environmental integration also play a major part in solar integration. Even greater attention must be paid to each element during the design, planning, and orientation of the house. There is one factor in particular that is critical: solar radiation. The house must be designed and constructed according to solar design principles in order to realize the maximum potential of the available insolation upon which the entire premise of the design is based. Thermal insulation also plays a very large part in the success or failure of such a design.

THE BENEFITS OF INSULATION

The amount of insulation required and the types required for houses in various parts of this country spans a tremendous range. The number of heating degree-days ranges all the way from 0 to over 10,000 in the continental United States and over 14,000 in parts of Alaska. Cooling requirements run anywhere from 0 hours per season to 3000 or more.

The thermal characteristics of houses must be adjusted to meet local conditions. To further confuse the issue, this can be done from marginal efficiency, average efficiency, absolute maximum efficiency, or anywhere in between.

Costs Versus Benefits

Much is said about the cost-effectiveness of the various individual measures that can be taken in either new or existing houses to increase thermal efficiency. We hear much, also, about *payback periods*. This is the length of time required for one project or another to pay for itself in terms of money saved in operating costs. The cost of wrapping your water heater with fiberglass insulation will be returned to you in 2.6 years. The cost of adding storm sash for a particular house will be recovered in 8.9 years, and so forth. But there are problems with payback periods and cost-effectiveness computations. They are often improperly evaluated. Many homeowners don't bother making improvements unless they figure they can save big bucks in a season or two.

There are a number of different ways to calculate cost-effectiveness and at best they are estimates. Numbers of this sort can be played with to reflect various factors that might or might not be true or hold true. Another problem is that little attempt is made to look at the potential long-range picture. Instead, we tend to think in terms of how long we might live in this particular house, how quickly we might get our money back by making a certain investment in thermal efficiency, how a certain project will work out with respect to a 6-year home-improvement loan or an 11-year mortgage, or whatever.

We seldom stop to consider what the long-term effect will be of spending $500 for a storm sash. Over the 50-year life of the storm sash, how much will the present owner and future owners save in terms of dollars? How much will the presence of the storm sash increase the value of the property of 10 or 20 or 30 years hence? What will the addition of the storm sash mean to the longevity of the structure by virtue of the added protection afforded? Over that period of 50 years, how much fuel or energy will be conserved that can be put to some useful purpose? By the same token, making a decision between the installation of average thermal insulation and super-efficient thermal insulation in a new house should be based not on what will happen in terms of cost or conservation over the course of the first owner's 20-year mortgage, but rather what the total effect will be over the 50-year or 100-year life of the house.

Admittedly, this concept might strike you as being overly altruistic. Why should you pay for something that some other person is going to benefit from? Well, you'll do that anyway. If you build a sound, practical, livable house the chances are excellent, barring disaster, that you are only one of several who will benefit over the years from that house. Taking the near-term, self-centered viewpoint is not only dismally shortsighted, it's as often as not, impractical and uneconomical to boot.

Expenditures made now for thermal efficiency of whatever specific sort will pay both tangible (including tax) and intangible benefits to you during your period of occupancy and then will be returned to you again in added dollars when you sell the property. House buyers are becoming more and more aware of what constitutes a thermally efficient and economical house. Even if they are not familiar with the specifics, they can get a good idea just by checking utility bills and maintenance costs. In the future, those houses that are economical to operate and are thermally efficient (along with other attributes) will be the ones that are most marketable and will command the highest prices.

If you can do the work yourself, the actual cash outlay will not be all that great and the value of your property will be greatly enhanced. Having the work done for you is more expensive, but is still well worth the price so long as you get full value for the money spent. Don't fall prey to one of the many rip-off artists or scams that are currently drifting about in this field. In addition, today's house built to the highest levels of thermal efficiency and effectiveness will be far more capable of accepting retrofits of the hyper-sophisticated heating-cooling-ventilating equipment and methods that will be coming on line during the next decade and after.

Effectiveness

The following example was developed by ASHRAE as a sample problem showing how heat loss rate is calculated in a house. The example appears in Chapter 24, "Heating Load," in the 1977 Fundamentals Handbook, *ASHRAE HANDBOOK & Product Directory*. A specific house (Fig. 6-6) was "designed" without the inclusion of any thermal insulation and then the same house was considered *with* thermal insulation. The results are enlightening.

The design parameters of the uninsulated house are as follows:

❑ The location is Syracuse, NY.

❑ The winter design conditions are an outside temperature of −10 F, with 11 mph wind speed.

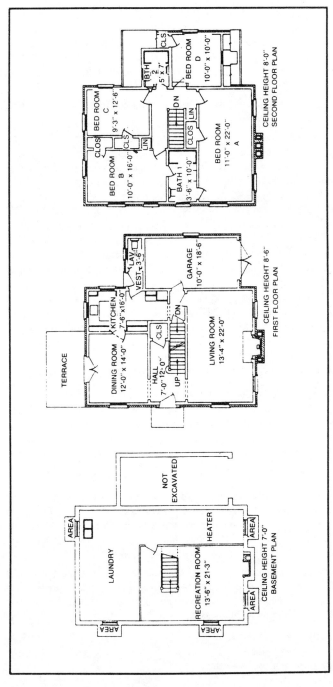

Fig. 6-6. Floor plans for the hypothetical house used in comparing the thermal performance with and without thermal insulation (reprinted with permission from the 1977 Fundamentals Volume, ASHRAE HANDBOOK & Product Directory).

243

☐ Assume an indoor temperature of 75 F.

☐ Assume the attic to be unheated.

☐ Assume the ground temperatures to be 32 F next to basement walls and 50 F under the garage and basement floors.

☐ Assume that all first and second floor windows are fitted with storm sash. The garage, however, is not.

The construction details and heat transfer coefficients of the building sections are as follows:

☐ House walls—0.29. Stud frame, wood exterior sheathing, building paper, brick veneer, interior metal lath, and plaster.

☐ Dormer walls—0.26. Same construction, except wood siding instead of brick veneer.

☐ Attic walls—0.42. Stud frame, wood exterior sheathing, building paper, brick veneer.

☐ Basement walls—0.10. Poured concrete 10 inches thick.

☐ Roof—0.44. Rafter frame, wood sheathing, and asphalt shingles.

☐ Ceiling, second floor—0.74. Metal lath and plaster.

☐ Windows, house—0.45 Double-hung wood windows averaging 70 percent glass.

☐ Windows, garage and basement—1.13. Steel casement.

☐ French doors—0.85. Doors are 50 percent glass.

☐ Floor, bedroom D—0.26. Yellow pine subflooring, maple finish flooring; metal lath and plaster ceiling below.

☐ Floor, basement and garage—0.10. Subbase of 3-inch cinder-aggregate concrete. Finish floor of 4-inch stone aggregate concrete.

The specific details of exterior doors are not noted in this listing, but they are included in the heat loss calculation sheet. The value for the doublehung wood windows are taken from Table 4-8 as 0.53 times the application factor, which by interpolation is 0.85. The value for the French doors is obtained in much the same way by using the value of 1.13 from the table for all glass construction and interpolating an application factor of 0.75.

When all of the room-by-room details are worked out and listed, they result in the compilation in Table 6-1. As you examine the table, be sure to check the explanatory notes that accompany it in order to understand how the figures were arrived at. More important to us in this discussion, however, is the total heat loss in Btuh—113,950.

The next step is to recalculate the heat loss for the same house after construction improvements have been made and thermal insulation has been added. These changes result in revised (and improved) overall heat transfer coefficients as follows:

☐ House walls—0.13

☐ Dormer walls—0.12.

☐ Basement walls—same.

❑ Roof—0.53.
❑ Ceiling, second floor—0.15.
❑ Windows and French doors—same.
❑ Floor, bedroom D—0.18.

Refer to Table 6-2 which shows the summary of the heat losses of the uninsulated house. On the "Design Totals" line, you will see the total heat loss of 113,950 Btuh. On the next line, "Operating Totals," you will see that the total loss is only 99,890. The difference lies in the infiltration loss; it has been halved. The reason, as is explained in Chapter 4, is that infiltration is initially calculated on the basis of all exposed exterior building sections. For air to actually infiltrate equally through all sides of a closed house at once is a physical impossibility—the roof would blow off.

An arbitrary assumption is made that infiltration at any given time will most likely take place only on the windward side and not on the leeward side. This presumably would amount to about half of the exposed exterior surfaces. Hence, the figure is downgraded to half. Note, too, in the "Percentages" line that infiltration amounts to only 14 percent of the total heat loss. This is quite low for a conventional frame house of this sort. In many older houses, especially those poorly built or not properly maintained, infiltration can amount to as much as 50 percent of the total.

Now turn to Table 6-3. This is the summary of heat losses from the insulated house. Primarily due to the added insulation, the design total heat loss has been reduced to 75,230 Btuh. Halving the infiltration loss as before, the operating total heat loss from the insulated house is 61,170 Btu every hour. There is a saving of 38,720 Btu of heat per hour. That's the equivalent, in the uninsulated house, of putting a pair of 5500-watt electric heaters out on the back porch and letting them run continuously.

The number of degree-days of heat required in the Syracuse area each heating season averages 6756. We'll assume that both houses are heated with No. 2 heating oil that has a value of 140,000 Btu per gallon and have heating system efficiencies of 70 percent. The operating heat loss of the uninsulated house is 99,890 times 6756 (degree-days) times 24 (hours per day) equals 16,196,564,160. Then, 85 (design temperature difference) times 0.70 (rated full load efficiency) times 140,000 (fuel heating value) equals 8,330,000. Dividing 16,196,564,160 by 8,330,000 equals 1944.37.

In this case, we can neglect the correction factors because they happen to make very little difference. The owner of the uninsulated house will burn about 1994 gallons of fuel oil over a heating season to keep his house warmed to 75 F.

Now let's see how the owner of the insulated house will fare. Following the same formula: 61,170 (operating heat loss) times 6756 (degree-days) times 24 (hours per day) equals 9,918,348,480. The design temperature difference, rated full load efficiency, and fuel heating value remain the same (or 8,330,000). Then 9,918,348,480 divided by 8,330,000 equals 1190.68. Again, we can neglect the correction factors. Fuel consumption for the insulated house is down by 754 gallons. That is a substantial

Table 6-1. Heat Loss Calculation Sheet for the Uninsulated Version of the Hypothetical House
(Reprinted with Permission from the 1977 Fundamentals Volume, ASHRAE HANDBOOK & Product Directory).

A	B	C	D	E	F	G
Room or Space	Part of Structure or Infiltration Air Changes	Net Exterior Area and Air Volume	U-value Coefficient, (Btuh)/((ft²)(F)	Temp. Diff.,[a] F	Heat Loss, (Btuh)	Totals, (Btuh)
Bedroom A and Closet	Walls	238 ft²	0.29	85	5870	
	Glass	40 ft²	0.45	85	1530	
	Ceiling	252 ft²	0.74	44.8[d]	8350	
	Infiltration (1)[g]	2016 cfh[b]	0.018[c]	85	3080	18,830
Bedroom B and Closet	Walls	156 ft²	0.29	85	3840	
	Glass	40 ft²	0.45	85	1530	
	Ceiling	170 ft²	0.74	44.8[d]	5630	
	Infiltration (1)[g]	1360 cfh[b]	0.018[c]	85	2080	13,080
Bedroom C and Closet	Walls	114 ft²	0.29	85	2810	
	Glass	27 ft²	0.45	85	1030	
	Ceiling	129 ft²	0.74	44.8[d]	4280	
	Infiltration (1)[g]	1032 cfh[b]	0.018[c]	85	1580	9,700
Bedroom D and Closet	Walls	118 ft²	0.29	85	2910	
	Glass	20 ft²	0.45	85	770	
	Ceiling	110 ft²	0.74	44.8[d]	3640	
	Floor over garage	110 ft²	0.26	40[c]	1140[p]	
	Infiltration (1)[g]	880 cfh[b]	0.018[c]	85	1350	9,810
Bathroom 1	Walls	30 ft²	0.29	85	740	
	Glass	14 ft²	0.45	85	540	
	Ceiling	55 ft²	0.74	44.8[d]	1820	
	Infiltration (1)[g]	440 cfh[b]	0.018[c]	85	670	3,770
Bathroom 2	Walls	79 ft²	0.26	85	1750	
	Glass	9 ft²	0.45	85	340	
	Ceiling	35 ft²	0.74	44.8[d]	1190	
	Floor over garage	35 ft²	0.26	40[c]	360	
	Infiltration (1)[g]	280 cfh[b]	0.018[c]	85	430	4,070
Living Room	Walls	267 ft²	0.29	85	6580	
	Walls (adjoining garage)	94 ft²	0.39[f]	40[c]	1470	

Room	Item	Area	U-factor	Δt	Btu
Dining Room	Walls	166 ft²	0.29	85	4090
	Glass (doors)	35 ft²	0.85	85	2530
	Glass (windows)	20 ft²	0.45	85	770
	Floor	168 ft²^b			
	Infiltration (1.5)^j	2140 cfh^b	0.018^c	85	3270
					10,660
Kitchen and Entrance to Garage	Walls	96 ft²	0.29	85	2370
	Walls (adjoining garage)	51 ft²	0.39^f	40^e	800^p
	Glass	18 ft²	0.45	85	690
	Door	17 ft²	0.51	40	350
	Floor	125 ft²			
	Infiltration (1.5)^j	1595 cfh^b	0.018^c	85	2440
					6,650
Lavette and Vestibule	Walls	82 ft²	0.29	85	2020
	Walls (adjoining garage)	85 ft²	0.39^f	40^e	1330^p
	Glass	9 ft²	0.45	85	340
	Door	19 ft²	0.51	85	820
	Floor	30 ft²			
	Infiltration (1.5)^k	383 cfh^b	0.018^c	85	590
					5,100
Entrance Hall	Walls	39 ft²	0.29	85	960
	Door	21 ft²	0.38	85	680
	Ceiling^f	87 ft²	0.74	44.8^d	2990
	Infiltration (2)^l	1110 cfh^b	0.018^c	85	1700
					6,330
Garage	Walls	167 ft²	0.29	50^e	2420
	Glass	53 ft²	1.13	50	3000
	Doors	44 ft²	0.51	50	1120
	Infiltration (1.5)^m	2360 cfh^b	0.018^c	50	2120.
	Floor	29 ft^s	0.81	50	1180
	Gain adjoining rooms				-5100^p
					4,740
Recreation Room^q	Walls	220 ft²	0.10	43	950
	Glass	8 ft²	1.13	85	770
	Floor	287 ft²	0.10	25	720
	Infiltration (1)^n	2010 cfh^b	0.018^c	85	3080
					5,520
				TOTAL	113,950

247

Table 6-2. Summary of Heat Losses of the Uninsulated House in Btuh (Reprinted with Permission from the 1977 Fundamentals Volume, ASHRAE HANDBOOK & Product Directory).

Room or Space	Walls	Ceiling and Roof	Floor	Glass and Door	Infil- tration	Totals
Bedroom A	5870	8350	—	1530	3080	18,830
Bedroom B	3840	5630	—	1530	2080	13,080
Bedroom C	2810	4280	—	1030	1580	9,700
Bedroom D	2910	3640	1140	770	1350	9,810
Bathroom 1	740	1820	—	540	670	3,770
Bathroom 2	1750	1190	360	340	430	4,070
Living Room	8050	—	—	1910	5730	15,690
Dining Room	4090	—	—	3300	3270	10,660
Kitchen	3170	—		1040	2440	6,650
Lavette	3350	—	—	1160	590	5,100
Entrance Hall	960	2990	—	680	1700	6,330
Garage	−1180[a]	−1500[b]	1180	4120	2120	4,740
Recreation	950	—	720	770	3080	5,520
Design Totals	37,310	26,400	3,400	18,720	28,120	113,950
Operating Totals[c]	37,310	26,400	3,400	18,720	14,060	99,890
Percentages[d]	37	27	3	19	14	100

[a] Wall heat loss of 2420 Btuh minus wall heat gains of 1470, 800, and 1330 Btuh.
[b] Heat gains of 1140 and 360 Btuh.
[c] Based on 0.5 computed infiltration.
[d] Based on operating totals.

reduction over that of the uninsulated house. When dollars are attached to these figures, they become even more impressive. Assume a cost of $1.25 per gallon. The owner of the uninsulated house will shell out $2430 for fuel. The owner of the insulated house will get by with $1488.75 for a savings of $941.25. That will buy a lot of thermal insulation. And to make matters worse, if the owner of the uninsulated house is in the 40 percent marginal tax bracket, he would have to earn approximately an extra $2350 to pay for his fuel.

Given the climate conditions upon which this example is based, a new house would not be constructed today with thermal resistance as low as that of even the insulated house cited. The thermal properties of the insulated house could probably now be considered as more or less average for an older house. A new one would be much better equipped to combat that sort of climate and enjoy even greater savings. The final figures shown in the example are merely an estimate, nothing more. There are few things more variable than just the weather. The heating bill for this year might well be less than last year and could easily be higher for the next couple of years. A 1-year basis for estimating potential savings simply is not time enough.

That being so, let's look at a longer time period. Degree-day figures for various locales are based upon long-term averages spanning many years. They are quite accurate for past periods because they were taken from actual hourly temperature readings. It follows that they will probably also be accurate for long-term future periods, plus or minus only a few degree-days. A decade should be a relatively safe basis for calculation. The owner of the insulated house can be relatively well assured of saving a bit over $9400. If we assume the life of the house to be 100 years—not at all unlikely for a well-built structure, if it is properly maintained—the savings amounts to just over $94,000. The savings in fuel oil, assuming that our fuel oil supply lasts that long, amounts to over 75,000 gallons.

The difference in operating costs between the two houses is large enough that recovery of insulation cost could probably be gained in a couple of years or so. You can use this same general system, for comparing different levels of thermal efficiency on a whole-house basis, just by plugging in different U values and heat loss numbers in Btuh for various sections of the house. But let's suppose your interest lies in a much smaller scale and you want to find out if it is worthwhile to install double-glazed windows rather than single-glazed. Let's further assume that 500 square feet of glass is involved. We'll say that both kinds of

Table 6-3. Summary of the Insulated Version of the Example House (Reprinted with Permission from the 1977 Fundamentals Volume, ASHRAE HANDBOOK & Product Directory).

Room or Space	Walls	Ceiling and Roof	Floor	Glass and Door	Infil- tration	Totals
Bedroom A	2620	2770	—	1530	3080	10,000
Bedroom B	1720	1870	—	1530	2080	7,200
Bedroom C	1260	1470	—	1030	1580	5,340
Bedroom D	1300	1220	790	770	1350	5,430
Bathroom 1	330	610	—	540	670	2,150
Bathroom 2	870	280	250	340	430	2,170
Living Room	3630	—	—	1910	5730	11,270
Dining Room	1830	—	—	3300	3270	8,400
Kitchen	1430	—	—	1040	2440	4,910
Lavette	1520	—	—	1160	590	3,270
Entrance Hall	430	960	—	680	1700	3,770
Garage	−580[a]	−1040[b]	1180	4120	2120	5,800
Recreation	950	—	720	770	3080	5,520
Design Totals	17,310	8,140	2,940	18,720	28,120	75,230
Operating Totals[c]	17,310	8,140	2,940	18,720	14,060	61,170
Percentages[d]	28	13	5	31	23	100

[a] Wall heat loss of 1080 Btuh minus wall heat gains of 680,370 and 610 Btuh.
[b] Heat gains 790 and 250 Btuh.
[c] Based on 0.5 computed infiltration.
[d] Based on operating totals.

windows are all glass (to avoid bothering with correction factors for sash). Single glass has a U of 1.10 in winter and insulating glass, with a one-half inch air space between the panes has a U of 0.49 in winter.

For 500 square feet, the total loss for the single glass would be 550 Btuh and the loss for the insulating glass would be 245 Btuh, per square foot. We can use the same temperature difference as in the previous example, 85 F, and the same number of degree-days, 6756. Then you can use a simple formula to determine how much heat will be lost through these two kinds of glass over an entire heating season.

For the single glass, this would be 550 times 24 times 6756, divided by 85, which equals 1,049,167 Btu. For the double glass, the figures would be 245 times 24 times 6756, divided by 85, which equals 467,356 Btu. Subtracting one from the other, there is a saving of 581,811 Btu over an average heating season. That doesn't look like much and it really isn't. It's only a small fraction of the total seasonal heat load for the entire house. Is it enough to bother with?

Let's say the house is heated electrically. That would mean the installation of the double glass would save 170.5 kilowatt hours of electricity per heating season (1 watt equals 3.413 Btu, 1 kilowatt equals 1,000 watts). At 6¢ per kilowatt hour, the annual saving would be $10.23 (not very impressive). If you were to burn No. 2 fuel oil at 60 percent efficiency—resulting in a useful heat input of 84,000 Btu per gallon—and the cost of the fuel oil were $1.25 per gallon, you would save $8.63. That is even less impressive.

The cost-effectiveness depends primarily upon two factors: the additional cost of the double glazing over the single and the time period over which the windows will be amortized. Round the savings off to $10.00 for simplicity. Over the course of a 20-year mortgage, the saving would be $200. If the double glazing cost an extra $1.00 per square foot, at the end of 20 years you would still be $300 behind (not counting interest). Over a 100-year house life span, the initial cost would be returned two-fold; the payback period would be 50 years. Over a short term, double glazing is not worth the effort. Over the long term, it certainly is if the windows last that long.

There are other factors to be considered. Double-glazing almost always cuts down on infiltration and that results in a further slight saving. The interior surface of double-glazing does not become as cold as single glass. This makes a somewhat more comfortable interior and also reduces cold air drop and drafts across the floors. In most instances, double glazing will either reduce or sometimes entirely prevent condensation and frost on the interior surfaces.

Double glazing is also somewhat more sound-proof than single glazing. On the other hand, double glazing does somewhat reduce the amount of light entering the house and also excludes a certain amount of insolation that might be beneficial. Outward visibility is also reduced by a small amount.

Moisture Control, Ventilation, and Infiltration

The presence of excessive amounts of water vapor, or of any amount of free moisture, within a structure and the proper admittance of outside air into the structure are two factors that must be considered as insulating plans are being developed for a new house or for renovating an existing house. These factors are inextricably interrelated with thermal performance. They also bear upon the structural integrity of the house over time and upon the ultimate comfort level of the living quarters and maintenance/operating costs.

Excess moisture and outside air admittance give rise to three elements of construction (or renovation) that must receive attention. These are the control of moisture, the control of and provisions for ventilation, and the control of infiltration. In this context, ventilation is the voluntary admittance of outside air, by whatever means, and it bears a close relationship with some aspects of moisture control. Infiltration is the involuntary admittance of outside air and can also be interwoven with both ventilation and moisture control. As a matter of convenience, I will discuss them separately.

MOISTURE CONTROL

Moisture control in a house is comprised of two different elements: protection against moisture and the control of water vapor. Moisture or better yet, *free moisture,* is just that—a puddle on the floor, rain on the windowsill, drips from a leaky pipe. *Water vapor* is a gas.

When an excessive amount of water vapor gets into the wrong places within the structure—a very common circumstance—that's not desirable and it can be destructive. Unfortunately, there are many instances where free moisture appears in a house—sometimes unnoticed, too—and that situation is also undesirable and it too can be destructive. The presence of free moisture often means that the amount of water vapor in the atmosphere will also be added to, by evaporation, perhaps causing more problems. For a number of reasons, both water vapor and free moisture must be controlled within the house.

Free Moisture

Damage to the structure resulting from inadvertent admission of free moisture can be immediate in some cases and slow and insidious in others. The effects are familiar to many homeowners: water-staining, degradation of plaster or wallboard, buckled paneling, blistered or scaling paint, lifted flooring, and so on. Fungus growth, mildew, dry rot and wet rot can occur and are much more serious problems if the framework of the house is involved. Thermal insulation can be, and often is, destroyed by quantities of water entering the building sections. There are several causes of these difficulties and the best insurance against them is top-notch quality construction.

Wind-driven Rain. It is not at all unusual for damage to a house to occur as a result of rainwater, and occasionally even fine snow, being driven into the fabric of the structure. Water can be forced into joints in the exterior siding, around window frames and sash, into door frames and thresholds, and into outside lighting fixtures. Water can leak or be driven behind chimney or vent pipe flashing, into masonry joints, through imperfect finish roofing. Even a simple house has a good many potential points of entry and the only way to avoid the problem is to build the structure right and to keep up with the maintenance chores over the ensuing years.

Leaky roofs are not to be tolerated. The damage that can result (often hidden) is sometimes substantial. Wet cap or roof insulation doesn't work at all and structural rotting (not to mention damage to the interior partitions and finish) is a good likelihood. Both the roof underlayment and the finish roof covering should be of top quality and properly applied. It should be replaced *before* it finally reaches the stage of complete deterioration from natural weathering. Proper flashing should always be installed. The roof design should be such that there is no opportunity for water to stand or for snow to build up to harmful depths. Structural strength and rigidity should be ample to withstand the test of time and weather. Because the roof of a house bears the greatest brunt of the weather yet, must be called upon to give the greatest amount of protection, it should be constructed in the best possible fashion. Skimping just doesn't make sense.

Perhaps the next most problematical area is the windows. This is particularly true for those on the "storm-sides" of the house. They abound with seams and cracks that are likely to become larger, rather than smaller, with time and repeated use. Window units must be properly installed with cracks fully caulked and the trimwork sealed to the house. An operating sash must be fully weatherstripped. All windows should have a flashing strip applied above them, unless they are permanently protected by a projection, and should be fitted with a drip cap as well. Exterior sills should have good projection past the exterior siding. They should have a drip groove or lip at the bottom. A tight-fitting storm sash gives good weather protection to the sash and inner parts of the frame. Stopped-in glass should be well sealed into the stops with a top-grade glazing sealant. Windows in foundation walls are especially prone to leakage. And more so if they are close to the ground and subjected to splashing or nearby ice buildup. Basement windows at grade level, or below-grade in window wells, must be particularly well sealed. They are best protected with clear plastic bubbles made for the purpose.

Entry doors, especially if located on the weather side of the house, are highly susceptible to wind-driven moisture. It can enter the cracks around the trimwork and frame, seep down into the framing via cracks around the threshold area, and even be blown directly into the building through a gap at the door bottom. Exterior doors must be fully sealed with a good caulk. This is especially important at the threshold which should be completely weatherstipped. Flashing should be installed above the door unless its upper portion is protected by a projection. A self-sealing or weatherstripped type of threshold or door-bottom attachment should be installed. Another useful device is a drip shield that mounts along the outside of the bottom edge to divert water away from the door edge itself. The best way to protect an expensive entry door from the weather and ensure that no moisture will enter around the door itself is to fit a storm door. This gives full protection to the whole door opening area. Of course, the storm door unit itself should be thoroughly sealed against the entrance of moisture.

Sliding glass patio doors and French doors are often troublesome and especially if they are not properly installed. If they open directly onto an unprotected deck or patio, the area around the door bottom is particularly prone to leakage. Sometimes the moisture appears inside the house, but in many instances it seeps unnoticed down into the structure or creeps between the flooring layers. The door frame and trim, as well as the component parts of the door assembly itself, must be very well sealed with a top-quality elastomeric caulk. This is best done on the inside and the outside, but at least along the bottom of the door.

French doors can be treated in much the same way as any entry door. However, double doors must be properly fitted where they meet and they should be equipped with tight-fitting closure hardware (decorative barrel bolts, for instance) top and bottom so that they can be shut tightly against their stops and weatherstripping. The best protection is afforded by a storm door arrangement. They can be obtained for many kinds of patio doors or custom-made for any kind, but seldom are fitted.

Water leakage through and around bulkhead doors leading into cellars is a common circumstance. This is compounded by the location and door position of most types. Damage is not usually a problem because the only building sections normally involved are the concrete floor and walls of the bulkhead entryway. Some are also fitted with floor drains to carry off water. But this is a nuisance and does add unnecessarily to the water vapor content of the interior air. About all that I can suggest as a cure for the problem is to originally install the bulkhead in as protected a location as possible, construct it and the entryway in the best possible fashion, and seal off every crack and cranny you can find. The doors themselves should be completely weatherstripped and kept in proper alignment.

The exterior siding of a house, again on the weather side in particular, takes a severe beating. The whole purpose of the siding is to keep moisture out of the building sections. It's surprising how often it fails to do that. Wind-driven rain can enter through poorly fitted joints, uncaulked or badly caulked seams, loose pieces, failed paint or waterproofing, and cracked or damaged siding.

All types of siding must be carefully fitted and installed and properly secured according to the manufacturer's instructions. Wood siding, except for cypress, redwood, and cedar (all of which can be allowed to weather naturally), should be kept painted or stained or at least coated with a preservative and water-repellant. Horizontal butt joints (as between sheets of plywood siding) should be thoroughly caulked, or better yet, flashed. Horizontal lap joints should have plenty of overlap. Vertical joints in horizontal siding (such as channel-lap boards) should be scarfed rather than butted and corner boards or other trim should be properly sealed.

The entire exterior surface of a house and everything that is a part of it, from thresholds to chimney caps, is endlessly subjected to extremes of weather conditions. Most of these areas conspire in one way or another to allow the entry of moisture into the structure. The passage of time, settling, and weathering only serves to compound the difficulties. A new house must be carefully constructed in the best possible fashion to minimize these potential problems and an existing house must be routinely maintained and repaired as necessary.

Groundwater Leakage. Perhaps the most common of all leakage problems in houses is groundwater leakage. There might only be some slight seepage through the basement walls from time to time, dampness every once in a while, or perhaps some seasonal leakage of a minor nature (and maybe not every year at that). Or streams of water may gurgle through the walls and have to be removed by a sump pump. Some houses have drainage gutters molded into the concrete floors; the water runs in one side of the house and out the other!

Groundwater moves through the earth at various levels and pressures. When the water table rises high enough, the water can enter a basement. Surface runoff can saturate the ground as a result of heavy rains or spring snowmelt. Water dripping from the eaves of a house can easily saturate the ground around the foundation enough to allow moisture to seep through the walls. It often happens that the presence of the house itself creates a moderate level of moisture in the soil area around it.

There are several ways to reduce the likelihood of excessive amounts of groundwater around the house. Location is the first consideration. A swamp or a marsh isn't a good place to build a house. This is especially true with a full basement (it'll be full, all right). The site should be dry in all seasons of the year, with no evidence of springs or underground streams, and should be pitched so that water drains away from the house. No watersheds or watercourses should lead to the site or be within a hundred feet or so.

The final grade around the house should be sloped away for at least 20 feet in all directions. Dense vegetation is best kept away so that the ground can dry satisfactorily after it does become soaked. The house should also be equipped with roof guttering and downspouts to carry away roof runoff from storms. Downspout discharge should be routed into drainaways, drainage ditches, or even drywells if necessary (but never septic tanks) to keep excessive moisture away from the foundation walls.

But the most important item of all—critical if the basement is to be used for living quarters and hypercritical in earth-sheltered house designs—is to adequately damp-proof or waterproof the basement (or house) walls. Groundwater can build up ample hydrostatic pressure to seep through ordinary poured concrete foundation walls and cinder blocks and concrete blocks are quite porous. Bad mortar joints are a common leak point in block walls. The joint between the footings and either poured concrete or block walls is another likely source. If any cracks have developed in either type of wall—and they almost inevitably will over a period of time—free moisture can easily find its way inside.

If there is any appreciable amount of water in the surrounding soil, it will surely find its way through either untreated or cracked basement walls. Just a minor amount of dampness will add to water vapor in the air. If the walls are furrred and insulated, the value of the insulation will be substantially diminished. Rot and degradation of the materials will slowly set in. If the amount of moisture is substantial, finishing the basement will be impossible until the leaks are permanently stopped. It is not at all unusual for sump pump installations to be required. Unfortunately, basement leakage problems often don't appear until quite some while after the house has been built and the basement or earth-sheltered living quarters have been finished; then it's a disaster.

Ice Dams. The buildup of ice dams on roofs is a common cause of water leakage. Sometimes the water leaks into the living quarters and alerts the homeowner to the problem, but often moisture seeps unnoticed down into the walls or other cavities. By the time the problem is recognized, a considerable amount of damage may have been done. Repairs, which might also entail some renovation, are often difficult. Usually they are disruptive for the occupants and they are always expensive.

Ice dams are often caused by insufficient cap insulation and this is usually coupled with inadequate or no attic ventilation. Enough heat builds up in the attic to melt some of the snow on the roof surface. The water runs down the roof until it gets to the colder eave area of the roof; there it freezes. The ridge of ice continues to grow and creep up the roof. It can also accumulate inside the eaves, along the inside surfaces of the upper siding or sheathing, and force its way beneath shingles, roof underlayment, and decking (Fig. 7-1).

As it does so, the expansive force drives the component parts of the building sections apart. This makes room for even more ice and water. Meanwhile, the meltwater continually pockets in growing puddles above the ice dam and eventually finds its way into the structure to run down into walls, soak cap insulation, ruin ceilings, and so forth.

At high altitudes, the strong winter sun can melt snow on the upper portions of a roof, but have no effect on the overhang portion. Water has been known to back up 4 and 5 feet on a roof in such circumstances and circumventing properly installed flashing. Flat or very shallow-pitched roofs are particularly subject to strange ice-dam and water-pooling effects. Such roofs seldom work out very well in harsh-winter country. In most places low-pitched roofs are a constant source of trouble.

There really is only one practical approach to avoiding ice dam problems and it encompasses several points. First, stay away from flat roofs or very shallow-pitched roofs in snow country as far as conventional residential construction practices are concerned. Many designers do use them and some of these roofs give no trouble for many years. But as many discouraged homeowners will tell you, it's a chancy proposition and the likelihood of eventual failure is good.

When a conventional roof is built (or replaced), 90-pound smooth mineral-surfaced roll roofing can be laid between the roofing felt and the finish roofing. This will minimize the possibility of water getting into the roof assembly.

Make sure that the attic floor, or cap, is heavily insulated to allow as little heat as possible to escape into the attic area to warm the underside of the roof. At the same time, provide for excellent ventilation throughout the attic area. This helps to keep the attic dry and to dissipate what little heat does escape the living quarters below. As a result, the entire roof surface remains cold, not much melting takes place, and ice dams are less likely to form (Fig. 7-2). An additional method is to remove the snow from the edges of the roof so that any ice buildup that does occur is minor and of no consequence. This is the most effective, surest, and least costly method. The job can be done readily with a long-handled snow rake made just for the purpose. Often there is no need for a ladder.

Vapor Barriers

A vapor barrier is any material or substance that will not admit the passage of water vapor or will do so only at an extremely slow rate. The permeability of a material is a measure of its capacity to allow the passage of liquids or gasses. *Water vapor permeability* is the property of a substance to permit the passage of water vapor and is equal to the *permeance* of the substance when 1 inch thick. The measure of water vapor permeability is the *perm*. This equals the number of grains, squared, of water vapor passing through a material or substance 1 foot square, per hour, per inch of mercury difference in vapor pressure. About all you really have to remember is that any material that has a perm rating of 1.0 or less is considered a vapor barrier. It will not allow the passage of any appreciable or harmful amounts of water vapor. Any material with a rating higher than 1.0 (and that accounts for most of them) is a "breather" or *breathable material* that will permit the passage of water vapor in whatever degree its perm rating indicates. The higher the perm number, the greater the amount of water vapor will pass through the material in a given time; 0.0 is totally impermeable.

Vapor barriers must be installed in houses built in all geographical locations where winter condensation problems occur (Fig. 7-3A) for protection against damage or poor thermal performance. The usual rule of thumb that was followed in the past was that any house constructed with building sections having a coefficient of thermal transmission of 0.25 or less were best protected with barriers.

While that U factor wasn't bad in many places years ago, today it isn't good. Most houses built in winter country today have vapor barriers installed as a matter of course. Those in severe winter country often have double barriers. One barrier is an integral part of the insulation and another is built in as a separately installed sheet barrier. Vapor barriers are equally important in warm climes where mechanical cooling is a standard feature of many houses. Water vapor in the warm and humid outside air can penetrate unprotected building sections and especially in walls and ceiling/roof assemblies. This unnecessary latent heat gain adds greatly to the cooling load of the house, increases cooling costs, and can also decrease comfort.

Vapor barrier materials are almost always installed in the building sections as close as possible to the living-quarters surface of the section or to the heated/cooled or conditioned side. Instructions often indicate that a barrier should be placed "on the warm side" of the construction.

Many thermal insulation products marketed these days include integral vapor barriers. Mineral batt and blanket material is faced with asphalt-

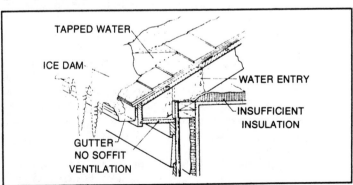

Fig. 7-1. Improper roof construction, insufficient ceiling insulation, and no eave ventilation can easily cause ice dam problems.

257

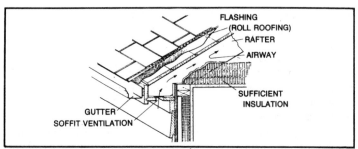

Fig. 7-2. Ice dams can be avoided in most cases by installing plenty of cap insulation, providing ample ventilation in the attic, and properly flashing the eave edge of the roof.

impregnated or foil-covered kraft paper. The foam plastic type of insulating sheathings are also usually foil-covered, often on both sides, and some kinds of plastic foam insulants are also relatively impermeable. It is best to ascertain just what the perm rating of various insulation products might be before depending upon them as vapor barriers. Faced mineral wool is often installed without any additional vapor barrier, but is just as often covered by a supplementary barrier. A supplementary barrier is recommended and especially when the insulation is installed dished between framing members. Other types of insulation must be installed in conjunction with a separate vapor barrier.

The most commonly used vapor barrier material is clear polyethylene sheet—"construction plastic." It is inexpensive and very effective. It comes rolled in huge sheets and it can be rapidly stapled in place. The standard 4-mil thickness is suitable. However, 6-mil is just as easy to obtain and a bit less susceptible to puncturing or slitting.

Foil-backed wallboard is an excellent vapor barrier and fine for retrofitting an existing house. Oil-based paints are relatively impermeable and they can be used to retrofit a vapor barrier to an existing house. There are also special vapor barrier paints made for the purpose. Impermeable slab, board, or sheet plastic foam insulation can be installed.

Heavy, reinforced, asphalt impregnated kraft paper works well and it can be bought in roll form. Roll roofing (90-pound weight) is sufficiently impermeable and also fairly long-lived, but expensive. Aluminum foil is excellent; in a 1-mil thickness its perm rating is 0. Foil on heavy kraft paper at a weight of about 12 pounds per 100 square feet is also very good (perm 0.002, approximately). Some vinylized or plasticized wallpapers or fabric wallcoverings have a very low perm rating and are useful in retrofitting during remodeling.

Exterior-grade plywoods with exterior glue have a low perm rating because of the waterproof gluelines within the sheets. If properly applied they make a good vapor barrier. Engineered grades of exterior plywood, as well as MDO and HDO types, are even better. And of course there are numerous other materials that are impermeable. Examples are sheet

258

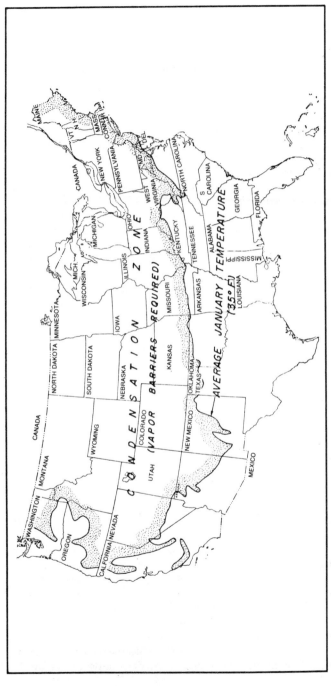

Fig. 7-3. This map shows the areas of the country where winter condensation problems are prevalent and vapor barriers should be installed. Vapor barriers are also needed in many of the remaining sections for protection against summer humidity.

metals, sheet plastics, glass, fiberglass panels, and so on. So by choosing your materials and working carefully, you can effectively seal off your entire living space within a continuous vapor barrier.

Vapor barriers, whether separate or integral with insulation and whether fitted to new houses or old ones, should be installed at the following locations and made as "seamless" as possible. Typical installations are shown here and in Chapter 9.

Crawlspaces. Open crawlspaces need not be treated. Unventilated or ventilated crawlspaces, heated or unheated, must be treated. The crawlspace floor is particularly important. Cover it with polyethylene sheeting, roofing felt, roll roofing, or a similar material to prevent moisture from rising from the ground and condensing on the underside of the first floor (Fig. 7-4). If the crawlspace is insulated with mineral wool, the integral vapor barrier will serve; position it face-upward. The inside of the crawlspace walls should also be covered.

Concrete Slabs. To prevent moisture from rising through the concrete, lay a vapor barrier over the gravel cushion before the concrete is poured (Fig. 7-5). The usual choice is polyethylene sheeting (generally the extra-heavy black variety). Care must be taken that it isn't damaged during the pouring. Foamed cellular glass insulation is an excellent (though more expensive) choice. It will provide vapor barrier and insulant at the same time with much less likelihood of damage. It must be properly fitted and sealed.

Basement Walls. The walls of heated basements should be fitted top to bottom with a vapor barrier. In some instances, a paint type might serve. The usual choice when finishing the area is an integral barrier on the insulation or the finish wallboard, a separate polyethylene sheet, or a combination. Often an extra damp-proofing sealer is applied to the walls before insulation is installed. The principal barrier should lie just behind the finish wall covering.

Floors. Concrete floors, whether slab-on-grade or basement, can be subject to more or less permanent dampness (or worse) if there is no vapor barrier beneath them. If they are to retrofitted with a finish flooring of some sort, the upper surface of the concrete should be sealed beforehand. Special sealers should be used when certain finish flooring such as carpeting or floor tile is to be laid. Note that some flooring products are not suitable for use on below-grade concrete slabs. If a wood floor is to be built, the slab should be first sealed. One possibility is to coat the floor with asphalt or an asphaltic mastic and then bed the sleepers in it. Insulation is then fitted between the sleepers and the whole affair is covered with polyethylene sheet before the subflooring or finish flooring is put down. Figure 7-6 shows a very similar arrangement.

Conventional framed-floor constructions over unheated crawlspaces, whether open, closed, or ventilated, are fitted with both insulation and vapor barrier. An integral barrier is often considered sufficient. An example is when faced mineral wool is installed between the floor joists with the

260

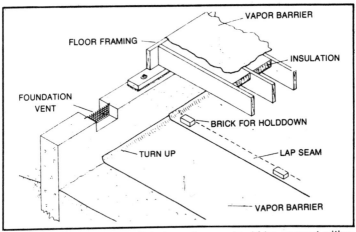

Fig. 7-4. The floor of a ventilated crawlspace should be covered with a vapor barrier ground cover to protect the underside of the house from condensation.

vapor barrier upward and close to the underside of the subflooring. Unfaced mineral wool batts and most other types of insulants require a separate vapor barrier. Polyethylene sheet is the easiest to use. It can be laid between the subflooring and the underlayment or between the under-

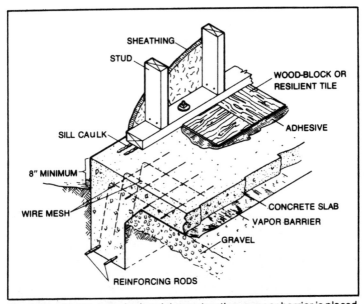

Fig. 7-5. In this thickened-edge slab construction, a vapor barrier is placed between the gravel cushion and the poured concrete. The same arrangement is used for other types of slab-on-grade construction.

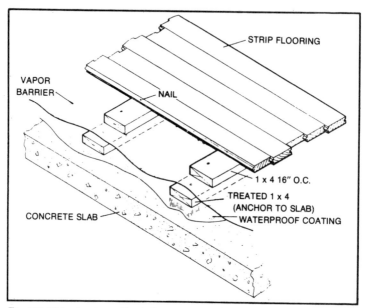

Fig. 7-6. This simple method of constructing a finish floor over a concrete slab affords double protection against moisture. It is a sealer or water-proofer on the slab itself and a vapor barrier suspended above.

layment and some kinds of finish flooring (such as nailed hardwood strip). Sheet vinyl flooring makes a good vapor barrier, but does usually have some seams and does not usually cover the entire floor out to all of the edges to seal with the wall vapor barrier. It is not often laid in every room of a house, but it is useful in retrofitting.

Walls. In new construction, house walls are generally fitted with faced mineral wool batt or blanket insulation. Sometimes the facing alone is depended upon as a sufficient vapor barrier. A supplementary polyethylene barrier does a better job, fully seals the walls, and has the advantage that the material can be lapped over to seal with both the floor and the ceiling vapor barriers. This will thoroughly cover all of the framing joints in the process. Foil-backed gypsum board also makes an effective barrier for this purpose and it is especially useful in retrofitting when it is used to directly cover an old existing wall. The manufacturers' application criteria and installation instructions must always be observed for these products to work properly. Other types of insulants than mineral wool generally must be covered by a separate barrier. Polyethylene sheet seems to be the most useful and effective (Fig. 7-7).

When an existing house is retrofitted with insulation blown into the wall cavities, the likelihood of hidden condensation occurring is quite good. Fitting a suitable vapor barrier is difficult unless the house is being extensively remodeled. Liberal applications of oil-based or vapor barrier paints are useful in this situation. Particular attention must be paid to sealing off all of the cracks around trimwork attached to outside walls. Vinylized or other relatively impermeable wall coverings, whether papers, fabrics, paneling, or wallboard, also serve well. If the remodeling is extensive, often it is possible to fit polyethylene sheet to the interior of outside walls beneath new wall covering and trimwork.

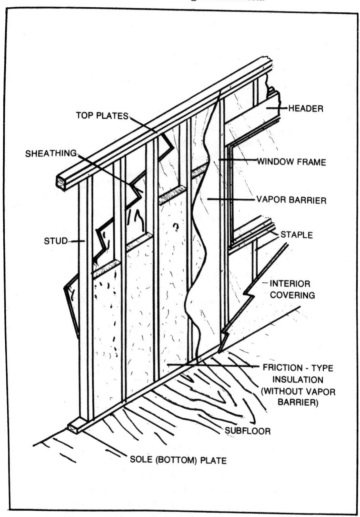

Fig. 7-7. A polyethylene sheet vapor barrier is easy to apply to frame walls where no integral barrier is provided with the insulation or where a supplementary barrier is preferred. Although the barrier is cut off at top and bottom, a better arrangement would be to leave a flap that would overlap both floor and ceiling barriers to seal the interior off completely.

Masonry veneered walls are fitted with a vapor barrier in the same manner as any conventional framed wall, because that is indeed what the interior section of the wall is. Either an integral or a separate barrier, or both, is positioned to the inside of the wall. A full masonry wall is another matter. If the wall is solid, a vapor barrier should be fitted to the inside surface. This can be a damp-proofing coating beneath or as a part of an applied interior finish or polyethylene sheeting between the interior surface of the masonry and the backside of a finish wall covering such as paneling.

In many circumstances, a foil-backed wallboard product will also serve relatively well. In a cavity type of masonry wall, the vapor barrier can be placed on the interior of the wall beneath the finish or on the outside surface of the inner section of the wall. A portion of the cavity should remain empty if an insulating material is installed in it and the outer course should be constructed as usual (permeable and fitted with weep holes at the base). This will allow dissipation of moisture that might otherwise accumulate between the two courses.

When vapor barriers are applied to walls, particular attention should be paid to fitting the material around eletrical outlet boxes, exhaust fans, light fixtures, registers, plumbing, or whatever. The problem is that considerable water vapor can escape through the cracks around the equipment, travel from the warm side of the wall to the cold side and condense on the sheathing or siding. This is especially true if the insulation is poorly fitted at the top and bottom (Fig. 7-8). Taping the vapor barrier tightly in place to seal the cracks is often possible and application of an elastomeric caulk to fill all cracks will likewise do the job. Though this is a seemingly small thing, it is easy to take care of and can be important for full protection.

Ceiling/Roof Assemblies. Vapor barriers are fitted to ceiling/roof assemblies in much the same fashion as to walls. The facing of mineral wool batt or blanket insulation often is adequate if the stapling flanges are secured to the edges of the ceiling joists or roof rafters and the flanges overlap. But if they are dished, or if other kinds of permeable insulation are installed, a separate vapor barrier should be installed. The usual choice is polyethylene sheet that is stapled directly to the edges of the joists or rafters. This can be done before or after the insulation is installed. It depends upon the type of material and the dictates of the construction.

In situations where insulation is being retrofitted to an existing, unprotected house, a vapor barrier should also be fitted to the ceiling/roof assembly if possible. In some instances this might have to consist of painting the ceilings with an oil-based paint or vapor barrier paint or putting up a relatively impermeable finish covering such as foil-backed gypsum board. A few types of ceiling tiles are also relatively impermeable and others can be made so by applying a finish (on either front or back). However, the vapor barrier thus provided will not be effective if the tiles are placed in a suspended-ceiling grid.

Not all authorities agree upon the need for a vapor barrier in ceiling/roof assemblies. Much depends upon the prevailing climate conditions and the construction of the house. There is substantial practical experience to suggest that *if* the ceiling is very well insulated and *if* the attic is very well ventilated, no ceiling vapor barrier is needed wherever winter outside design temperatures are higher than −20F.

Below that temperature, both heavy ceiling insulation *and* a vapor barrier are required. Evidence also suggests that in houses where no combustion air is required (i.e., heating by electric resistance equipment or fuel-fired equipment fed only by outside combustion air) a ceiling vapor barrier not only is unnecessary, but undesirable. In such situations there is often a sufficient buildup of interior water vapor to require dehumidification even during the heating season. If the ceiling vapor barrier is absent, the excess moisture will migrate upward and be exhausted through the vents in a well-ventilated attic, causing no harm.

While the presence of vapor barriers is almost always essential, at least in certain parts of the house, their use and placement is sometimes

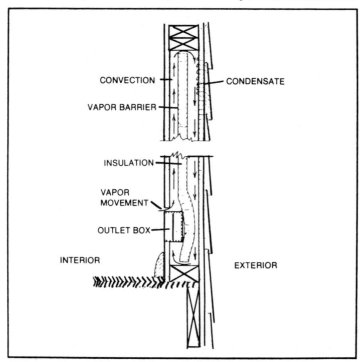

Fig. 7-8. This sketch shows the importance of completely sealing off cracks around equipment installed in walls or ceilings. This is especially true in cases where the walls are not filled with insulation or the installation is a poor one.

open to question. Especially with regard to ceiling/roof assemblies, their installation cannot always be reduced to a simple rule of thumb that covers all situations. Judgement must be exercised and local custom and experience can be a good guide.

Doors. Doors are not subject to damage from water vapor. They are not customarily fitted with a vapor barrier. However, a liberal coating of oil-based paint on the interior surface will stop any outward migration of water vapor. A storm door will afford protection against the entrance of wind-driven free moisture.

Windows. Condensation on windows is a common occurrance and it can lead to such difficulties as lifting paint, degradation of the glazing putty, rotting sash, and seepage of water down into the wall. If the inside temperature is 70 F and the relative humidity only 10 percent, condensation will form on a single-glazed window when the outside temperature is −10 F. If the inside relative humidity is 20 percent, it will form at an outside temperature of +7 F. At −10 F outside, condensation will not occur until the indoor relative humidity reaches 38 percent (if the window is fitted with storm sash).

The best way to avoid window condensation problems is not to lower the indoor relative humidity, but to install tight-fitting storm sash on all windows. If condensation occurs between the window and the storm sash, venting the storm sash with two or three small vent holes at top and bottom will often take care of the problems without admitting any appreciable additional amount of infiltrating air into the house. The installation of double-glazed windows will also take care of all but the most severe condensation difficulties and triple-glazing will virtually eliminate it.

Windows that are covered each night with interior insulating shutters seldom will frost over even if only single-glazed. Older types of aluminum-framed or steel-framed windows are prone to developing thick layers of frost all over the inside surfaces. Often this is to the point of rendering the window inoperable. Newer types built with thermal breaks do not have this problem as often, but they are still less desirable than wood-framed or vinyl-clad windows.

VENTILATION

Adequate ventilation *is* an absolute must in any residence. The essential aspects to consider are the ventilation of the interior living quarters and the ventilation of the structure.

Interior Ventilation

Adequate ventilation provides a continuous supply of oxygen to the occupants. In many houses, ventilation supplies combustion air to fuel-fired heating equipment, wood stoves, fireplaces, and gas-fired cooking ranges. It also disperses and carries away unsavory odors, tobacco smoke, and the like. In many older houses, much of this is accomplished simply through the infiltration into the structure of fresh outside air. The average replacement rate of the entire volume of inside air in such houses is usually considered to be about once every hour. This is more than sufficient to do the job most of the time. Rates as low as 0.25 changes per hour are considered healthful, but do little to ensure a continuous supply of what most of us would call "fresh" air.

Most new, tightly-built houses have an infiltration rate of approximately 0.5 air changes per hour. Some houses might have a bit less. Because of this continual "tightening-up" of new houses, many local building codes now require that all heating apparatus, including fireplaces and woodstoves, be equipped with facilities for introducing outside combustion air into the units rather than taking that air from inside the house. Also, infiltration in any house, whether new or old, is usually insufficient to take care of peak loads of cooking odors and such. Normal practice is to install a cooking range hood or kitchen wall fan to provide forced ventilation as needed.

Ventilation of the interior is also necessary at times to cool the living spaces or to vent excessive amounts of water vapor in the air. This can be partially accomplished by the simple expedient of opening windows and doors (especially in good weather), but there are many times when heavy or peak loads of heat or water vapor cannot be satisfactorily ejected in this way. It is essential that bathrooms be fitted with exhaust fans and laundry equipment be vented to the outside. Heat or high moisture content in the air in a laundry room can be exhausted by a wall or ceiling vent fan operated manually or controlled by a humidistat. Clothes driers should be directly vented to the outside. Bathroom vent fans are commonly wired to turn on with the bathroom light. They can also be controlled by a timer or be manually operated.

Structural Ventilation

Adequate ventilation of certain parts of the structure is extremely important in order to help prevent the formation of condensation within or on the building sections during the heating season and it is also effective in decreasing the amount of water vapor that enters the building during the cooling season. In addition, it will help to dry out any free moisture that might enter. There are two areas of particular concern. One occurs only in houses with crawlspaces. The other is common to all houses—roofs. Floor, wall, or ceiling sections are not commonly ventilated, at least in this country, because there is no need. There is one exception to this. In some circumstances when foil-covered foam plastic insulating sheathing is applied to wall exteriors, vent strips must also be installed to allow air circulation. Follow the manufacturers' installation instructions to the letter in such situations.

Crawlspace Ventilation. Open crawlspaces need no further attention and neither do crawlspaces that are already hyperventilated (such as an otherwise open crawlspace skirted with latticework, for instance). But closed, unheated perimeter crawlspaces do need to be ventilated. If the crawlspace does not have a vapor barrier ground cover, it should be fitted with vent openings through the walls (Fig. 7-9) in the ratio of one square

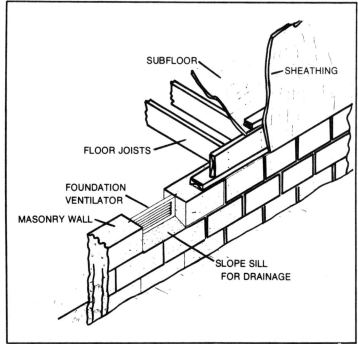

Fig. 7-9. Typical foundation ventilator installation.

foot of net free ventilating area to every 150 square feet of crawlspace floor area (with a minimum of four ventilators). If a vapor barrier ground cover is in place, the ratio can be decreased to 1 square foot of net free ventilating area for every 1500 square feet of crawlspace floor (with a minimum of two ventilators). The "not free ventilating area" refers to completely open, unobstructed ventilating space. When screening or louvers are placed over a ventilating opening (screening should always be used and louvers often must be), the opening is restricted to a certain degree. To find the actual size for ventilators fitted with screening or louvers, refer to Table 7-1. For best results, ventilators should be placed in the corners of the crawlspace walls to allow a good flow of air into the interior corners of the crawlspace area. Otherwise, there will be dead air pockets there and a consequent buildup of moisture.

Roof/Attic Ventilation. The critical parts of a house for proper ventilation are the attic spaces and roof areas if a buildup of water vapor and its attendant difficulties are to be avoided. Regardless of the style of roof, free-flowing ventilating air should be allowed to continuously move through the open space between it and the insulation layer over the living quarters. Where the ceilings are insulated and fitted with vapor barriers, the attic space, space behind knee walls, or space between the ceiling joists and a flat or slightly-pitched roof should be vented. If the insulation and vapor barrier are installed in the roof rafters themselves, ventilating space should be left between the underside of the roof sheathing and the upper surface of the insulation.

There are any number of specific arrangements for introducing a constant flow of ventilating air. In general, the object is to provide both inlets and outlets wherever possible to allow good cross ventilation. Failing that, a sufficient number of ventilators of appropriate size must be installed, usually at approximately the same level in the structure, so that at any given time—depending upon outside air motion conditions—some will act as inlets and others as outlets. The best arrangement is to position inlet vents as low as possible in the roof assembly and the outlet vents as close to the ridge as possible. This allows a natural stack effect to operate and a certain amount of air movement will almost always take place regardless of wind conditions. If the ventilators are in the same plane, ventilation is less positive and less effective.

The sketches in Fig. 7-10 show general venting arrangements for gable-roofed houses. Arrangements for hip roofs are shown in Fig. 7-11 and arrangements for flat roofs are shown in Fig. 7-12. The figures to the right of the illustrations are ratios. They indicate the vent opening in

Table 7-1. Determine the Actual Ventilator Size Required to Accommodate the Desired Net Free Ventilating Area.

Obstructions in ventilators—louvers and screens[1]	To determine total area of ventilators, multiply required net area in square feet by:[2]
¼-inch-mesh hardware cloth	1
⅛-inch-mesh screen	1-¼
No. 16-mesh insect screen (with or without plain metal louvers)	2
Wood louvers and ¼-inch-mesh hardware cloth[3]	2
Wood louvers and ⅛-inch-mesh screen[3]	2-¼
Wood louvers and No. 16-mesh insect screen[3]	3

[1]In crawl-space ventilators, screen openings should not be larger than ¼ inch; in attic spaces no larger than ⅛ inch.

[2]Net area for attics determined by ratios in figures 22, 23, and 24.

[3]If metal louvers have drip edges that reduce the opening, use same ratio as shown for wood louvers.

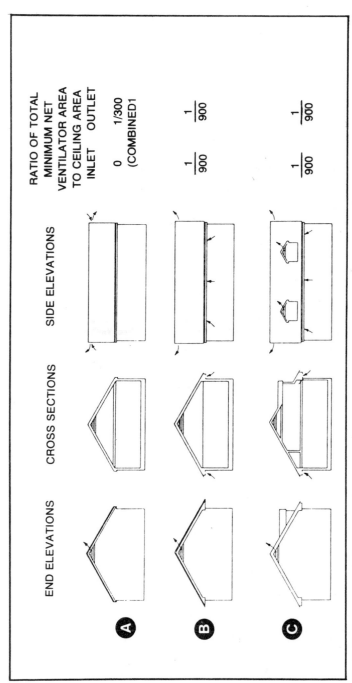

Fig. 7-10. Arrangements for ventilating gable roofs. Note the roof airway in the cross section in C.

square feet (upper number) and the corresponding ceiling area in square feet (lower number). Figure 7-10 (B and C), 1 square foot of net free ventilating area is required for every 900 square feet of ceiling area—for both inlets and outlets. These vents should be screened or louvered. Use Table 7-1 to determine actual vent opening sizes. An airway between insulation and roof sheathing in an insulated roof assembly is shown in Fig. 7-13 and also as a part of Fig. 9-16.

Inlet vents are usually installed in the soffit beneath the roof over-hang. Where there is no soffit, vents can be cut directly into the frieze boards.

Vents should be fully screened; use nothing larger than No. 16 mesh insect screening. Vertical vents should be weather-protected with louvers. All vents must be installed in weatherproof fashion, sealed, caulked, and flashed as necessary. Vents should be positioned so that they are in no danger of becoming obstructed by fallen leaves or drifting snow. All vents must be constructed and set so that no appreciable amount of wind-driven rain or fine snow, can enter the structure.

INFILTRATION

Infiltration/exfiltration is one of the most important factors in the heat loss/gain of a house. Cold air leaking into a house in winter must be warmed and at the same time a roughly equal amount of air already warmed is lost. Fuel must be burned in compensation. The cold entering air is also very dry and serves to drive the interior relative humidity down. If the interior air is not humidified, the thermostat set-point must be kept overly high to provide decent comfort levels.

When warm air enters in summer it imposes an additional load upon the cooling system. At the same time, a certain amount of cooled air is lost through exfiltration. When the warm air is also very humid, yet another

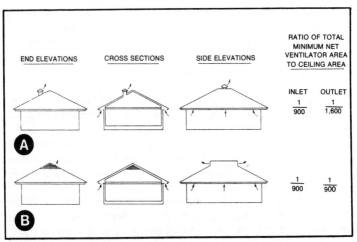

Fig. 7-11. Ventilating arrangements for hip-roofed houses.

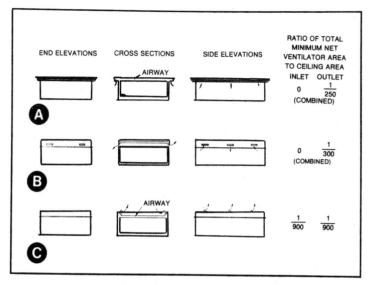

END ELEVATIONS	CROSS SECTIONS	SIDE ELEVATIONS	RATIO OF TOTAL MINIMUM NET VENTILATOR AREA TO CEILING AREA INLET OUTLET
A	AIRWAY		0 $\frac{1}{250}$ (COMBINED)
B			0 $\frac{1}{300}$ (COMBINED)
C	AIRWAY		$\frac{1}{900}$ $\frac{1}{900}$

Fig. 7-12. Ventilating arrangements for flat-roofed houses. Both B and C are constructed with parapets, while A has overhanging eaves.

cooling load is imposed. The cooling equipment must extract the excessive water vapor from the air.

Infiltration control is most easily achieved during construction of a new house. Basement walls must be properly built. Windows, doors, and bulkheads must be properly installed, sealed and caulked. The joint between the foundation top and the sill must be sealed with a sill sealer and caulk. The framing members of the structure should be of good grade, kiln-dried, and carefully fitted so as to minimize the difficulties of shifting, settling, and warping. Exterior sheathing for both walls and roofs should be the sheets rather than boards and they should be nailed *and* glued to the framing. All exterior joints and seams, everywhere, must be fully caulked and sealed. Exterior siding (preferably sheets) should be carefully fitted and applied with nails and glue. In many types of construction, the interior wall covering can also be glued in place.

If the roof directly covers the living spaces (as opposed to a ventilated attic), particular care should be taken to make the sections as tight against infiltration as possible.

Windows are critical. They must be fully sealed to the structure with no cracks or gaps anywhere that might admit air. The windows should be low-infiltration double- and triple-glazed. Vinyl-clads with integral mounting flanges are good in this respect.

Doors must also be well sealed around their frames and trimwork and completely weatherstripped (including the threshold). Tight-fitting storm doors are essential to infiltration reduction and an air-lock type of entryway is even better.

Fireplace and stove flues must be fitted with tight dampers. Airtight stoves and enclosed fireplace units are preferred. Outside combustion-air ducts should be installed wherever possible.

Ventilating fans and clothes dryer vents must be fitted with automatic closures.

In short, every crack, gap, and opening in the house must be sealed up and the building sections must be built with materials inherently resistant to air passage and in a fashion that precludes excessive infiltration. In addition, the proper installation of a full insulating envelope and a full, well sealed vapor barrier will greatly aid in the process of cutting potential excessive infiltration.

Everything in this section applies equally to existing houses. The problem is that good infiltration control is much more difficult and can't be approached in quite the same way—nor as effectively. Many older houses, and especially those that were built several decades or more ago, have serious infiltration problems. Except in cases of extensive renovation or complete rebuilding, the problem can't be tackled from the inside of the structure. Most control measures have to be externally applied.

The starting point is almost always with windows and doors. Storm doors and sash must be fitted. Weathered, worn, ill-fitting sash or window units should be replaced or at least completely weatherstripped. All door

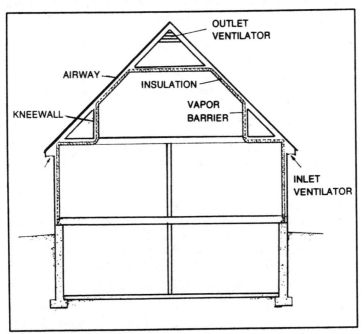

Fig. 7-13. The kneewall area and the peak are connected by an above-insulation airway for complete circulation.

and window frames and trimwork must be caulked with a top-grade elastomeric caulk. Doors must be fully weatherstripped or replaced if they are in bad shape. If airlock entryways can be added (either inside or outside), so much the better.

Unused fireplaces should be closed up, in-use fireplaces should be fitted with tight dampers and glass doors. Stove chimneys, whether masonry or metal, must be equipped with tight-fitting dampers, too, and replacement of nonairtight stoves with airtight models is well worth considering (they'll provide more heat for less fuel anyway).

Old airways should be plugged and entry points of cables and pipes should be thoroughly sealed off. The sill-foundation joint can be caulked from the inside and the joint between the lower edge of the exterior siding and the foundation wall can usually be filled with a sealer or caulk. A search should be conducted to locate any cracks or gaps in the exterior that might allow air to enter floor, wall, or ceiling cavities. These must be plugged, filled, or covered.

Often air leaks can be discovered on the inside of the house on a windy day. Checking about by watching the smoke trail from a burning incense stick is one aromatic approach. Leaks can be blocked off with patching plaster, putty, caulk, or even a bit of cellophane tape for a temporary repair.

Many more possibilities open up when remodeling or renovation takes place. Old siding can be replaced with new sheet-type siding or interlocking metal or vinyl siding that is underlaid with insulating sheathing or at least roofing felt. Window frames and door frames can be heavily caulked when the old siding is removed.

New interior wall, floor, or ceiling coverings can be underlaid with a polyethylene sheet vapor barrier or the new materials can be foil-backed. Retrofitting wall or ceiling insulation will prove helpful. Floors over open or ventilated crawlspaces can be fitted with insulation and a vapor barrier that will also reduce infiltration. Joints between the finish flooring and the mopboards on the outside walls can be caulked and then fitted with a trim molding set in more caulk. Much the same can be done at the wall-ceiling joint if necessary.

In short, any practical method that you can think of that will prevent outside air from coming in will be of help. There is one caution. Don't position an infiltration barrier that is also impermeable to water vapor—such as a polyethylene sheet—on or near the exterior of outside building sections. Air will be kept out, but water vapor will be trapped inside the sections and damaging condensation is sure to result.

Insulation Applications

8

Everyone can understand what happens if the planks, caulked seams, and glue joints of a wood boat hull aren't properly constructed or if they are loose, weak, and ill-fitting. All that water that's supposed to be on the outside will come inside. Much the same is true of a house. If the insulation barrier is poorly fitted, improperly done, skimpy and ill-conceived, all that cold (or warm) air that is supposed to stay outside will come inside. The homeowner had best have a stout heating/cooling system and a fat wallet on hand if he wants to remain comfortable.

It's an absolute must that insulation types and values be properly selected for certain specific applications and then be properly installed. Proper installation commonly does not get proper consideration. In very few houses will you find fault-free insulation installations and than includes jobs done by professional installers. It would seem obvious to anyone that if the roof of the house is not properly put together and the roof covering does not have full integrity, it will leak. Exactly the same is true of an insulation envelope. If not done just right, it will leak. Perhaps the difference is that leaking water is easy to see.

To do a good job you need knowledge of what's involved and a willingness to exercise enough patience to make sure that *all* of the insulation is installed just right and with full coverage. You must make sure that the house is constructed tightly and that the vapor barriers are properly put in. You have to be as picky, picky, picky as the worst of fussbudgets if you want to get the most from your insulation dollar.

SELECTING INSULANTS

Selecting the insulants to use for residential insulating applications is generally not a difficult job. This is especially true for straightforward wood-frame house construction. Of the several kinds readily available, fiberglass batt or blanket and various of the rigid foam boards are probably now the most widely used.

In selecting insulants that will nicely fulfill your requirements, you'll first probably want to check the cost of the material as delivered to your job site or as installed if you're not doing the work yourself. Relate that to the thermal efficiency and effectiveness that you will gain. The ratio of cost to benefits should be to your liking. You don't want to be underinsulated. That will mean you'll pay out more in the long run than you have to for heating/cooling system operating costs. And you might also pay more than you have to for a heating system that's bigger than you need. On the other hand, you don't want to overinsulate to the point where it becomes impossible to recapture a large portion of the initial cost for insulating.

You must also assess the various physical characteristics of the insulants. For example, if one of your goals is a high level of safety in the house, of which fire safety is a large part, then noncombustible insulants would be of more interest to you than those that are combustible. Relative water vapor permeability will be important if you live in a damp climate. Such factors as dimensional stability, potential for corrosiveness, or a susceptibility to insect or rodent damage should figure in your plans. Whatever the specifics, the idea is to choose an insulant that you feel will do the best job for you under your particular circumstances. A do-it-yourselfer will often choose one kind over another because of its ease of installation.

Fiberglass batts and blankets work well in most ceiling, wall and floor cavities, but they would be totally unsuitable to insulate the perimeter edge of a slab because they would crush flat and have no value whatsoever. On the other hand, a rigid cellular glass insulant is ideal for insulating slab perimeters and foundation walls. But while it could be used to insulate above a ceiling, for instance, the cost and the difficulty of installation would be too high for the amount of thermal performance gained when compared to other types of insulants that are better suited for that application. Because cellular glass insulation is totally noncombustible and extremely stable, there are some advantages in applying it to a residential ceiling area.

Loose-fill mineral wool insulants might have a tendency to settle in vertical cavities unless blown into place under just the right pressure, but they are far less apt to settle when placed horizontally as in an attic floor. Even if they do settle, they can often be readily topped off with a bit more. A plain reflective insulant in the walls of a house located in a harsh far-northern climate would be ineffective, but quite suitable in some benign southern climates.

The actual thickness, or the thickness versus the R value, of an insulant can also be of consequence. This can be especially true when retrofitting insulants to an existing house. For example, there might not be room enough to install suitably thick fiberglass batts to achieve a desired R value. This would mean installing a thinner material with a lower k to achieve the desired results. You could add insulation to the exterior walls of your house by furring the outside with 2 x 2s, placing 1½-inch, R-4.75

fiberglass batts in the bays and then covering the insulation with new exterior siding.

But that's a whole lot of work and expense when you can accomplish the same objective by covering the original exterior siding with a layer of R-5 rigid foam insulating board and then putting on the new siding. At the same time, you'll create a better seal against infiltration. By mounting the exterior siding on three-fourth inch furring strips placed over the insulating sheathing, you can gain an extra R-2 (assuming the sheathing is foil-faced).

The list of possibilities goes on and on, but the point is that there is at least one optimum insulant for every application. There is no such thing as a single insulant that will answer all purposes in any particular house. You'll end up using two or three kinds, most likely. By checking all the facts and details carefully and giving some thought to the different applications involved in your own house, you'll definitely end up with a better than usual insulating job.

WHERE TO INSULATE

Every building section of the structure that bounds a space having a design temperature significantly lower than the desired regular indoor temperature, whether actually exposed to the outdoors or not, should be insulated to a degree that reduces heat transfer and infiltration/exfiltration to the lowest possible practical degree. This is just as true where natural and mechanical cooling are required to lower indoor temperatures to a comfortable level and where heating is necessary to maintain the indoor temperature.

Foundations

Perimeter foundations should always be insulated if they enclose a heated space and they sometimes are insulated even when the space remains unheated. It is not always necessary to insulate an entire foundation. A heated basement that is large aboveground is really little more than a first floor and the walls should be insulated to the same degree as the other exposed walls of the house. This can be done within the wall cavities or on the outside of the walls (or any combination thereof). It is not always necessary to insulate beneath the basement floor, although this is often done.

If a basement is partially below grade and is heated, any aboveground portions of the walls that are of frame construction must be fully insulated just as are other exterior frame walls. Above-grade masonry sections must also be insulated. This can be done on the outside, on the inside, or within the wall section itself (or all three). The below-grade portions of masonry walls should also be insulated, although not necessarily to full depth. The hollow cores of concrete or cinder blocks can be filled. This does help somewhat.

Another common practice is to apply an insulant that completely covers the inside surface of the masonry walls. This is particularly advantageous where the interior of the basement will be finished to provide additional living space. Insulation can also be applied to the exterior of the masonry walls. In this case it need extend no more than approximately 2 feet below grade level. Any greater depth usually does little good insofar as heat transfer is concerned (except in very cold climates). There is no need to insulate beneath the basement floor. However, doing so will provide a somewhat warmer floor and afford a greater degree of comfort.

Sometimes a basement floor is finished with a wood subfloor for the sake of appearance and in this case an insulant can be placed between the sleepers that support the flooring. This too will add substantially to overall comfort even though the savings in actual heat loss is minimal.

If the foundation is a poured concrete slab-on-grade, insulation is essential. Perimeter edge insulation is generally all that is required; the interior portion of the slab is left uninsulated. For comfort, an unheated concrete slab—that is, one that does not incorporate heating system ducts—should not be used in locales where the winter weather is severe even when the slab is insulated around the edges. The heated type of concrete slab which contains perimeter heating ducts can be used in any climate and edge insulation is an absolute must for comfort and operating economy.

Although interior slab areas are generally not insulated underneath, they often are on the upper surface. Laying wall-to-wall carpeting and padding in itself provides a considerable amount of insulation and increases comfort levels remarkably. Wood flooring is sometimes installed on slab surfaces. In that case, an insulant can be placed between the slab and the flooring materials. As with the basement floor, the savings in heat loss are rather small but general comfort is increased substantially.

Well-ventilated crawlspaces are generally not insulated at all. There is no need and the space remains unheated and at virtually the same temperature as the outdoors. Many crawlspaces are designed for minimum ventilation year-round, and many are fitted with vent ports that are meant to be open in summer for full ventilation and closed up tight in winter to reduce ventilation to a relatively modest order of infiltration. The walls or floor of a crawlspace fitted with permanently-open vents need not be insulated. The underside of the house floor should be insulated instead. The same is true of crawlspaces fitted with operable vents. The theory is that the vents might inadvertently be left open during cold weather and allow a substantial heat loss through an uninsulated house floor.

And unvented crawlspace can be treated in either of two ways. The house floor can be thoroughly insulated and the crawlspace walls and floor left alone—this is the usual course today—or the crawlspace itself can be fully insulated. In years past, it used to be fairly common practice—nowadays not recommended and not allowed in most places—to actually make the crawlspace a part of the heating system. In effect, the whole crawlspace area was turned into a huge plenum chamber and the heat from the crawlspace was distributed upward through the first floor into the living quarters. In such circumstances, the walls and floor of the crawlspace must be fully insulated. The house floor is not insulated.

Another situation found in many older houses is where the crawlspace opens either completely or partially into a full basement area. If the basement is heated, the crawlspace is too. In this case, the above-grade portions of the crawlspace walls—together with the surface area extending 2 feet below grade—should be insulated. The crawlspace floor generally remains uninsulated. However, there is no reason why it could not be covered.

There are occasions—particularly in severe winter climates—where the interior surfaces of unvented crawlspace walls are covered with an insulant and the floor of the house is heavily insulated. The crawlspace floor might or might not be left uninsulated. It would seem at first glance that because the house floor is insulated there is little point in extending the coverage to the crawlspace walls. It is true that the overall heat loss down through the house floor and out through the crawlspace walls will be decreased only to a slight degree by the addition of insulation to the crawlspace walls.

What does happen is that the wide and often abrupt temperature swings that are characteristic of severe winter climates are not as readily transmitted to the unheated interior of the crawlspace if the walls are insulated. This more even (and slightly higher) intermediate temperature of the crawlspace in turn creates less of an effect upon the floor temperatures of the house. The variations are somewhat fewer and farther between. This leads to a more even and more comfortable average floor temperature in the house and it might also somewhat reduce cycling of the heating system.

In other words, insulating the crawlspace walls creates a buffer zone against winter weather that is more effective than the walls alone and results in a somewhat greater level of comfort. Whether or not any significant dollar savings are actually realized is a point for conjecture and of course it depends upon individual circumstances. Often as not, this sort of installation is made primarily because it's not very expensive or difficult. And "it's worth a try" if nothing else. At least all of the insulation bases are well covered.

Sills

In any kind of house construction where the structure is built atop a continuous-wall foundation—whether the house is wood-framed, post-and-beam, dome, log, or what have you—there is some sort of sill construction. The sill is a structural member that rests atop the foundation and upon which the structure of the house rests. There are several forms. In a post-and-beam house the sill might be a large beam such as an 8 x 8. In a conventional wood-frame house, the sill is usually called a sill plate and consists of a 2 x 6 or 2 x 8 laid flat on the foundation top. For our purposes, the sills that are set upon posts or piers, on unheated crawlspace, or full on basement foundation walls are of no consequence. Those that are a part of full heated basements or heated crawlspaces are of consequence.

The top of a foundation wall is almost never smooth and even. The surface is nubbly, rough, and often irregular with occasional slight dips and rises. Even though wood is compressible to some degree and even though the wood sills are surmounted by the heavy weight of the house structure pressing constantly downward, the bottom of a sill or sill plate almost never conforms exactly to the top of a foundation wall. There are always gaps and cracks through which air and heat can readily enter or escape. This crackage has to be sealed (Fig. 8-1). The material most often used is called sill sealer. This is a special fiberglass insulant that is sandwiched between the foundation top and the sill. The material compresses into place and neatly fills the voids. Other materials such as compressable foam gasketing might also be used.

Floors

The underside of the first floor of a house that is built upon an unheated basement or crawlspace, a ventilated crawlspace, or an open pier or post foundation must be fully insulated. The usual procedure is to place insulation between the floor joists or floor-frame beams. This is a particularly common method where the underfloor area is fully enclosed by a full-perimeter foundation.

If the foundation is open and unskirted, however, the exposed surface of the insulant is subjected to the cooling effects of air currents or even wind circulating beneath the house. The area is also susceptible to mechanical damage by children, pets, and small wild critters roaming about beneath the building. Strong winds can actually create enough suction to pull unsecured lightweight batts of fiberglass out of the joist cavities. For the sake of both mechanical and thermal protection, the open bays are often closed off with a rigid covering. This might be simply a weatherproof gypsum wallboard or an exterior sheathing that provides additional insulating value.

So-called cold floors—in this sense, floors that are exposed to low or intermediate design temperatures—can also be insulated from above. This is done by placing a layer of insulation between the subflooring and the finished flooring. A surprising amount of thermal resistance can also be added to a floor section by laying down carpet padding, preferably of the extra-heavy felt variety, and a thick wall-to-wall carpet.

Walls

All of the exterior walls of a house, as well as those that are exposed to intermediate temperatures, must be fully insulated. The common procedure in the past has been to install an insulant in the wall cavities between the framing studs. In some geographic areas this is about all that is necessary even today. The insulant might not even have to be of full wall-cavity thickness. In the colder parts of the country, however, that system has not been substantially upgraded. There are several methods used depending upon how much thermal resistance is deemed necessary or desirable.

At the least, the wall cavities of standard 2 x 4 stud walls are filled to full depth ((3½ inches). Varying degrees of thermal resistance can be added by applying an insulating exterior sheathing to the outside faces of the studs or, in retrofits, right over the old siding or sheathing. In some cases, more thermal resistance is added by covering the inside of the wall frame with an insulating sheathing material as well.

Where an even higher R value is required, there are three more possibilities. One that has recently come into widespread use consists of framing the walls with 2 × 6s or even 2 × 8s. The size of the these studs allows them to be placed farther apart, usually on 24-inch centers, so the cost for the larger wall-framing structural materials is not greatly increased overall. This allows a greater depth of wall cavities that can be filled with an insulant or a combination of insulant and reflective air space. The wall can also be covered inside or outside, or both, with an insulating sheathing material.

Another method, now being recognized as "super-insulation" construction, actually makes use of two separate wall frames, one inside the other (Fig. 8-2). A conventional stud-framed wall is built in the usual fashion around the perimeter of the house and covered with an exterior sheathing and exterior siding. The wall cavities are filled with an insulant. Then a second, identical wall frame is built around the perimeter of the house, but to the inside of the first and positioned to leave an air space of an inch or more between the two.

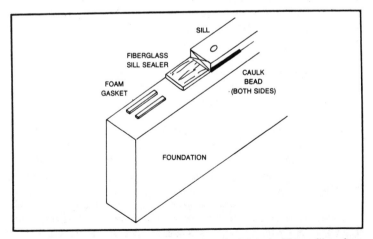

Fig. 8-1. If the basement or crawlspace is to be heated, either a fiberglass sill sealer, double foam gasket strips, or a similar sealer should be placed between the sill plate and the foundation. In addition, a bead of elastomeric caulk should be run along the bottom edge of the sill plate on each side.

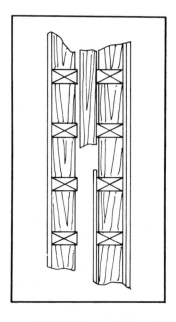

Fig. 8-2. This cross section, looking directly down from above, shows the construction arrangement for a "super-insulation" double stud-wall construction. A mineral wool insulation is placed in the cavities between all of the studs. The air space between the wall frames can be left empty, filled with more mineral wool insulation, or insulating sheathing can be secured to the inner edges of the outer wall frame. Other combinations of insulants and plane air spaces can also be used.

This interior wall frame is likewise filled with an insulant and then covered and decorated in the conventional fashion. The result is a wall section of very high thermal resistance and about a foot or more of thickness. This construction has fringe benefits. It provides ample room between the two sections for pipes, wires and ducts. There is space to build in pocket shutters for windows. The great thickness provides deep reveals for windows. This is fine for shading, protection, architectural emphasis, and putting out potted plants. The wall is practically soundproof.

Somewhat similar systems are available from manufacturers of factory-built houses or "kit" houses and are adaptable to houses of construction other than conventional frame style as well. For example, one manufacturer of log houses offers a double-wall system (Fig. 8-3) where both inner and outer walls can be 3 or 4 inches thick. The logs are tightly interlocked at all corners and intersections and a wide air space is left between the sections. The air space can be left open if no further R value is needed or it can be filled with an insulant for even greater thermal resistance.

A manufacturer of solid-wall houses, where the walls are constructed of solid wood beams stacked one atop another, provides a special system whereby a core of foam insulant is laminated between two thick layers of wood (Fig. 8-4). This provides a solid-wall construction that is natural wood on the inside and the outside. Because of the foam core, it has a much higher thermal resistance than a solid timber wall of comparable thickness.

Sandwich-wall construction is offered by several manufacturers. With this method, a complete full-length wall frame is made with structural members that range from conventional 2 x 4s all the way up to 2 x 14s. The sections are often made in full house lengths, 40 feet or more, with window and door openings built in. An inside covering, typically a plasterboard, is glue-bonded under heat and pressure to one side of the framework using huge sheets that are practically seamless. Then the wall cavities are prewired for electricity and filled with a foam insulant. The outside of the framework might or might not then be covered with an exterior sheathing glue-bonded in place.

As you can imagine, this kind of wall construction has tremendous thermal resistance against any kind of infiltration. Whether or not systems and materials of this sort will become available for use in some way in job-site construction remains to be seen.

Masonry house walls can be handled in several different ways. If the wall is covered with a masonry veneer, such as brick, stone or stucco, the usual construction method is to apply the masonry materials to the exterior of an otherwise ordinary framed wall covered with an exterior sheathing (Fig. 8-5). Stone and brick are spaced out from the sheathing about an inch, while stucco is generally applied to metal lath nailed to the wall frame. Here the cavities in the wall frame can be insulated in the usual way and another layer of insulating sheathing might be applied to the interior as well. The exterior sheathing board can also be of the insulating variety. The situation is not much different than a conventional wall.

If the wall construction is solid masonry or is a so-called cavity wall where an air space is left between an inner and an outer masonry section (Fig. 8-6), there are several possibilities that can be used. First, the interior of the masonry wall can be furred with wood strips and insulation placed between the strips and against the masonry. This can then be covered with a standard wall covering or an insulating sheathing plus a wall covering. If the wall is composed partly or wholly of hollow-cored block or

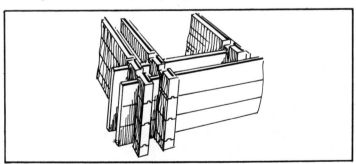

Fig. 8-3. This double-wall construction is made up of thick timbers that interlock at all corners and intersections. The void can be left empty or filled partly or wholly with insulation. A wall construction of exceptionally high *R* value can be obtained (courtesy of Pan Abode Cedar Homes).

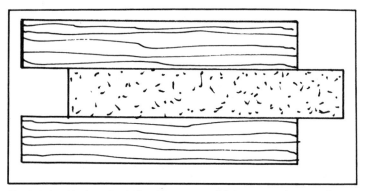

Fig. 8-4. A typical method of making up a solid, tongue-and-groove house wall timber by laminating a layer of foam insulant between two layers of wood. A wide range of thicknesses, sizes, and configurations is possible, along with high *R* value.

tile, the cores can be filled with an insulant. The cavity of a cavity-wall construction can be partly filled with an insulant. However, in many instances a cavity of small depth should remain for venting. This depends upon both the nature and construction of the wall section and the nature of the insulant.

Insulation can also be applied directly to the exterior of a masonry wall. This is a particularly effective way to retrofit insulation to an existing uninsulated or insufficiently insulated solid-masonry house. This will mean a greatly increased thermal resistance plus a huge thermal mass. The outside surface of the insulant can then be covered with a siding or, in some cases, stucco. Even a special paint can be directly applied to provide a wholly new exterior finish.

In certain kinds of houses, such as a Cape Cod style, a *knee wall* is used to box out the unusable low area beneath the sloping ceilings of the second floor or attic when that area is used as living space and is heated. These walls, typically about 4 to 5 feet high, are insulated in the same fashion as any wall. Undereaves areas are calculated for heat loss on the basis of an unheated space. The usual procedure is to place an insulant between the wall studs in the usual fashion, but an interior insulating sheathing might also be used if you prefer.

Doors

There is no insulating to be done to doors in the usual sense of the word. There are some alternatives to consider when you select either new or replacement doors for your house. Wood exterior doors have a reasonably good insulating value just as they are and the thicker the door the greater the value. Doors with thin rails and stiles and even thinner inset decorative panels don't do much to keep the cold out. Heavy, thick, solid-wood doors without panes of glass do. The presence of windows in a door, even small ones, does much to destroy its insulating value.

Steel doors, available in a wealth of decorative style and colors, that are filled with a foam insulant make an excellent choice. For a given thickness, most of them have a higher R value than wood doors and at the same time they are not subject to warping, sticking, and the various other ills that wood doors sometimes suffer. A core of urethane or isocyanurate will afford the greatest R value and any metal door should be constructed with a thermal break. This means that the construction of the door is such that the metal cladding is discontinuous from the inside to the outside. Heat can much less easily be transmitted in either direction. The conductive metal surface is broken by a nonconducting barrier of high thermal resistivity. Magnetic weatherstripping that always seals the door tightly against infiltration is also a good idea.

If the doors that are commercially available don't appeal to you for one reason or another, you can make your own exterior doors and at the same time incorporate a high degree of thermal resistance. For example, a bulky slab door made of two layers of three-fourth inch white cedar with a 1-inch core of polyisocyanurate sandwiched between them would result in an R of over 10. That is twice that of a good insulated steel door. Better yet, the cost would likely be substantially less.

Any exterior door will give better thermal performance if it is fitted with a storm door. If the storm door is properly installed and is tight, considerable added insulating value is gained not only by virtue of the R value of the storm door itself, but also that of the dead air space between

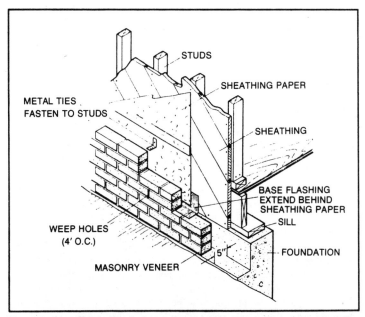

Fig. 8-5. A typical method of constructing a brick-veneered house wall.

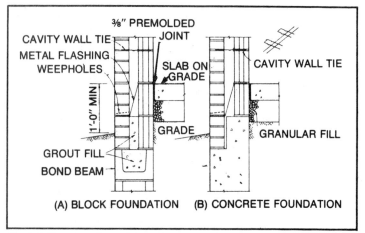

Fig. 8-6. Cross sections of two typical cavity wall constructions. Note that no foundation or wall insulation is shown. In most parts of this country, at least some should be installed for full protection against heat gains/losses (courtesy of the Portland Cement Association).

the two doors. The common metal-framed combination screen/storm doors that are mostly glass essentially provide only the dead air space. At the same time, they cut down on the rate of infiltration that would take place through the crackage around the single exterior door. A heavy slab door with no glazing provides considerably more R value. However, this is at the expense of easy visibility and the need to replace it with a screen door in warm weather. Either type will provide added protection against weathering for an often-expensive decorative exterior entry door.

Windows

Windows present quite a challenge to those interested in conserving energy because they have the lowest thermal resistance of any of the various building sections. The challenge is to admit the greatest amount of light, allow the greatest amount of outward visibility, satisfy the need for admittance of fresh summer breezes, and at the same time cut the potential heat loss or gain through them to the barest minimum. Easy to say, but tough to do.

Window Units. Ordinary flat, single-thickness glass is the biggest offender in the heat loss department and it really doesn't matter much how thick the glass is. You can make a significant improvement by simply installing insulating (double-glazed) glass instead. Most factory-built window units for residential use are available in either form. The value of the glazing is dependent upon the thickness of the air gap that separates the two panes. A one-half inch air space allows a considerably better U value than does a one-eighth inch air space.

Triple glazing has also become popular over the past few years in areas with very severe winter weather. These units consist of a double-glazed sash assembly with a movable or removable third sash panel on the outside—much like an integral storm window. Triple-glazing further reduces heat loss, but for many installations the cost-effectiveness is poor. However, you must also consider the advantage of reduced cold air fall down the walls and onto the floor and the somewhat warmer interior surface of the window unit. Both factors add a bit to comfort. There also is a disadvantage to multiple-glazed units. Each added layer of glass reduces the amount of light coming into the house (and the outward visibility) by 10 percent.

The kind of sash and framing in which the glazing is mounted also has an effect upon the heat transmission characteristics of the window unit. The first consideration is the amount of the total opening area within the window frame that the sash occupies. If the glass is stopped-in in a structural frame, it occupies virtually 100 percent of the area. If the sash holding the glazing is bulky, the sash portion itself might occupy as much as 40 percent of the opening area and the glazing the remaining 60 percent. Adjustments can be made to determine the U value of windows with varying ratios of sash to glass (see Chapter 4).

Wood frames and vinyl-clad wood frames transmit less heat and they also have a substantially higher inside surface temperature than do solid metal-frame windows. The newer types of metal-frame windows are fitted with thermal breaks to alleviate this problem. By and large, wood-frame windows remain the most effective against heat transfer. Some frame/sash arrangements allow less infiltration than others and fixed glass is generally the best in this respect. Most manufacturers will supply specific U values for their own products.

Another possibility is to use insulating glass with the interior surface of one pane treated with a special low-emittance coating. (There are several possibilities for such coatings, each with different characteristics). The coating serves to further reduce transmission heat loss, but at some cost to visibility and also to the admittance of beneficial heat from the sun in winter.

Another idea that has been proposed is a reversible sash double-glazed with clear glass on one side and a special heat-absorbing glass on the other. Any of several kinds of heat-absorbing glass, each with somewhat different properties, might be used. Operable vents should be positioned above and below the heat-absorbing glass, in the sash frame. During winter, the reversible sash would be positioned with the heat-absorbing glass facing in so that most of the heat absorbed by the inner pane would be circulated back into the room. In summer, the sash would be reversed and heat from the sun would be dissipated to the outdoors instead of being brought into the room (Fig. 8-7).

Double-glazing and triple-glazing are relatively new to residental construction. You can still use the old tried and true method of putting up storm sash in the fall and taking it down in the spring. Fitting storm sash to single-glazed windows is just about as effective as installing double-glazed

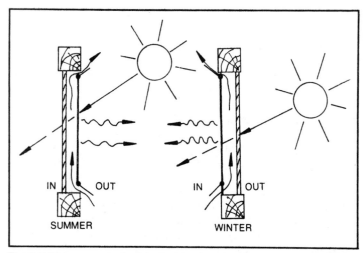

Fig. 8-7. The concept of using double-glazed sash with one coated pane allows the sash to be positioned in summer to keep the sun's heat out. It can be reversed in winter to collect the sun's heat within the living space.

units. There is less initial cost, more flexability, less expense in case of breakage, and the not uncommon problem of double-glazing losing its inner seal and clouding up between panes is completely avoided.

One exception to windows insulated in the usual sense is a system developed by Zomeworks of Albuquerque, New Mexico. It is called the Beadwall. Basically, this is a window wall—a large expanse of glass reaching from floor to ceiling or therabouts and generally quite wide—rather than a window unit of the sort that is inserted into a relatively small opening in a wall. The construction consists basically of inner and outer full-sized sheets of plate glass that are built right into the structure. They cannot be opened. Their primary purpose is to emit large quantities of sunlight to the interior of a house designed for passive solar heating. The secondary purpose is admittance of light and outward visibility.

The two panes of glass are separated by a deep air space. Dimensions vary with design specifications. A reversible vacuum/blower unit is built into the structure along with storage containers for a large quantity of tiny foam plastic beads. The beads can be blown into the space between the glass sheets to fill it entirely and form an opaque wall of high thermal resistance. This can be done manually or automatically under control of a time clock or a photocell. During the daytime, the beads are sucked back out of the space into their storage containers to admit light and sunshine. The system is much like opening and closing a set of drapes except that the Beadwall has a far greater effectiveness against heat transfer.

Window Accessories. There are other means of reducing heat loss through window areas. For want of a better term, I will call them window accessories. Probably none of these items should be depended upon for a permanent or consistent reduction in heat loss or heating system operating costs. All of them are dependent upon occupant participation to put them into effect. Unless the devices are in place, they do no good and a large part of the time they are *not* in place. Even when these devices are automated, they are only operational part of the time and usually not on a consistent basis. Futhermore, even automatic devices have manual overrides that frequently come into use.

While the various window accessories can indeed reduce heat loss to some extent, and also reduce heating costs, their presence should not be figured into the heat loss calculations for determining average seasonal heating costs or for sizing the heating system. They should be installed as an energy conservation measure.

Heat loss or gain through window areas can be reduced by the simple expedient of covering the windows. The window accessories most commonly used for the purpose are venetian blinds, draperies of various sorts, roll shades, and shutters. Venetian blinds do little to improve heat loss characteristics, although they do have some effect by blocking radiation. Heavy draperies can do a much better job if they are tightly fitted to the window frame at the sides and are enclosed at the top in a valance. Preferably, they should also be tightly fitted and closed to the window frame at the bottom edge.

There is a multitude of different kinds of drapes with a wide variation in R value. Those that are specifically designed to lessen heat transfer are the best, but even in this group some are far more effective than others. Very heavy materials with reflective or insulating linings, but otherwise of more or less conventional style and design, will do a good job if fitted properly.

Newer, special designs—some of them use the louver principle—made of the latest in insulating-fabric materials and operating in tightly-fitted tracks offer the highest R value. They are specifically designed just for the purpose of reducing heat loss or gain through windows. Their biggest drawback is that their appearance might leave something to be desired. It depends upon your personal tastes.

The manufacturers provide insulating values for their products, but corroboration from independent test reports is a good idea wherever possible. It has been shown that with a properly-fitted, rather ordinary drapery in place, the winter U value of a single-glazed window/drape unit can be brought as low as 0.88 (R-1.14) as opposed to U-1.13 without. Special thermal draperies can afford a total R of 4 or 5 or even more.

It's interesting to note that ordinary roller-type pull-down shades that have been standard equipment for decades in homes all around the country are virtually as effective in reducing heat loss through windows as are standard draperies if the shades fit relatively close to the window frame.

Table 8-1 shows the seasonal energy expenditure for a window in New York City in terms of kBtu (100-Btu units) per square foot of window area. It was assumed that the roll shades remain fully lowered for 12 hours

**Table 8-1. Seasonal Energy Expenditure for a Window in New York City
(KBtu/Sq. Ft.) (- Denotes Energy Input Required from Mechanical System).**

GLAZING	SHADING	NORTH		EAST		SOUTH	
		Wint.	Sumr.	Wint.	Sumr.	Wint.	Sumr.
Single	None	−84	−43	−38	−76	+29	−59
Single	roll shade	−69	−15	−23	−26	+45	−20
	Savings	15	28	15	50	16	39
Storm/double	None	−25	−37	+14	−65	+71	−51
Storm/double	roll shade	−19	−13	+21	−23	+81	−18
	Savings	6	24	7	42	10	33

Savings roll shade + double compared to no roll shade + single		65	30	17	53	52	41

	Winter U-Values		
Type of Glass	Shade Up	Shade Down	
Single glass	1.13	0.88	
Storm/double	0.55	0.49	

per day and a heating season of 4714 degree-days was used. The compass directions given are for the window exposures. West is not listed because it is assumed to be the same as east. Under the given conditions, a north-facing window fitted with a roll shade accounted for a saving of 15,000 Btu per square foot for the heating season. Summer savings were even greater.

Internal window shutters are old devices that were common in many houses of the Colonial era in this country and they were then called Indian shutters. The purpose was for protection against Indian attacks.

Today's thermal shutters are made quite differently and have substantially higher R values. Such shutters can be easily made in the home workshop and fitted tightly to the window openings as either hinged or removable panels. When set in place, they provide an opaque-wall section of reasonable thermal resistance (Table 8-2). They can also be installed in new houses in pocket form where they slide back into cavities or pockets built into the walls at each side of the windows. Factory-built units are becoming available on a fairly widespread basis. Their cost is quite reasonable if they are home-built. They have the advantage of not only reducing heat loss through windows, they also provide improved comfort near windows, reduce sound transmission from outside, and afford privacy. They have the disadvantages of possible storage problems when they are not in use and they must be manually set in place and removed on a regular basis for best results.

Band Joists

Most houses have a band joist area around the perimeter of the house where the end and header joists of the first-floor frame rest atop the foundation. This area is of different construction than the remainder of the wall area and is generally of less thermal resistance. If the basement or crawlspace of the house is unheated, the underfloor area will be insulated and this automatically takes care of the band joist area. When the basement or crawlspace is heated, however, the underfloor area is unlikely to be insulated. This leaves the band joist area at least partly unprotected. This area around the entire perimeter of the house should be fully insulated.

A second band joist area occurs in many houses at the second-floor level. This area is not present where the roof rafters and the ceiling joists rest directly on top of the top plate of the first-floor walls. But if a full floor-frame assembly is constructed to rest upon the first-floor wall top plate, header and end joists are used to close off the second-floor joists and they form a band joist area. When there is no insulation present above the first-floor ceiling, the band joist area is left unprotected. It should be fully insulated between the first-floor ceiling and the second-floor subflooring.

If there is insulation present above the first-floor ceiling, between the floor joists, the insulant might not be of a thickness equal to the full depth of the joists. This leaves some part of the band joist area exposed. Insulation should be fitted to all of these exposed portions. The same applies to a band joist area located between a second and third floor. Note that sometimes the band joist area does not go entirely around the house. For instance, in some 1½-story designs thermal protection will be needed at the gable end walls, but not at front or rear walls.

Table 8-2. Insulating Values of Various Insulating Panel Materials.

MATERIAL	RESISTANCE (for 1" thickness)	U-value of window with 1" panel	U-value of window with 2" panel
Expanded polystyrene, extruded, plain	4.00	0.20	0.11
Expanded polystyrene, molded beads	3.57	0.22	0.12
Expanded polyurethane	6.25	0.14	0.07
Cork (¾ inch)	1.68	0.39	
Cork/paper bd/cork (¾)	2.56	0.29	—
Plywood (¾ inch)	0.93	0.55	—

Header Areas

Header areas are found in most houses above each window and door—regardless of their specific location. The cross section of these areas is different than the rest of the wall area and is also of lower thermal resistance than a fully insulated wall. Nothing can be done to insulate solid headers themselves, but hollow box headers should be filled with an insulant as they are constructed. If the interior or exterior of the wall section will be covered with an insulating sheathing board, heat loss through header areas will be reduced somewhat. It will still be proportionately greater than for the remainder of the wall. If ordinary noninsulating sheathing is to be used, consideration should be given to covering just the header areas with an insulating sheathing board of the same thickness as the noninsulating type that will be used on the remainder of the wall. This procedure will bring the heat loss characteristics of the header sections more into line with the rest of the wall.

Ceilings

Any ceiling area that is exposed to a lower temperature than the inside design temperature should be heavily insulated. Natural heat flow is upward so ceiling areas can be the sources of tremendous heat losses. The area to be insulated might consist of an entire ceiling below an unheated attic or below a shallow-pitched shed or flat roof otherwise uninsulated. Or it might only be a portion of a ceiling lying below a small cold area such as the unused and unheated space behind a kneewall.

In most cases, the insulant is placed between the ceiling joists. Sometimes, particularly in severe winter climates, additional insulation is placed on top of the joists as well to gain added R value. Ceilings can be further insulated by applying an insulating plaster as a finish or by putting up acoustic ceiling tile that has good thermal as well as acoustic properties.

Another possibility, especially effective in retrofitting old houses with high ceilings, is to build a dropped-ceiling frame. The space between the old and new ceilings can then be fitted with insulation and the new ceiling itself could be composed of a finish material with good thermal properties for added R. A grid-type ceiling can also be used. This consists of a metal framework into which either ordinary or insulating large-sized ceiling tiles can be fitted. Some of these tiles are especially made with high R value.

Roofs

In many houses, it is necessary to insulate the roof rather than a ceiling. The most common arrangement is to fill the cavities between the roof rafters with an insulant and then cover the rafter faces with an interior covering such as plasterboard. The treatment is virtually identical with walls except that the R value of the insulant must generally be considerably higher. As with walls, an insulating sheathing can be applied to the interior rafter faces before putting on a finish covering in order to gain additional R value.

Some flat, shed, or very shallow-pitched roofs are not insulated between the framing members, but rather upon the roof deck itself. Sometimes this is done instead of putting insulation between the ceiling joists directly below the roof. Sometimes both systems are used together for better thermal performance. In this situation, there are several possibilities and a number of different materials that might be used.

The conventional method is to apply an insulating roof decking made just for the purpose. This thick, fibrous material looks much like overgrown ceiling tiles. It comes in various sizes, thicknesses, and R values. A built-up finish roof covering made of layers of hot-mopped tar and heavy roofing felt topped with a thick layer of roofing stone or gravel is applied directly on the roof decking.

Another possibility, now becoming fairly common in residential construction, is to apply a decking of plywood or tongue-and-groove planks to the roof frame. Then a heavy layer of insulation is put on, followed by a layer of roof sheathing, and the finish roof covering. By varying the insulation type, thickness, and R value, various kinds of roof constructions can be made up and the thermal performance tailored to the climatic conditions in whatever degree is preferred.

The specifications of many house designs call for the ceiling framework to be either wholly or partially open to view. The structural members are finished and become part of the interior decor. This limits or eliminates the space between the roof framing members where thermal insulation is conventionally applied. Therefore, different methods must be used. There are two common procedures.

If only the lower portion of the structural members is to be left open to view, a relatively thin insulant can be placed in the spaces between the structural members and up against the underside of the roof decking. The insulant is then covered with plasterboard or some other finish covering and trimmed out with molding to complete the job.

Many plans call for the entire depth of the structural members to be exposed and the underside of the roof decking is finished to form the ceiling. In this case, there is no alternative but to apply the insulant to the exterior of the roof—atop the ceiling/decking. The insulant is then covered with a sheathing. This in turn is covered with the finish roofing. This is the better system of the two. It is simpler, easier, and less costly to apply and it affords considerably better thermal performance overall. In addition, the amount of insulation that can be applied is not limited as it is in the spaces beneath the roof decking. As high an R value as is preferred can be installed.

Ducts

Central forced-air heating systems, central mechanical cooling systems, and air conditioning systems that are used for both heating and cooling year-round all employ a distribution system of ductwork to move the conditioned air to the various parts of the house. Ductwork should always be routed through the conditioned areas of the house rather than through unconditioned attics or crawlspaces. By doing so, heat losses through the walls of the ducts from warm air traveling through them will simply be added to the heated space and not lost into an unheated area. By the same token, heat gained through the duct walls when the equipment is in a cooling mode will simply serve to help in cooling the conditioned air around the duct. But in the interest of system efficiency, ductwork that travels through conditioned spaces often is insulated anyway so that the proper amount of cool or warm air will exit at the air outlet where it is supposed to. If it is absolutely necessary that some ductwork travel through unconditioned spaces, then it must be heavily insulated to prevent unwarranted heat gains or losses that would reduce the efficiency of the system and elevate operating costs.

Existing uninsulated ductwork can be externally wrapped or enclosed with an insulant wherever it is accessible (Fig. 8-8). The same can be done to ductwork being installed in new construction. A general-purpose insulant can be used and there are also several special types made for the purpose. In new construction the usual procedure is to install preinsulated duct sections as needed. This ductwork might have an insulating material applied to either the inside or outside or the duct sections themselves might be made of an insulating material. Whatever method you follow, it's wise to select duct insulation or insulating ductwork with a sufficiently high thermal resistance to maintain full efficiency of the heating system, minimize any potential losses, and yet remain cost-effective.

Piping

Insulating the piping in your house might well be a good idea and there are numerous special insulants made for the purpose. Hot water supply and return pipes in hydronic heating systems must be heavily insulated (Fig. 8-8) where they pass through unheated spaces in order to prevent excessive cooling of the fluid before it reaches the heating units. In the interest of efficiency, it certainly does no harm to insulate heat pipes that pass through heated spaces as well. The domestic hot water supply piping coming from water heaters can also be insulated. This increases the efficiency of the hot water system to some degree and will also help to minimize unnecessary heat gain in mechanically cooled spaces.

Generally, it is unnecessary to insulate cold water pipes, but there are two exceptions. One is when the piping is exposed to low temperatures (a situation to be avoided if possible). In that case, they should be fitted with heat cables and then well insulated to prevent the possibility of a freeze-up. The second situation involves metallic cold-water piping that tends to form condensation on the outer surfaces. This is the familiar "sweating" problem. Excessive condensation on pipes seldom has any consequential effect upon heat loss or gain. However, extreme circumstances can add excessive moisture to the air which then must be "wrung out" by an air conditioning system. It can cause mildew, fungus attack, rot, and be generally damaging to parts of the house in some circumstances. This possibility can be avoided by the simple expedient of insulating the offending pipe sections.

Water Heaters

Over the years unit water heaters have been notorious wasters of heat and energy. Most households use large quantities of hot water and the process of generating that hot water often accounts for a substantial percentage of the total fuel and/or energy costs of a house. In the past, water heaters have been poorly insulated. Usually they contain only a skimpy, thin, and often poorly installed layer of mineral wool insulation between the storage tank proper and its sheet-metal outer shell. The result is that an excessive quantity of heat is lost to the atmosphere. This requires extra fuel or energy to keep the stored hot water at its desired temperature. Frequently this is 100 F or more above room air temperature. In theory, the heat escaping from the water heater is disbursed into the room and thereby lowers the number of Btu's that must be pumped into that room by the heating system to maintain the set ambient temperature. The heat is not completely lost because it is put to use within the room. But in practice, this heat is generated in a very inefficient and costly manner and does little good.

Unit water heaters, whether electric or gas-fired, should be thoroughly insulated so that as much heat as possible is retained within the storage tank and the burner or elements are called upon to reheat the water as infrequently as is practically possible. Freestanding heaters can be externally wrapped with an insulant. Unit water heaters that are built in (such as certain under-counter models) can be thermally protected by installing insulants in or around the cubicle in which they are contained. Any unit water heater can be enclosed by constructing a relatively tight-fitting structural framework around them or by building an enclosure into the house framework specifically for the purpose. In either case, the enclosure should be heavily insulated.

TOOLS AND EQUIPMENT

A few insulants require highly specialized equipment (as well as expertise) that cannot even be rented in most places, much less be found in

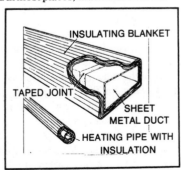

Fig. 8-8. Sheet metal duct wrapped with insulation. Heating pipes should be similarly treated and domestic hot water piping is also often insulated.

INSULATING BLANKET

TAPED JOINT

SHEET METAL DUCT

HEATING PIPE WITH INSULATION

the home mechanic's workshop. The remaining insulants probably require fewer tools and equipment to install than any other average do-it-yourself project (Fig. 8-9).

The insulants that are most easily installed by the do-it-yourselfer are mineral wools of either the batt or blanket variety, pouring types like vermiculite, ceramic and perlite, rigid types such as sheathing sheets, slabs, or board varieties, and reflective insulants.

Those that can be readily installed in *some* applications include loose-fill cellulose and loose-fill mineral wool. Advanced do-it-yourselfers can successfully cope with insulating concrete and perlite or vermiculite concrete. These materials do require some knowledge, and preferably some experience, in concrete work.

Those insulants that must be left to the experts include spray-on cellulosic-fiber insulation, foamed-in-place types such as urea-formaldehydes and urethanes, applications where a loose-fill mineral wool (usually called "blowing wool") must be blown into the house cavities, and applications where cellulosic blown insulation must be similarly installed. For the most part, the installation of this latter group of insulants is well beyond the scope of the do-it-yourselfer.

Installing reflective foil insulation requires the least amount of gear. You'll want a carpenter's retractable steel tape measure; a 10-foot size is about the handiest. A carpenter's or zigzag rule is perfectly suitable and actually you could probably get by with a decent yardstick.

You'll need a straightedge; practically anything will serve including a fairly straight length of board. A carpenter's square is handy for making true 90-degree trim cuts. Use a pencil or scriber for marking cutting lines and a pair of sharp shears about 6 or 8 inches long for cutting the material. A utility knife is best for in-place trimming.

Use a staple gun to attach the insulation. A heavy duty, hand-operated stapler loaded with one-fourth inch or five-sixteenth inch staples works best. An electric stapler is more difficult to use in many instances because the housing of the staple gun overhangs the stapling point. You can't work it into close quarters and you run the risk of damaging the delicate foil. A hammer stapler is easy to use, but definitely not recommended for an inexperienced installer because of the possibility of missing the mark and ruining the foil.

The first consideration in working with any of the mineral wools—fiberglass, rock, or slag—is self-protection. A dust mask is an absolute must because the tiny mineral fibers shake loose and float about you in a cloud all the time. Inhaling the glassy particles is dangerous and having a chunk of mineral fluff suddenly drop into your mouth when you are installing the material overhead is definitely disconcerting—to say the least.

A pair of safety goggles to keep the particles out of your eyes is a smart idea. The fibers are extremely irritating to the skin (though this bothers some people far more than others) and they are also difficult to thoroughly wash away. This means that in the interest of comfort a uniform

296

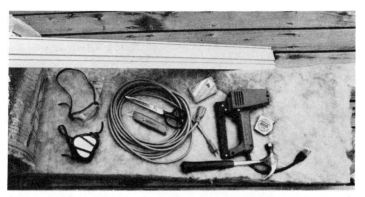

Fig. 8-9. This modest assortment of tools and equipment is all that's needed to install mineral wool batt or blanket insulation: tape measure and straightedge, shears and utility knife, hammer for driving in stubborn staples, a stapler (electric shown here) and staples, safety goggles, and dust mask. Not shown is duct tape for making repairs (if needed).

is in order. Wear a cap, a long-sleeved shirt buttoned at cuffs and throat and with the collar turned up and use lightweight leather gloves as much as possible when you handle the material.

The tiny glass fibers are invisible when stuck into your skin and impossible to pull out with tweezers. If you can't get rid of an irritating fiber or two, coat the irritated area of skin with woodworkers' white glue, Duco plastic cement or any other glue that forms a tough skin. Let the glue dry thoroughly, then peel it off. Usually the glass fibers will pull right out. Then coat the skin with a good hand lotion.

As far as tools are concerned, they're just the same as for reflective foil. You'll need a straightedge, measuring tape, pencil or scriber, and shears. Thick batts or blankets are most easily cut with extra-long shears (10-inch or even 12-inch). Batts and blankets that are faced with kraft paper or foil-surfaced paper have thick stapling flanges along each side. They are best fastened with a hand-operated stapler and five-sixteenth inch or three-eighths inch staples (one-fourth inch staples are sometimes a bit short). Electric or hammer staplers will work, but not as easily and they require more caution. Friction-fit batts don't have to be secured; just stuff them into place.

Insulants that are poured are no problem at all. If you'll be working in an enclosed area, wear a dust mask. These materials can raise great clouds of irritating dust when being dumped with great abandon into large areas like an attic floor. The material can be poured directly from the bags— even into concrete block cores. When pouring into vertical cavities, occasional prodding with a long, slender stick will insure that no air pockets are being left. When the material is poured into horizontal cavities, it must be smoothed out to uniform depth. This can be done with a narrow, short-handled rake turned upside down or you can make a leveling board from a scrap of wood.

Placing loose-fill mineral wool isn't much of a problem. Depending upon how much of it you'll be handling and where, you'll probably want the same protective gear that should be worn while installing mineral wool batts and blankets. Fluffing the wool into place can raise quite a cloud of glass particles. A rake or a leveling board is needed to level the material to uniform depth in horizontal cavities.

The materials and equipment you will need to install the various kinds of insulating sheathing and board or slab insulants vary somewhat depending upon the nature of the material. These insulants include ordinary asphalt-impregnated fiberboard sheathing, molded or extruded polystyrene foam with or without a foil skin, foil-faced polyurethane and isocyanurate insulating sheathing, and cellular glass board, block, and sheet.

At least some amount of fitting is required in practically every application. That means you'll need a measuring tape, a straightedge, and a carpenter's square for laying out the pieces to size. To mark with, a pencil works fine on some materials. In other instances, a mechanical scriber such as scratch awl works better. The foamed plastic materials can be readily cut with a sharp, thin-bladed knife if the thickness is not too great. An ordinary utility knife works fine. The material can also be easily sawed with a carpenter's crosscut handsaw or a portable electric circular saw. However, this tends to leave ragged edges. Fiberboard sheathing can also be cut easily with a handsaw, but a circular saw is much faster. This procedure raises huge clouds of fibrous dust. A dust mask and safety goggles will be a necessity.

No safety equipment is needed when working with the rigid plastic foams and you can safely handle all of these materials with your bare hands. That's not so, however, with cellular glass insulants. This material is very abrasive. It is somewhat akin to a pumice block and it will quickly abrade your skin if you handle much of it. Wear stout leather gloves to avoid that problem.

This material cuts easily enough that a power saw is wholly unnecessary. The usual procedure is to wrap tape around one end of a carbide-tipped industrial hacksaw blade and make the cuts by hand. Ordinary hacksaw blades can be used the same way. However, the teeth won't last long (depending upon the specific kind of blade). Don't use a choice carpenter's handsaw. The abrasiveness of the material will file the saw teeth to nubs.

Rigid insulants are generally secured to the building either with mechanical fasteners—usually nails—or with adhesives. Sometimes a combination of the two is used. You'll need a hammer for the first method. A regular 16-ounce carpenter's claw hammer works fine. If you have a great deal of nailing to do, you'll find that wielding a 13-ounce head is considerably easier on the arm. If you opt for the gluing method, you'll need a small-size cartridge-type caulking gun. Most of the adhesives are packed in standard cartridges. In some applications the insulant need not be fastened at all, but just set in place.

In some instances, you will need other hand tools as well. For instance, an adhesive or mastic supplied in bulk has to be applied with a small putty knife, an old round-tipped table knife or some similar tool. With some kinds of insulating sheathing board, it's desirable to fill the joints between boards or planks with a special sealer or caulking. This will require a putty knife or perhaps a small trowel of the kind that masons use to point up brick work. As an alternative to shears or a utility knife, some insulating materials can be readily cut with a linoleum knife or carpet knife.

Cellulose fiber insulation can be placed by hand in horizontal cavities such as beneath an attic floor (though even here it is best blown into place). If you do choose to install the material by hand, all you'll need is a rake or leveling board to adjust the fill to the desired even depth. You should also wear a mask. It has been found that the chemicals used to treat cellulose insulation for fire retardancy sometimes separate from the material to the extent of leaving a noticeable residue of powder in the bags in which it is packed.

To be on the safe side, it's wise to use not an ordinary dust mask, but a respirator of the kind approved for use with chemical dusts. These respirators are readily available and they usually contain a charcoal filtration unit suitable for use with agricultural chemicals. Wearing gloves and safety goggles is a good idea.

9 Installing Insulation

The integrity of a building's thermal envelope must be complete. The integrity of a thermal envelope can be defined as unimpaired soundness. Consider as an example the space shuttle *Columbia*. That incredibly complex, but fragile ship is completely covered with thousands of highly-specialized insulating tiles. The tiles (manufactured by Johns-Manville, one of the largest makers and suppliers in the country of fiberglass building insulation) are made of 99.8 percent pure silica fibers mixed in a slurry with a binder and then formed into the desired shapes. The purpose of this insulant is to protect the *Columbia* against heat gain. In this case, the gain comes not from the rays of the sun, but from the intense heat buildup caused by friction as the airship reenters the earth's atmosphere at high speed.

Without this insulation envelope, the ship would be reduced to an incinerated blob. Not long after *Columbia's* spectacular initial launch into space in April of 1981, observers discovered that a few of the insulating tiles had broken away and disappeared during the lift-off. There was much concern at this because the integrity of the thermal envelope had been breached; it was no longer sound and complete.

The question was whether or not the degree of failure of the thermal envelope would be sufficient to imperil the spaceship. The subsequent successful reentry of the ship into the earth's atmosphere, followed by an incredibly smooth and beautiful landing on Rogers Dry Lake in California, proved that (in this case at least) the broken integrity of the envelope caused no substantial harm. But neither was it 100 percent effective.

The thermal envelope of your house can be considered in much the same way. Only complete integrity of the envelope will allow 100 percent effectiveness and efficiency. If you "lose a tile" by failing to insulate a small spot, ignoring a rip or a thin spot—or because of some other oversight, mistake, or lapse in quality workmanship—the practical result will be just

300

a slight diminution of what might have been. The chances are pretty slim that you'll ever notice the difference. Let such errors and omissions in insulation installation begin to multiply, however, and the effects pile up rapidly. A sloppy insulating job can result in about half the intended effectiveness and efficiency.

I will assume throughout most of this discussion that you'll be doing the work yourself and in that case your principal allies in getting the job done right will be care, thought, and patience.

In the event that you don't want to do your own insulating or cannot because of the nature of the type of insulant you prefer, I suggest that you make use of the information that follows to verify the work done by the professionals that you hire.

BATTS AND BLANKETS

In terms of square footage, probably more mineral fiber batt and blanket insulation is installed, both by do-it-yourselfers and by professionals, in residences than is any other kind of insulation. The material is obtainable anywhere, relatively effective, inexpensive, and it's easy to install.

Mineral fiber batt and blanket insulation, which includes rock and slag wool and fiberglass, only has its full rated R value when it is dry and at full loft—the specified thickness of the material. It is tightly compressed when packaged, but it usually will fluff back out of its own volition shortly after being unpacked. If a piece looks skimpy, usually a gentle shake or a few slaps will restore its loft. When it is installed, it should not be compressed at any point, nor should any attempt be made to fluff it out further or stretch it. A small amount of compression is acceptable when fitting the material and especially with friction-fit batts between framing members. Ends should be cut a bit long to insure a snug fit with no air gaps between the material and the framing or other building materials.

The insulation should always conform tightly to its surroundings and not show any gaps or openings. Fitting the insulation properly to an odd-shaped space involves cutting the material to the same shape, but just a tad larger, and fitting it carefully in place like a piece of jigsaw puzzle. Batts or sections of blankets that meet end to end should fit snugly together and can be slightly interwoven by manipulating the material around a little bit. But they should not be jammed together. If electrical boxes, pipes, wires, or ductwork are likely to compress the material more than just a tiny bit, it is usually better to cut a shallow notch or chase from the material for a clean fit. Care must be taken when installing the material against a curved surface so that it is not unduly compressed along the curve.

Most mineral wool batt and blanket insulation is attached to a kraft paper facing, which may or may not be foil-covered, that has integral stapling flanges along each side for easy attachment. The facing not only supports the insulation and affords some mechanical protection, but also constitutes a vapor barrier. There are two methods of attaching the material. One way is to lay the stapling flanges on the faces of the framing members where they will overlap one another and provide a relatively unbroken vapor barrier (Fig. 9-1). Care must be taken that the flanges lie flat and smooth and that the staples or other fasteners are driven fully home. Otherwise, difficulties will arise when the time comes to apply the wall covering.

The other method is used mostly with foil-covered insulation. The material is "dished" into the cavities between the framing members by positioning the stapling flanges on the sides of the framing members with the leading edge of each flange flush with the edge of the framing member (Fig. 9-2). This dishes the material inward from one-half an inch to three-fourth an inch and provides a reflective air space after the wall covering is attached. This allows a slightly improved R value.

Care should be taken that the flanges lie fully flat on the sides of the framing members. This sometimes takes a bit of fiddling around. If there are gaps where the flanges are puckered and out of alignment (Fig. 9-3), the integrity of the vapor barrier will be impaired. An easy path for infiltration will be formed and, if the gaps are large enough, convective loop currents can establish themselves within the wall cavities. All of these problems reduce the effectiveness and efficiency of the insulation.

Where a batt or section of blanket end butts up against a framing member, the facing should lap over the outside face of the member or be folded up against the side of it, to seal the end off completely (Fig. 9-4). In order to preserve the integrity of the vapor barrier any rips, slits, or tears in the facing (Fig. 9-5) should be repaired before the wall covering is put on. It's a good idea to make a close inspection just prior to installation of the wall covering (or ceiling, flooring, etc.) and make any repairs that are necessary. You can do this by gluing a patch of scrap facing over the damaged area or by covering it with a strip of aluminized duct tape.

Mineral fiber batt and blanket insulation is most easily trimmed or cut to size with a pair of long, sharp shears. Be sure to make your cuts clean and square and not cockeyed and scraggly. Small custom-fitted pieces should be about one-half inch larger all around than the opening into which it will fit. Larger pieces, should be about three-fourth of an inch larger. When you fit the material into place, this will leave a small overlap of facing for stapling and sealing.

Accurate cutting is important for a good fit. However, precise measurements of the sort used in cabinetmaking are entirely unimportant. When fitting small pieces, or long and narrow ones, you will probably find it easier to peel the facing off the insulation, fit the insulation tightly enough so that it stays in place by itself, and then staple a properly-sized piece of facing over it. Staples are most often used to secure the material because they are cheap, fast, and easy. But you can use common tacks or some other fastener as well. Whatever you use, make sure that they are driven fully home. A spacing of about 6 to 8 inches apart is usually ample;

corners should be tightly fastened, and don't be afraid to use closer spacing anywhere that seems to be indicated.

Foundations

Let's go through a whole-house mineral wool batt or blanket insulation installation to see what's needed, step by step. First, let's consider full-basement foundation walls. Mineral fiber insulants can't be used beneath basement floors or on the outside of any kind of foundation walls. But they can be used inside. For example, where a wood floor is to be built up over a concrete floor, a common procedure is to seal the concrete floor with a damp-proofer and then lay sleepers—2 x 4s on edge, for instance—to support the subflooring or finish flooring material.

By maintaining either 16- or 24-inch centers for the sleepers, you can easily insert batts or blanket into the cavities before laying the flooring. If the concrete slab is sealed, no vapor barrier is necessary. One can be added for double protection. For best results, make sure that the insulation is uniformly placed and there are no gaps or skimped spots.

Basement walls can be insulated with mineral fiber in a couple of ways. One common method is to nail nominal 1 x 2 furring strips horizontally at the top and bottom of the wall and vertically every 16 or 24 inches on centers. Secure the strips with masonry nails. (Caution: Be sure to

Fig. 9-1. One method of installing faced mineral wool batt or blanket insulation is to overlap the stapling flanges on the outer edges of the framing members. The vapor-barrier facing is continuous and unbroken and it also presents a better barrier against infiltration. However, the finish covering must then be spaced out from a foil-faced insulation. Also, the stapling flanges of paper-faced insulation may interfere with the smooth placement of wallboard directly on the framing members.

Fig. 9-2. A common method of applying faced mineral wool insulation is to "dish" the material between the framing members. The stapling flanges are attached to the sides rather than the front edges. This provides a plane air space for foil-faced insulation and also ensures that the finish covering can be easily applied.

wear safety goggles when driving masonry nails.) It is essential that the below-ground portion of the masonry walls be free from dampness or leaks. Coat the walls with a good waterproofer if there is any possibility of moisture appearing. Staple mineral wool masonry wall insulation to the furring strips. Make sure to avoid gaps and air spaces (Fig. 9-6). If the insulation does not have an integral vapor barrier, apply a separate 4-mil polyethylene sheet and then cover the walls with paneling or wallboard. Alternatively, you can provide both vapor barrier and wall covering at the same time by applying foil-backed gypsum wallboard.

The second method is the more cost-effective in cold climates and consists of building a light frame wall to match the dimensions of the masonry walls. Nominal 1 x 3 stock is fine for the top and sole plates; use 2 x 3 dimension stock for studs. Set the studs on 16- or 24-inch centers, nail the sole plate to the concrete floor with masonry nails, and fasten the top plate to the underside of the first-floor joists or to nailing blocks attached to them. The whole framework should be spaced out from the masonry wall approximately 1 inch. Then cut several long, 1½ inch wide strips of mineral wool insulation and remove the wool from the facing. Separate the strips to approximately 1¼-inch to 1½-inch thickness and pack a full-length strip between the masonry wall and the back edge of each wall frame stud. Then staple 3½-inch thick batts or blankets between the studs. The facing on the insulation will serve as a vapor barrier, but common practice

Fig. 9-3. A very common mistake is to leave mineral wool batt or blanket insulation poorly fitted and installed with the facing puckered, the stapling flanges gapped open, and the ends improperly secured. In this instance, the insulation was installed too early in the construction—before the house was closed up. The insulation got wet, the facing shrank when it dried and pulled away from the staples. Numerous pieces had to be replaced.

is to install a secondary barrier for extra protection. Either foil-backed gypsum board or a separate polyethylene sheet will do the job.

Floors over unventilated crawlspaces can be insulated by placing the insulation in the floor cavities or by insulating the crawlspace itself.

Fig. 9-4. The ends of faced mineral wool insulation should be cut a bit long and then carefully folded in and stapled to completely seal them off.

Fig. 9-5. The vapor barrier facing of mineral wool insulation is easily damaged. This large tear is a common fault, caused when a carpenter swung a long board around and a corner jabbed the facing. All such damage should be repaired before the insulation is covered up.

Insulating the floor is generally the more economical method, but sometimes there are reasons to opt for the crawlspace method.

To insulate the crawlspace, first smooth out the ground fairly well and clean out any debris. Then lay a vapor barrier over the entire floor. Ordinary 30-pound roofing felt has often been used for this purpose, but unfortunately it is short-lived if there is much moisture present in the ground. If you do use felt, overlap each strip by about 2 inches and adhere the seams with cold roofing cement.

A better solution (and easier) is to lay out a sheet of polyethylene. The heavy-duty black "construction plastic" that's available at most lumberyards works fine. This material unfolds from the roll in very large sheets, so you might be able to lay down a completely seamless vapor barrier. If not, simply overlap individual pieces by about a foot. No sealing is necessary. Whatever you use, the vapor barrier should be folded up the foundation walls for a distance of about 6 inches. Stick the edges down with a mastic. Ordinary roof patching compound works well.

Lay long lengths of blanket insulation across the crawlspace area. Fasten one end of each length to the sill plate, drape it down along the foundation wall and out across the crawlspace floor (Fig. 9-7). Carry it up the wall on the opposite side, fold the end into place, trim if necessary, and secure that end to the sill plate. Take care to not compress the insulation unduly when curving it down the wall and then out across the floor. But at the same time, the insulation should lie as flat as possible (without

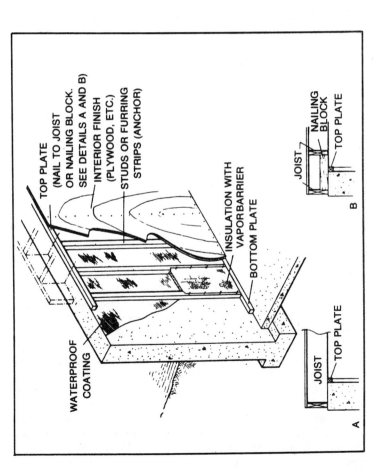

WATERPROOF COATING

TOP PLATE (NAIL TO JOIST OR NAILING BLOCK. SEE DETAILS A AND B)

INTERIOR FINISH (PLYWOOD, ETC.)

STUDS OR FURRING STRIPS (ANCHOR)

INSULATION WITH VAPOR BARRIER

BOTTOM PLATE

A

JOIST

TOP PLATE

B

JOIST

NAILING BLOCK

TOP PLATE

Fig. 9-6. A basement wall can be insulated by first installing furring strips as shown, stapling faced mineral wool in place, and then covering with a finish material.

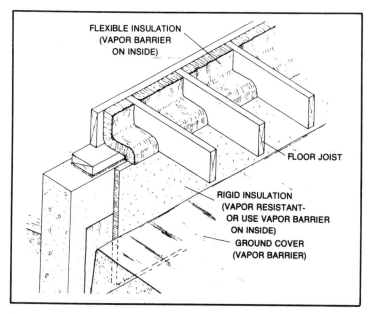

Fig. 9-7. Alternative methods of insulating crawlspace walls. The mineral wool can be placed only at the top of the walls, covering the sills and band joists, with the wall surface itself covered with a rigid insulation. One problem with this method (if thick mineral wool is used) is in making the folds in the material and keeping it in proper position. The mineral wool could be extended to the crawlspace floor instead of using the rigid insulation and could be continued across the crawlspace floor as well. Note the way in which the vapor barrier is installed.

crushing) against the wall and be tucked into the corner formed by the wall/floor joint.

The insulation can be held in place by setting a few bricks or small rocks on top of it. The vapor-barrier facing should be uppermost. Wherever necessary, trim the insulation to fit and seal around floor joists. Each subsequent strip should be nested tightly against the edge of the previous one. If you want, you can fold the stapling flanges upward and staple them together using an ordinary office-type desk stapler. This is not essential.

One problem with this type of arrangement—although it is thermally quite effective—is that if later access is needed to parts of the crawlspace for repair work or whatever, the insulation can be easily damaged and/or displaced. If sufficient care is exercised, boards or scraps of plywood can be laid down first and taken up after the work is done. The insulation will compress in the meantime, but it should regain its full loft a short time after the boards have been removed. It will be necessary to inspect the insulation and make repairs as necessary.

At the same time the crawlspace or the basement walls are insulated, the band joist areas must also be taken care of. End joist areas are most easily handled by cutting long strips of blanket to a suitable width and setting them along the length of the end joists. The vapor barrier faces into the warmer area. Fasten the insulation through the stapling flange to the underside of the subflooring above. The cut lower edge, which will have no stapling flange left on it, will rest partly upon the sill. If the material is thick it will overlap somewhat. Calculate the width of the strip for a tight fit so that it can be partially held in place by friction.

The insulation can also be "crowded" in place in an insulated crawlspace installation by pushing the crawlspace wall insulation tight against it. Header joist areas are most easily insulated by cutting short sections from batts or blanket and then standing the pieces up on edge between the floor joists, against the header and with the vapor barrier facing into the basement or crawlspace (Fig. 9-8). Use the stapling flanges at each side to secure the material to the floor joists.

Floors

Insulating a floor section over an unheated basement is not a difficult chore. Doing the same in a cramped crawlspace or under a house set low on open piers can be much more of a struggle. Unfortunately, it's not usually possible to install mineral fiber blanket or batt insulation in floor cavities by working from above before the subflooring is laid because of the danger that the insulation will become soaked by rain or snow before the house can be closed in. The job is almost always done from below and there are several variations on the theme.

When insulation is installed in floors above unheated areas, the vapor barrier must face upward toward the heated area. Though friction-fit batts have no integral vapor barrier, they are the easiest to install in underfloor areas. All that's required is to stuff the batts, trimmed to size if need be, up into the cavities between the framing members and tuck them tightly against the underside of the subflooring. This means that a vapor barrier must be separately installed. This can be done by laying polyethylene sheet over the subflooring and then putting underlayment over that. The finish flooring is then laid on the underlayment.

If the floor specifications do not call for a multiple-layer floor where a polyethylene vapor barrier can be laid, an insulation with an integral vapor barrier will have to be used. Laying polyethylene over the floor joist tops and then putting down the subflooring will work only if the subflooring can be kept completely dry during construction. If rainwater leaks through the subflooring, it forms huge blisters of water in the stretchable plastic sheeting. These blisters must then be "popped" and drained and the vapor barrier patched. It never does regain its original shape or effectiveness.

Faced batt or blanket is cut to fit if necessary and then pushed up into the cavities between the framing members, with the facing upward. This material tends not to cling very well to the framing members. It must be secured or restrained if it shows signs of slipping downward or when it is installed in a well-ventilated crawlspace or in an open foundation arrangement (also true of friction-fit batts under these latter conditions).

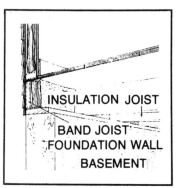

INSULATION JOIST

BAND JOIST

FOUNDATION WALL

BASEMENT

Fig. 9-8. The band joist area (both headers and ends) in a heated crawlspace or basement should be fully insulated. Cut pieces of mineral wool to fit and stand them in place as shown with the vapor barrier facing turned to the inside of the building.

There are several ways that you can go about this. One is to apply several daubs of mastic or construction adhesive (available in caulking-gun cartridges) to the face of the insulation. Then push the insulation into place so that the adhesive sticks to the underside of the subflooring (Fig. 9-9).

Another method is to stuff the insulation into place, then pull the wool aside slightly at several points alongside the framing members and reach up in with a stapler, staple the facing to the underside of the subflooring, and then work the wool back into place.

Both of these methods place the facing directly against the subflooring. This means that there is no air space between them for ventilation. Also, if the insulation is foil-faced the potential thermal resistance of the reflective foil is negated. There is no reflective plane air space.

When you want to leave a space between the insulation facing and the underside of the subflooring, there are four common methods of restraining the insulation or supporting it at just the right depth in the cavities between the framing members.

One method is to slip the insulation into place to the desired depth and then jam heavy wire rods (pointed at each end and made for just this purpose) crosswise between the joists (Fig. 9-10). This method requires that the insulation bottom surface be above the lower edge of the joists by a half inch or more. The second method is an alternative to the first and uses lengths of springy lath or other wood strips jammed between the joists instead of wire rods (Fig. 9-11).

With the remaining two methods, the insulation is pushed up into the cavities between the floor joists so that its bottom surface is more or less even with the lower edges of the joists. Drive a series of small nails or brads partly into the joist edges and spaced 18 inches or so apart, then lace wire—ordinary soft iron mechanics' wire works fine—back and forth diagonally from nail to nail.

The last method involves laying out runs of poultry netting ("chicken wire") and stapling it to the bottom edges of the floor joists (Fig. 9-12). This method affords the greatest amount of support and protection for the insulation.

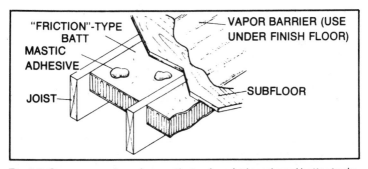

Fig. 9-9. One easy way to make sure that unfaced mineral wool batts stay in place when installed under a floor is to place globs of mastic on the insulation. Push the wool up against the floor to make an adhesive bond. Then very gently straighten the wool to full loft and final position.

An additional method, not often used, but certainly the best, is to cover the entire underside of the floor with sheets of sheathing—either plain or insulating. Whatever is used should not act as a second vapor barrier. It should have a certain amount of permeability to allow the free outward passage of water vapor. Although this method is more expensive and a good deal more work, it also affords complete mechanical protection for the insulation as well as a certain amount of added R value.

More often than not, a few irregularities and obstructions are encountered during the process of insulating beneath a floor. Irregular or odd-sized cavities should be filled with pieces cut to fit snugly. For small

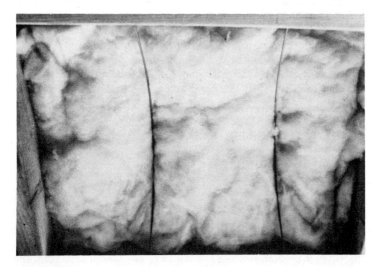

Fig. 9-10. Mineral wool batt or blanket insulation can be easily kept in place by jamming special pointed-tip wire restraining rods in place below the material.

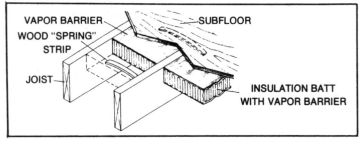

Fig. 9-11. Scraps of lath or other wood strips will effectively hold mineral wool batt or blanket insulation in place in an underfloor installation.

cavities, it is often easier to remove the facing and install that first, then cut the wool to size and slip it into place. Very small or very narrow cavities make the installation of the facing or vapor barrier practically impossible. If there is only a small total area left without a vapor barrier, probably it can be ignored with no detrimental effects.

If there is a large amount, a polyethylene sheet vapor barrier is best installed between the subflooring and the underlayment or finish flooring. In any event, all small cavities and even narrow spaces between structural members should be stuffed full of wool loosely enough to approximate standard density.

Pipes and wires should be carefully fitted around by slitting the insulation as necessary and working both the vapor barrier and the wool closely around them. Cracks around a soil stack or other pipes should be carefully stuffed full so that they are well sealed. Electrical wires should never lie within the insulation. They should be either above or below and wires should not compress the insulation at any point. Normally, one will not find piping running parallel with the floor in an unheated area, but this does happen. If there is any possibility of freeze-up, the pipe should lie above the insulation. Failing that, the pipe should be wrapped with a heat tape and then individually wrapped with a pipe insulant.

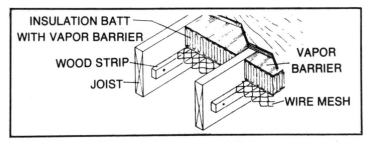

Fig. 9-12. Wire mesh will hold underfloor mineral wool batt or blanket insulation in position and also afford it some mechanical protection. The mesh is shown here supported by and attached to wood nailing strips secured to the joist sides. It could also be stapled directly to the joist sides or in long runs across the joist bottom edges.

312

Walls

Stud-framed walls are insulated by cutting the batts or blanket about three-fourths of an inch long at each end and slipping the insulation into the cavities between the studs (Fig. 9-13). If the material must be trimmed to width, allow an extra three-fourths of an inch. Position the insulation and stretch the facing, which should face inward to the conditioned area, to free it from folds and wrinkles. Slip your fingers along between the sides of the insulation and the sides of the studs. Make sure that the wool lies flat and is evenly distributed into the outside corners of the cavity. Fold the stapling flanges out flat against the edges of the studs and staple them down tight. Pull them free of bulges and wrinkles as you do so. The stapling flanges will overlap to provide an unbroken vapor barrier.

If there is a possibility that the stapling flanges might interfere with the application of the interior finish covering or if the insulation is foil-faced and a plane air space should be left to gain added R value, then the insulation should be dished. Instead of stapling the flanges to the stud edges, push the insulation back a bit and staple the flanges to the sides of the stud. The flange edges should be flush with the stud faces. Make sure the wool fits snugly in place at top and bottom, fold the excess facing into flanges, and staple them down. When the insulation is dished, an additional polyethylene sheet vapor barrier is recommended.

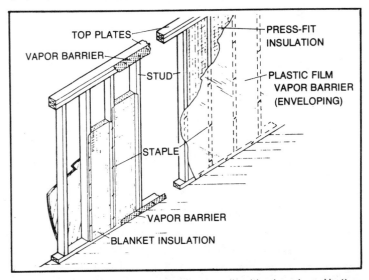

Fig. 9-13. Two methods of insulating frame walls with mineral wool batt or blanket insulation. On the left, faced material is installed with the stapling flanges across the stud edges. No additional vapor barrier is needed. The insulation could also be dished between the studs. In that case, a supplementary polyethylene sheet vapor barrier should be installed. On the right, friction-fit batts are stuffed between the studs and then covered with a vapor barrier.

Electrical wiring often causes problems when insulating exterior walls. The usual procedure for installing cables, following the National Electrical Code, is to pass them through holes drilled through the centers of 2 x 4 studs or plates or through holes placed at least 2 inches inboard from either edge of larger framing members. Where vertical cable runs pass through top or sole plates, simply slit the insulation slightly to fit around the cable at the point of entrance or exit. Lap the cut facing around the cable and bend the cable outward and down so that it will pass over the insulation facing without compressing it (Fig. 9-14). This presupposes that some slack has been left in the cable that will allow them to be bent outward slightly.

If they have been pulled up tight, another problem arises. If you place the insulation either over or behind the wires, the insulation will be unduly compressed on one side and there will be a sizable air space left on the other. Both situations impair the effectiveness of the insulation. Although it's a lot of work, the best arrangement is to bring the cables forward as far as possible and then cut a full-length channel in the insulation somewhat wider than the cable.

Slide the insulation behind the cable so that the cable lies in the channel. It is not a good idea to make a slit in the insulation so that the cable ends up being surrounded by insulation. This can create a potential fire hazard because the thermal insulation also impedes the normal transfer of heat away from the wire. If the wire becomes hot while being used, it cannot cool properly and the added thermal insulation can lead to a breakdown of the electrical insulation if the normal operating temperature rating of the cable is exceeded.

Because the cable should be left open to the air, this means a break in the vapor barrier facing. This should then be covered with another vapor barrier. A sheet of polyethylene over the studs will do the job or you can glue a strip of scrap facing over the channel. The same situation occurs with cables that are run vertically through stud after stud across a wall section. There is almost never any slack so the wires cannot be bent either inward or outward. You can cut a length of insulation to fit from the sole plate level to just beneath the horizontal cables and secure it in place. Then tuck a bit of loose wool behind the cables and install another length from the cables to the top plate. Cover the channel with vapor barrier material.

There are always electrical boxes for convenience outlets and wall switches mounted on outside wall frames. The boxes extend back into the wall cavity for at least 2½ inches, often more, and the electrical cables loop out of the back of the boxes and take up even more space. If mineral wool insulation of a thickness equal to the depth of the wall cavities is being installed, it is not a good idea to try and stuff the full thickness of the material behind the box. The compression is so great that the insulation has practically no value at that point and a large gap is left all around the outlet box as well. If the outlet boxes are metal, as most are, they will transfer a substantial amount of heat (plastic outlet boxes are less of a problem).

The best arrangement is to make a full cutout in the insulation to accommodate the outlet box. Before you put the insulation in place, pack scraps of mineral wool—not too tightly—between the back of the box and the exterior sheathing/siding and over and around the wires coming out of the box. There's no danger of overheating here if the cables are either brought forward to the outside of the insulation or laid back against the exterior sheathing because the passage through the insulation is so short.

Slip the full length of insulation in place and tuck the edges of the cutout carefully around the box. Fill with more scraps of wool if there are any gaps or open spaces. Incidentally, the edges of foil-faced insulation, in particular, should be trimmed so that they do not lap over into the electrical box. The aluminum foil is an electrical conductor.

Some folks have also packed scraps of mineral wool into the box itself and behind and around the convenience outlet or switch. This is probably a good idea from a house heat-loss standpoint, but whether or not it is from an electrical standpoint is another question because of the overheating possibility. The National Electrical Code has nothing specific to say on the subject.

It is not usual practice to install water pipes in exterior walls, especially in hard-winter country, but occasionally they are. Here the insulation should be slit and fitted around the pipes as closely as possible so that they are fully nested in the mineral wool—unless they are all the way forward in the wall cavity. In that case, the insulation can usually be slipped behind small pipes or tubing. Channels should be cut for larger pipes.

Fig. 9-14. Fit faced mineral wood batt or blanket insulation carefully around electrical wires by slitting the facing and wrapping it tightly in place, and then stapling.

If the holes cut in the framing members through which the pipes run are substantially oversized and exit into an unheated space, fill the gaps with scrap mineral wool packed in tightly. Then seal around the pipe with an elastomeric caulking compound. Be sure to use one capable of withstanding 200 F temperatures if hot-water pipes are involved. Ductwork, vent pipes, electrical wires or anything else routed into the wall cavities from an unheated space should be similarly treated before the wall insulation itself is put into place. The object is to seal off unwanted air currents and reduce the possibility of infiltration/exfiltration.

One aspect of wall insulation sometimes neglected, are the gaps in frames of doors and windows. These gaps should be thoroughly filled with strips of mineral wool poked into place with a putty knife, kitchen knife, or whatever else might suit. The mineral wool will fit into cracks as narrow as an eighth of an inch if you work at it. The effort is worthwhile. The material should be packed in fairly tight but not jammed solid. The density here will often be much greater than that of the wall insulation itself, but that's all right. After all the gaps are filled, cover the entire width of the framing members, gap, and window or door frame with a vapor barrier material (Fig. 9-15)—either insulation facing or polyethylene strips—wide enough that the material extends a couple of inches out into the window or door opening itself. After you put the wall covering on, fold the excess back over the outside surface of the covering and staple it down. It will be hidden when the finish trim is put on and will form a tight, unbroken seal.

There's nothing that can be done in the way of insulating headers above doors and windows with mineral wool insulation once the walls have been built. The only opportunity to use wool in this instance is when box-type headers are built. During construction, the interior of the boxes can be filled with fitted chunks of insulation.

Usually the vapor barrier facing is not included. It is a good idea, if you'll not be putting up full-length sheets of polyethylene as a supplementary vapor barrier, to cover the entire door and window header areas with either polyethylene or scrap pieces of insulation facing so that the vapor barrier for the entire wall section is complete.

Knee walls are insulated in exactly the same fashion as exterior walls (Fig. 9-16). Make sure that the insulation fits snugly at top and bottom, against the sole and top plates, and flange the facing out at top and bottom for a good vapor-barrier seal. The top plate of the wall frame in this instance is slanted downward to match the pitch of the roof rafters. This particular point has a good potential for heat loss if the insulation is not well fitted.

Instead of cutting the upper end of the insulation square and jamming it into place, which can cause either excessive compression or a gap (and sometimes both), the best arrangement is to cut the end of the insulation on an angle slightly less than that of the top plate so that the material rests snugly against the framing members at all points. If there is access into the unheated space behind the knee wall, you can crawl around in back and

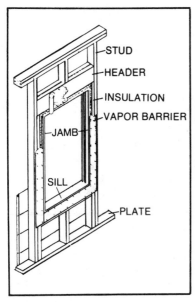

STUD

HEADER

INSULATION

VAPOR BARRIER

JAMB

SILL

PLATE

Fig. 9-15. Cracks and gaps around windows and doors, between the framing members and the window or door frames, should be filled with scraps of mineral wood, and then covered with a vapor barrier. Though not shown here, the vapor barrier can be extended out into the window or door opening and then folded back beneath the finish trim to make a better seal.

straighten all the insulation out and snug it into corners and against framing members at the edges. That is an opportunity that you don't have with other kinds of wall construction.

There's one other spot that sometimes is forgotten. It is common practice to make up wall corners or intersections with full-length studs separated by scrap pieces in order to gain the required stud spacings (Fig. 9-17). There are also corner and intersection arrangements that leave full-length or part-length open channels between the framing members that are partially hidden. Be sure to fill all such spaces with scrap mineral wool packed in to about average density. Cover the corner or intersection framing with vapor barrier material as necessary so that it is completely sealed off.

Ceilings

There are several methods by which ceilings can be insulated with mineral wool batt or blanket insulation. Unfaced batts can be stuffed up into place from below. Following that, a polyethylene sheet vapor barrier is stapled to the underside of the ceiling joists. Alternatively, the batts can be placed from above after a vapor barrier and finish ceiling has been installed. Faced batts or blanket, either plain or foil, are generally slipped into the joist openings and the flanges stapled either to the bottom edges of the joists or to the joist sides—just as in a wall installation. Alternatively, they can be shoved down into position from above after the finish ceiling has been installed.

The place to start is in the band joist area (if there is one). Cut short sections of batt or blanket to fit snugly into the space between joists in a

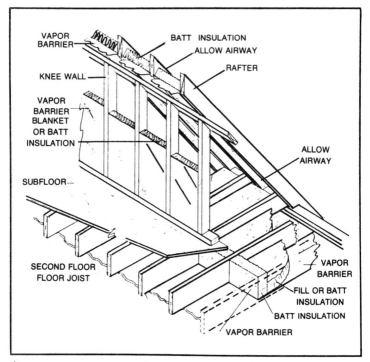

Fig. 9-16. A typical knee wall construction and the placement of mineral wood insulation. Note the method of insulating the unheated portion of the floor and the upended pieces that seal off the ceiling joist cavities directly below the knee wall.

header joist area or full-length strips for end joist areas (Fig. 9-18). Secure them by stapling or with mastic with the vapor-barrier facing inward, toward the heated (or cooled) space. Place the batt or blanket material between the joists (Fig. 9-19). Start at the outside ends of the bays. The insulation should extend fully over the top plate of the wall or butt tightly against the band joist insulation. If there is a gap between the top plate of the wall and the bottom surface of the insulation, pull off thin strips of wool to fill the gaps all the way across and to the full depth of the plate. The insulation should not block eave ventilation. There should be a gap of at least an inch between the outermost top edge of the insulation and the bottom surface of the roof sheathing or decking (Fig. 9-20). In some cases, it might be necessary to trim off the top edge across the end of the insulation on an angle to provide a suitable air gap.

Ceiling joists often overlap one another at their ends, just as do floor joists, creating an awkward spot to insulate properly because of the transitional gap that is left. The easiest way to handle this situation is to cut the batt or blanket length to stop exactly at the joist overlap.

Then start with a new batt or blanket length butted snugly against the first and continue running the insulation (Fig. 9-21). Wherever pipes or wires are encountered, they must be worked around in much the same fashion as in floors and walls. The critical point is to make sure that the insulation fits snugly everywhere. Great care should be taken that all of the stapling flanges and insulation edges lie tightly against framing members without any gaps. Rising warm air currents will quickly find their way through them and the integrity of the vapor barrier is also breached.

Wherever batts or lengths of blanket meet end to end, make sure they fit snugly against one another. It does no harm to run a strip of duct tape across the facing (Fig. 9-22) to seal the joint (unnecessary if a supplementary polyethylene sheet vapor barrier will be installed as well).

The thickest mineral wool batt or blanket insulation available today is 6½ inches (or R-19). In many areas of the country, this provides insufficient insulation for a ceiling. The usual recourse in to install a second layer, and sometimes even a third, on top of the principal installation. There are several points to keep in mind with this arrangement.

The second layer of insulation should not have a vapor barrier facing. It should be made up of unfaced batts. If these are unavailable to you, you

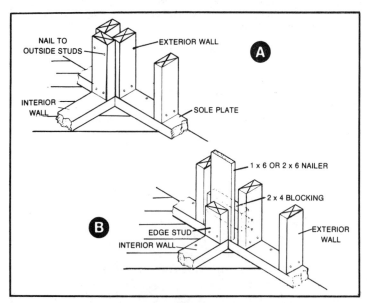

Fig. 9-17. Two typical methods of wall intersection framing. The arrangement for wall corners are similar and there are other methods as well. Most of them contain large gaps (which are quickly concealed as the sheathing is applied) that should be filled with scraps of mineral wool and covered with a vapor barrier as necessary. Timing of this part of the insulating job is important and it may well have to be done considerably before the other insulation is installed.

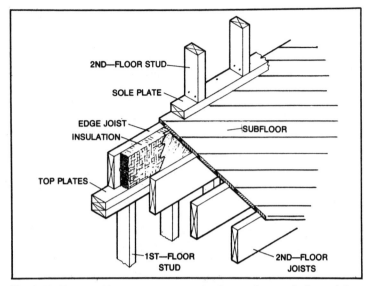

Fig. 9-18. The band joist area between the first and seconds floors (plat-form framing method). The area, here an end (edge) joist, must be insulated for full thermal protection by installing mineral wool batt or blanket material, vapor barrier facing inward, as shown. A header joist area would be handled in much the same way, but with short pieces tucked between the floor joists.

must peel the wool off and discard the facing. The usual procedure is to lay the batts (or blanket lengths) at right angles to the ceiling joists. This serves to cover the framing members and improve thermal performance at those points. It also provides plenty of support for the insulation. In some

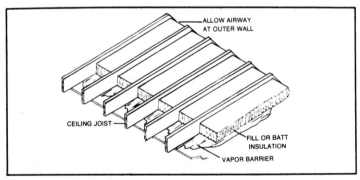

Fig. 9-19. Insulating most kinds of ceilings with mineral wool batt or blanket insulation consists merely of placing the material between the ceiling joists with a vapor barrier facing the conditioned living space. An airway must be left for ventilation through the eaves. This sometimes requires trimming the outer edges of the insulation as it is installed.

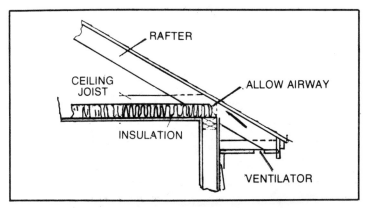

Fig. 9-20. This cross section shows how the ceiling insulation extends to cover the wall top plate, but leaves sufficient space for ventilation between it and the roof sheathing.

cases, this arrangement can also afford a plane air space between the two layers.

Care should be taken that the ventilating space along the eaves is not blocked off. This might take some trimming of the insulation and some careful arranging. Also, electrical cables must be routed over the top of the second layer of insulation and never between the two. This is because of the potential for overheated wiring. It is especially dangerous in an unvented attic area that can become very hot in summer. The wires can, however, safely pass upward through the insulation. The edges and ends of the batts or blanket lengths should fit snugly together and none of the material should be overly compressed at any point.

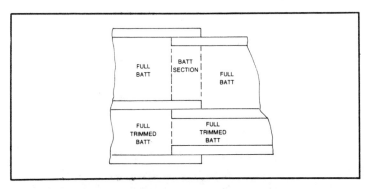

Fig. 9-21. Ceiling and floor joists are frequently overlapped, usually outside-and-outside, and sometimes outside-and-inside. If full pieces of mineral wool insulation are installed, large gaps are left at the joist ends. For a snug, effective fit, trim the insulation even with the joist ends and butt two or three pieces together.

Fig. 9-22. Where two batts or blanket lengths of faced mineral wool insulation butt together in a ceiling installation, a strip of duct tape will close off the joint, keep the pieces aligned, and seal the vapor barrier.

Special precautions must be taken when insulating, or reinsulating, around or over recessed ceiling lighting fixtures that protrude up into the cavities being insulated. The National Electrical Code specifies that—unless the lighting fixture is of a special kind that is clearly marked and approved for high-temperature service or for installation in cavities where thermal insulation will be in direct contact with the fixture—it must be installed in accordance with certain rules.

The fixture must be spaced at least one-half inch from any combustible material, it shall be so installed that any adjacent combustible material will not be subjected to temperatures of over 90 C (194 F), that no thermal insulation shall be installed within 3 inches of the fixture, and that thermal insulation cannot be so installed above the fixture that the free circulation of air is impeded. In the interest of fire safety, don't pack insulation around standard recessed ceiling lighting fixtures. Leave a 3-inch clearance all around the sides and plenty of free space above the fixture to allow circulation of air and escape of heat that builds up when the fixture is in operation (Fig. 9-23).

Roofs

Roofs are insulated with mineral wool batts or blankets in much the same way as are ceilings. In most such cases, the underside of the roof assembly *is* a ceiling. Generally, the batts or blankets are placed from below by stuffing them between the rafters. Either friction fit batts or faced insulation can be used. The former should be covered with a polyethylene sheet vapor barrier. The latter can be so treated or not.

Faced batts or blanket can be stapled to the lower edges of the rafters to form an unbroken vapor barrier or they can be stapled to the sides of the rafters. The insulation should always extend out over any wall top plates to provide complete coverage. It is usually best to leave an air space of about an inch or more between the insulation and the underside of the roof sheathing or decking to allow for ventilation. If this is not possible, then the insulation should be covered with a supplementary polyethylene vapor barrier sheet. Otherwise, everything that has been said about ceiling insulation installations applies to roof insulation as well.

There is one circumstance, albeit an unusual one, where the insulation is applied above the roof decking or sheathing. This is sometimes called a thermal roof. In the thermal roof arrangement, the roof frame and the underside of the roof decking or sheathing is left open to view and finished to complement the interior decor. Insulation must be placed on the outside.

Sheathing or decking is laid across the roof rafters or beams in the usual fashion. Then a gridwork is built of dimension stock on the upper surface of the sheathing or decking. This can be of whatever depth is required to hold the necessary mineral wool insulation. If the insulation consists of friction-fit batts, a vapor barrier should be laid first, over the sheathing. This is generally considered unnecessary if faced batts or blanket are used.

The insulation is installed in the gridwork with the vapor barrier facing down, toward the conditioned space. Then the whole affair is covered with another layer of sheathing—three-eighth plywood is sufficient—and topped with a finish roofing (Fig. 9-24).

Where substantial thermal resistance is required of the roof section, this arrangement is not feasible because it will not allow for a sufficient thickness of mineral wool. With the advent of several types of high-R insulants of relative thinness, the job can be more easily done in other ways anyway.

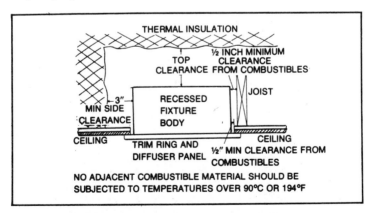

Fig. 9-23. Certain requirements must be followed when insulating around a standard recessed ceiling lighting fixture unless the fixture is specifically approved for direct contact with thermal insulation. The exact top clearance is not spelled out by the National Electrical Code, but it must be sufficient to allow heat from the fixture to escape.

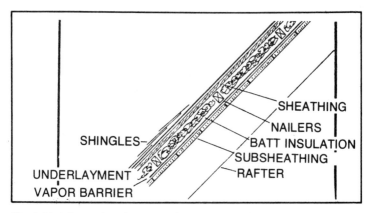

SHEATHING

NAILERS

SHINGLES— BATT INSULATION

SUBSHEATHING

UNDERLAYMENT RAFTER

VAPOR BARRIER

Fig. 9-24. A thermal roof construction can be insulated with mineral wool by securing a grid of nailing strips to the roof decking, installing the insulation in the grid, and then applying an outer sheathing and finish roofing.

Electric water heaters can be insulated (Fig. 9-25) even by an amateur do-it-yourselfer with excellent results. Use either mineral wool insulation of the same type as is used in floors, walls, and ceilings or purchase a ready-made water tank insulating kit. Gas water heaters should *not* be insulated by an amateur using bulk materials in a cobbled-up arrangement. It *can* be done by purchasing an approved kit made especially for the purpose. Both electric and gas kits include all necessary materials and complete instructions.

To insulate an electric water heater with bulk material, you'll need a roll of 3½-inch, R-11 fiberglass insulation with either plain or foil facing (batts won't work because they're too short). Unroll a length of insulation, stand it on edge, and wrap it around the tank. Mark it for a proper fit—neither loose nor tight but just snug—and cut the length from the roll.

Cut enough additional strips of the same length so that when you stack them atop one another they will cover the entire height of the tank. Trim the top piece so that it extends 3½ inches above the top of the tank. Then wrap the bottom piece around the tank, with the bottom edge resting on the floor, and secure it with a couple of tabs of duct tape across the joint. Continue doing the same thing with the remaining lengths until the entire tank wall is covered.

As you place the lengths, mark the locations of the cover of the electrical connection box and the access plates that expose the elements. Make cutouts through the insulation that are somewhat larger than the plates. Don't discard the cutouts; put them back into place as plugs that can be removed at any time for service work. If the cold water supply pipe for the tank runs close alongside the surface of the tank shell, you can wrap the insulation right over it. If there is room enough, slip it between the pipe and the tank. The overflow pipe coming from the relief valve should be left

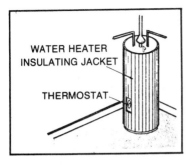

Fig. 9-25. Either gas or electric storage-type water heaters can be insulated by wrapping them with faced mineral wool blanket. The reduction in operating cost can be substantial.

WATER HEATER INSULATING JACKET

THERMOSTAT

out in the open. If need be, you can extend the pipe from the valve for more clearance.

After everything is arranged to your satisfaction, stick strips of tape over all of the seams and the joints at the cut ends of the lengths. Then cut out a circular piece of insulation—this will probably have to be made up of a pair of half-circles—of the same diameter as the tank.

If you'd like a full-dress installation, cut the fiberglass to the same diameter as the tank, but the facing to a 7-inch greater diameter, so that the extra facing will cover the exposed fiberglass edge of the topmost length. Set this piece in place and make a notched cutout that permanently exposes the safety relief valve. Under no circumstances should this valve be covered. To finish the job, wrap the hot water outlet pipe with pipe insulation wherever it is accessible.

SHEATHINGS

The various kinds of insulating sheathings probably rank second in popularity to mineral wool insulations and they are often used in combination with one another. Sheathings can be applied by simply cutting the sheets to fit and nailing them in place, or gluing them, or both. They are not as universal in application as mineral wool, but on the other hand they can do some jobs better.

Foundations

Insulating sheathing is not designed or intended to be used exposed on the exterior of foundation walls. Many types will not stand up to continued exposure to sunlight or moisture. Using those that are faced with reflective foil would be pointless and also more expensive than installing other insulants better suited for the purpose.

Insulating sheathings can be used on the interior of foundation walls in some circumstances. In a full basement, for instance, the arrangement is much the same as for mineral wool insulations. Furring strips are fastened to the foundation wall and then the insulating sheathing can be applied to the masonry wall between the furring strips or secured to the furring strip surfaces leaving an air space between the insulating sheathing and the masonry wall (or both). The job can also be done with adhesive only and no furring, as Fig. 9-26 shows. The sheathing must then be covered with plasterboard, paneling, or some similar material to finish the job. It should not be left exposed.

Securing the sheathing is simple enough. A few dabs of adhesive will hold sheets to the masonry wall until they are covered by another material and sheets can be fastened to the furring strips with adhesive or short nails. When fitting sheets of sheathing between furring strips, be careful to cut them accurately so that there are no gaps at the edges. Special channel or clip systems of fastening either the insulating sheathing or the finish wall covering are available. These afford an easy means of providing a three-fourth inch air space within the wall cavity in order to make a reflective facing effective.

Insulating sheathings can also be used to cover the interior walls of crawlspaces. There are a couple of exceptions. Plastic foam sheathings should not be used in crawlspaces where there is any possibility that flammable materials such as points or thinners might be stored or in crawlspaces having access doors or hatches of more than 2 x 2 feet in size. Also, some local building codes require that plastic foams be covered with a barrier of one-half inch plasterboard—even in an empty crawlspace.

Wherever installation of plastic foam or other types of insulating sheathing board can be reasonably and feasibly installed on crawlspace walls, the job is not a difficult one. Sheets of the material are secured

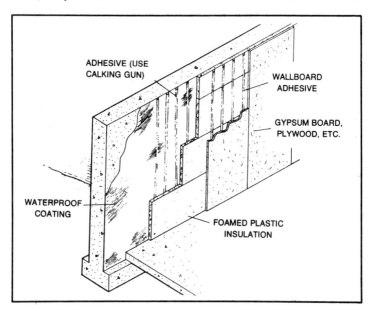

Fig. 9-26. There are a number of methods of insulating basement walls with insulating sheathing or other rigid insulants. This drawing shows how both insulation and wall covering can be installed with adhesive. Be sure to use an adhesive that is compatible with the insulation.

directly to the walls with an adhesive. The pieces should be closely fitted and the seams butted tightly. The material should extend from grade level or somewhat below to the underside of the floor joists. Alternatively, the sheathing can be notch-cut to slide up between the floor joists and butt against the underside of the subflooring. Depending upon the nature of the band joist area and the floor insulation, any spaces between the insulating sheathing and the band joist should be filled with insulation. Mineral wool does a good job there.

There is one circumstance where certain types of insulating sheathings, particularly foil-faced polystyrene, can be used to insulate the exterior of foundations walls. This is done when continuous long sheets of sheathing are applied to the frame walls of the house. Instead of ending at the bottom level of the exterior siding, the material is extended in an unbroken sheet to a point at least 2 feet below the finished grade. In this case, the material cannot be left unprotected. It should be covered with a suitable material that can withstand the rigors of weather and moisture. Use one-eighth inch cement-asbestos board or a similar material. This exterior covering should extend upward for 3 or 4 inches underneath the exterior siding. The siding itself and the fill dirt at the foundation will serve to hold both covering and insulation in place.

Floors

There are several applications where insulating sheathing is advantageous in floor constructions. One example is applying the material to the underside of floor joists to enclose the floor insulation over a ventilated or open crawlspace. Plastic foam sheathings are, however, not a good choice here because of their flammability and because local codes might require an additional covering of plasterboard as well.

Another possibility arises when a wood floor is to be built upon a concrete floor as part of a basement-finishing project or upon a slab foundation. A three-fourth inch thickness is generally more than enough for this purpose, no matter what the R value of the material, because heat lost through the interior portions of slab floors is minimal and not much thermal resistance is required to greatly improve the comfort factor.

After a vapor barrier has been laid, nominal 1-inch furring strips or 2-inch sleepers can be fastened to the concrete with masonry nails. Their spacing on centers depends upon the type of wood flooring that will be laid down. Sections of insulating sheathing can be laid between the furring strips or sleepers in much the same way a masonry wall is insulated with the same material. The final step is to put down a subflooring or finish flooring in the conventional manner (Fig. 9-27).

Insulating sheathing can also be used in a conventional wood-framed floor construction. After the subflooring (usually plywood) has been put down, the sheets of insulating sheathing can be laid directly atop a polyethylene vapor barrier. No fastening is necessary and the sheets should be carefully fitted for minimal joint. As the pieces are placed, the

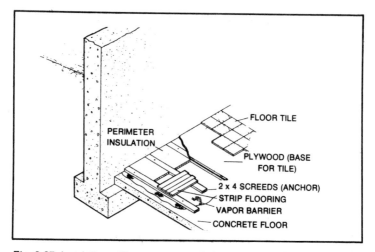

Fig. 9-27. Insulating either a new or existing concrete basement floor is simple when a wood floor is built up on the slab. Just insert strips of insulating sheathing or other rigid insulation between the floor sleepers and lay the finish flooring on top. In relatively mild climates, the perimeter insulation alone will serve well. In colder climates, cover the entire slab.

locations of the floor joists below should be marked on the insulation surface with a chalk line. Then the insulation is covered with a layer of plywood or particle board underlayment and fastened down with ring-shank nails. The final step is the application of finish flooring. This arrangement is sometimes used in second-floor constructions with certain types of insulating sheathings, not to improve thermal performance, but because a substantial reduction in annoying and intrusive impact noise transmitted into the first-floor living space can be gained.

Walls

The principal use of insulating sheathing is to cover house walls—framework and all. This method greatly improves thermal performance through those parts of the walls where studs and other framing members are located. The sheathing is quite often used in conjunction with mineral wool or other insulation placed within the wall cavities. Generally, the material is applied to the exterior of the building. This can be done in several ways.

One common method is to apply the insulating sheathing directly to the studs as a substitute for ordinary exterior sheathing. However, insulating sheathing is not a structural material and adds no strength to the framework of the walls. This means that under most building codes all of the wall frames must be strengthened at each corner. The usual procedure is the same one that has been used for decades for the same purpose. A diagonal brace, usually a nominal 1 x 4, is let into the outside edges of the

328

wall studs, running from sole plate to top plate (Fig. 9-28). This provides the necessary rigidity to the house frame.

Alternatively, the insulating sheathing can be applied over an exterior sheathing that does have structural strength. This involves first applying conventional sheathing in one of three ways; fiberboard sheathing (which also has reasonably good thermal properties) over the entire wall framework; plywood exterior sheathing over the entire framework; or plywood sheathing at the wall corners only (usually in full 4-foot widths wherever possible) and fiberboard sheathing at all other points. The method that is chosen usually depends upon the desired degree of structural strength and rigidity of the house frame and the dictates of local building codes. The insulating sheathing is then applied over the conventional sheathing.

Insulating sheathing can be applied, following manufacturers' recommendations, by nailing it in place, gluing it to the frame, or using both nails and glue. Only adhesives that have been recommended for use with the specific insulants should be used. Some adhesives are incompatible with some insulants. Nailing should be carefully done so as not to damage the material. Pieces should be cut and trimmed to fit snugly in place with joints and seams well-fitted. Most insulating sheathing materials are relatively delicate and don't take kindly to being bounced and banged

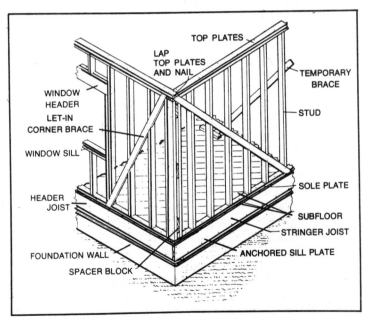

Fig. 9-28. If the wall framing is to be covered with insulating sheathing alone, let-in braces must be installed as shown at all corners to provide structural rigidity.

around. A reasonable amount of care should be taken in handling and applying the sheets.

Many commonly available insulating sheathings are faced on each side with aluminum foil or foil and paper. This serves as a skin for the insulant, imparts greater strength to the material, acts as an excellent vapor barrier, and allows added R value when applied in conjunction with a plane air space. If you install an insulating sheathing flat against an exterior sheathing and then apply an exterior siding directly against the insulating sheathing, you will gain no added value from the foil facing. However, if you apply nominal 1-inch furring strips over the insulating sheathing and then put on the exterior siding, you will gain approximately R-2 in thermal resistance by virtue of the enclosed air space and the reflective surface. It would also be possible (though it is not usually done) to install furring strips between the exterior sheathing and the insulating sheathing to gain a second air space.

Insulating sheathing affords an excellent barrier against infiltration of outside air and that potential can be maximized by proper installation. Where the insulating sheathing is applied directly to the studs, a glued and nailed application is more infiltration-proof than an installation made with nails alone. If the material is applied over conventional exterior sheathing, the sheets should be arranged to overlap and cover the joints between the sheets of the regular exterior sheathing.

Further sealing with an approved elastomeric caulk at joints between the insulating sheathing and other parts of the framework—at window and door frames, for instance—is a good idea. The sheathing should be fully sealed off at the bottom edges to prevent air flow up into the wall section and should also be tightly sealed as necessary along the top edges. The seams along the sides of the sheets, or where cut pieces abut one another, should be filled by troweling in a recommended or specified sealing compound. If all of these minor details are properly taken care of, the house will have an unbroken exterior skin that will vitrually eliminate infiltration/exfiltration.

Note that some insulating sheathing products are designed to be installed under certain circumstances so that some ventilation can take place in order to remove excess water vapor that might otherwise accumulate. This arrangement can reduce the potential for low infiltration and the installation must be carefully made for good results.

It is also possible to install insulating sheathing on the interior of walls. This arrangement is becoming much more common nowadays and especially with some kinds of manufactured or "kit" houses. It is a good arrangement when it's desirable to increase the thermal resistance of log, solid-wall, or timber-wall houses without changing the exterior appearance of the house. The insulating sheathing is simply applied either directly against the inside wall surface or on furring strips and secured with either nails, glue, or both.

The material can be applied to the inside of a conventional stud wall frame in exactly the same way as it is to the outside. Whatever the specifics, the material should be tightly fitted and well sealed. In all cases, it should be covered with an interior finish material such as plasterboard, finish planking, or wall paneling. Though the interior installation is likely to be a bit more difficult because of the need to fit the material around interior partition walls, electrical outlet boxes and what have you, the end result is equally effective.

Insulating sheathing is also an ideal material to include in masonry wall constructions. For example, where a conventional frame wall is to be veneered with brick or stone, the insulating sheathing can be applied to the wall frames in the usual fashion (provided proper bracing is also installed) or a layer of insulating sheathing can be applied over the conventional exterior sheathing. Then the brick or stone veneering is laid up as usual. Because it is common practice to leave an air space between the veneer and the sheathing, a foil-faced insulating sheathing will automatically provide extra R value.

By the same token, insulating sheathing can also be installed in the space left between the inner and outer masonry courses of a masonry cavity wall. Typically, this kind of construction consists of an interior course of concrete block and an exterior course of brick. There is a space of anywhere from about 1 to 4 inches between the two. It is a fairly simple matter to insert panels of insulating sheathing into the cavity (Fig. 9-29).

However, this must generally be done as the construction proceeds rather than after a wall assembly is finished. Special tie wires are generally positioned in the mortar joints of both masonry courses in order to tie the courses together and strengthen the wall. This means that the insulating sheathing must be fitted around or over these ties and the materials should also be secured to the outside face of the inside masonry course. This can be done by driving nails through the material and into the green mortar joints. Alternatively, dabs of adhesive can be used.

It is also possible to apply insulating sheathing to the exterior (or interior) of masonry walls, though this would be an unusual application—especially in new construction. This would involve securing the insulating sheathing either directly to the masonry wall or to furring strips fastened to the wall. The insulating sheathing cannot be left exposed to the outdoors, however, and additional finish siding of some sort would then have to be applied. Any kind of wood, steel, or aluminum siding might be used. Another possibility would be to secure metal lath over a protective vapor barrier and plaster on a coating of stucco.

The header areas of the windows and doors are a source of greater heat loss (or gain than other sections of the wall. In some cases, it is about the same as the wall cross section through the studs and in some instances it can be even less than that.

When insulating sheathing is applied over the entire wall, either inside or outside, the problem is largely taken care of. However, a typical conventional stud wall insulated only with mineral wool in the wall cavities

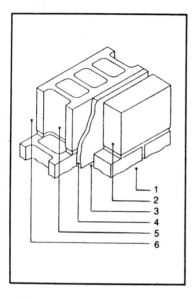

Fig. 9-29. Typical insulated brick (or other unit masonry) cavity wall construction: (1) outside air; (2) face brick; (3) air space; (4) insulation; (5) concrete block; (6) inside air.

and sheathed only with plywood or fiberboard will have somewhat improved thermal performance if the header areas are further protected with insulating sheathing. This can be easily done at very little cost simply by substituting small pieces of same-thickness insulating sheathing at the header areas. This is best done on the outside. If the interior wall is covered with plasterboard and then a second layer of finish covering (such as wall planking or paneling), the header areas could be covered on the inside with insulating sheathing of the same thickness as the plasterboard and then covered with the finish material.

Ceilings

Insulating sheathings are not commonly applied to ceiling areas. There is no particular reason why they cannot be. In most constructions, it would probably be necessary and certainly easier to apply the material from below by securing it to the underside of the ceiling joists. An additional application of mineral wool blanket or loose-fill insulation between the joist cavities would cover the upper surface of the insulating sheathing and also add considerably to the overall U. The lower surface of the insulating sheathing would then have to be covered with a fire-resistant material such as plasterboard. Ordinary acoustic ceiling tile probably would not serve unless treated for fire retardancy or composed of a mineral substance.

Applying the insulating sheathing to a ceiling is no different than a wall frame. Seams and joints should be tight and filled or caulked. The materials should be well secured to the joints with nails or with a combination of nails and adhesive. Ring-shank nails will give greater holding power (although most insulating sheathings are so lightweight that there is little pulldown tendency because of gravity). And as with walls, leaving a plane air space in the construction section will allow you to take advantage of the foil facing and a ceiling area is a good place to do so.

Roofs

There are several kinds of insulating sheathings that can be used to improve the thermal performance of roof assemblies. Some products work better than others and a few types are not recommended for roof applications because of possible shrinkage, damage due to continuous temperature cycling, and the possibility of temperatures within the roof construction that could exceed the maximum temperature rating of the material, causing degradation. When using the material in this application, be sure to select one that will properly withstand the rigors of the conditions under which it will function.

Insulating sheathing can be applied to the underside of roof rafters in a finished living space where it effectively forms a part of a roof/ceiling assembly. A typical application would be the upper story of a 1½-story house such as the "expanded attic" of a Cape Cod style. The material is generally used in conjunction with mineral wool insulation placed between the rafters in order to gain a higher thermal performance in the most effective manner.

The sheathing can be nailed or glued directly to the bottom edges of the rafters. In most instances, it would also be applied to the underside of a series of collar tie beams rather than going all the way up into the roof peak. This allows a ventilating area so that fresh air can travel up from the eaves, behind the insulation, and into the space above the collar tie beams to be exhausted through louvers placed in the gable ends. The sheathing should then be covered with plasterboard or some other finish wall covering.

Insulating sheathing can also be applied directly to the underside of the roof decking or sheathing where the roof rafters or beams are to be left exposed. The sheathing should be tightly fitted between the rafters or beams, sealed at all edges, and then covered with plasterboard or other finish material. The visible joints at the rafter or beam edges can be covered with strips of trim molding (Fig. 9-30).

A more common arrangement is to apply the insulating sheathing to the outside of the roof decking or sheathing. One possibility for doing so is to fasten a border strip around the perimeter of the roof sheathing. The strip should match the thickness of the insulating sheathing. A vapor barrier might or might not have to be laid upon the sheathing. This depends upon the nature of the insulating material. Then the sheets are laid on the roof surface and secured with just a few nails to hold them in place. The finish roofing is put on and fastened with nails long enough to go through the insulating sheathing and into the roof decking. An alternative to this method—especially useful where the insulating sheathing is more than an inch thick—is to cover the insulating sheathing with another sheathing layer, such as three-eighth inch plywood, to form an outer skin. The finish roofing is then fastened to the outer sheathing (Fig. 9-31).

Yet another possibility consists of building up a full grid on top of the roof decking or sheathing as is done when installing mineral wool insulation. The insulating sheathing is then fitted into the grids and sealed in place. Then a second outer sheathing of three-eighth inch plywood can be applied to cover the grid and the finish roofing secured to the outer layer. Alternatives to the outer plywood sheathing would be nailing strips to which cedar shingles or shakes are attached, a sheet steel roof could be fastened directly to the grid work members, or aluminum sheet roofing could be applied with just a few added nailing strips for extra support.

BOARDS AND SLABS

Board and slab insulants are made of a variety of materials such as polystyrene, polyurethane, polyisocyanurate, or cellular glass. Various shapes, sizes, and thicknesses (and R values) are readily available, including blocks and tapered slabs. Most of these materials are unfaced and they have a variety of possible uses.

Foundations

Probably the most widespread application for board and slab insulants in residential construction is in protecting foundations. These materials can be applied to the interior of crawlspace walls in exactly the same way as insulating sheathings are. The most convenient method of attachment usually is by adhesive, but be sure to use one that is compatible with the insulation and will not "melt" it. Boards and sometimes slabs—depending upon the degree of thermal performance required—can be secured to the above-grade portions of heated-basement foundation walls and extended to a depth of 2 feet below grade. The pieces should be well-fitted and precisely cut. They can be held in place by a combination of pressure from the bottom edge of the exterior siding, dabs of adhesive on the foundation wall, and the backfilled earth pressing against them. Because of the possibility of mechanical damage and degradation from sunlight and mois-

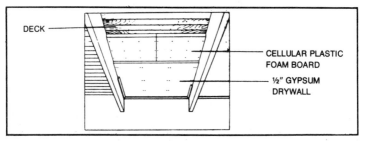

Fig. 9-30. This drawing shows how insulating sheathing can be applied to the underside of a roof decking between exposed rafters or beams. Trim molding hides the joints between the rafter sides and the wallboard.

334

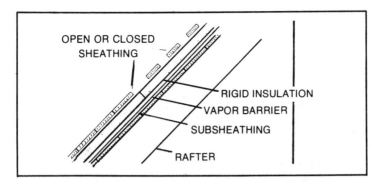

OPEN OR CLOSED
SHEATHING

RIGID INSULATION
VAPOR BARRIER
SUBSHEATHING
RAFTER

Fig. 9-31. This is an increasingly popular method of constructing a thermal roof. Insulating sheathing or rigid insulation is secured to the roof decking or sheathing with the finish roofing applied on top. An outer sheathing or nailer strips might or might not be required. It depends upon the type of finish roofing.

ture, the insulation should be covered with cement-asbestos board or some other similar material.

Boards and slabs of various sizes and thickness can also be employed for all kinds of below-grade exterior foundation wall insulation. Some, especially cellular glass, are particularly useful for insulating earth-sheltered houses where their application extends to roof sections as well. In such circumstances, great care must be taken to adequately waterproof the masonry construction and to protect the insulating material from the incursion of moisture as well. Applications of this sort tend to be complex and each individual situation is best enginered according to on-site conditions.

Slab insulations, and often boards as well, are widely used for perimeter insulation under concrete slabs. In this instance, the relative "crushability" of the material is of importance and a sturdy material has to be selected. Typically, the insulation extends back into the field of the floor for about 2 feet. Less than 2 feet is generally considered inadequate and more is often not essential. However, there are some instances where it is deemed desirable to lay board or slab insulation under the entire concrete slab. This is especially true in a thermal-mass design where the slab will store heat.

Perimeter insulation can be arranged in several different ways. One of the most common methods is shown in Fig. 9-32. Here a continuous foundation wall with a notched top is poured first and then a layer of gravel and/or sand is compacted and leveled within the foundation perimeter. A vapor barrier—polyethylene sheet is most commonly used—should be laid across the entire filled area and wrapped up the face of the notch of the foundation wall. The barrier can be extended upward several inches to overlap the wall vapor barrier for a complete seal. Slab or board insulation is laid on top of the vapor barrier around the entire perimeter of the foundation. It should extend back for a minimum of 1 foot and preferably for 2 feet. A strip of insulation is cut to stand on edge against the foundation wall notch face. It is sized to leave a gap of about one-fourth inch at the top. A strip of wood one-fourth inch thick and the same width as the insulation thickness should be laid on the upper edge of this perimeter insulation belt.

The concrete for the floor slab is poured directly on the insulation at the edges and upon the vapor barrier in the remaining area. If reinforcing mesh is bedded in the concrete, care must be taken to not puncture the vapor barrier or damage the insulation. After the concrete has cured, the wood strips are removed—leaving a gap.

This gap can be filled with a hot tar seal provided the specific insulating material is capable of withstanding both the heat and the volatile solvents in the tar. Some insulations cannot so an elastomeric caulk or some other type of sealing compound must be used. Be sure to get the correct recommendations for the kind of insulation that you will be using. Any type of finish flooring can then be applied.

Another possibility for slab perimeter insulating is shown in Fig. 9-33. In this grade-beam construction, the slab or board insulation is placed against the inside sloping face of the grade beam and should extend

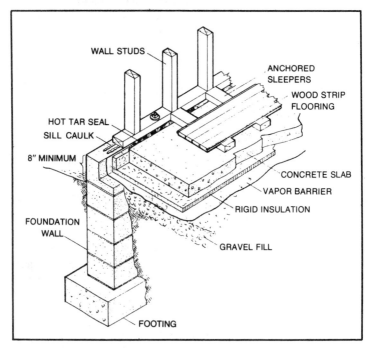

Fig. 9-32. This method of perimeter insulation of slab-on-grade foundations is effective and neither difficult nor expensive.

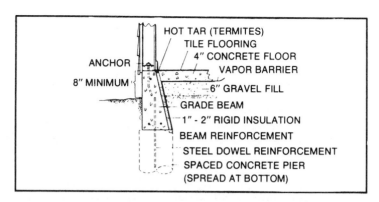

Fig. 9-33. This method of insulating a slab-on-grade foundation places the rigid insulation against the inside face of the grade beam. The same approach can be used on a straight-wall foundation (either block or poured concrete).

to a depth of 18 to 24 inches below the outside grade level. Note again the hot tar seal (primarily a termite prevention procedure) along the top edge of the insulation. Depending upon the specific insulant being used, other types of seals might be called for, and indeed, on many occasions no seal at all is included.

If the concrete slab includes perimeter heating system ducts, the insulating situation is a bit different. Figure 4-11 shows this arrangement; notice the inclusion of a continuous vapor barrier. Slab perimeter insulation can also be placed on the outside of the foundation wall. In this case, the insulation covers the entire above-grade area of the foundation wall and usually extends to about 2 feet below the finished grade. This is undoubtedly the simplest method of application, but it does not provide protection back under the lip of the slab perimeter.

Floors

Insulating boards and slabs can also be used to provide thermal protection in floor assemblies. Their application and installation is very much like that of the insulating sheathings. About the only difference is that there are more pieces to handle (because they are generally smaller) and there is no foil facing to be concerned with. For example, to insulate poured concrete floors, whether basement floors or poured-on-grade foundation slabs, just cover the entire floor area instead of only the perimeter section with the material before pouring the concrete.

There are two potential problems here. One is mechanical damage from reinforcing wire, shovels, etc., and the other is that the pieces of insulation might shift about during the pouring process. Due care and caution must be exercised as the concrete is placed so that the pieces don't get out of alignment, break, or become otherwise damaged. Cellular glass is probably the toughest insulant as far as being damage-proof is concerned.

These materials can also be used to insulate between a concrete floor and a built-up wood floor by simply fitting the boards or slabs between the floor sleepers and sealing them in. A vapor barrier or damp-proofing coating should be applied over the concrete first. Another possibility is the same sandwich construction mentioned earlier in the discussion of insulating sheathings. The insulating material is placed between a subfloor and an underlayment or finish floor in conventional wood-frame floor construction. In this situation, the boards or slabs are simply cut to fit as necessary, laid out on the subfloor, and secured with a just enough nails to hold them in place as the underlayment or finish floor is laid. Seams and joints, especially where the insulant is fitted around pipes and wires, should be well sealed.

Masonry Walls

Insulating board and slab can be applied to practically any kind of masonry wall. They can be used to insulate the exterior of the shallow foundation walls or grade beams that are a part of slab-on-grade construction. And that they also can be applied to crawlspace walls. Another application is full-height heated basement walls. Boards of 2-foot width can be secured directly to the foundation walls with adhesive between the furring strips that will support the finish wall covering. The mechanics of this installation are just the same as for insulating sheathing or mineral wool installations.

Boards and slabs are also commonly used in core or cavity masonry wall constructions. Slabs are often preferred because of their (usually) greater thickness and their ease of handling and installing as the masonry wall is built. In a core wall, the material is simply set in place. Sometimes there is no need for an additional vapor barrier and the masonry materials are built right up around it. Cavity wall construction is similar except that the insulation is generally secured to the outside face of the inside wall and an air space is left between it and the inside face of the outside course.

Some types of slab and board insulation, notably cellular glass, can be applied directly to the exterior of a masonry wall. Adhesive alone is generally sufficient to secure this material in place. It has the added advantage that it can be directly finished by applying a coat of stucco or even a specially-formulated vinyl emulsion paint. The same material can be used on the interior of masonry walls with equal ease and need not be covered with a fire-retardant finish material such as plasterboard. The finish can be a directly-applied plaster or paint (Fig. 9-34).

Roofs

Insulating board and slab materials have seen relatively common use over the past few years in roof construction. They can be placed on the inside of a roof between the rafters or beams just as can the insulating sheathings. The pieces can be held in place with adhesive or by finish support moldings nailed to the rafters or beams. Some types of insulants, such as polyurethane, should be covered with plasterboard or some similar material. Other types, such as cellular glass, do not have a combustibility problem and can be directly finished if preferred.

It is much more common, however, for these materials to be applied to the exterior of the roof. The material can be laid on top of the roof sheathing or decking, just the same as with insulating sheathing, and closed at all edges by a trim strip. The pieces need only be secured sufficiently to hold them in place as the finish roofing is being applied. Some designs call for an added layer of sheathing to which the finish roofing can be applied. In other cases that step can be eliminated. A gridwork system can also be used whereby the grid is made up on the surface of the sheathing or decking. The pieces of insulation are fitted into the grid spaces and then the whole is covered with the final roofing layer.

Board and slab insulation is at its best on flat roofs. There are a number of different design possibilities and special tapered block stock is

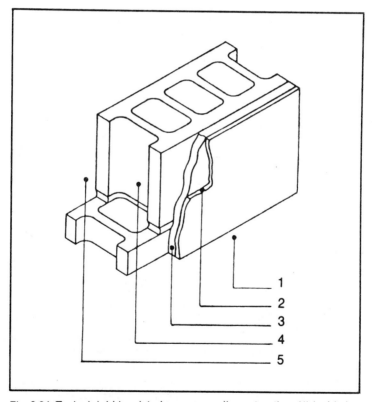

Fig. 9-34. Typical rigid-insulated masonry wall construction: (1) inside (or outside) air; (2) interior (or exterior) finish; (3) insulating sheathing or rigid insulation; (4) masonry block; (5) outside (or inside) air.

made for just this purpose. By properly arranging the tapered blocks, positive water drainage on a flat roof can be easily achieved. The blocks are pitched toward strategically positioned drainpipes or downspouts. A flat roof deck of suitable strength must first be laid. Then, depending upon the nature of the roof assembly, a layer of reinforced gypsum board or perhaps ordinary fiberboard might or might not be laid down.

The next step is to position the insulating blocks, boards, or slabs. Tapered blocks must be properly sequenced to achieve the proper drainage system. The insulation is then typically covered with either a barrier sheet, a membrane sheet, or a layer of one-half inch fiberboard for further protection.

Then several alternate layers of roofing felt and hot tar are applied, with a topping of roofing stone as a finish. A relatively new alternative to this traditional method of applying the finish layers is to cover the insulation with a sealed sheet membrane. This is then covered with a layer of roofing stone ballast to hold everything in place.

POURS AND FILLS

There are a number of applications in residential construction where loose-fill or poured insulants can be used if the seasonal heating and cooling requirements are not overly stringent. They have the advantages of being very easy to install, easy to handle, and easy on the pocketbook. If they are properly put in, they will do an excellent job of insulating. In all cases, proper density and coverage are the most important factors.

Foundations

Poured insulants such as perlite and vermiculite are widely used to fill the hollow cores of concrete or cinder block foundation walls. The type of wall, the height or thickness involved doesn't matter. The walls should be well damp-proofed on the exterior—both above and below grade. If the top of the foundation wall is to be capped with solid blocks or if the top course is to have its cores filled with mortar, then the insulation must be placed before that part of the job is done. I mention this because masons sometimes get one jump ahead of the insulation installer. And then it's too late.

Installing a poured insulant is simplicity itself. Just pour the material directly from the bag into the cores of the blocks. Use a long, slender rod to periodically stir the material about a bit as you pour it into the voids. Make sure that it doesn't hang up anywhere and leave a void. However, don't mash the insulation down into the cores with a stick. Try for an even density throughout the entire core column without packing it down. Perlite generally will cause little difficulty in this respect and neither will the relatively fine vermiculite specifically graded for insulating masonry. The coarse vermiculite sometimes will. Once the material is in place and all of the cores are full, immediately close the cores off by applying a top course of solid masonry, fill the top-course cores with mortar, or cover it with polyethylene sheet.

Floors

A poured insulation works very nicely to insulate beneath a wood floor built on top of a concrete slab such as might be done when converting a heated basement to a family room. The arrangement is much the same as when insulating with mineral wool or insulating board. The concrete slab should first be sealed with a damp-proofer or covered with a polyethylene sheet vapor barrier, or both, and then the sleepers can be laid down.

Pour the insulation between the sleepers. Keep the density as even as possible. Then lay the subflooring or finish flooring. This must be done with some degree of care so as not to displace the insulation. A 1½-inch depth of insulation is generally sufficient to give good thermal protection and added floor comfort in all but the coldest climates.

Walls

Pour-type insulations are not generally recommended for installation in vertical wall cavities. They do have a tendency to settle to some degree and in new construction other kinds of insulants with higher R value and greater ease of installation are most frequently chosen. There is another difficulty, too, as those who have worked on walls filled with sawdust are well aware. When the occasion arises to cut a hole in the wall to mount a new switchbox or to make some repair, the insulation pours forth. Then there arises the interesting question of how best to reinsulate.

However, this is not to say that pour-type insulations have not or cannot be used in walls. The trouble is, it's the very devil of a job to install because the wall construction must be completed, then holes must be drilled through the top plates and the insulation poured in. Positioning the material is difficult and so is getting a uniform density. It is also nearly impossible to completely fill the wall cavities. All in all, neither the process nor the result is particularly satisfactory.

There is one method of application that works fairly well and that is blowing the material in under slight pressure. This process has been used by a few do-it-yourselfers with reasonable success, but it is not a recommended procedure.

Loose-fill insulation, either cellulosic or mineral wool, is widely used to insulate house walls. However, the material must be positioned with special blowing apparatus that completely fills the wall cavities to a predetermined density. This is a job for professional installers and not one that can be satisfactorily undertaken by do-it-yourselfers (unless, of course, you happen to be a do-it-yourselfer who is in the insulation business).

Pour-type insulation can be included in the cavities of masonry wall constructions. This requires a closed-cavity type of wall that does not have weep holes through the bottom course of the exterior wall section for venting and drainage purposes. After the wall has been built to full height, but before it is capped, the material is simply poured into the space, agitated a bit with a long slender rod during the process to assure even distribution and relatively even density.

Ceilings

Both poured and loose-fill insulations are commonly used to insulate above ceilings. Although more often installed as a retrofit in existing houses, they are also used in numerous new constructions.

Poured insulants are put in after the finish ceiling (or a ceiling backer) has been put up, by pouring the material between the joists, raking it out and leveling it (Fig. 9-35). Where eaves ventilation has been provided, blocking strips must be built in at the ends of the joists to prevent the loose material from spilling out into the eaves areas and either filtering down through the vents or blocking them. Also, any gaps that exist around soil stacks, vent pipes, wires and such must be completely sealed off before the insulating begins or the material will dribble down through the cracks. For the same reason, blocking must be put into place around a chimney opening. The wood members should be at least 2 inches away from the chimney surface.

There is an alternative to blocking at a chimney and barriers at the eaves and that is to install short strips of unfaced mineral wool batt or blanket material to accomplish the same purpose without the problem of trying to fit and nail in pieces of wood. The mineral wool batts can be stuffed in place in the usual fashion without much difficulty. If it is necessary to place barrier batts in a shallow eaves area, often it is easiest to do that part of the insulating from below before the ceiling is put up.

Loose-fill mineral wools can be installed above a ceiling in much the same fashion as poured types. Putting the material in place by hand is not recommended by insulation companies and for a good reason. The thermal performance of mineral wool is dependent upon its installed density and completeness of coverage and putting the loose-fill in and then raking it level by hand almost invariably results in some degree of nonuniformity and differences in density from point to point. This in turn means uneven thermal performance. However, having the insulation unevenly in place is a good deal better than not having the insulation at all. If the job is carefully done the result is likely to be satisfactory.

The key is to make sure that you do not cover any more than the specified square footage of ceiling area per bagfull of material than is indicated on the chart printed on the bag for the particular *R* value that you want (Fig. 9-36). By installing the correct number of bags for the square footage that you have to cover and then carefully raking and leveling the material, you should end up with nearly as uniform a job as a professional installer achieves with his special blowing equipment. As with the pour-type insulants, ventilated eave areas should be blocked so as to permit adequate ventilation, but prevent the insulation from either spilling out into the eaves area or being blown back into the attic by breezes coming through the vents (Fig. 9-37). Cracks around pipes and wires can be filled with bits of the loose-fill and clumps of the material can be packed between

342

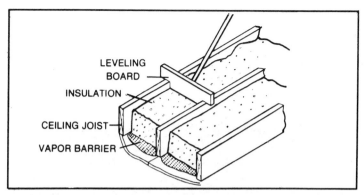

Fig. 9-35. Insulating a ceiling with poured insulation consists of pouring the material in place between the ceiling joists then raking it out level and to the proper depth/density.

framing members and chimney walls to fill that gap if it is not too wide. Otherwise, use chunks of mineral wool batt or blanket stuffed in place as necessary. Do *not* use the faced variety.

REFLECTIVES

The reflective insulations that are available for use in residential construction come in three different forms: foil-facing or backing attached to another insulating material, plain aluminum foil designed especially for this purpose, and kraft paper/foil expandable combinations that provide multiple plane air spaces within the building cavity.

In all cases, at least one plane air space must be included in the building section if the reflective foil is to function. Insulants with reflective coverings must be recessed into the building cavities or the finish covering must be spaced out on furring strips from the foil surface in order to gain the added benefit of the reflective surface. Even greater thermal performance can be obtained by installing two foil-faced insulants with a plane air space between them. An exmaple is foil-faced mineral wood batts recessed into the wall cavities and covered by foil-backed gypsum board. Plain reflective insulations must be separately installed, but they can be used in conjunction with other insulants if you prefer (i.e., foil within wall cavities and insulating sheathing applied to the exterior).

Foundations

Reflective insulation typically is installed to improve the thermal performance of heated basement walls only when the space is to be finished and made into living quarters. The first step is to nail horizontal furring strips across the top and bottom of the wall and then install vertical furring strips on 16-inch centers across the entire wall surface. Window openings must likewise be furred around (Fig. 9-38). Cut lengths of reflective insulation to fit between the furring strips from floor to ceiling. Have a slight overlap at each end. Position the foil at one top corner and staple the flange to the furring strip about every 8 inches. Pull the flange taut as you go (Fig. 9-39).

Then start at the opposite top corner and stretch the material tight; this will expand the folded paper backing and provide an added plane air

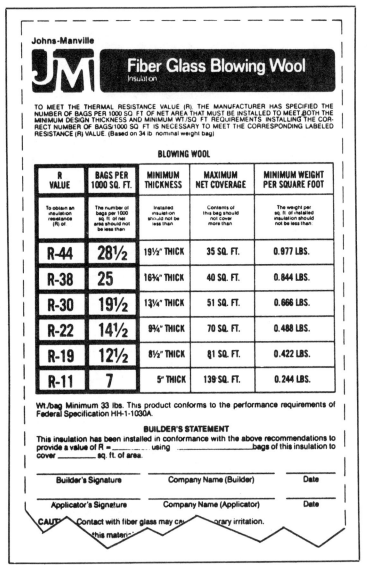

Johns-Manville

Fiber Glass Blowing Wool
Insulation

TO MEET THE THERMAL RESISTANCE VALUE (R), THE MANUFACTURER HAS SPECIFIED THE NUMBER OF BAGS PER 1000 SQ FT OF NET AREA THAT MUST BE INSTALLED TO MEET BOTH THE MINIMUM DESIGN THICKNESS AND MINIMUM WT./SQ. FT REQUIREMENTS. INSTALLING THE CORRECT NUMBER OF BAGS/1000 SQ. FT IS NECESSARY TO MEET THE CORRESPONDING LABELED RESISTANCE (R) VALUE. (Based on 34 lb. nominal weight bag)

BLOWING WOOL

R VALUE	BAGS PER 1000 SQ. FT.	MINIMUM THICKNESS	MAXIMUM NET COVERAGE	MINIMUM WEIGHT PER SQUARE FOOT
To obtain an insulation resistance (R) of	The number of bags per 1000 sq. ft. of net area should not be less than	Installed insulation should not be less than	Contents of this bag should not cover more than	The weight per sq. ft. of installed insulation should not be less than
R-44	28½	19½" THICK	35 SQ. FT.	0.977 LBS.
R-38	25	16¾" THICK	40 SQ. FT.	0.844 LBS.
R-30	19½	13¼" THICK	51 SQ. FT.	0.666 LBS.
R-22	14½	9¾" THICK	70 SQ. FT.	0.488 LBS.
R-19	12½	8½" THICK	81 SQ. FT.	0.422 LBS.
R-11	7	5" THICK	139 SQ. FT.	0.244 LBS.

Wt./bag Minimum 33 lbs. This product conforms to the performance requirements of Federal Specification HH-1-1030A.

BUILDER'S STATEMENT

This insulation has been installed in conformance with the above recommendations to provide a value of R = _____ using _____ bags of this insulation to cover _____ sq. ft. of area.

_____	_____	_____
Builder's Signature	Company Name (Builder)	Date
Applicator's Signature	Company Name (Applicator)	Date

CAUTION: Contact with fiber glass may cause temporary irritation.

Fig. 9-36. This sample label is typical of those found on bags of blowing/pouring wool. Unless the requirements are followed, the thermal performance will be below par (courtesy of Johns-Manville.

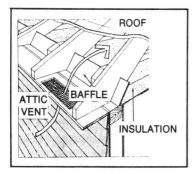

Fig. 9-37. When poured insulation or loose-fill insulation is placed in an attic floor, ventilated eaves must be kept open and the insulation prevented from spilling into them by installing wood baffles, as shown here, or sections of mineral wool batt to serve the same purpose.

space (Fig. 9-40). Pull the insulation smooth and staple down the entire length (Fig. 9-41) and then across the top and bottom. Be sure to treat the insulation gingerly. It can be damaged very easily.

Where the insulation must be stapled to furring strips that are spaced on less than 16-inch centers or must be fastened over odd-shaped areas, staple a full-size piece into place first and then trim as necessary with a sharp utility knife. The expandable type of insulation cannot be expanded, but there is no alternative. Even in such circumstances, the insulation will provide an R value of at least 3.0. (With single-thickness foil this makes no difference.)

When you encounter electrical outlet boxes, turn the power off first (aluminum foil is an excellent conductor of electricity) and then apply the material right over the boxes. After the insulation has been fastened down, carefully cut out around the boxes with a utility knife (Fig. 9-42) and then tape the cut edges of the insulation into place with masking, cellophane, or some similar tape. When the insulating job has been completed, check carefully for any damage, make repairs as necessary, and then immediately install the wall covering to protect the insulation.

Note that an added measure of thermal performance can be achieved by following either of two somewhat different procedures. One method is

Fig. 9-38. Furring out masonry basement walls in preparation for installing reflective foil insulation. The job is the same as for installing mineral wool or rigid foam insulants (courtesy of Alfol Inc.).

345

Fig. 9-39. The expandable foil insulation is attached at one upper corner first and then stapled through the flange into the edge of the furring strip (courtesy of Alfol Inc.).

to apply 1½-inch furring strips instead of the usual three-fourth inch variety, recess the reflective insulation halfway into the wall cavities (this requires some careful stapling), and then apply a foil-backed plasterboard to the furring strips. The second method is to put up three-fourth inch furring strips and apply the foil insulation as discussed above. Then install a second set of three-fourth inch furring strips directly over the first. Fasten foil-backed gypsum board or a similar wall covering to the second set of furring strips. Either procedure adds another plane air space that is reflective on both surfaces. The gain in thermal performance would be around R-3, depending upon conditions.

Floors

The expandable type of reflective insulation works well in floor constructions and can be installed either flush with the floor joist bottom edges or recessed within the floor cavities. The flush installation is faster, but the recessed installation affords a bit of added protection for the insulation. It is a little less susceptible to mechanical damage.

Fig. 9-40. The reflective insulation is pulled taut to expand it and then stapled at the opposite top corner (courtesy of Alfol Inc.).

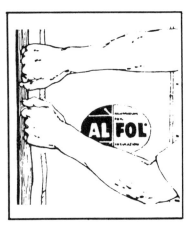

Fig. 9-41. Once the top is secured, the reflective insulation is stapled down its length. Keep it taut and smooth during the process (courtesy of Alfol Inc.).

To install this kind of insulation, cut the lengths of material 3 inches longer at each end than the length of the floor cavity. Expand the insulation for a portion of its length (Fig. 9-43). Secure a corner of one end to a floor joist. Leave the extra 3 inches folded downward. Drive several staples along one side, through the stapling flange and 8 to 12 inches apart. Then pull the material tight across the cavity and staple down the other side (Fig. 9-44). Continue alternating back and forth. Keep the insulation smooth and tight as you go (Fig. 9-45) until the entire length is in place. Staple down the 3-inch tab at each end to complete the seal (Fig. 9-46).

The entire job can be done by one person. However, keeping the unfastened material up out of the way as you work can sometimes be a problem. The material is easily damaged. The job will go faster and easier if you have a helper to hold the material in place and stretch it out as you smooth and staple it. Irregular and narrow sections are best handled by stapling the material in place first and then cutting off the excess with a utility knife. The thermal performance at these areas will not equal that of the full-width cavities, but that can't be helped.

Fig. 9-42. Switch and outlet boxes are covered over with the reflective foil insulation (turn the power OFF first). Then the insulation is cut away from around the boxes and the cut edges of the insulation are taped in place (courtesy of Alfol Inc.).

347

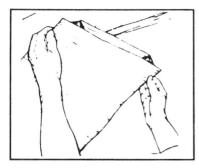

Fig. 9-43. Start a reflective-foil flooring installation by expanding one end of a strip of insulation and positioning it between the floor joists (courtesy of Alfol Inc.).

To install the insulation around pipes and wires, make slits at the appropriate points and work the material around the obstruction. Finish off by taping the slit edges together and to the pipes or cables. If there is some danger that the insulation might be damaged by activities taking place in the area below the floor, it's a good idea to cover it with a layer of fiberboard sheathing, gypsum wallboard, or some similar material.

Plain foil or foil-backed paper insulation that is nonexpandable is installed in the same way. It too can be installed either flush or recessed (Fig. 9-47). There might not be stapling flanges to work with and great care must be taken not to tear the foil.

Walls

The use of reflective insulation in conventional frame walls has largely fallen into disfavor over recent years. It is more difficult to work with than other kinds of insulation and it is effective only under certain conditions. Other materials frequently do a better job at less overall cost. However, it still does have its uses and its adherants. Plain foil or an expandable type of insulation with kraft paper backing to form multiple plane air spaces can be used. Installation can be either flush or recessed

Fig. 9-44. Staple one end of the expandable reflective foil insulation strip in place on each side. Leave a 3-inch extra flap and pull the material taut as you staple (courtesy of Alfol Inc.).

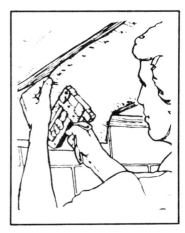

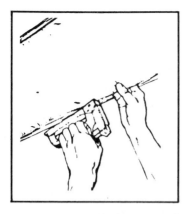

Fig. 9-45. Continue to fit the insulation, smooth and taut, into place between the floor joists and staple every 8 inches or so along the flanges (courtesy of Alfol Inc.).

into the wall cavities and the job is done in exactly the same way as a floor or masonry foundation wall installation.

The insulation should be carefully fitted at all studs and other framing members and smoothly fastened in place. Joints around electrical boxes should be sealed with tape and pipes or wires in the wall cavities should be positioned so as not to interfere with the material. In most cases, the recessed application will afford the greatest R value. This is especially true if the walls are covered with a foil-backed gypsum wallboard. Further thermal performance can be achieved by covering the exterior of the wall frames with a foil-backed insulating sheathing. There is a potential here for a total of as many as five plane air spaces. Two of them are reflective on both surfaces.

There is really only one situation where either single-layer or expandable reflective insulation can be used in masonry wall construction. That is on the interior of a wall that is to be finished with plasterboard, paneling, or the like. In this situation, the installation would be made in exactly the same way as for a basement wall. Apply the material to furring strips nailed to the interior surface of the masonry.

Fig. 9-46. To finish the run of insulation, staple the flap securely to the sill plate at each end of the strip (courtesy of Alfol Inc.).

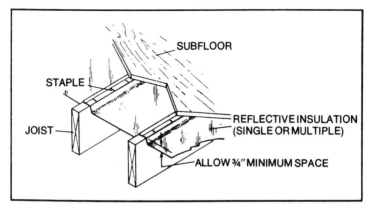

Fig. 9-47. This sketch shows how either single or multiple reflective foil insulation can be installed in a floor from above. Generally, this is not practical with platform-framing construction, but it might be in a balloon-framed house where the roof can be built and the house closed up before the subflooring is laid.

Ceilings

Under most circumstances, reflective insulations are not widely used in ceiling installations. However, foil-faced mineral wool batt or blanket insulation is commonly used in this application. Here the reflective covering faces down into the heated area. But there is one application in particular where the installation of a reflective insulation, generally of the single-layer type, is of considerable value.

In a hot-dry climate where cooling is the principal consideration, the reflective foil can be spread over the entire attic floor area. This can be done either alone or in conjunction with a mineral wool or other insulation below it. This places a vapor barrier *above* the mass thermal insulation, but the arrangement works satisfactorily in a hot, dry climate where the likelihood of damaging condensation forming beneath the vapor barrier is slim. The effect of this insulating procedure is to substantially reduce the cooling load by reflecting radiant energy away from the living spaces below. The installation process is a bit tedious, but not difficult. It merely consists of covering the whole exposed area tightly with foil, shiniest side up. The foil can be overlapped and crimped into place as necessary and secured with staples wherever it will not stay put of its own accord.

Roofs

A reflective insulation is not normally used in roof sections. On the other hand, there are situations where a reflective foil can prove of considerable worth in a roof construction by deflecting a portion of the radiant energy that would otherwise be imposed upon a cooling system. The situation is much the same as for the ceiling arrangement just discussed. A plane air space must be left in order for the reflective insulation to be effective. This can be achieved by stapling the material between the rafters or across their lower edges in the same way as it is applied in a floor construction.

Alternatively, either plain aluminum foil, builder's foil, or a foil-faced rigid insulation can be applied to the roof sheathing. The finish roofing is secured to furring strips on top of the reflective surface. The finish roofing itself can be reflective, bright aluminum roofing sheets.

Note, however, that these applications are somewhat unusual and are more oriented toward reducing cooling loads by deflecting incident solar energy than they are toward reducing heating loads by diminishing heat transfer through conductance and convection. Reflective foils are also sometimes employed to reflect radiant energy *into* a heated living space in order to increase the amount of free sun's heat in a solar heating design. If you have some thoughts about installing reflective insulations either alone or in conjunction with other insulants for these purposes, it would be wise to check your plans with a local architect or heating/cooling engineer before proceeding.

PROFESSIONAL INSTALLATIONS

All of the above insulations can be readily installed by the do-it-yourselfer in retrofit or new-construction applications. By proceeding carefully and paying attention to the small details, you can achieve an excellent insulating job. Often it will be better than might be done by a contractor.

Sometimes the insulation is installed by workers who might well be excellent professional carpenters or masons or whatever, but they are not professional insulation installers. Sometimes the material is installed by professional insulation contractors who are really not very professional. It doesn't take much cash or knowledge, or any experience, to set up shop as a "professional insulation specialist." If you plan to have your insulating work done by professionals, how do you know what you are getting into?

First, beware of telephone, direct mail, advertising, or door-to-door solicitations for insulating work. The products and services offered might well be legitimate, but they also might not be (Fig. 9-48). In all cases, you should thoroughly check the references and recommendations of any insulating company or any building contractor who agrees to do insulating work. Make sure that the company is a recognized, reputable, and fully professional organization.

There are plenty of sources where you can find information on contractors, insulation or otherwise, who operate in your area. The Chamber of Commerce or a Better Business Bureau are good possibilities and your telephone book will list local or regional contractors' associations headquartered nearby.

Another good possibility is a state association of insulation manufacturers or installers. You can also check with local building department officials. They might be able to give you some solid, practical information and advice. References, if you can obtain them, can be directly checked and financial standing can be determined through a bank or credit reporting company. A general reputation can be ascertained by talking with other contractors, customers of the company involved, or perhaps friends or neighbors who are knowledgeable.

However you go about it, the bottom line is to thoroughly check and double check all of the details before you engage a contractor to do any insulating (or other) work. Read the fine print of the contract, review its contents with your attorney, and be sure that you understand and agree with all of the clauses before you sign it. There are some insulants that are best installed only by a professional insulation installer who has the expertise and the equipment to do the job properly. The following are insulants that can *only* be installed in *any* application by a pro:

☐ Mineral-fiber blowing wool must be professionally installed in walls and any other enclosed cavities and it is best when professionally placed in open cavities as well. For those who are interested in the specifics of such installations, the Mineral Insulation Manufacturers Association, 382 Springfield Avenue, Summit, NJ 07901, offers a technical guide booklet on the subject, called *Mineral Wool "Blowing Wool."*

☐ Dry cellulose insulation must be professionally installed in walls and in other closed cavities. It is also best blown into open horizontal cavities. The process is much the same for installing blowing wool.

**INSULATION
MANUFACTURER OF URETHANE FOAM
FACTORY SECONDS
BUY DIRECT AND SAVE!
4′x8′ sheets, ½ to 4″ THICK FOIL FACED, 9 R'S
PER INCH (1″ OF FOAM IS WORTH 2″ OF FIBROUS
GLASS IN INSULATION VALUE)**

Fig. 9-48. Proceed with caution when you are about to hire someone to install insulation for you or when you are tempted by an advertisement such as this one. What causes the material to be factory seconds? Is the material fully usable? What are the real savings, if any? What are "9 R's? Presumably that means R-9. But the listed R value of urethane (or polyurethane) insulation is typically 6.25, not 9, at a density of 1.5 pounds per cubic foot. What is the density of this material? Where does the other R-2.75 come from? Are they including, somehow, the "value" of the foil facing? It probably won't reach that high anyway. Is the foil on one or both sides of the material? The last statement that 1 inch of foam is worth 2 inches of fibrous glass in insulating value is virtually meaningless. Beware!

☐ Insulating concretes, including the vermiculite and perlite varieties, are best handled by professional masons unless the homeowner has some experience in and knowledge of concrete work in general.

☐ The spray-type insulants must be installed by professionals who know their business. These include spray-on cellulosic fiber, urethane foams, urea-formaldehyde foams, and any others of that ilk.

I can't overstress the importance that any professional you hire to install insulation must do a competent, top-quality, and fully-effective job for you. In many cases, you will be able to keep an eye on the job as it progresses. You'll be able to spot deficiencies as they occur and have them corrected. I strongly suggest that you do just that. But don't make a pest of yourself. That only slows the job down and antagonizes the workmen.

With the blown or foamed-in-place insulations that are installed in closed cavities, there is really no way you can inspect the insulating job. That's all the more reason to choose a top-notch, reputable contractor to do the work. Once the job is finished and buttoned-up, you'll have to live with the results.

RETROFITTING

Retrofitting insulation in an existing house that has insufficient insulation, or perhaps none at all, is sometimes fairly simple, often a difficult chore, and usually a combination of the two. The effectiveness of the completed job often depends much upon the ingenuity of the installer. Insulants are commonly used in various combinations in order to achieve maximum thermal performance with the least amount of expense and renovation. The blowing wools and cellulose are used principally for retrofitting.

In order of "thermal performance," ceilings or roofs deserve the first attention in retrofitting. This is followed by the walls and then the floors. Windows are very important, as are doors and ducts, and sealing against infiltration can be a critical factor. There is no way that I can tell you exactly how to go about retrofitting insulation to your house, because there are so many different detailed possibilities. I can give you some ideas that might point you in the right direction. The insulation itself is installed in existing houses in just the same way as in new construction. The problem generally lies in gaining easy access to the proper spot to install the material.

Foundations

The foundation is perhaps the easiest area in the house to retrofit. Board, slab, or sheathing insulation can be secured to the exterior of foundation walls with little difficulty. Dig the earth away from the foundation walls to a depth of a couple of feet, wash the walls down thoroughly, let them dry *completely,* and then glue the insulation in place. Make sure that it is tucked up tight to the bottom edge of the exterior siding/sheathing and caulk all seams. Apply an exterior cover over the insulation, if necessary, for solar and mechanical protection and then backfill the earth.

The inside surfaces of crawlspace walls can be insulated by any of the methods used in new construction. The job is done in exactly the same way. The interior surfaces of heated basement walls can likewise be covered by any of the previously discussed methods and materials. If the walls have not been previously sealed or damp-proofed, this must be done and it often entails thoroughly cleaning the wall surfaces. If the walls have been painted or whitewashed and there is any evidence of flaking, don't depend upon adhesives alone to hold insulation and the wall covering in place—use nails.

Floors

Existing floor assemblies that have no insulation in them can be easily insulated from below—just as in new construction. If an insufficient amount of insulation has already been installed, you can put more in without removing the old. However, don't use a material that has a vapor barrier attached. Another possibility arises if a new finish floor is to be laid in the house. That involves putting down first a layer of rigid insulation, then an underlayment, and that is followed by the new finish floor. This system works best when the entire floor of the house is being replaced.

Concrete slab floors—whether basement, slab-on-grade foundation, or perhaps in a garage that is being converted to living space—can be easily insulated by first damp-proofing the concrete, then laying a vapor barrier, followed by flooring sleepers. Install rigid or pour-type insulation between the sleepers and then put down the finish floor. If the concrete is cracked or broken, the damage should be repaired with a top-quality epoxy repair cement. Unevenness can be compensated for by shimming the floor sleepers as necessary. Perhaps the most critical factor is to completely seal the floor and the floor/wall joint to prevent the entry of moisture.

Walls

Retrofitting walls can be ticklish, but there are alternatives that will serve to greatly improve thermal performance. Probably the most common retrofit, if the wall cavities are empty, is to have them blown full of blowing wool or cellulose (Fig. 9-49). Urea-formaldehyde foam has also been widely used in the past, but its popularity has now greatly decreased.

If the walls contain some insulation, but not enough, or if the homeowner wants some insulation other than a foamed-in-place or blown variety, there are further possibilities. One is to remove the interior wall covering during a renovation project, strip out the insufficient old insulation if there is any, install mineral wool blanket or batt insulation, and then re-cover the walls and redecorate.

This is a laborious, dirty process and certainly not inexpensive. It is perfectly viable where an old house is being rebuilt. Another method, equally effective but less difficult, consists of covering the existing in-

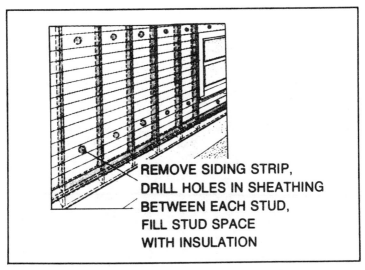

REMOVE SIDING STRIP,
DRILL HOLES IN SHEATHING
BETWEEN EACH STUD,
FILL STUD SPACE
WITH INSULATION

Fig. 9-49. This sketch shows the general method whereby existing house walls are retrofitted with a blowing insulant.

terior wall surfaces with a layer of insulating sheathing. That part of the job is simple. The real work is involved in extending the door and window frames, repositioning electrical boxes, and putting up new wallboard or paneling and trimwork.

The retrofit can also be done from the outside and sometimes this is the easiest course. There are two commonly used methods. One is to remove the old exterior siding, apply insulating sheathing, and then re-cover with new exterior siding (which can be spaced out on furring strips for added R value). The second method is to apply the insulating sheathing directly over the old exterior siding if it is smooth enough (Fig. 9-50) or to furring strips if it is not. Then install a new exterior siding. Often steel, aluminum, or vinyl siding with its own insulating backerboard is applied to improve thermal performance even more. The new siding can be applied on furring strips to gain an added plane air space.

Band Joists

The band joist area is sometimes neglected even in relatively new and otherwise fairly well insulated houses. This is a point worth checking. The band joist area in a full basement or a crawlspace might be fully accessible and can be easily retrofitted with a mineral wool batt insulation. A second-floor band area can sometimes be reached via an unfinished attic so that it too can be insulated (though usually not without a struggle). If this part of the house is not readily accessible, it's hardly worth bothering with. The time, trouble, and expense would far outweigh any benefits unless major renovation is in progress anyway.

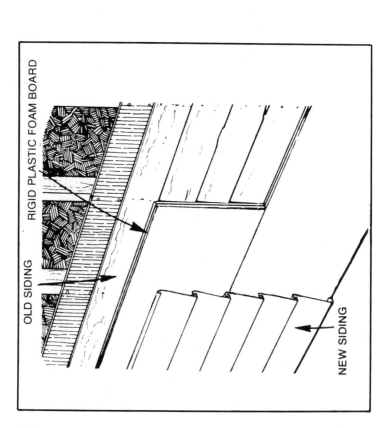

OLD SIDING　　RIGID PLASTIC FOAM BOARD

NEW SIDING

Fig. 9-50. Rigid insulation, either sheathing or some other form, can be applied right over old exterior siding in some cases with new siding applied over that. The new siding might have an integral insulating backerboard for further thermal protection.

Masonry Walls

Sometimes there is not much that can be done about improving the thermal performance of masonry walls. For instance, a masonry veneer on a conventional wood-frame wall can be retrofitted only by blowing or spraying insulation into the wall cavities if they are empty and if there is access for the equipment or by removing the existing interior wall covering and filling the cavities with mineral fiber blanket or batt. In conjunction with that—or alone if the walls cannot be filled—the existing interior wall covering can be retrofitted by applying a layer of insulating sheathing, followed by new wallboard or paneling.

Masonry cavity walls cannot be internally retrofitted because there is no practical access into the cavity. The only alternative to improving thermal performance for these and solid masonry walls is to cover either the inside or the outside with an insulating material. The inside can be protected in the same way that a basement wall is in new construction.

The outside could be completely covered with cellular glass, for instance, then painted or stuccoed to present an entirely new finish. This would also involve extending the window and door frames and rearranging the exterior trimwork. It might also entail some fitting work around the eaves and rake areas. This arrangement is ideal for an old stone, brick, or block house that is being completely renovated. It envelops and makes useful a huge thermal mass that was previously not used to advantage.

Ducts

Uninsulated ducts are commonly found in older houses in both conditioned and unconditioned spaces. In most instances, ductwork should be retrofitted with a blanket insulation or a specially-made duct insulation. This will reduce heat losses or gains, improve the efficiency of the heating/cooling equipment, and result in the maximum amount of warmed or cooled air being delivered to the registers. The job is done simply enough by wrapping the insulating material around the duct sections and taping it in place. Joints in the ductwork should be taped shut first. Use a special wide, aluminized duct tape made for the purpose.

There is one circumstance where insulating existing heat ducts might not be advisable. This is when the ductwork travels through an insulated, unventilated crawlspace. Duct heat loss is depended upon to keep the uninsulated floor above at a comfortable temperature and at the same time admit by transfer a certain amount of heat to the living space. This was not an uncommon practice years ago and many of those installations still exist. If such ductwork is fully insulated, the amount of heat in the crawlspace area is reduced, the floor above could become chilly, and additional heat would have to be pumped into the living space via the normal register route.

However, an arrangement of this sort is neither efficient nor conservative. It would be a good idea to investigate the possibility of fully insulating the ductwork to exclude all mechanically-generated heat from crawlspace. Depending upon the circumstances, this should lower overall heating requirements and cost by a reasonable amount.

Ceilings

There are a number of ways insulation can be retrofitted to ceiling areas. Perhaps the simplest, and a very popular one these days, is to add a layer of unfaced mineral wool insulation to an already existing layer above the ceiling. This is done by laying out batts or blanket at right angles to the ceiling joists in just the same way as is done in new construction. If no insulation exists in the ceiling, either batt, blanket, or loose-fill mineral wool, (cellulose or a poured insulant) can be placed between the ceiling joists and on top of the existing ceiling. If no vapor barrier exists, one should be laid or stapled in place before the insulating starts (Fig. 9-51) or a faced insulant should be used. The vapor barrier should be to the heated side of the insulation just above the ceiling itself. A second layer of insulation added above an original layer should not be faced with a vapor barrier. It should remain permeable.

Many older houses were made with a full attic floor that usually had single-thickness boards. Beneath those boards there might be no insulation whatsoever or there may be a thin layer of "cap" insulation of mineral wool or perhaps even sawdust. If there is plenty of open depth in the joist cavities, new insulant can be blown in to fill the area completely. This requires a professional.

Alternatively, you can tear up most or all of the floorboards and put in batt, blanket, loose-fill, or pour-type insulation right on top of the old ceiling. This is a tiresome, dirty, and difficult job.

Another possibility, also not an easy one, is to leave the flooring in place, lay down a layer of insulating sheathing, and cover the whole affair with plywood. This job can also be done from below by covering the existing ceiling with insulating sheathing and then applying a new finish ceiling of plasterboard. You could also consider making the finish ceiling of insulating plaster or insulating tiles. These can also be used in combination with other insulants to gain added R value.

If the ceiling is more than 7 feet 6 inches high, there are two more possibilities. One is to build a dropped-ceiling framework of nominal 1-inch boards and strapping. This will reduce the ceiling height by 6 inches or more. Then fill the framework with thick mineral wool batt insulation and apply a new finish ceiling. A second method is to install a metal grid type of dropped ceiling and fill the grid with special insulating ceiling tiles made just for the purpose. If a sufficiently deep drop can be managed, you might also put up a grid ceiling with insulating tiles and mineral wool batt or blanket secured above the ceiling. Sufficient space must be allowed to be able to lift the ceiling tiles into the gridwork frame.

If none of these solutions appeal to you, there is yet another possibility if the attic space is sufficiently large enough to be made into a den, an

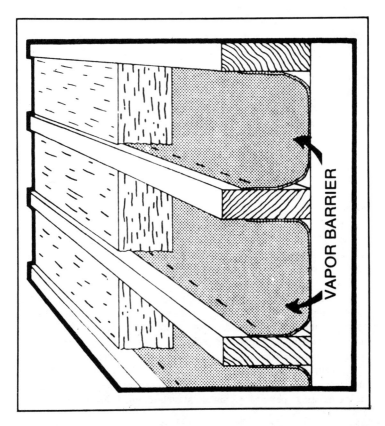

VAPOR BARRIER

Fig. 9-51. If there is no vapor barrier in an existing ceiling, one should be put in from above before retrofitting ceiling insulation.

office, a TV room, or whatever. Forget about trying to insulate the ceiling and instead install knee walls (if they are not already present). Insulate the knee walls and between the roof rafters just as in new construction. Finish the area with paneling, trimwork and some fresh flooring. Add some heat and electrical outlets and create a new living space.

Roofs

Where the undersides of existing roofs that are uninsulated or insufficiently insulated are accessible, insulation can be installed without much difficulty by following the same procedure as for new construction. If that isn't feasible or if there isn't enough physical space to allow sufficient insulation for the required or desired overall U there's no alternative but to install insulation on the exterior of the roof. This is definitely a major (and expensive) project, but depending upon the circumstances it may well be worthwhile whether the original finish roofing needs replacing or not. The heat loss through an uninsulated roof in a cold climate is tremendous and the costs could be rapidly recovered.

Although it is sometimes possible to apply insulation and a new finish covering right over the old finish roofing material, this is generally not a good idea and sometimes leads to more work than you originally anticipated. The best bet is to strip the old finishing roofing off completely. If the roofing felt underlayment is in good shape, it can be left. Otherwise it should also be removed and replaced. At the same time, check all of the flashing and sills in the roof sheathing and make any repairs or replacements that are necessary.

Once the roof deck is clean, clear, and in good shape, you can lay down insulation, new oversheathing, and a new finish roofing using methods and procedures that are commonly employed in new construction. Some new flashing, chimney crickets, and vent flanges might have to be replaced. In some cases this can provide complications where masonry chimneys or wall sections are involved.

Doors

Because you can't retrofit insulation to doors, the only solution to improving thermal performance at these points is to replace the doors or to add storm doors if there are none. If the existing entry doors are in poor condition, replacing them might be cost-effective over a reasonable period of time.

The actual job of replacing a door is not a difficult one if the doors are wood. They can be readily trimmed to fit the existing frame. Steel doors, however, are another matter because the framework must be fitted to the door. This can entail a good deal of ripping and tearing in order to fit a new frame into place. The job might not be worth the effort.

Storm doors are generally not too much of a chore to install. You can make your own wood storm doors or buy commercial ones and trim them to fit the existing openings. Commercial metal-framed combination storm/

screen doors are adjustable within certain ranges to fit odd-sized or cockeyed existing door frames. The doors come complete with installation instructions. Even an inexperienced do-it-yourselfer can install one over the course of a Saturday afternoon.

Windows

The retrofit situation with windows is about the same as for doors. You can't add insulation, so you must either add to the existing windows or replace them.

The easiest procedure to gain thermal performance from windows is to add storm sash to either the exterior or the interior—whichever is easiest. This is quite effective if the original windows are single-glazed, but is a marginal proposition if they are already double-glazed. If the existing windows are commercial units of fairly recent manufacture, you might be able to purchase factory-built storm sash from the same manufacturer (and sometimes from others) that will fit exactly in place. Nearly all manufacturers of modern double-glazed commercial window units offer optional storm sash for triple-glazing.

But in most cases, there is no recourse but to have the storm sash custom-made, window by window. Most building supplies dealers and lumberyards have contacts with door-and-sash mills who make storm sash to order. You shouldn't have much difficulty in obtaining them. There is also the possibility of making the storm sash yourself if you are good at woodworking or if you'd care to purchase commercial storm window kits. Commercial kits are comprised of aluminum channel and associated hardware that can be cut and fitted to individual window openings and then glazed with either plastic or glass. Properly installed, they are very effective. Just taping plastic film to either the inside or the outside window frames works well.

Actually changing existing single-glazed window units for double-glazed ones is a major proposition. It is worth investigating if you are contemplating a substantial amount of remodeling or renovation or if the old windows are in bad shape and they will soon have to be replaced anyway.

The specifics of the work depend entirely upon the nature of both the existing and the new windows. Seldom will you find a new commercial unit that will fit exactly in place of an old one (though this does happen). Generally, the job involves removing all interior and exterior trim and prying the old window unit out. Then you must enlarge, reduce or change the shape (or even the location) of the window opening to accomodate the new unit. Sometimes some of the exterior siding must be removed and a considerable amount of patching and rebuilding almost always is part of the job. When the circumstances are right, the change is well worth the effort.

One of the easiest and most effective ways to improve the thermal performance of window areas is to build thermal shutters for them. Although this should not be regarded as a permanent, round-the-clock improvement, some substantial savings can be realized if the shutters are regularly left open only when necessary and kept closed as much as possible. Several varieties of thermal shutters (as well as thermal drapes and curtains) are commercially available and they are also quite easy to construct in a home workshop. In cold climates, the cost of home-built shutters for an entire house can sometimes be recouped in one heating season.

Index

Edited by Steven Bolt

The Home Insulation Bible

by S. Blackwell Duncan

Today's homeowner faces two crucial problems: how to conserve energy, and how to put the brakes on skyrocketing home heating and cooling costs! The most obvious and probably least expensive solution could well be to update and improve the insulation in your home. This practical, money-saving manual can help you get the best insulation for the money in a new house, or in an older home. Jam-packed with solid, workable advice, it gives you hands-on, how-to-do-it info on selecting the most efficient home insulation *and* installing it for the least amount of money.

Every facet of home insulation is covered, from the basics of keeping a house heated or cooled, moisture and ventilation control and ways to estimate heat gains or losses, to how insulating materials work, the natural insulating qualities of various types of building materials, and the relative qualities of different commercial *and* noncommercial insulants—including spun glass, expanded polystyrene, foamed urethane, polyisocyanurate, heat-expanded loose fills, chopped cellulose, ceramic granules, and more. You'll get all the facts on calculating thermal resistance/conductivity of various insulators and find out how to calculate heating/cooling energy consumption and total costs for heating or cooling during a full season under a variety of conditions.

All the factors that can result in heat loss or gain in every type of house are explained. Included is information on the site, the building orientation, prevailing wind tracks, the sun's course at different seasons, and many other controllable *and* uncontrollable situations that you need to consider when you determine the insulation requirements for your home. Plus, there are step-by-step instructions on how to install different types of insulation in older homes and practical data on professional installation and retrofitting.

If you're a homeowner in search of a complete guide to saving on home heating and cooling costs by updating the insulation in your home, this is the sourcebook to have!

S. Blackwell Duncan is the author of several how-to books for TAB including *The Complete Book Of Outdoor Masonry* and *Plumbing With Plastic*.